T0271024

Spillover Effects of
China Going Global

Spillover Effects of
China Going Global

Joseph Pelzman

George Washington University, USA

NEW JERSEY · LONDON · SINGAPORE · BEIJING · SHANGHAI · HONG KONG · TAIPEI · CHENNAI · TOKYO

Published by

World Scientific Publishing Co. Pte. Ltd.

5 Toh Tuck Link, Singapore 596224

USA office: 27 Warren Street, Suite 401-402, Hackensack, NJ 07601

UK office: 57 Shelton Street, Covent Garden, London WC2H 9HE

Library of Congress Cataloging-in-Publication Data
Names: Pelzman, Joseph, author.
Title: Spillover effects of China going global / Joseph Pelzman
    (George Washington University, USA).
Description: New Jersey : World Scientific, 2016. | Includes indexes.
Identifiers: LCCN 2015050751 | ISBN 9789814603348 (hc : alk. paper)
Subjects: LCSH: Economic development--China. | New products--China. |
    Research, Industrial--China. | Technological innovations--China. |
    China--Commerce. | China--Foreign economic relations.
Classification: LCC HC427.95 .P396 2016 | DDC 330.951--dc23
LC record available at http://lccn.loc.gov/2015050751

British Library Cataloguing-in-Publication Data
A catalogue record for this book is available from the British Library.

In-house Editors: Dr. Sree Meenakshi Sajani/Qi Xiao

Typeset by Stallion Press
Email: enquiries@stallionpress.com

Printed in Singapore

I dedicate this book to the memory of my mother and father, Zina (ז״ל) and Abraham (ז״ל). Among the innumerable lessons they taught me, both in their words as well as by the model of their own lives, was our responsibility to look past unfounded fears of the cultural and national "other."

As passions may inevitably escalate during this important U.S. election year, and China's footprint continues to grow steadily on the world stage, it is all the more urgent for Western scholarship to look past the potential "fear factor" and assess the spillover effects of China going global in a fair and balanced manner.

Contents

List of Tables   xi

List of Figures   xxi

About the Author   xxiii

Chapter 1.   Introduction   1

Chapter 2.   An Overview of China's Export Growth   5

2.1   Theoretical Modeling of the Impact
of China's Exports   6

2.2   Decomposition of China's Exports   10

Chapter 3.   The Value-Added Chain in China's
International Trade   19

3.1   The Formal Model of the Value-Added Chain in
International Trade   21

3.2   The Value-Added Chain in China's International Trade:
Upstream Linkages or Looking Backward   26

3.3   The Value-Added Chain in China's International Trade:
Looking Forward   93

Chapter 4.   China's International Trade Competitiveness: An Assessment Based on Revealed Comparative Advantage (RCA) and Constant Market Share (CMS) Indexes   **113**

4.1   Competitiveness Based on RCA and Herfindahl Indexes   120

4.2   Competitiveness Based on Constant Market Share Decompositions   158

Chapter 5.   Evolution of China's International Trade Competitiveness in Textiles and Apparel Exports to the USA — Pre- and Post-MFA   **167**

5.1   The Control of Textile and Apparel Trade: The Early Years   178

5.2   Moving Away from the MFA: The Agreement on Textiles and Clothing   183

5.3   Review of Transition TMB Decisions: The First 20 Months   188

    5.3.1   Category 352/652 (Cotton and Man-made Fiber Underwear)   188

    5.3.2   Category 351/651 (Cotton and Man-made Fiber Pajamas and Other Nightwear)   189

    5.3.3   Category 434 (Men's and Boy's Wool Coats Other Than Suit Type)   190

    5.3.4   Category 435 (Women's and Girl's Wool Coats)   191

    5.3.5   Category 440 (Woven Wool Shirts and Blouses)   192

5.4   The ACT and the PRC   194

5.5   Estimating the Impact of Quota Removal: Methodological Considerations   196

    5.5.1   Import Demand   201

    5.5.2   Import Supply   202

5.6   Predicted Estimates of the Post-MFA PRC–India and PRC–Vietnam Competition Outcome   207

5.7   The Supply Side Response   230
       5.7.1   Cotton Fiber   231
       5.7.2   Textiles   232
       5.7.3   Apparel   236

**Chapter 6.   China's 10-Year WTO Experience:
                Applying Market Solutions
                to a Non-Market Player   239**

6.1   The Overall Reliance on AD Measures   244
6.2   The Sectoral Pattern of AD Measures, CVDs
       and Safeguards   254
6.3   US Measures Against the PRC as a Non-Market
       Economy   262

**Chapter 7.   Quantifying and Modeling PRC
                Foreign Aid — A Search for
                Markets, Infrastructure and
                Service Contracts and Resources   275**

7.1   Measuring PRC Foreign Aid   276
7.2   A Behavioral Model of PRC Foreign Aid   283
7.3   A Model of PRC Supply of Foreign Aid   286
7.4   Statistical Results   288

**Chapter 8.   China's Outward Investment
                Program — A Search for Technology   295**

8.1   A Review of FDI and its Spillover Effects   318
8.2   Innovation via M&A or Immigration of Skilled S&E
       Workers?   324
       8.2.1   The Decision to Innovate via Immigration . . .   325
       8.2.2   The Decision to Acquire R&D   327
8.3   Micro Data on the PRC Path to Acquire
       Foreign R&D   329

Bibliography   337

Index   351

List of Tables

2.1   Share of Total Imports in Total
      Expenditure (%)   8
2.2   Share of China's Imports in Total
      Expenditure (%)   9
3.1   Shares of China's 1995 Value Added Embodied
      in Gross Exports by Source Country and Source
      Industry Electrical and Optical Equipment (%) . . .   32
3.2   Shares of China's 2000 Value Added Embodied
      in Gross Exports by Source Country and Source
      Industry, Electrical and Optical Equipment (%) . . .   34
3.3   Shares of China's 2005 Value Added Embodied
      in Gross Exports by Source Country and Source
      Industry, Electrical and Optical Equipment (%) . . .   36
3.4   Shares of China's 2008 Value Added Embodied
      in Gross Exports by Source Country and Source
      Industry, Electrical and Optical Equipment (%) . . .   38
3.5   Shares of China's 2009 Value Added Embodied
      in Gross Exports by Source Country and Source
      Industry, Electrical and Optical Equipment (%) . . .   40
3.6   Shares of China's 1995 Value Added Embodied
      in Gross Exports by Source Country and Source
      Industry, Chemicals and Non-metallic Mineral
      Products (%)   42

3.7   Shares of China's 2000 Value Added Embodied in Gross Exports by Source Country and Source Industry, Chemicals and Non-metallic Mineral Products (%)   44

3.8   Shares of China's 2005 Value Added Embodied in Gross Exports by Source Country and Source Industry, Chemicals and Non-metallic Mineral Products (%)   46

3.9   Shares of China's 2008 Value Added Embodied in Gross Exports by Source Country and Source Industry, Chemicals and Non-metallic Mineral Products (%)   48

3.10   Shares of China's 2009 Value Added Embodied in Gross Exports by Source Country and Source Industry, Chemicals and Non-metallic Mineral Products (%)   50

3.11   Shares of China's 1995 Value Added Embodied in Gross Exports by Source Country and Source Industry, Machinery and Equipment nec (%)   53

3.12   Shares of China's 2000 Value Added Embodied in Gross Exports by Source Country and Source Industry, Machinery and Equipment nec (%)   54

3.13   Shares of China's 2005 Value Added Embodied in Gross Exports by Source Country and Source Industry, Machinery and Equipment nec (%)   56

3.14   Shares of China's 2008 Value Added Embodied in Gross Exports by Source Country and Source Industry, Machinery and Equipment nec (%)   58

3.15   Shares of China's 2009 Value Added Embodied in Gross Exports by Source Country and Source Industry, Machinery and Equipment nec (%)   60

3.16   Shares of China's 1995 Value Added Embodied in Gross Exports by Source Country and Source Industry, Basic Metals and Fabricated Metal Products (%)   62

3.17   Shares of China's 2000 Value Added Embodied
in Gross Exports by Source Country and Source
Industry, Basic Metals and Fabricated Metal
Products (%)   64

3.18   Shares of China's 2005 Value Added Embodied
in Gross Exports by Source Country and Source
Industry, Basic Metals and Fabricated Metal
Products (%)   66

3.19   Shares of China's 2008 Value Added Embodied
in Gross Exports by Source Country and Source
Industry, Basic Metals and Fabricated Metal
Products (%)   68

3.20   Shares of China's 2009 Value Added Embodied
in Gross Exports by Source Country and Source
Industry, Basic Metals and Fabricated Metal
Products (%)   70

3.21   Shares of China's 1995 Value Added Embodied
in Gross Exports by Source Country and Source
Industry, Wood, Paper, Paper Products, Printing
and Publishing (%)   73

3.22   Shares of China's 2000 Value Added Embodied
in Gross Exports by Source Country and Source
Industry, Wood, Paper, Paper Products, Printing
and Publishing (%)   75

3.23   Shares of China's 2005 Value Added Embodied
in Gross Exports by Source Country and Source
Industry, Wood, Paper, Paper Products, Printing
and Publishing (%)   77

3.24   Shares of China's 2008 Value Added Embodied
in Gross Exports by Source Country and Source
Industry, Wood, Paper, Paper Products, Printing
and Publishing (%)   79

3.25   Shares of China's 2009 Value Added Embodied
in Gross Exports by Source Country and Source
Industry, Wood, Paper, Paper Products, Printing
and Publishing (%)   81

3.26 Shares of China's 1995 Value Added Embodied
      in Gross Exports by Source Country and Source
      Industry, Transport Equipment (%)   83

3.27 Shares of China's 2000 Value Added Embodied
      in Gross Exports by Source Country and Source
      Industry, Transport Equipment (%)   84

3.28 Shares of China's 2005 Value Added Embodied
      in Gross Exports by Source Country and Source
      Industry, Transport Equipment (%)   86

3.29 Shares of China's 2008 Value Added Embodied
      in Gross Exports by Source Country and Source
      Industry, Transport Equipment (%)   88

3.30 Shares of China's 2009 Value Added Embodied
      in Gross Exports by Source Country and Source
      Industry, Transport Equipment (%)   89

3.31 China's Participation Index, Backward   94

3.32 China's Participation Index, Forward   95

3.33 China's Index of the Number of Production Stages in
      International and Domestic   98

3.34 China's Index of Distance to Final Demand   99

3.35 China's Domestic Value Added Embodies in Total
      Final Demand (Millions US Dollars)   101

3.36 China's Domestic Value Added Embodies in EU15
      Final Demand (Millions US Dollars)   103

3.37 China's Domestic Value Added Embodies in EU27
      Final Demand (Millions US Dollars)   104

3.38 China's Domestic Value Added Embodies in US Final
      Demand (Millions US Dollars)   105

3.39 China's Domestic Value Added Embodies in OECD
      Final Demand (Millions US Dollars)   106

3.40 China's Domestic Value Added Embodies in ASEAN
      Final Demand (Millions US Dollars)   107

3.41 China's Domestic Value Added Embodies in Hong
      Kong Final Demand (Millions US Dollars)   108

3.42 China's Domestic Value Added Embodies in Japan's
      Final Demand (Millions US Dollars)   109

3.43   China's Domestic Value Added Embodies in Korean
       Final Demand (Millions US Dollars)   110
3.44   China's Domestic Value Added Embodies in Chinese
       Taipe's Final Demand (Millions US Dollars)   111
3.45   China's Domestic Value Added Embodies in Thailand's
       Final Demand (Millions US Dollars)   112
4.1   PRC — Revealed Comparative Advantage Indexes
       Based on Domestic Value Embodied in Gross Exports
       and Gross Exports (Manufacturing Goods, to the
       World)   121
4.2   Competitiveness of PRC Exports RCA Index; World
       Market Shares and Herfindahl Index of Geographical
       Concentration Section I — Live Animals — Animal
       Products Measured by HS Categories   124
4.3   Competitiveness of PRC Exports RCA Index; World
       Market Shares and Herfindahl Index of Geographical
       Concentration Section II — Vegetable Products
       Measured by HS Categories   127
4.4   Competitiveness of PRC Exports RCA Index; World
       Market Shares and Herfindahl Index of Geographical
       Concentration Section III — Animal or Vegetable
       Fats Measured by HS Categories   130
4.5   Competitiveness of PRC Exports RCA Index; World
       Market Shares and Herfindahl Index of Geographical
       Concentration Section IV — Prepared Foodstuffs
       Measured by HS Categories   131
4.6   Competitiveness of PRC Exports RCA Index; World
       Market Shares and Herfindahl Index of Geographical
       Concentration Section V — Mineral Products
       Measured by HS Categories   135
4.7   Competitiveness of PRC Exports RCA Index; World
       Market Shares and Herfindahl Index of Geographical
       Concentration Section VI — Products of the
       Chemicals or Allied Industries Measured by HS
       Categories   136

4.8   Competitiveness of PRC Exports RCA Index; World
Market Shares and Herfindahl Index of Geographical
Concentration Section VII — Plastics and Rubber
and Articles thereof Measured by HS Categories . . .   139

4.9   Competitiveness of PRC Exports RCA Index; World
Market Shares and Herfindahl Index of Geographical
Concentration Section VIII — Raw Hides and Skins
Measured by HS Categories   140

4.10 Competitiveness of PRC Exports RCA Index; World
Market Shares and Herfindahl Index of Geographical
Concentration Section IX — Wood and Articles of
Wood Measured by HS Categories   141

4.11 Competitiveness of PRC Exports RCA Index; World
Market Shares and Herfindahl Index of Geographical
Concentration Section X — Pulp of Wood or of other
Fibrous Cellulosic Material Measured by HS
Categories   142

4.12 Competitiveness of PRC Exports RCA Index; World
Market Shares and Herfindahl Index of Geographical
Concentration Section XI — Textile and Textile
Articles Measured by HS Categories   143

4.13 Competitiveness of PRC Exports RCA Index; World
Market Shares and Herfindahl Index of Geographical
Concentration Section XII — Footwear Measured
by HS Categories   148

4.14 Competitiveness of PRC Exports RCA Index; World
Market Shares and Herfindahl Index of Geographical
Concentration Section XIII — Articles of Stones
Measured by HS Categories   149

4.15 Competitiveness of PRC Exports RCA Index; World
Market Shares and Herfindahl Index of Geographical
Concentration Section XIV — Natural or Cultured
Pearls Measured by HS Categories   150

4.16 Competitiveness of PRC Exports RCA Index; World
Market Shares and Herfindahl Index of Geographical

Concentration Section XV — Base Metals Measured
by HS Categories   151
4.17   Competitiveness of PRC Exports RCA Index; World
Market Shares and Herfindahl Index of Geographical
Concentration Section XVI — Machinery and
Mechanical Appliances Measured by HS
Categories   154
4.18   Competitiveness of PRC Exports RCA Index; World
Market Shares and Herfindahl Index of Geographical
Concentration Section XVII — Vehicles, Aircraft and
Vessels Measured by HS Categories   155
4.19   Competitiveness of PRC Exports RCA Index; World
Market Shares and Herfindahl Index of Geographical
Concentration Section XVIII — Optical,
Photographic, Cinematographic Measured
by HS Categories   157
4.20   Competitiveness of PRC Exports RCA Index; World
Market Shares and Herfindahl Index of Geographical
Concentration Section XIX — Arms and Ammunition
Measured by HS Categories   158
4.21   Competitiveness of PRC Exports RCA Index; World
Market Shares and Herfindahl Index of Geographical
Concentration Section XX — Miscellaneous
Manufactured Articles Measured
by HS Categories   159
4.22   Competitiveness of PRC Exports RCA Index; World
Market Shares and Herfindahl Index of Geographical
Concentration Section XXI — Works of Art Measured
by HS Categories   160
4.23   Decomposition of Changes in PRC Exports into CMS
Components (Various Years and Percent)   161
5.1   PRC Exports to the World of Textiles and Apparel
Products (Percentage Share by HS Category)   168
5.2   PRC Exports of Textiles and Apparel Products —
Top Five Import Markets (Million US Dollars
by HS Category)   171

5.3   Textile Categories Under MFA Quota for the PRC,
       Vietnam and India   176

5.4   OLS Estimates of the US Import Demand
       from the Vietnam with the PRC as the
       Presumed Competition (By T&A Category, 1995–2008)   210

5.5   OLS Estimates of the US Import Demand
       from the PRC with Vietnam as the
       Presumed Competitor (By T&A Category, 1995–2008)   214

5.6   OLS Estimates of the US Import Demand
       from the PRC with India as the
       Presumed Competitor (By T&A Category, 1995–2008)   219

5.7   OLS Estimates of the US Import Demand
       from India with the PRC as the
       Presumed Competitor (By T&A Category, 1995–2008)   224

6.1   China's Tariffs on Agricultural and Manufactured
       Products MFN Weighted Average (%)   242

6.2   Anti-Dumping Measures Imposed as Reported
       by WTO Members 1995–2014   246

6.3   Countervailing Measures Imposed as Reported
       by WTO Members 1995–2014   247

6.4   Safeguard Measures Imposed as Reported by WTO
       Members 1995–2014   249

6.5   Top 10 Anti-Dumping Targets, 1995–2014
       (number of measures in force)   252

6.6   Countries Targeting China for Anti-Dumping Measures,
       1995–2014   253

6.7   Countries Against Whom China is Imposing
       Anti-Dumping Measures, 1995–2014   255

6.8   Commodity Composition of China's CV and AD
       Measures, 1995–2014   260

6.9   US Antidumping and Countervailing Duty Orders
       in Place (1977–2009/2015)   267

6.10   USITC, Antidumping and Countervailing Duty Orders
       Against China, in Place, as of September 29, 2015
       (1984–2015)   268

7.1   PRC Aid Commitments by Recipient
      (2000–2012)   278
7.2   Summary Characteristics of the PRC Aid Data   . . .   289
7.3   GLM Estimates of PRCAID by Year   292
7.4   Estimates of PRC Aid Using a Random Effects
      GLS Estimator   294
8.1   Value of Chinese Cross-Border M&As, as Compared
      to the World and Developed Economies,
      1990–2012   298
8.2   The Top Non-financial TNCs from China, Ranked
      by Foreign Assets, 2011   299
8.3   Cross-border M&A Deals Worth Over $1 Billion
      Completed in 2012 by China   305
8.4   Potential Outcomes in a Cournot–Nash Duopoly R&D
      Acquisition Model   328
8.5   Cross-Border M&A Deals in Technology Worth
      More than $100 Million between 2005 and 2013   . . .   330
8.6   Cross-Border Incomplete and Troubled M&A Deals
      in Technology Worth More than $100 Million between
      2005 and 2013   332
8.7   Heard on the Street — PRC TNCs Purchases of Small
      Foreign Assets   333

List of Figures

2.1 Exports of Goods and Services as a Percent of GDP
China, Japan, Korea, Malaysia, Thailand, India . . .   11

2.2 Annual Growth of Exports of Goods and Services
China, Japan, Korea, Malaysia, Thailand, India . . .   12

2.3 Total Exports to the World by China, Thailand, India,
Korea and Malaysia, 2001–2012   12

2.4 Total Exports to Developed Market Economies
by China, Thailand, India, Korea and Malaysia,
2001–2012   13

2.5 Total Exports to USA by China, Thailand, India,
Korea and Malaysia, 2001–2012   14

2.6 Total Exports to EU28 by China, Thailand, India,
Korea and Malaysia, 2001–2012   14

2.7 Total Exports to Japan by China, Thailand, India,
Korea and Malaysia, 2001–2012   15

2.8 Total Exports to Africa by China, Thailand, India,
Korea and Malaysia, 2001–2012   16

2.9 Total Exports to Asia by China, Thailand, India, Korea
and Malaysia, 2001–2012   16

2.10 Total Exports to Latin America and the Caribbean by
China, Thailand, India, Korea and Malaysia, 2001–2012   17

3.1 Foreign Value-Added Content of China's Exports by
Major Categories as a Percent of Total Exports . . .   27

3.2   Origin of China's Foreign Value-Added Content
       of Exports, 1995–2009 (%)   30
5.1   Market Equilibrium with a Binding Quota   199
6.1   AD Measures, by HS Sector and Year   256
6.2   Safeguard Measures by HS Sector and Year   258
6.3   Countervailing Measures by HS Sector and Year . . .   259

About the Author

 Joseph Pelzman is a Professor of Economics, International Affairs and Law at George Washington University. He also serves as the Chairman of the Department's PhD Committee and its PhD Admissions Committee.

Professor Pelzman was a Fulbright Scholar at Ben Gurion University of the Negev, Israel (1995–1996) and Renmin University of China (2012–2013). He was a Visiting Professor of Law and Economics at Catholic University Law School (2001–2005); a Visiting Professor of Law at the Radzyner School Of Law, The Interdisciplinary Center, Herzliya, Israel (2001); Research Associate at The Maurice Falk Institute for Economic Research in Israel, The Hebrew University of Jerusalem, Jerusalem, Israel (1988–1997); Visiting Scholar and Fellow at The Russian Research Center, Harvard University (1991–1992); and Visiting Professor of Economics and Lady Davis Fellow, Department of Economics and Soviet and East European Research Center, The Hebrew University of Jerusalem (1984–1985).

Professor Pelzman has published numerous academic articles in a number of leading economics journals, including the *American Economic Review, Journal of Political Economy, European Economic*

Review, and *Southern Economic Journal.* His primary professional interests are in the areas of international trade, international trade law, and law and economics. His trade policy focus is on adjustment costs of international trade and "skill differentials" as determinants of the "new" comparative advantage.

His latest books both representing the outcome of his Fulbright fellowships include *The Economics of the Middle East and North Africa,* London: World Scientific Press, 2012 and *Spillover Effects of China Going Global,* London: World Scientific Press, 2016. His recent journal contributions include "'Womb for Rent': International Service Trade Employing Assisted Reproduction Technologies (ARTs)", *Review of International Economics,* 21, 3, August 2013; and "PRC Outward Investment in the US and Europe: A Model of R&D Acquisition", *Review of Development Economics,* 2015.

Chapter 1

Introduction

With the granting of Most Favored Nation (MFN) status by the US and Europe to the People's Republic of China (PRC) in the early 1980s, the trading world radically changed. The PRC's participation in the world trading community has not only expanded beyond all expectations, it has also transformed our understanding of the importance of dynamic comparative advantage and the importance of "global value-added chains" in transforming trade in commodities into trade in skills. China's increasing footprint in the global marketplace does not only include its merchandise exports. It also covers enormous natural resource flows from Latin America and Africa, and foreign direct investment in and out of the PRC. The major challenge to the global community of China's participation in the global economy is the resulting "spillovers" that it creates for its major trading and investment partners. These spillovers are treated as both negative and positive-sum rather than as zero-sum in the global international trade game.

For developed-country consumers, China's growing footprint presents the opportunity of acquiring low-cost consumer goods, across varying levels of sophistication and efficiency. Within the literature on global value-added chains, these products are generally referred to as downstream processed products, involving the flow of intermediates into China for processing and eventual exporting to developed market economies. The resulting interrelationship between the developed economies and the PRC in these products is obvious.

Equally important is the demand in China for developed country merger and acquisition (M&A) partners in many high value-added industries such as autos, computers, military equipment and digital entertainment.

China's developing-country neighbors are immediately affected by the major price and value competition that they face. India, Malaysia, Mexico, Pakistan, the Philippines, Thailand and Vietnam, among others face a reduction in exports attributable to China's growth in exports. As the value-added chain has expanded, the same countries are beginning to benefit from the PRC "spillover" in that they gain by participating in the PRC's product mix.

With China's growth expanding, even at less than double digit, its demand for raw materials, intermediate products, and skilled labor also expands. Relative to Western Europe and the United States, the growth in PRC demand for raw materials and other intermediates has altered the traditional OECD Development Assistance Committee (DAC) country foreign aid to the developing world. Unlike US and other DAC country-assistance programs, the PRC has used its expanded demand for raw materials and intermediates as an entrée to providing infrastructure-development assistance to many countries in Africa and Latin America at lower than world market prices. In so doing, the PRC can acquire the necessary inputs to their industrial projects, provide employment for much of its construction and services industries and, at the same time, provide basic infrastructure development to the developing countries. The resulting "spillover" effects in Africa and Latin America can be observed in improved local highway infrastructure, improved telecommunication services, expanded schools, hospitals and port facilities.

The rapid uncontrolled industrial development in the PRC has also created a major negative "spillover" effect in its large cities and countryside — air and water pollution. These pollutants do not honor country borders and consequently spillover international borders. The environmental challenges created by China's rapid growth and expanding international trade are both domestic and international in scope.

The goal of this volume is to investigate these "spillover" effects in depth. In Chapter 2, we present an aggregate overview of China's export growth in order to identify its overall "global footprint." Chapter 3 begins the process of decomposing this export growth. The first decomposition issue is — what portion of China's exports are Chinese in origin and what portion are imported inputs. In Chapter 4, we continue the investigation by assessing China's competitive advantage by focusing on our estimated Revealed Comparative Advantage (RCA) and Constant Market Share (CMS) Indexes. In Chapter 5, we review China's long-term successful sectors — Textile and Apparel — in light of the new competition rules developed by the WTO in the Uruguay Round in 2005 and applied to the PRC in 2008.

The experience of China's ten year participation in the WTO is discussed in Chapter 6. Despite the fact that the PRC gained enormously from its participation in the global economy, it endured a long process of litigation initiated by developed country WTO members who were struggling with outdated jurisprudence with respect to dumping and countervailing law and the application of countervailing duties to non-market economies. The bilateral litigation between the US and the PRC as the former struggled with domestic US trade law and WTO jurisprudence is explored in detail in this Chapter.

The PRC's search for raw materials and intermediate products altered its traditional Communist foreign aid program of the 1950's and 1960's. The new 21st century tied-aid program and its mix of infrastructural development and acquisition of payment in kind is investigated in Chapter 7. Continuing with this outward expansion, Chapter 8 focuses on China's outward investment strategy as a vehicle by which to acquire "start-up" companies in the US and Israel where the residual acquired component is new technology. Despite the attempts by the US Congress to limit PRC M&A activity on large ticket items, the PRC has been very successful in acquiring very small "start-up" companies with a clear cut agenda to introduce major innovation in its domestic market.

The question of the overall cost-benefit analysis of the spillover effect of China's policy of going global is left to the reader. Clearly the PRC leadership has concluded that they are on the correct development path, subject to periodic adjustments.

Chapter 2

An Overview of China's Export Growth

When the People's Republic of China (PRC) was granted Most Favored Nation (MFN) status by the United States in 1979, no one imagined that Chinese participation in the world trading community would have such a global impact. In the early post-MFN period, most of the analysts were unable to differentiate China from other Soviet type economies. Bayard *et al.* [1981, 1982], Pelzman [1986a, 1986b, 1992], were an exception in that they predicted a non-Soviet type response from the PRC. In fact, they predicted an expansion in Chinese exports in a single sector driven by offshore processing — textiles and apparel. When the quota system governing textile and apparel trade was dismantled in 2005 for most of the quota bound exporters and in 2008 for the PRC, bets were placed on India rather than China as the beneficiary. As Pelzman and Reese [1989] and Pelzman and Shoham [2009a] have demonstrated, betting on India was incorrect.

The current attention to PRC's export growth has been driven by three concerns: (1) the impact of China's export growth on world welfare and the consequences of a reduction in Chinese growth on its international trade[1]; (2) the shift in Chinese exports towards

---

[1]China's gross domestic product is reported to have grown 7.3 percent in the third quarter of 2014, its slowest rate of growth in more than five years. China, is expected to miss its annual GDP target of 7.5 percent for the first time since 1998. This slowdown is expected to have negative spillover effects on the world economy.

higher value-added products and (3) the bilateral imbalances created between the US and the PRC and the EU and the PRC [Lemoine and Ünal, 2012; Deer and Song, 2012].

2.1. Theoretical Modeling of the Impact of China's Exports

An understanding of the spillover effects of international trade is best described by the recent micro-level heterogeneity theoretical trade models examined by Melitz [2003], Melitz and Redding [2014], Eaton and Kortum [2002], Bernard *et al.* [2003] and Arkolakis *et al.* [2012], where trade elasticity and the share of expenditure on trade are sufficient statistics to measure the spillover effects of international trade. Using these models, Hsieh and Ossa [2011] present empirical estimates of the spillover effects of China's growth on its trading partners.

The starting point of this literature is the conventional CES utility functions across N countries and S industries, where it is assumed that each industry provides consumers with a continuum of differentiated products.

$$U_j = \prod_{s=1}^{S} \left(\sum_{i=1}^{N} \int_0^{M_{ijs}} x_{ijs}(v_{is})^{\frac{\sigma_s-1}{\sigma_s}} dv_{is} \right)^{\frac{\sigma_s-1}{\sigma_s}\mu_{js}}, \qquad (2.1)$$

where

$x_{ijs}(v_{is})$ represents the quantity of an industry s variety originating from country i consumed in country j;

M_{ijs} represents is the number of industry s varieties originating from country i available in country j;

σ_s represents the elasticity of substitution between industry s varieties and assumed to be greater than 1 and

μ_{js} represents the share of country j's income spent on industry s varieties.

To produce $x_{ijs}(v_{is})$ in country i, the literature assumes that firms will be employing a linear-production function with productivity differences governed by country specific heterogeneous technology. Labor inputs consist of both production labor and that required to deliver the end product to country j. Shipping the good to a destination requires a per-unit iceberg trade cost of $\tau_{ijs} \geq 1$.

Firms are assumed to face the following demand function:

$$x_{ijs} = \frac{p_{ijs}^{-\sigma_s}}{P_{js}^{1-\sigma_s}} \mu_{js} w_j L_j. \tag{2.2}$$

For a particular productivity level, a perfectly competitive firm from country i incurs a marginal cost to produce variety s affected by the specific wage rate (w_j) and the number of workers or consumers (L_j).

The two prices include the delivered price of variety s in country j (p_{ijs}) and a price index for all industry s varieties (P_{js}). Perfect competition forces marginal cost pricing:

$$p_{ijs} = \frac{\sigma_s}{\sigma_s - 1} \frac{\tau_{ijs} w_i}{\varphi}, \tag{2.3}$$

$$P_{js} = \left(\sum_{i=1}^{N} M_{ijs} p_{ijs} (\tilde{\varphi}_{ijs})^{1-\sigma_s} \right)^{\frac{1}{1-\sigma_s}}, \tag{2.4}$$

where φ is a measure of productivity and $\tilde{\varphi}_{ijs}$ represents the productivity of the representative firm in industry s of country i selling to country j.

The most fascinating element of these models is that regardless of the specific competition framework one assumes for the domestic or foreign firms, the models all produce identical aggregate outcomes. The models yield the same expressions for trade flows, price indexes and welfare gains from trade. Labor-market clearing results in an equilibrium where the left-hand side of Equation (2.5) presents the fraction of country i's labor devoted to cover both fixed and variable costs and on the right-hand side the expected number of workers required to enter industry s.

$$\left[\sum_{s=1}^{S} \frac{(\theta_s + 1)(\sigma_s - 1)}{\theta_s \sigma_s} \mu_{js} \right] L_i = \sum_{s=1}^{S} M_{is}^e (\theta_s + 1) f_{js}^e. \tag{2.5}$$

The key coefficients controlling trade are CES price indexes that consumers face and trade shares. Trade shares are driven by trade costs and cross price elasticities, θ_s, σ_s.

Tables 2.1 and 2.2 reproduce the share of total imports and the share of imports from the PRC, relative to total manufacturing expenditure for China's trade partners for 1995, 2001 and 2007 [Hsieh and Ossa, 2011, Tables 4 and 5]. While the size of manufacturing imports from China has grown on average from 5.3 percent to 14.7 percent in total manufacturing imports, its share of total manufacturing expenditure increased from 1.1 percent to 3.9 percent over the 1995–2007 period. This reflects the growing footprint of China in world trade.

Hsieh and Ossa [2011], using industry specific estimates of σ_s ranging from 1.7 to 19.5 and estimates of θ_s ranging from 0.8 to 22.0 predict the spillover effects of China's growth and continued export expansion, *ceteris paribus*. Overall, they predict

Table 2.1   Share of Total Imports in Total Expenditure (%)

	1995	2001	2007
USA	15.8	21.4	21.8
Argentina	11.2	11.7	19.7
Brazil	9.1	15.9	13.9
Canada	36.1	38.4	40.0
France	32.0	38.1	40.0
Germany	22.1	30.3	33.9
India	10.7	11.1	17.9
Italy	20.3	25.6	28.2
Japan	4.8	7.3	11.5
Mexico	30.6	34.5	31.7
Russia	—	18.3	22.4
UK	28.1	30.8	35.0
Africa	23.4	22.1	31.9
Other Asia	23.5	23.0	23.5
Other Europe	24.1	27.8	28.3
Other LA	20.6	19.7	26.1
Average	20.8	19.7	26.1

Source: Hsieh and Ossa [2011, Table 4]. Data represent the share of manufacturing imports relative to total manufacturing expenditure. The data is updated by the authors from the NBER-UN and NBER-CES databases.

Table 2.2 Share of China's Imports in Total Expenditure (%)

	1995	2001	2007
USA	2.3	3.5	5.6
Argentina	0.6	0.9	2.7
Brazil	0.5	0.6	1.7
Canada	1.4	2.1	4.6
France	1.2	1.8	3.4
Germany	1.2	1.9	3.5
India	0.6	1.0	4.0
Italy	0.9	1.3	2.8
Japan	1.1	2.2	4.6
Mexico	0.5	1.2	3.9
Russia	—	1.2	3.3
UK	1.3	2.5	4.2
Africa	1.4	1.5	4.7
Other Asia	2.3	3.6	6.8
Other Europe	1.1	1.7	3.5
Other LA	1.0	1.5	3.7
Average	1.1	1.8	3.9

Source: Hsieh and Ossa [2011, Table 5]. Data represent the share of manufacturing imports from China relative to total manufacturing expenditure. The data is updated by the authors from the NBER-UN, NBER-CES and the China Annul Bureau of Statistic's Annual Survey of Industrial Production databases.

that only 3.0 percent of the worldwide benefits of Chinese-increased productivity spillover to other countries. Their explanations for this small spillover effect are based on their presumptions that (1) the Chinese productivity changes do not spillover over to China's export sector, thus limiting the terms of trade effect; (2) there is a limited correlation between China's growth in productivity and the trade elasticity, θ_s constraining the home market effect and (3) the share of Chinese imports in total expenditure of its trade partners is still fairly limited.

These estimates should be viewed as a first approximation of the "real" spillover effects of China's expansion. These estimates would be much larger if the authors considered the strong linkages between

China and its Asian trade partners in the full spectrum of trade in intermediate inputs along with trade in end products.

2.2. Decomposition of China's Exports

The significance of China–Asia integration can be best assessed by focusing on a decomposition of China's global exports by country. The inter-Asian connection of these trade patterns is a reflection of the fact that the magnitude of China's footprint in international trade is not just governed by the size of their total exports but also by the linkages developed with its immediate Asian neighbors. One of the spillover effects of China's massive footprint is the inclusion of other Asian economies in the world-trading network, either as part of the Chinese value-added network or as independent participants.

In Figure 2.1, we compare the total exports of China, India, Korea, Malaysia, Thailand and Japan, relative to their GDP, in the period 1980–2012. It is striking that China's total exports of goods and services relative to GDP is not as substantial as that of its Asian neighbors, Korea, Malaysia and Thailand. As Rodrik [2006] and Lin and Li [2006] point out, using total exports to GDP as a measuring instrument, China's exports do not seem quite so exceptional. However, this standard is too simple. We are ignoring the "large country effect." Countries such as India and the PRC are expected to be more self-sufficient, simply because of their large size, and endowment. Despite China's growth and what appears to be the export driver to that growth, its size makes it less dependent on foreign trade. Having said that, the fact that China in 2012 exported 27 percent of its GDP is very impressive.

In Figure 2.2, we present the annual export growth rates of each of these Asian competitors. Despite the fact that the annual growth rates are moving in the same cycle over the entire 1980–2012 period, the annual cycles in growth rates for the PRC are far more limited. Overall, the comparisons in both figures make the export performance of the PRC look less exceptional than one would expect. What then leads to the large spillover effect?

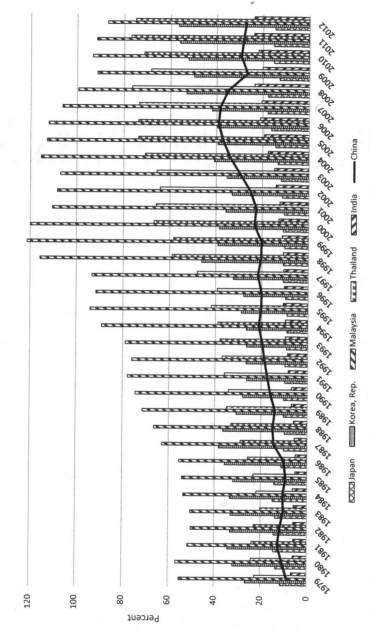

Figure 2.1   Exports of Goods and Services as a Percent of GDP — China, Japan, Korea, Malaysia, Thailand, India

Source: UN, COMTRADE

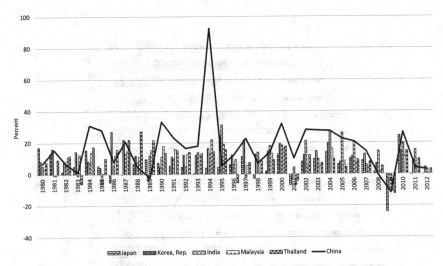

Figure 2.2   Annual Growth of Exports of Goods and Services of China, Japan, Korea, Malaysia, Thailand, India

Source: UN, COMTRADE

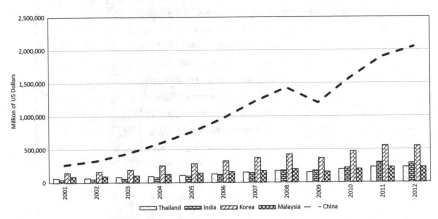

Figure 2.3   Total Exports to the World by China, Thailand, India, Korea and Malaysia, 2001–2012

Source: UN, COMTRADE

Beginning with the data contained in Figure 2.3, we clearly see that the answer to this question lies in the sheer magnitude of China's footprint on world trade. PRC exports deflated by their GDP hides the impact of the dollar value of PRC exports. In Figure 2.3, we provide a comparative look at China's total exports relative to its Asian competitors, India, Korea, Malaysia and Thailand, over the period 2001–2012. The difference in size is mind boggling. China's exports in 2012 to the world are four times as large as its major competitor — Korea. Comparing China to India is equally telling. China's total exports to the world in 2012 was seven times that of India. That is, it is not just the "large country effect" but rather the price competitiveness of PRC exports which leads to this very large footprint.

As we outline the direction and amount of trade by major groupings, the magnitude of China's footprint is obvious across other geographic groups. Figure 2.4 presents China's total exports to the developed countries. China's total exports in 2012, to this market, is five times as large as that from its major competitor — Korea.

Likewise, China's exports is ten times as large as that of India. Figures 2.5–2.7 present a comparison of China's total exports to the United States, EU28 and Japan, respectively. The differential in magnitude of China's total exports to these destinations, relative to its Asian competitors, highlights the extreme size differential of

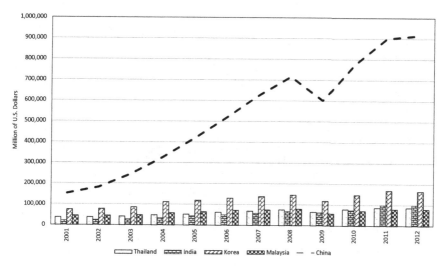

Figure 2.4   Total Exports to Developed Market Economies by China, Thailand, India, Korea and Malaysia, 2001–2012
Source: UN, COMTRADE

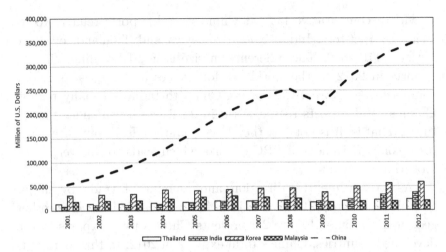

Figure 2.5 Total Exports to USA by China, Thailand, India, Korea and Malaysia, 2001–2012

Source: UN, COMTRADE

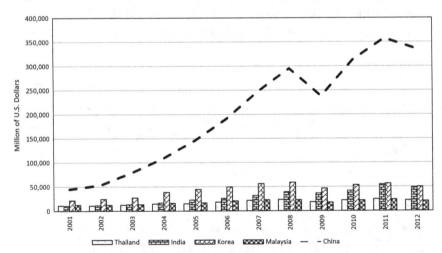

Figure 2.6 Total Exports to EU28 by China, Thailand, India, Korea and Malaysia, 2001–2012

Source: UN, COMTRADE

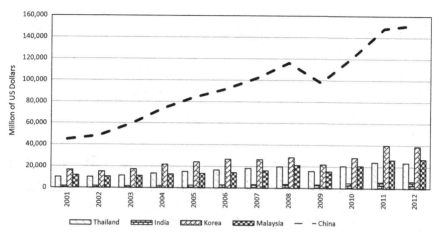

Figure 2.7   Total Exports to Japan by China, Thailand, India, Korea and Malaysia, 2001–2012

Source: UN, COMTRADE

China's presence in the industrialized countries. This observation speaks to the competitiveness of Chinese firms and not to the PRC as an incorporated State-Owned Enterprise (SOE).

Shifting the direction of trade to developing countries one would expect that China's major export competitors would have a more significant presence. Figures 2.8–2.10 present a comparison of China's total exports to Africa, Asia and Latin America and the Caribbean, respectively. The differential in magnitude of China's total exports to these destinations, relative to its Asian competitors, continues to exist. Despite the fact that the absolute exports from China are smaller, the differential relative to its Asian competitors remains.

Overall, a review of these aggregate trade flows supports the view that the PRC's footprint in exports, between 2001 and 2012, is more "global" than that which is exclusively relegated to develop market economies.

A number of questions are raised by looking at China's total exports. First, we have the country of origin issue: what portion of China's exports are Chinese in origin and what portion are imported

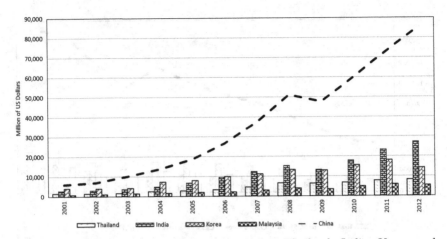

Figure 2.8   Total Exports to Africa by China, Thailand, India, Korea and Malaysia, 2001–2012

Source: UN, COMTRADE

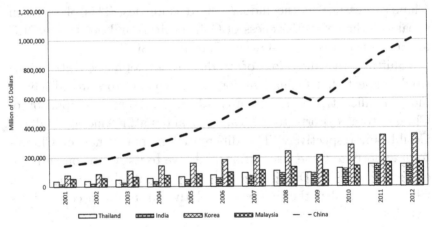

Figure 2.9   Total Exports to Asia by China, Thailand, India, Korea and Malaysia, 2001–2012

Source: UN, COMTRADE

inputs? Second, we have the diversification issue: what has happened to the bundle of goods that are exported to the industrialized countries? Do we observe a concentration of products or a diversification? Third, have China's exports increased in sophistication? Is the

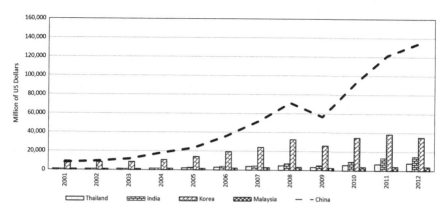

Figure 2.10 Total Exports to Latin America and the Caribbean by China, Thailand, India, Korea and Malaysia, 2001–2012
Source: UN, COMTRADE

conclusion reached by Amiti and Freund [2010], that

> *"the skill content of China's exports increased from 1992 to 2005, but the increase was driven almost entirely by China's processing exports. . . . There was little skill upgrading found in China's non-processing exports,"*

correct? Finally, can we estimate China's export competitiveness? In particular, is the expansion in China's competitiveness driven by new products, new markets or both? In Chapter 3, we take up the first and third questions — what portion of China's exports are Chinese in origin, what portion are imported inputs and are these exports becoming more sophisticated? In Chapter 4, we present estimates of China's revealed comparative advantage (RCA), its geographic and product diversification and tie it to the sophistication issue raised by Amiti and Freund [2010]. A detailed review of the trade performance of China's Textile and Apparel industry with its major consumer markets — the USA and the EU, before and after the collapse of the Multi-Fiber Arrangement (MFA) in 2008 is presented in Chapter 5.

Chapter 3

The Value-Added Chain in China's International Trade

The magnitude of China's footprint in international trade, while significant, disguises a more complex reality of China's participation in the global economy. With China's accession into the WTO, there has been a rising investment in information and communications technology (ICT), as well as investment in domestic education and human capital development. The outcome of these trends is observed in China's exports when they are measured in terms of value added. This result is in conformity with the general principles of "globalization," where what matters in a country's "competitiveness" is its ability to utilize intermediate goods and services from other countries without having to develop a whole integrated industry. As Baldwin [2009] and Baldwin and Venables [2010] have pointed out, what matters more today is "what you do" rather than "what you sell." In that vein participating in a global network enhances competitiveness by providing access to cheaper, more differentiated and better quality inputs as well as technological spillovers.

The popular concept of "supply chains" in economics originates from the basic idea that today's goods and services do not have "parents" in the traditional country of origin definition [Pelzman and Shoham, 2010]. In a world where we have international production networks across firms, industries and countries, the reality of international trade is bound up in what Coe and Hess [2007] refer to as the international fragmentation of production. As Hudson [2004] points out, the shift in our understanding of "supply chains" as being "networks" represents the increasingly complex interactions among global producers and suppliers.

Historically, there were two key drivers for this enormous flow of intermediate goods and services. The first of these was the drastic reduction in transaction costs. The cost of moving products across the many layers in intermediate producers — such as transport and port costs, freight and insurance costs, tariffs, costs associated with non-tariff measures, mark-ups by importers and wholesalers — all have dropped drastically. Add to that the continuous reduction in barriers to trade arising from successive rounds of global trade liberalization, and you have a clear cost incentive for entering into the global production networks [Grossman and Rossi-Hansberg, 2008; Baldwin, 2009]. Liberalization of investment through multilateral and bilateral investment agreements (BIT) further spurred these interrelationships as firms use FDI to spread their production activities across many countries thus leading to a further expansion of production networks.

The second driver to this expansion of production networks is less expensive and far more reliable telecommunications, information management software and increasingly powerful computers (ICT). This second driver noted by Baldwin [2009] significantly decreased the cost of coordinating complex activities over long distances across global production networks. This has also transformed many non-tradable and tradable services. In particular, as the OECD has pointed out, despite the fact that distribution, sales and production activities were the first movers in these global production networks, they have led the way for R&D and decision-making activities to locate internationally [OECD, 2011a, 2011b, 2011c].

China's participation in the global value-added network has been discussed in the literature substantially. Anecdotal stories about China's value added in such items as the IPhone and IPad [Linden *et al.*, 2009; Dedrick *et al.*, 2009; Dierickx and Cool, 1989; Korkea-maki and Takalo, 2010] have even reached the popular press. In order to get beyond the individual product and industry case studies, we look for trends using the database created at the OECD–WTO-Trade in Value Added (TiVA) which links national Input–Output (I–O) tables with bilateral trade data to develop inter-country I–O tables.

3.1. The Formal Model of the Value-Added Chain in International Trade

In order to better understand the tracking of international trade via value-added chains we summarize the methodology applied by Koopman *et al.* [2010] as it was implemented at the OECD–WTO–TiVA database. The starting point for the conceptual framework is the standard 2×2 model, where each country produces differential tradable goods i ranging from 1 to N in T sectors.[1] Tradable goods include final, intermediate and raw material goods. Countries can treat these products as direct consumer goods or as intermediate inputs. For the data base, it is assumed that each country exports both intermediate and final goods to the other.

In this framework, it is assumed that country j's output must be used as an intermediate good or a final good at home or abroad, or

$$X_j = A_{jj}X_j + A_{jk}X_k + Y_{jj} + Y_{jk}, \quad j, k = 1, 2, \qquad (3.1)$$

where X_j is the $N \times 1$ gross output vector of country j, Y_{jk} is the $N \times 1$ final demand vector from country k for final goods produced in j and A_{jk} is the $N \times N$ I–O coefficient matrix, giving intermediate use in k of goods produced in j. The 2×2 production and trade relationship can be restated in matrix notation applied by the OECD–WTO–TiVA:

$$\begin{bmatrix} X_1 \\ X_2 \end{bmatrix} = \begin{bmatrix} A_{11} & A_{12} \\ A_{21} & A_{22} \end{bmatrix} \begin{bmatrix} X_1 \\ X_2 \end{bmatrix} + \begin{bmatrix} Y_{11} & Y_{12} \\ Y_{21} & Y_{22} \end{bmatrix}. \qquad (3.2)$$

Rearranging terms, we have:

$$\begin{bmatrix} X_1 \\ X_2 \end{bmatrix} = \begin{bmatrix} I - A_{11} & -A_{12} \\ -A_{21} & I - A_{22} \end{bmatrix}^{-1} \begin{bmatrix} Y_{11} + Y_{12} \\ Y_{21} + Y_{22} \end{bmatrix} = \begin{bmatrix} B_{11} & B_{12} \\ B_{21} & B_{22} \end{bmatrix} \begin{bmatrix} Y_1 \\ Y_2 \end{bmatrix}, \qquad (3.3)$$

---

[1] The rationale for adding the T sectors is that while trade occurs across N possible goods, the I–O table is limited to only T sectors.

where B_{kj} is the $N \times N$ Leontief inverse matrix, representing the total requirement matrix that gives the amount of gross output in producing country k required for a one-unit increase in final demand in country j. Y_j is a $2N \times 1$ vector that gives the global use of j's final goods. That is:

$$X = (I - A)^{-1}Y = BY, \tag{3.4}$$

where X and Y are $2N \times 1$ vectors, and A and B are $2N \times 2N$ matrices.

In order to decompose international trade into transactions in intermediate and final demands requires measuring domestic and foreign contents, first for production, and then for international trade. Let V_k be the $1 \times N$ direct value-added coefficient vector. Each element of V_s gives the share of direct domestic value added in total output. This is equal to one minus the intermediate input share from all countries (including domestically produced intermediates):

$$V_j \equiv u\left(I - \sum_k A_{kj}\right), \tag{3.5}$$

where u is a $1 \times N$ unity vector. One can consider V to be a $2 \times 2N$ matrix of direct domestic value added for both countries:

$$V \equiv \begin{bmatrix} V_1 & 0 \\ 0 & V_2 \end{bmatrix}. \tag{3.6}$$

The unique contribution of the OECD–WTO–TiVA data base as explained by Koopman [2010] is their creation of a "direct value-added share" (VAS) matrix by source:

$$VAS \equiv VB = \begin{bmatrix} V_1 B_{11} & V_1 B_{12} \\ V_2 B_{21} & V_2 B_{22} \end{bmatrix}. \tag{3.7}$$

Within the VAS matrix, the individual elements represent domestic VAS of domestically produced products in a particular sector at home. For example, $V_2 B_{21}$ denote the share of country 2's value added in a particular product. The first N columns in the VAS matrix includes all value added, domestic and foreign, needed to produce one additional unit of domestic products in country 1. The second

N columns present VAS for production in country 2. This matrix is expanded to $N \times N$ countries. Because all value added must be either domestic or foreign, the sum along each column is one:

$$V_1 B_{11} + V_2 B_{21} = V_1 B_{12} + V_2 B_{22} = u. \qquad (3.8)$$

In order to link the value-added shares to exports the OECD–WTO-TiVA data base [Koopman *et al.*, 2010] denote E_{jk} to represent an $N \times 1$ vector of gross exports from j to k.

$$E_{j*} = \sum_{k \neq j} E_{jk} = \sum_{k} (A_{jk} X_k + Y_{jk}) \quad j, k = 1, 2, \qquad (3.9)$$

$$E = \begin{bmatrix} E_{1*} & 0 \\ 0 & E_{2*} \end{bmatrix} \qquad (3.10)$$

and

$$\hat{E} = \begin{bmatrix} \mathrm{diag}(E_{1*}) & 0 \\ 0 & \mathrm{diag}(E_{2*}) \end{bmatrix}, \qquad (3.11)$$

where E is a $2N \times 2$ matrix and $\hat{E}$ is a $2N \times 2N$ diagonal matrix.

Combining the VAS matrix and an export matrix as weights produces a $2 \times 2N$ matrix $VAS\_\hat{E}$ the sectoral measure of VAS by source country:

$$VAS\_\hat{E} \equiv VB\hat{E} = \begin{bmatrix} V_1 B_{11} \hat{E}_1 & V_1 B_{12} \hat{E}_2 \\ V_2 B_{21} \hat{E}_1 & V_2 B_{22} \hat{E}_2 \end{bmatrix}. \qquad (3.12)$$

The elements of this matrix captures all upstream sectors' contributions to value added in a specific sector's exports. For example, for the famous Chinese iPhone case $VAS\_\hat{E}$ includes value added in the electronics component sector itself as well as value added in inputs from all other sectors (such as glass, rubber, transportation and design) used to produce the iPhone for exports by China.

Domestic and foreign content of exports and value-added exports are different concepts. Despite the fact that both concepts measure the value generated by factors employed in the producing country, domestic content of exports is independent of where that value is used. Value-added trade, on the other hand, depends on how a country's exports are used by importers. It is the value added generated by country 1 but absorbed by country 2. Consequently, the OECD–WTO-TiVA data base [Koopman *et al.*, 2010] define related measures of domestic and foreign contents in sector level gross exports, not sector level value-added exports. Because the latter depends on who absorbs the value added, it has to be defined in terms of final demand after zeroing its diagonal,

$$VÂT \equiv \hat{V}BY = \begin{bmatrix} \hat{V_1} & 0 \\ 0 & \hat{V_2} \end{bmatrix} \begin{bmatrix} B_{11} & B_{12} \\ B_{21} & B_{22} \end{bmatrix} \begin{bmatrix} Y_{11} & Y_{12} \\ Y_{21} & Y_{22} \end{bmatrix}. \tag{3.13}$$

In Equation (3.13), Y_{kj} is an N by 1 vector and Y is $2N$ by 2 final demand matrix. $\hat{V_j}$ is a N by N diagonal matrix with direct value-added coefficients along the diagonal. The resulting $VÂT$ is a $2N$ by 2 value-added production matrix, its diagonal elements represent each country's production of value added absorbed by itself while its off diagonal elements constitute the $2N$ by 2 bilateral value-added trade matrix. It excludes value added produced in the home country that returns home after processing abroad.

The aggregate (2×2) measure of value added by source in gross exports is given by:

$$VAS\_E \equiv VBE = \begin{bmatrix} V_1 B_{11} E_{1*} & V_1 B_{12} E_{2*} \\ V_2 B_{21} E_{1*} & V_2 B_{22} E_{2*} \end{bmatrix}. \tag{3.14}$$

VAS_E represents the OECD–WTO-TiVA data base's [Koopman *et al.*, 2010] the value added by source measure. Diagonal elements of VAS_E define the domestic value added in each country's exports. Off-diagonal elements give the foreign value added embodied in each country's exports.

Gross exports are decomposed into foreign value (FV) added and domestic value (DV) added as follows:

$$DV = \begin{bmatrix} V_1 B_{11} E_{1*} \\ V_2 B_{22} E_{2*} \end{bmatrix} = \begin{bmatrix} V_1 (I - A_{11} - A_{12}(I - A_{22})^{-1} A_{21})^{-1} E_{1*} \\ V_2 (I - A_{22} - A_{21}(I - A_{11})^{-1} A_{12})^{-1} E_{2*} \end{bmatrix},$$
$$\tag{3.15}$$

$$\text{FV} = \begin{bmatrix} V_2 B_{21} E_{1*} \\ V_1 B_{12} E_{2*} \end{bmatrix} = \begin{bmatrix} u(A_{21} - A_{12}(I - A_{22})^{-1} A_{21}) \\ \times (I - A_{11} - A_{12}(I - A_{22})^{-1} A_{21})^{-1} E_{1*} \\ u(A_{12} - A_{21}(I - A_{11})^{-1} A_{12}) \\ \times (I - A_{22} - A_{21}(I - A_{11})^{-1} A_{12})^{-1} E_{2*} \end{bmatrix}.$$

$$(3.16)$$

The OECD–WTO-TiVA data base [Koopman *et al.*, 2010] accounts for a country importing its own value added, which has been exported but returns home after being processed abroad. *VAS_E* attributes foreign and domestic contents to multiple countries when intermediate products cross borders in the $N \times N$ cases.

In the $N \times N$ cases, the OECD–WTO-TiVA data base [Koopman *et al.*, 2010] provide all value-added components despite the various complications. Production, value-added shares, and sources of value added in gross exports are given by:

$$X = (I - A)^{-1} Y = BY,$$
$$VAS = VB, \qquad\qquad (3.17)$$
$$VAS\_E = VBE.$$

With N countries and N sectors, X and Y are $NN \times 1$ vectors; A and B are $NN \times NN$ matrices; V and VAS are $N \times NN$ matrices; E is a $NN \times N$ matrix and VAS_E is a $N \times N$ matrix.

Summing over all trading partners for all goods, the OECD–WTO-TiVA database [Koopman *et al.*, 2010] provides the key decomposition equation that states that a country's gross exports to the world is the sum of the following five broad terms:

$$E_{j*} = DV_j + FV_j$$

$$= V_j B_{jj} \sum_{k \neq j} Y_{jk} \qquad\qquad (a)$$

$$+ V_j B_{jj} \sum_{k \neq j} A_{jk} X_{kk} \qquad\qquad (b)$$

$$+ V_j B_{jj} \sum_{k \neq j} \sum_{l \neq j,k} A_{jk} X_{kl} \qquad\qquad (c)$$

$$+ V_j B_{jj} \sum_{k \neq j} A_{jk} X_{kj} \tag{d}$$

$$+ FV_j, \tag{e}$$

$$\tag{3.18}$$

where [Koopman *et al.*, 2010, p. 14] notes that (a) DV added embodied in the exports of final goods and services absorbed by the importer; (b) DV added embodied in exports of intermediate inputs used by the importer to produce its domestically needed products; (c) DV added embodied in intermediate exports used by the importer to produce goods for third countries ("indirect value-added exports"); (d) DV added embodied in intermediate exports used by the importer to produce goods shipped back to the source country ("reflected domestic value added") and (e) value added from foreign countries embodied in gross exports ("foreign value added used in exports").

Summing (a)–(c) generates each country's value-added exports to the world. Summing (a)–(d) generates domestic content in a country's gross exports. As such, the OECD–WTO-TiVA database [Koopman *et al.*, 2010] captures only the direct effect and the first round of the indirect effect in the value-chain stream. If the value-chain stream consists of multiple segmentations, then the only way to capture the full order of the decomposition is by using information on domestic final demand in the importing country to obtain domestic value added embodied in the intermediate goods used by direct importers to produce domestically-needed final goods. This estimate is the best that can be provided by this data set. In that case, one can obtain a full-order decomposition, using the five value-added components to account for 100 percent of the country's gross exports only when trade values are summed over all sectors and all trading partners (total exports to the world).

3.2. The Value-Added Chain in China's International Trade: Upstream Linkages or Looking Backward

In Figure 3.1, we begin decomposing China's foreign trade in terms of value added. The data shown in Figure 3.1 is the foreign

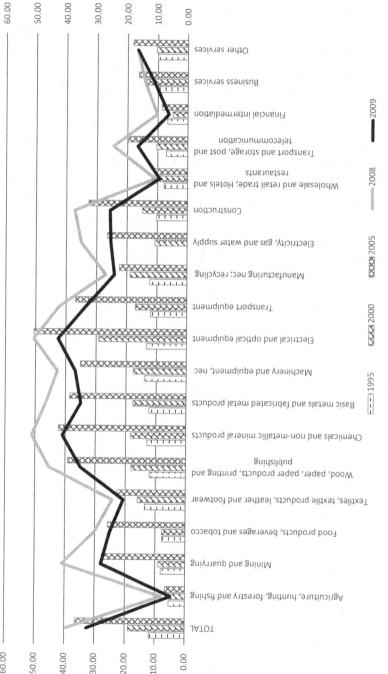

Figure 3.1 Foreign Value-Added Content of China's Exports by Major Categories as a Percent of Total Exports

Source: OECD–WTO_Statistics on Trade in Value Added (TiVA)

content of China's exports by major categories over the 1995–2009 period. This represents looking backward along the value chain. The foreign content of China's exports increased significantly in all manufacturing sectors between 1995 and 2009. The electrical equipment industry had the highest percentage at 43 percent in 2009, triple the percentage in 1995. Chemicals and minerals, machinery, and basic metals industries also had relatively high shares.

The size of foreign value added in a country's total exports clearly depends on its size and patterns of specialization. Smaller economies tend to have higher shares of foreign value added embodied in their exports; larger economies have a wider variety of domestically sourced intermediate goods available and are therefore less reliant on foreign imports of intermediates. Countries with substantial natural resources, such as the United States, have lower ratios of foreign value added in exports as much of its agricultural activities require fewer intermediate goods in the production process.

China's exports are highly heterogeneous and therefore display varying degrees of foreign value-added content. This is not surprising given that variations in foreign value-added content of exports is determined by China's economic structure and export composition. Moreover, it is determined by technical characteristics of specific production functions and sophistication in support services which tend to facilitate the fragmentation and outsourcing that we observe in China's exports.

Another important factor that we observe in Figure 3.1 is that the foreign value added is very large in basic industries that make heavy use of imported primary goods such as mining, basic metals, chemicals and rubber and plastics. Fragmentation is also significant for those sectors which produce what is considered high technology intensive products. Parts and components are often produced in one country and exported to another in which they are assembled. This international division of labor is found in China's electrical machinery, television and communication equipment, computing machinery and motor vehicle industries.

Increased production standardization is a major factor explaining the increased foreign value added in China's exports. Van Assche and

Gangnes [2007], Ma and Van Assche [2010] and Van Assche [2012] point out that when firms push the specialization envelope to its extreme form — referred to as "modulization" — the production process is compartmentalized into a very unique set of fixed I–O technical coefficients. Consequently, components can be brought in from a variety of sources as long as they meet the required technical specification. The more a product is standardized in this way, the easier it becomes to shift country of origin for many of the required components. Products that are composed of different "modules" can be assembled using components from other producers because the end product has a pre-determined standard that has been codified with no room for improvising. This process of developing and accepting international standards for products is part of the process of "globalization" that China accepted early in its outreach program. The major spillover effect of this process for China has been the codification of transactions and creation of new kinds of tradable services. Products that do not have this "modality" characteristic require components to be specifically adjusted to each other, thereby limiting the separability of production activities.

For China, the global value-added chain goes beyond the separability of the production function it also involves extending its frontiers to include many of its East Asian neighbors as part of its "global factory." The clearest sign of the positive spillover effect of its large footprint in international trade is the inclusion of neighbors as components of its export ventures. Figure 3.2 presents the origin of China's total foreign value added in its exports. It is not surprising to find that the foreign value added of China's exports originates largely in neighboring economies. The majority of China's exports over the period 1995–2009 embody intermediates sourced from within Asia. Exports of components originating from Taiwan, Korea and Japan are exported to China for final assembly.

The primary explanation for this geographical clustering is due to the importance of distance for general cost reduction in joint planning and inspection of production processes and the importance of distance to local transportation hubs. The empirical studies point out that despite the reduction in transportation costs they are

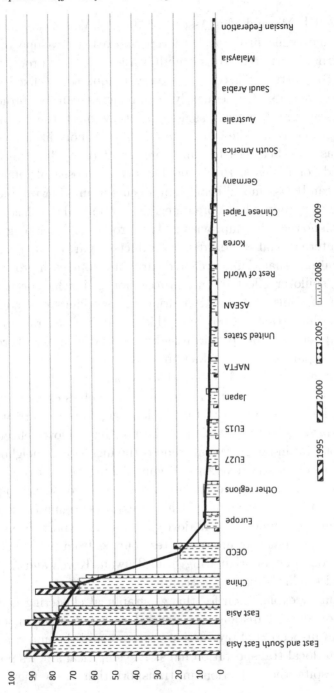

Figure 3.2   Origin of China's Foreign Value-Added Content of Exports, 1995–2009 (%)

Source: OECD–WTO Statistics on TiVA

still much larger than tariff duties and when calculated in terms of 'weight-to-value' ratios remain significant [Harrigan, 2010; Van Assche, 2012; Hummels, 2007]. In addition to transport costs and general production coordination costs, the time for delivery of final and intermediates is also crucial for the firm operating across borders in a global value-added network. Hummels and Schaur [2012] and Harrigan and Venables [2006] point out that the adoption of 'just-in-time' techniques forces firms to locate production of time-sensitive components closer to their hubs.

Tables 3.1–3.5 presents the shares of China's value added embodied in gross exports by source country and source industry for one of the high tech sectors — electrical and optical equipment for the years 1995–2009, respectively. Given the coverage differential in Chinese data in the period pre- and post-2005, we believe that presenting each year's data can present a more accurate snapshot of the composition of the upstream value-added changes. The most obvious data change is the spillover effect of adding other Asian economies to the Chinese upstream operation. While there has been an increase in linkages with Thailand, Cambodia and Vietnam, Malaysia shows the largest increase in this sector. Despite that fact that the OECD continues to represent a large upstream partner, the data is actually referring to two major OECD participants, the US and Japan. While we normally think of upstream value in terms of tradable components, the data continue to point to a large and growing requirement for upstream business services.

The next major Chinese export with high value-added content is the chemicals and non-metallic mineral products sector. Considered to be a medium-high technology sector, the chemicals sector generally known to be the sector with the highest vertical foreign direct investment (FDI) and is the main source of intra-firm trade — trade between foreign affiliates. Large firms in this sector, including Chinese SOEs, have extensive upstream activities (exploration, recovery, transport) and downstream activities (refining, chemicals, marketing and retail).

In Tables 3.6–3.10, we present the evolution of China's value-added content in the chemicals and non-metallic mineral

Table 3.1 Shares of China's 1995 Value Added Embodied in Gross Exports by Source Country and Source Industry Electrical and Optical Equipment (%)

	Total	Japan	Korea	East Asia	ASEAN	East and South East Asia	China	Chinese Taipei	United States	OECD	EU27	EU15	NAFTA
TOTAL	100	3.83	0.97	92.94	0.8	93.75	86.68	1.08	1.9	9.35	1.81	1.71	2.14
Agriculture, hunting, forestry and fishing	2.29	0	0.02	2.12	0.05	2.17	2.1	0	0.04	0.1	0.02	0.02	0.04
Mining and quarrying	4.42	0.01	0.01	3.56	0.13	3.7	3.54	0.01	0.06	0.33	0.04	0.04	0.11
Food products, beverages and tobacco	0.47	0	0	0.42	0.01	0.43	0.41	0	0.01	0.03	0.01	0.01	0.01
Textiles, textile products, leather and footwear	1.34	0.06	0.07	1.26	0.01	1.27	1.07	0.05	0.01	0.18	0.02	0.02	0.01
Wood, paper, paper products, printing and publishing	1.73	0.13	0.05	1.4	0.06	1.46	1.18	0.03	0.1	0.41	0.07	0.07	0.14
Chemicals and non-metallic mineral products	10.06	0.37	0.21	9.04	0.11	9.16	8.21	0.22	0.3	1.2	0.25	0.24	0.33
Basic metals and fabricated metal products	8.18	0.51	0.14	7.47	0.03	7.5	6.71	0.1	0.11	1.08	0.21	0.19	0.14

												NAFTA
Machinery and equipment, nec	4.36	0.04	0.01	4.22	0.01	4.23	4.17	0	0.03	0.14	0.05	0.05	0.03
Electrical and optical equipment	43.4	1.26	0.16	42.57	0.15	42.72	40.69	0.33	0.32	2.03	0.27	0.26	0.32
Transport equipment	0.56	0.03	0	0.51	0	0.51	0.47	0	0.01	0.06	0.02	0.02	0.01
Manufacturing nec; recycling	0.87	0.02	0.01	0.85	0	0.85	0.82	0.01	0	0.04	0.01	0.01	0
Electricity, gas and water supply	2.13	0.12	0.02	1.97	0.01	1.98	1.78	0.04	0.03	0.24	0.04	0.04	0.04
Construction	0.13	0.02	0	0.08	0	0.08	0.05	0	0.02	0.07	0.02	0.01	0.02
Wholesale and retail trade; Hotels and restaurants	7.74	0.26	0.05	7.18	0.07	7.24	6.73	0.1	0.12	0.63	0.14	0.13	0.15
Transport and storage, post and telecommunication	3.82	0.22	0.07	3.31	0.05	3.36	2.95	0.04	0.13	0.65	0.16	0.14	0.15
Financial intermediation	3.92	0.16	0.05	3.56	0.05	3.61	3.23	0.06	0.09	0.48	0.11	0.11	0.1
Business services	4.26	0.54	0.08	3.28	0.05	3.33	2.58	0.04	0.48	1.49	0.31	0.29	0.5
Other services	0.32	0.07	0.01	0.13	0.01	0.14	0	0.04	0.03	0.2	0.06	0.05	0.04

Source: OECD–WTO Statistics on TiVA

Table 3.2   Shares of China's 2000 Value Added Embodied in Gross Exports by Source Country and Source Industry, Electrical and Optical Equipment (%)

	Total	Japan	Korea	East Asia	ASEAN	East and South East Asia	China	Chinese Taipei	United States	OECD	EU27	EU15	NAFTA
TOTAL	100	8.06	2.36	83.82	1.88	85.7	70.86	1.93	4.47	22.05	5.55	5.38	4.86
Agriculture, hunting, forestry and fishing	1.79	0.03	0.01	1.55	0.06	1.61	1.51	0	0.03	0.13	0.03	0.03	0.03
Mining and quarrying	4.43	0.01	0.01	2.91	0.23	3.13	2.87	0.01	0.03	0.44	0.08	0.07	0.08
Food products, beverages and tobacco	0.51	0.04	0	0.44	0.01	0.45	0.4	0	0.01	0.08	0.01	0.01	0.01
Textiles, textile products, leather and footwear	1.02	0.05	0.04	0.93	0.01	0.94	0.8	0.04	0.02	0.14	0.02	0.02	0.02
Wood, paper, paper products, printing and publishing	1.8	0.19	0.05	1.31	0.06	1.38	1.05	0.02	0.13	0.58	0.14	0.14	0.16
Chemicals and non-metallic mineral products	9.58	0.76	0.28	7.91	0.28	8.19	6.5	0.32	0.45	2.13	0.5	0.48	0.49
Basic metals and fabricated metal products	7.4	1.02	0.18	6.05	0.08	6.14	4.51	0.34	0.32	2.16	0.44	0.42	0.37

Machinery and equipment, nec	1.67	0.21	0.03	1.29	0.02	1.31	1	0.04	0.12	0.53	0.15	0.15	0.12
Electrical and optical equipment	43.81	2.84	1.16	38.86	0.64	39.5	34.21	0.42	1.95	8.24	2.08	2.06	2.02
Transport equipment	0.83	0.04	0.01	0.73	0.01	0.74	0.69	0	0.02	0.12	0.05	0.04	0.02
Manufacturing nec; recycling	0.34	0.14	0	0.29	0	0.29	0.14	0.01	0.01	0.18	0.02	0.02	0.02
Electricity, gas and water supply	3.32	0.25	0.05	3.04	0.04	3.08	2.66	0.05	0.06	0.49	0.08	0.08	0.07
Construction	0.26	0.09	0.01	0.19	0	0.19	0.09	0	0.01	0.16	0.04	0.04	0.01
Wholesale and retail trade; Hotels and restaurants	8.42	0.75	0.18	7.12	0.2	7.32	5.83	0.29	0.26	1.74	0.43	0.4	0.3
Transport and storage, post and telecommunication	4.66	0.42	0.08	3.72	0.08	3.8	3.09	0.08	0.26	1.21	0.34	0.32	0.28
Financial intermediation	4.4	0.39	0.09	3.59	0.08	3.67	2.88	0.14	0.19	1.03	0.24	0.24	0.2
Business services	5.05	0.67	0.16	3.42	0.06	3.48	2.39	0.14	0.55	2.31	0.77	0.76	0.58
Other services	0.7	0.16	0.02	0.46	0.01	0.47	0.24	0.01	0.06	0.38	0.11	0.11	0.06

Source: OECD–WTO Statistics on TiVA

Table 3.3   Shares of China's 2005 Value Added Embodied in Gross Exports by Source Country and Source Industry, Electrical and Optical Equipment (%)

	Total	Japan	Korea	Malaysia	East Asia	ASEAN	East and South East Asia	China	Chinese Taipei	United States	OECD	EU27	EU15	NAFTA
TOTAL	100	7.96	7.02	2.7	72.17	7.2	79.37	49.47	6.66	4.75	30.26	7.98	7.54	5.48
Agriculture, hunting, forestry and fishing	1.87	0.02	0.04	0.06	1.53	0.1	1.63	1.47	0	0.03	0.15	0.03	0.02	0.04
Mining and quarrying	5.35	0.01	0.03	0.24	1.98	0.54	2.52	1.92	0.02	0.06	0.93	0.1	0.08	0.19
Food products, beverages and tobacco	0.51	0.03	0	0.01	0.4	0.03	0.42	0.36	0	0.01	0.08	0.02	0.02	0.01
Textiles, textile products, leather and footwear	0.44	0.02	0.02	0	0.33	0.02	0.35	0.26	0.02	0.02	0.09	0.02	0.02	0.02
Wood, paper, paper products, printing and publishing	1.52	0.17	0.09	0.04	0.95	0.09	1.04	0.66	0.04	0.11	0.62	0.16	0.15	0.15
Chemicals and non-metallic mineral products	8.14	0.86	0.67	0.34	5.39	0.73	6.12	3.43	0.4	0.58	3.05	0.79	0.74	0.64
Basic metals and fabricated metal products	7.41	1.16	0.46	0.06	5.54	0.18	5.71	3.67	0.25	0.29	2.82	0.65	0.6	0.36

Machinery and equipment, nec	1.75	0.22	0.07	0.07	1.1	0.1	1.2	0.78	0.02	0.16	0.8	0.31	0.3	0.17
Electrical and optical equipment	42.21	2.16	3.27	1.34	34.17	3.81	37.98	24.59	4.01	1.49	9.29	2.02	1.93	1.64
Transport equipment	0.62	0.1	0.06	0	0.43	0.02	0.45	0.27	0.01	0.04	0.3	0.09	0.08	0.05
Manufacturing nec; recycling	1.25	0.28	0.04	0	0.98	0.01	1	0.63	0.03	0.06	0.46	0.08	0.07	0.06
Electricity, gas and water supply	2.84	0.22	0.16	0.04	2.39	0.12	2.5	1.84	0.14	0.06	0.63	0.14	0.12	0.07
Construction	0.23	0.06	0.01	0.01	0.11	0.01	0.13	0.02	0.01	0.01	0.16	0.06	0.05	0.02
Wholesale and retail trade; Hotels and restaurants	8.03	0.82	0.53	0.27	5.56	0.68	6.25	3.3	0.69	0.35	2.64	0.75	0.7	0.43
Transport and storage, post and telecommunication	4.64	0.72	0.38	0.07	3.08	0.26	3.34	1.56	0.22	0.27	2.16	0.59	0.54	0.32
Financial intermediation	4.39	0.39	0.21	0.09	3.39	0.19	3.58	2.43	0.27	0.18	1.16	0.28	0.27	0.21
Business services	7.5	0.6	0.91	0.04	3.97	0.27	4.24	1.77	0.4	0.96	4.46	1.71	1.65	1.03
Other services	1.3	0.12	0.07	0	0.87	0.04	0.91	0.52	0.12	0.07	0.47	0.19	0.18	0.08

Source: OECD–WTO Statistics on TiVA

Table 3.4 Shares of China's 2008 Value Added Embodied in Gross Exports by Source Country and Source Industry, Electrical and Optical Equipment (%)

	Total	Japan	Korea	Malaysia	East Asia	ASEAN	East and South East Asia	China	Chinese Taipei	United States	OECD	EU27	EU15	NAFTA
TOTAL	100	6.6	5.86	2.35	73.17	6.47	79.64	54.57	5.2	4.41	26.06	6.39	5.92	5.08
Agriculture, hunting, forestry and fishing	2	0.02	0	0.06	1.66	0.12	1.78	1.64	0	0.04	0.1	0.02	0.02	0.05
Mining and quarrying	6.91	0.01	0.03	0.18	2.3	0.44	2.74	2.25	0.01	0.1	1.15	0.09	0.08	0.23
Food products, beverages and tobacco	0.57	0.03	0	0.01	0.47	0.03	0.5	0.44	0	0.01	0.07	0.02	0.02	0.01
Textiles, textile products, leather and footwear	0.44	0.01	0.02	0	0.36	0.02	0.38	0.32	0.01	0.01	0.06	0.02	0.02	0.01
Wood, paper, paper products, printing and publishing	1.47	0.13	0.07	0.03	0.96	0.08	1.04	0.74	0.03	0.11	0.51	0.12	0.11	0.14
Chemicals and non-metallic mineral products	7.94	0.66	0.59	0.25	5.44	0.6	6.04	3.87	0.29	0.6	2.64	0.64	0.6	0.65
Basic metals and fabricated metal products	7.33	0.99	0.4	0.04	5.44	0.13	5.57	3.86	0.19	0.38	2.67	0.59	0.54	0.48

Machinery and equipment, nec	1.73	0.18	0.07	0.03	1.14	0.05	1.19	0.87	0.02	0.1	0.72	0.33	0.32	0.11
Electrical and optical equipment	40.94	1.63	2.99	1.22	34.68	3.4	38.08	26.98	3.02	1.26	6.98	0.84	0.79	1.33
Transport equipment	0.6	0.11	0.03	0	0.46	0.02	0.48	0.31	0.01	0.03	0.25	0.07	0.06	0.03
Manufacturing nec; recycling	1.29	0.24	0.03	0	1.01	0.02	1.03	0.72	0.02	0.07	0.45	0.1	0.09	0.07
Electricity, gas and water supply	2.21	0.18	0.07	0.02	1.79	0.09	1.88	1.45	0.07	0.06	0.48	0.12	0.11	0.07
Construction	0.22	0.06	0.01	0.01	0.1	0.01	0.12	0.03	0.01	0.02	0.15	0.05	0.04	0.02
Wholesale and retail trade; Hotels and restaurants	8.43	0.75	0.36	0.25	6.03	0.68	6.7	4.12	0.62	0.33	2.28	0.61	0.56	0.42
Transport and storage, post and telecommunication	4.37	0.61	0.27	0.07	2.83	0.27	3.1	1.6	0.18	0.25	1.85	0.54	0.5	0.29
Financial intermediation	4.36	0.3	0.13	0.07	3.43	0.15	3.58	2.69	0.24	0.14	0.91	0.24	0.23	0.16
Business services	7.83	0.59	0.75	0.11	4.12	0.34	4.47	2.03	0.37	0.84	4.33	1.79	1.67	0.93
Other services	1.36	0.11	0.04	0	0.93	0.03	0.96	0.64	0.11	0.06	0.45	0.2	0.19	0.08

Source: OECD–WTO Statistics on TiVA

Table 3.5 Shares of China's 2009 Value Added Embodied in Gross Exports by Source Country and Source Industry, Electrical and Optical Equipment (%)

	Total	Japan	Korea	Malaysia	East Asia	ASEAN	East and South East Asia	China	Chinese Taipei	United States	OECD	EU27	EU15	NAFTA
Total	100	6.32	5.39	2.23	74.64	5.96	80.59	57.42	4.74	4.52	25.16	6.07	5.58	5.18
Agriculture, hunting, forestry and fishing	2.12	0.02	0	0.04	1.84	0.1	1.93	1.81	0	0.04	0.11	0.02	0.02	0.05
Mining and quarrying	5.8	0.01	0.03	0.12	2.01	0.43	2.44	1.95	0.02	0.07	1.09	0.07	0.06	0.18
Food products, beverages and tobacco	0.63	0.03	0	0.01	0.55	0.02	0.57	0.51	0	0.01	0.07	0.02	0.01	0.01
Textiles, textile products, leather and footwear	0.54	0.01	0.02	0	0.48	0.02	0.5	0.44	0.01	0.01	0.06	0.01	0.01	0.01
Wood, paper, paper products, printing and publishing	1.57	0.13	0.07	0.02	1.07	0.06	1.13	0.84	0.02	0.14	0.54	0.1	0.09	0.17
Chemicals and non-metallic mineral products	7.79	0.63	0.48	0.22	5.61	0.53	6.14	4.17	0.3	0.55	2.35	0.54	0.5	0.59
Basic metals and fabricated metal products	6.74	0.8	0.28	0.04	5.05	0.11	5.16	3.84	0.13	0.27	2.17	0.51	0.46	0.37

Machinery and equipment, nec	1.73	0.14	0.09	0.03	1.17	0.05	1.22	0.92	0.01	0.11	0.69	0.3	0.29	0.12
Electrical and optical equipment	40.56	1.71	2.57	1.23	34.43	3.14	37.57	27.38	2.72	1.33	6.71	0.83	0.76	1.42
Transport equipment	0.63	0.1	0.04	0	0.48	0.02	0.5	0.33	0.01	0.04	0.26	0.06	0.05	0.05
Manufacturing nec; recycling	1.36	0.23	0.03	0	1.1	0.02	1.12	0.82	0.02	0.06	0.41	0.08	0.07	0.07
Electricity, gas and water supply	2.17	0.19	0.12	0.02	1.79	0.09	1.88	1.36	0.11	0.04	0.5	0.11	0.1	0.05
Construction	0.25	0.06	0.01	0.01	0.11	0.02	0.13	0.03	0.01	0.02	0.17	0.06	0.05	0.02
Wholesale and retail trade; Hotels and restaurants	8.59	0.65	0.36	0.23	6.35	0.6	6.95	4.66	0.56	0.31	2.09	0.56	0.5	0.39
Transport and storage, post and telecommunication	4.37	0.58	0.29	0.07	2.82	0.25	3.07	1.61	0.18	0.27	1.88	0.52	0.47	0.3
Financial intermediation	4.91	0.29	0.15	0.07	3.96	0.15	4.11	3.3	0.17	0.18	0.94	0.21	0.2	0.2
Business services	8.64	0.61	0.79	0.11	4.65	0.34	4.99	2.57	0.37	0.99	4.66	1.87	1.74	1.09
Other services	1.6	0.11	0.04	0	1.17	0.03	1.2	0.9	0.1	0.06	0.45	0.19	0.18	0.08

Source: OECD–WTO_Statistics on TiVA

Table 3.6 Shares of China's 1995 Value Added Embodied in Gross Exports by Source Country and Source Industry, Chemicals and Non-metallic Mineral Products (%)

	Total	Japan	Korea	East Asia	ASEAN	East and South East Asia	China	Chinese Taipei	United States	OECD	EU27	EU15
TOTAL	100	2.1	1.19	91.75	1.03	92.78	87.08	1.07	2.08	8.16	1.69	1.59
Agriculture, hunting, forestry and fishing	6.5	0	0.03	6.17	0.08	6.25	6.13	0.01	0.08	0.21	0.04	0.04
Mining and quarrying	8.89	0.01	0.01	7.28	0.27	7.55	7.25	0.01	0.11	0.58	0.06	0.06
Food products, beverages and tobacco	1.07	0	0.01	0.97	0.02	0.99	0.96	0	0.02	0.07	0.02	0.02
Textiles, textile products, leather and footwear	3.27	0.15	0.17	3.11	0.02	3.13	2.66	0.13	0.03	0.41	0.05	0.04
Wood, paper, paper products, printing and publishing	1.98	0.13	0.06	1.6	0.07	1.67	1.36	0.04	0.12	0.44	0.08	0.08
Chemicals and non-metallic mineral products	47.86	0.54	0.46	45.87	0.23	46.1	44.34	0.45	0.61	2.17	0.43	0.41
Basic metals and fabricated metal products	2.86	0.18	0.05	2.57	0.02	2.58	2.29	0.04	0.05	0.42	0.1	0.09

Machinery and equipment, nec	1.43	0.03	0.01	1.32	0	1.33	1.28	0	0.02	0.11	0.04	0.04
Electrical and optical equipment	0.96	0.19	0.02	0.8	0.03	0.83	0.5	0.06	0.06	0.34	0.06	0.06
Transport equipment	0.55	0.03	0.01	0.5	0	0.5	0.47	0	0.01	0.07	0.02	0.02
Manufacturing nec; recycling	0.71	0.02	0.01	0.69	0	0.69	0.66	0.01	0	0.03	0.01	0.01
Electricity, gas and water supply	3.31	0.07	0.03	3.12	0.02	3.14	2.96	0.05	0.04	0.2	0.04	0.03
Construction	0.13	0.01	0	0.07	0	0.08	0.05	0	0.02	0.06	0.02	0.01
Wholesale and retail trade; Hotels and restaurants	7.94	0.14	0.06	7.32	0.07	7.4	6.99	0.1	0.13	0.53	0.13	0.12
Transport and storage, post and telecommunication	4.7	0.17	0.09	4.09	0.07	4.15	3.75	0.05	0.17	0.67	0.16	0.14
Financial intermediation	3.67	0.11	0.06	3.3	0.06	3.36	3.02	0.06	0.09	0.43	0.11	0.1
Business services	3.85	0.29	0.09	2.87	0.06	2.93	2.41	0.04	0.48	1.24	0.28	0.27
Other services	0.3	0.04	0.01	0.1	0.01	0.11	0	0.03	0.03	0.18	0.06	0.05

Source: OECD–WTO_Statistics on TiVA

Table 3.7 Shares of China's 2000 Value Added Embodied in Gross Exports by Source Country and Source Industry, Chemicals and Non-metallic Mineral Products (%)

	Total	Japan	Korea	East Asia	ASEAN	East and South East Asia	China	Chinese Taipei	United States	OECD	EU27	EU15
TOTAL	100	2.75	1.67	88.1	1.56	89.66	81.71	1.73	2.21	10.52	2.44	2.34
Agriculture, hunting, forestry and fishing	5.32	0.02	0.01	4.69	0.13	4.82	4.65	0.01	0.08	0.28	0.05	0.05
Mining and quarrying	11.06	0.01	0.01	7.97	0.42	8.4	7.95	0.01	0.03	0.59	0.11	0.1
Food products, beverages and tobacco	0.97	0.02	0.01	0.84	0.02	0.87	0.81	0	0.02	0.08	0.02	0.01
Textiles, textile products, leather and footwear	2.97	0.1	0.14	2.78	0.03	2.81	2.4	0.13	0.04	0.34	0.04	0.04
Wood, paper, paper products, printing and publishing	1.79	0.1	0.05	1.34	0.07	1.41	1.16	0.02	0.11	0.43	0.1	0.1
Chemicals and non-metallic mineral products	43.38	0.84	0.64	41.04	0.43	41.46	38.82	0.66	0.59	2.88	0.61	0.59
Basic metals and fabricated metal products	2.08	0.19	0.07	1.69	0.02	1.71	1.33	0.1	0.09	0.54	0.13	0.12

Machinery and equipment, nec	1.37	0.13	0.02	1.08	0.02	1.1	0.88	0.04	0.08	0.36	0.11	0.11
Electrical and optical equipment	2.01	0.21	0.2	1.52	0.06	1.58	1.04	0.06	0.18	0.8	0.19	0.19
Transport equipment	0.74	0.03	0.01	0.67	0.01	0.68	0.63	0	0.01	0.08	0.03	0.03
Manufacturing nec; recycling	0.2	0.04	0	0.17	0	0.17	0.12	0	0.01	0.06	0.01	0.01
Electricity, gas and water supply	5.59	0.11	0.05	5.38	0.03	5.41	5.14	0.06	0.05	0.28	0.04	0.04
Construction	0.19	0.03	0	0.14	0	0.14	0.1	0	0.01	0.07	0.02	0.02
Wholesale and retail trade; Hotels and restaurants	8.17	0.25	0.13	7.31	0.12	7.43	6.63	0.28	0.15	0.82	0.2	0.19
Transport and storage, post and telecommunication	5.13	0.2	0.08	4.34	0.08	4.42	3.94	0.09	0.22	0.83	0.22	0.2
Financial intermediation	4.55	0.16	0.09	3.78	0.07	3.85	3.37	0.12	0.15	0.68	0.18	0.18
Business services	3.94	0.26	0.13	2.99	0.04	3.03	2.46	0.12	0.35	1.19	0.33	0.32
Other services	0.54	0.06	0.02	0.38	0	0.38	0.28	0.01	0.04	0.19	0.05	0.05

Source: OECD–WTO Statistics on TiVA

Table 3.8   Shares of China's 2005 Value Added Embodied in Gross Exports by Source Country and Source Industry, Chemicals and Non-metallic Mineral Products (%)

	Total	Japan	Korea	East Asia	ASEAN	East and South East Asia	China	China Taipei
TOTAL	100	5.61	2.91	68.42	3.17	71.58	57.78	1.81
Agriculture, hunting, forestry and fishing	5.12	0.03	0.1	3.9	0.16	4.06	3.77	0
Mining and quarrying	15.4	0.02	0.01	4.31	1.02	5.33	4.24	0.04
Food products, beverages and tobacco	1.24	0.03	0.01	0.76	0.04	0.8	0.71	0
Textiles, textile products, leather and footwear	0.81	0.02	0.02	0.64	0.02	0.66	0.57	0.02
Wood, paper, paper products, printing and publishing	1.78	0.15	0.05	1.09	0.04	1.13	0.87	0.02
Chemicals and non-metallic mineral products	42.61	1.99	1.52	35.77	1.12	36.89	31.34	0.85
Basic metals and fabricated metal products	2.65	0.31	0.11	1.95	0.03	1.97	1.46	0.07
Machinery and equipment, nec	1.58	0.19	0.03	1.03	0.02	1.05	0.79	0.02
Electrical and optical equipment	1.4	0.31	0.08	0.81	0.08	0.9	0.32	0.1
Transport equipment	0.68	0.12	0.06	0.51	0.01	0.52	0.32	0
Manufacturing nec; recycling	1.05	0.2	0.03	0.83	0.01	0.83	0.59	0.02
Electricity, gas and water supply	4.32	0.2	0.09	3.76	0.06	3.82	3.37	0.08
Construction	0.21	0.05	0.01	0.09	0.01	0.09	0.03	0.01
Wholesale and retail trade; Hotels and restaurants	5.75	0.53	0.21	3.85	0.19	4.04	2.76	0.3
Transport and storage, post and telecommunication	4.51	0.59	0.21	2.93	0.12	3.05	1.98	0.1
Financial intermediation	3.77	0.29	0.09	2.85	0.1	2.95	2.37	0.07
Business services	5.73	0.49	0.24	2.51	0.1	2.61	1.62	0.08
Other services	1.39	0.09	0.04	0.86	0.02	0.88	0.68	0.04

	India	Russian Federation	Saudi Arabia	United States	Australia	Germany	OECD
TOTAL	1.26	2.38	3.15	4.55	1.85	1.57	22.75
Agriculture, hunting, forestry and fishing	0.05	0.13	0	0.15	0.12	0.01	0.47
Mining and quarrying	0.58	0.72	2.56	0.15	0.99	0.01	2.41
Food products, beverages and tobacco	0.01	0.01	0	0.04	0.02	0.01	0.15
Textiles, textile products, leather and footwear	0.01	0	0	0.02	0	0	0.1
Wood, paper, paper products, printing and publishing	0.01	0.07	0	0.13	0.02	0.04	0.56
Chemicals and non-metallic mineral products	0.17	0.69	0.4	1.63	0.11	0.52	7.25
Basic metals and fabricated metal products	0.02	0.08	0	0.13	0.05	0.09	0.89
Machinery and equipment, nec	0.01	0.03	0	0.14	0.01	0.14	0.67
Electrical and optical equipment	0.01	0.01	0	0.14	0	0.09	0.78
Transport equipment	0	0.01	0	0.03	0.01	0.03	0.31
Manufacturing nec; recycling	0.06	0	0	0.05	0	0.02	0.34
Electricity, gas and water supply	0.02	0.13	0.01	0.1	0.03	0.03	0.57
Construction	0.01	0	0	0.02	0.02	0.01	0.14
Wholesale and retail trade; Hotels and restaurants	0.1	0.24	0.03	0.28	0.08	0.08	1.65
Transport and storage, post and telecommunication	0.06	0.14	0.02	0.29	0.14	0.09	1.83
Financial intermediation	0.05	0.02	0.02	0.17	0.05	0.03	0.87
Business services	0.08	0.06	0.05	1.02	0.18	0.33	3.37
Other services	0.01	0.04	0.04	0.08	0.02	0.05	0.4

Source: OECD–WTO Statistics on TiVA

Table 3.9 Shares of China's 2008 Value Added Embodied in Gross Exports by Source Country and Source Industry, Chemicals and Non-metallic Mineral Products (%)

	Total	Japan	Korea	East Asia	ASEAN	East and South East Asia	China	United States	Australia	Germany	Brazil	Russian Federation	Saudi Arabia	OECD
TOTAL	100	3.72	1.91	66.57	2.65	69.21	59.73	3.97	2.67	1.42	1.43	2.35	3.68	19.48
Agriculture, hunting, forestry and fishing	4.92	0.02	0.01	3.84	0.17	4.01	3.82	0.15	0.02	0	0.16	0.15	0	0.26
Mining and quarrying	19.76	0.02	0.01	4.72	0.8	5.52	4.67	0.23	1.81	0.01	0.55	0.55	3.24	3.07
Food products, beverages and tobacco	1.15	0.02	0	0.85	0.07	0.92	0.82	0.03	0.01	0.01	0.02	0.01	0	0.11
Textiles, textile products, leather and footwear	0.82	0.01	0.01	0.69	0.02	0.71	0.66	0.01	0	0	0.01	0	0	0.06
Wood, paper, paper products, printing and publishing	1.72	0.09	0.03	1.06	0.04	1.11	0.93	0.11	0.01	0.04	0.04	0.08	0	0.42
Chemicals and non-metallic mineral products	41.09	1.2	1.1	35.2	0.84	36.04	32.41	1.61	0.07	0.44	0.1	0.73	0.31	5.63
Basic metals and fabricated metal products	2.42	0.2	0.08	1.82	0.02	1.84	1.52	0.12	0.05	0.07	0.05	0.08	0	0.68

Machinery and equipment, nec	1.47	0.11	0.03	0.99	0.02	1.01	0.85	0.06	0.01	0.13	0.01	0.08	0	0.49
Electrical and optical equipment	0.98	0.17	0.06	0.65	0.07	0.71	0.36	0.09	0.01	0.04	0.01	0.01	0	0.43
Transport equipment	0.61	0.11	0.03	0.49	0.01	0.5	0.35	0.02	0.01	0.03	0	0.01	0	0.22
Manufacturing nec; recycling	1.03	0.13	0.02	0.79	0.01	0.81	0.64	0.05	0	0.03	0	0	0	0.27
Electricity, gas and water supply	3.16	0.14	0.03	2.67	0.04	2.71	2.47	0.09	0.04	0.03	0.03	0.11	0.01	0.43
Construction	0.23	0.03	0	0.07	0.01	0.08	0.03	0.02	0.05	0.01	0.01	0	0	0.16
Wholesale and retail trade; Hotels and restaurants	5.85	0.4	0.1	4.02	0.2	4.22	3.28	0.23	0.1	0.09	0.11	0.27	0.02	1.42
Transport and storage, post and telecommunication	4.01	0.41	0.13	2.53	0.13	2.66	1.9	0.23	0.13	0.08	0.1	0.13	0.01	1.45
Financial intermediation	3.57	0.18	0.04	2.78	0.08	2.86	2.49	0.12	0.11	0.03	0.03	0.02	0.02	0.68
Business services	5.81	0.41	0.2	2.49	0.11	2.6	1.75	0.75	0.24	0.33	0.17	0.07	0.03	3.31
Other services	1.4	0.07	0.02	0.9	0.02	0.92	0.78	0.06	0.02	0.06	0.03	0.04	0.03	0.39

Source: OECD–WTO_Statistics on TiVA

Table 3.10 Shares of China's 2009 Value Added Embodied in Gross Exports by Source Country and Source Industry, Chemicals and Non-metallic Mineral Products (%)

	Total	Japan	Korea	East Asia	ASEAN	East and South East Asia	China	China Taipei
TOTAL	100	3.98	2.1	66.64	3.13	69.76	59.06	1.21
Agriculture, hunting, forestry and fishing	4.95	0.02	0.01	3.9	0.16	4.07	3.87	0
Mining and quarrying	17.59	0.01	0.01	3.91	0.93	4.84	3.86	0.03
Food products, beverages and tobacco	1.21	0.03	0.01	0.91	0.07	0.98	0.87	0
Textiles, textile products, leather and footwear	1	0.01	0.02	0.9	0.02	0.92	0.86	0.01
Wood, paper, paper products, printing and publishing	1.79	0.11	0.04	1.16	0.04	1.2	0.99	0.01
Chemicals and non-metallic mineral products	40.67	1.37	0.88	34.24	1	35.24	31.35	0.6
Basic metals and fabricated metal products	2.38	0.19	0.09	1.79	0.02	1.81	1.49	0.02
Machinery and equipment, nec	1.52	0.1	0.06	1.02	0.02	1.03	0.85	0.01
Electrical and optical equipment	1.17	0.18	0.1	0.79	0.11	0.89	0.45	0.06
Transport equipment	0.65	0.12	0.05	0.52	0.02	0.54	0.35	0
Manufacturing nec; recycling	1.09	0.14	0.02	0.87	0.01	0.88	0.69	0.01
Electricity, gas and water supply	2.86	0.15	0.06	2.4	0.05	2.45	2.12	0.06
Construction	0.27	0.04	0	0.08	0.01	0.09	0.03	0.01
Wholesale and retail trade; Hotels and restaurants	6.16	0.37	0.16	4.33	0.25	4.58	3.55	0.2
Transport and storage, post and telecommunication	4.13	0.42	0.18	2.52	0.15	2.67	1.8	0.07
Financial intermediation	4.02	0.19	0.07	3.16	0.1	3.26	2.85	0.04
Business services	6.84	0.45	0.31	3.02	0.14	3.16	2.07	0.06
Other services	1.68	0.07	0.03	1.13	0.02	1.15	0.99	0.03

	United States	Australia	Brazil	Germany	Russian Federation	Saudi Arabia	OECD
TOTAL	4.38	2.88	1.5	1.48	1.87	3.26	20.87
Agriculture, hunting, forestry and fishing	0.18	0.07	0.22	0	0.12	0	0.36
Mining and quarrying	0.18	1.55	0.4	0.01	0.54	2.63	2.89
Food products, beverages and tobacco	0.04	0.03	0.03	0	0.01	0	0.15
Textiles, textile products, leather and footwear	0.01	0	0.01	0	0	0	0.06
Wood, paper, paper products, printing and publishing	0.13	0.02	0.05	0.03	0.05	0	0.48
Chemicals and non-metallic mineral products	1.76	0.21	0.15	0.4	0.49	0.46	5.86
Basic metals and fabricated metal products	0.1	0.05	0.07	0.08	0.06	0	0.67
Machinery and equipment, nec	0.08	0.01	0.01	0.15	0.04	0	0.55
Electrical and optical equipment	0.09	0	0.01	0.04	0.01	0	0.49
Transport equipment	0.03	0.01	0	0.03	0.01	0	0.27
Manufacturing nec; recycling	0.05	0	0	0.03	0	0	0.28
Electricity, gas and water supply	0.06	0.04	0.03	0.04	0.1	0.01	0.45
Construction	0.03	0.05	0.01	0.01	0.01	0	0.18
Wholesale and retail trade; Hotels and restaurants	0.23	0.13	0.15	0.09	0.19	0.02	1.46
Transport and storage, post and telecommunication	0.27	0.19	0.11	0.09	0.11	0.02	1.62
Financial intermediation	0.16	0.11	0.04	0.03	0.02	0.02	0.75
Business services	0.91	0.37	0.19	0.39	0.07	0.04	3.91
Other services	0.07	0.03	0.04	0.06	0.03	0.05	0.43

Source: OECD–WTO Statistics on TiVA

products sector. In the pre-2000 period, the value-added content was less than 20 percent. In the period that followed the value-added content doubled to 51 percent in 2008 and then declining to 40 percent in 2009. Part of this variation is a function of data issues and part as a result of changes in PRC legislation concerning the joint venture activity. With 2005 (Table 3.8), China's value-added portfolio adds Saudi Arabia, Russia and Australia who provide minerals and ores. The total value added as a percent of China's exports rises to 42 percent. In 2008 (Table 3.9), China added Brazil to the list of countries supplying it with raw materials. The major distinction that one observed in the upstream trail for China's chemicals and non-metallic mineral products sector is that the OECD suppliers are primarily in the same sector, while the non-OECD countries are providing raw material inputs. Overall, the output of this industry largely consists of intermediate products used in further stages of production. China's full participation in this sector exposes it more intensely to the competition of imported inputs and the importance of exclusive technology at all intermediate stages.

The importance of machinery and equipment, nec., exports and value-added exports to Japan and Germany are well known. In Tables 3.11–3.15, we present the evolution of China's value-added content in the machinery and equipment, nec., sector. The value-added chain in the early period demonstrates a very large intra-industry link across firms in the machinery sector. That pattern is maintained after 2005 (Tables 3.14 and 3.15) when China adds Australia, Germany and Russia into its value-added source countries.

Foreign value added is very large in basic industries that make heavy use of imported primary goods such as, basic metals and fabricated metal products. China's participation in this value-added chain has grown from 1995 to 2009, from 12 percent to 34 percent. This sector is viewed as medium to low technology. Tables 3.16–3.20 present the evolution of China's value-added content in the basic metals and fabricated metal products sector. The data show that China has increased its participation in the international sourcing of intermediates. Not only has it increased the share of value added in its exports, it has also added to the list of countries from whom it sources

Table 3.11 Shares of China's 1995 Value Added Embodied in Gross Exports by Source Country and Source Industry, Machinery and Equipment nec (%)

	Total	Japan	East Asia	East and South East Asia	China	China Taipei	United States	OECD
TOTAL	100	3.56	92.12	92.99	86.11	1.06	1.95	9.49
Agriculture, hunting, forestry and fishing	2.69	0	2.49	2.55	2.47	0	0.04	0.11
Mining and quarrying	5.98	0.01	4.89	5.06	4.87	0.01	0.07	0.4
Food products, beverages and tobacco	0.55	0	0.49	0.5	0.48	0	0.01	0.04
Textiles, textile products, leather and footwear	1.76	0.08	1.65	1.67	1.42	0.07	0.02	0.23
Wood, paper, paper products, printing and publishing	1.66	0.12	1.33	1.4	1.13	0.03	0.1	0.38
Chemicals and non-metallic mineral products	9.9	0.35	8.9	9.02	8.09	0.22	0.27	1.14
Basic metals and fabricated metal products	11.32	0.66	10.38	10.42	9.38	0.14	0.13	1.39
Machinery and equipment, nec	32.74	0.06	32.51	32.52	32.43	0.01	0.05	0.21
Electrical and optical equipment	4.6	0.91	3.98	4.09	2.61	0.25	0.23	1.47
Transport equipment	0.96	0.04	0.89	0.89	0.84	0.01	0.01	0.09
Manufacturing nec; recycling	1.03	0.02	1.01	1.01	0.97	0.01	0	0.05
Electricity, gas and water supply	2.79	0.12	2.61	2.63	2.42	0.04	0.03	0.25
Construction	0.15	0.02	0.1	0.1	0.07	0	0.02	0.08
Wholesale and retail trade; Hotels and restaurants	8.92	0.24	8.3	8.37	7.87	0.1	0.12	0.63
Transport and storage, post and telecommunication	4.88	0.23	4.27	4.33	3.89	0.05	0.15	0.73
Financial intermediation	4.74	0.16	4.32	4.38	3.99	0.06	0.1	0.52
Business services	4.97	0.47	3.85	3.91	3.2	0.04	0.56	1.55
Other services	0.36	0.07	0.14	0.15	0	0.04	0.03	0.22

Source: OECD–WTO_Statistics on TiVA

Table 3.12 Shares of China's 2000 Value Added Embodied in Gross Exports by Source Country and Source Industry, Machinery and Equipment nec (%)

	Total	Japan	Korea	East Asia	ASEAN	East and South East Asia	China	China Taipei	United States	OECD
TOTAL	100	3.56	1.36	89.16	1.13	90.29	82.44	1.52	2.04	11.38
Agriculture, hunting, forestry and fishing	1.89	0.01	0.01	1.68	0.05	1.73	1.66	0	0.02	0.1
Mining and quarrying	6.7	0.01	0.01	4.69	0.28	4.96	4.66	0.01	0.02	0.55
Food products, beverages and tobacco	0.56	0.02	0	0.5	0.01	0.52	0.48	0	0.01	0.05
Textiles, textile products, leather and footwear	1.36	0.04	0.05	1.26	0.01	1.27	1.12	0.05	0.02	0.14
Wood, paper, paper products, printing and publishing	1.29	0.08	0.03	0.94	0.05	0.99	0.82	0.02	0.07	0.31
Chemicals and non-metallic mineral products	7.48	0.35	0.2	6.48	0.18	6.66	5.67	0.21	0.22	1.14
Basic metals and fabricated metal products	11.28	0.81	0.2	10.04	0.08	10.12	8.57	0.45	0.23	1.81
Machinery and equipment, nec	34.4	0.52	0.04	33.42	0.05	33.48	32.74	0.1	0.29	1.29

Electrical and optical equipment	4.62	0.36	0.46	3.68	0.11	3.79	2.75	0.08	0.3	1.61
Transport equipment	1.26	0.04	0.01	1.16	0.01	1.17	1.11	0	0.02	0.12
Manufacturing nec; recycling	0.25	0.04	0	0.22	0	0.22	0.17	0.01	0.01	0.07
Electricity, gas and water supply	4.68	0.13	0.04	4.48	0.02	4.5	4.26	0.04	0.03	0.29
Construction	0.23	0.04	0.01	0.18	0	0.19	0.14	0	0.01	0.09
Wholesale and retail trade; Hotels and restaurants	7.77	0.33	0.1	6.9	0.1	7	6.21	0.24	0.13	0.89
Transport and storage, post and telecommunication	5.95	0.23	0.06	5.16	0.07	5.23	4.76	0.07	0.2	0.84
Financial intermediation	5.5	0.2	0.06	4.66	0.07	4.72	4.21	0.12	0.16	0.76
Business services	4.11	0.27	0.09	3.2	0.03	3.23	2.71	0.1	0.28	1.15
Other services	0.65	0.07	0.01	0.5	0	0.51	0.4	0.01	0.03	0.19

Source: OECD–WTO Statistics on TiVA

Table 3.13 Shares of China's 2005 Value Added Embodied in Gross Exports by Source Country and Source Industry, Machinery and Equipment nec (%)

	Total	Germany	Japan	Korea	United States	China	China Taipei	OECD	East Asia	ASEAN	East and South East Asia
TOTAL	100	2.83	6.87	2.91	3.96	64.9	1.97	24.3	77.14	2.33	79.48
Agriculture, hunting, forestry and fishing	2.59	0	0.02	0.03	0.04	2.22	0	0.14	2.27	0.06	2.32
Mining and quarrying	7.79	0	0.01	0.01	0.06	3.69	0.01	1.17	3.72	0.46	4.19
Food products, beverages and tobacco	0.64	0	0.02	0	0.01	0.51	0	0.07	0.54	0.01	0.55
Textiles, textile products, leather and footwear	0.51	0	0.01	0.02	0.01	0.37	0.01	0.07	0.41	0.01	0.42
Wood, paper, paper products, printing and publishing	1.35	0.04	0.12	0.04	0.09	0.69	0.01	0.46	0.87	0.04	0.91
Chemicals and non-metallic mineral products	6.8	0.18	0.53	0.42	0.39	3.79	0.19	2.04	4.96	0.32	5.28
Basic metals and fabricated metal products	12.11	0.35	1.27	0.48	0.4	7.71	0.27	3.4	9.73	0.13	9.86

Machinery and equipment, nec	31.09	0.82	1.09	0.2	0.75	26.88	0.08	3.77	28.25	0.22	28.47
Electrical and optical equipment	5.98	0.36	0.85	0.59	0.46	1.6	0.68	2.95	3.73	0.51	4.24
Transport equipment	1.31	0.06	0.23	0.15	0.08	0.63	0.01	0.63	1.02	0.02	1.03
Manufacturing nec; recycling	2.06	0.04	0.3	0.06	0.09	1.26	0.02	0.57	1.63	0.01	1.65
Electricity, gas and water supply	4.03	0.05	0.18	0.08	0.06	3.3	0.05	0.51	3.62	0.04	3.67
Construction	0.2	0.02	0.05	0.01	0.01	0.03	0.01	0.14	0.1	0.01	0.1
Wholesale and retail trade; Hotels and restaurants	6.9	0.14	0.66	0.22	0.27	3.91	0.28	1.92	5.16	0.21	5.37
Transport and storage, post and telecommunication	4.95	0.14	0.62	0.21	0.26	2.5	0.09	1.86	3.53	0.12	3.66
Financial intermediation	3.96	0.05	0.33	0.1	0.15	2.61	0.08	0.91	3.16	0.07	3.23
Business services	6.2	0.5	0.47	0.28	0.79	2.29	0.1	3.3	3.31	0.09	3.4
Other services	1.51	0.06	0.1	0.03	0.06	0.9	0.06	0.39	1.11	0.01	1.12

Source: OECD–WTO_Statistics on TiVA

Table 3.14   Shares of China's 2008 Value Added Embodied in Gross Exports by Source Country and Source Industry, Machinery and Equipment nec (%)

	Total	Japan	Korea	East Asia	ASEAN	East and South East Asia	China
TOTAL	100	5.58	2.38	75.98	2.13	78.11	66.37
Agriculture, hunting, forestry and fishing	2.63	0.01	0	2.33	0.07	2.4	2.31
Mining and quarrying	9.58	0.01	0.01	4.04	0.37	4.41	4.01
Food products, beverages and tobacco	0.69	0.02	0	0.61	0.02	0.63	0.59
Textiles, textile products, leather and footwear	0.52	0.01	0.01	0.45	0.01	0.46	0.42
Wood, paper, paper products, printing and publishing	1.29	0.09	0.03	0.86	0.04	0.9	0.73
Chemicals and non-metallic mineral products	6.5	0.4	0.3	4.83	0.28	5.12	3.99
Basic metals and fabricated metal products	11.73	1.06	0.41	9.34	0.09	9.44	7.68
Machinery and equipment, nec	31.34	0.83	0.24	28.51	0.14	28.65	27.39
Electrical and optical equipment	4.87	0.6	0.52	3.28	0.43	3.72	1.77
Transport equipment	1.25	0.27	0.06	1.01	0.01	1.02	0.67
Manufacturing nec; recycling	2.04	0.23	0.04	1.6	0.02	1.63	1.32
Electricity, gas and water supply	2.99	0.14	0.04	2.61	0.03	2.63	2.4
Construction	0.22	0.04	0	0.09	0	0.1	0.04
Wholesale and retail trade; Hotels and restaurants	7.3	0.58	0.15	5.52	0.21	5.73	4.52
Transport and storage, post and telecommunication	4.61	0.5	0.17	3.18	0.15	3.33	2.36
Financial intermediation	3.84	0.24	0.06	3.11	0.06	3.17	2.72
Business services	6.95	0.45	0.29	3.42	0.16	3.58	2.42
Other services	1.65	0.09	0.02	1.19	0.01	1.21	1.03

	China Taipei	United States	Australia	Germany	Russian Federation	Saudi Arabia	OECD
TOTAL	1.27	3.67	1.16	2.9	1.11	1.15	22.81
Agriculture, hunting, forestry and fishing	0	0.04	0.01	0	0.02	0	0.1
Mining and quarrying	0.01	0.1	0.57	0.01	0.19	1.05	1.46
Food products, beverages and tobacco	0	0.01	0	0	0	0	0.06
Textiles, textile products, leather and footwear	0.01	0.01	0	0	0	0	0.06
Wood, paper, paper products, printing and publishing	0.01	0.09	0.01	0.04	0.03	0	0.4
Chemicals and non-metallic mineral products	0.13	0.4	0.02	0.16	0.13	0.06	1.72
Basic metals and fabricated metal products	0.19	0.51	0.17	0.33	0.22	0	3.26
Machinery and equipment, nec	0.05	0.5	0.01	0.91	0.17	0	3.51
Electrical and optical equipment	0.38	0.36	0	0.29	0.01	0	2.07
Transport equipment	0	0.05	0	0.07	0.01	0	0.54
Manufacturing nec; recycling	0.01	0.11	0	0.05	0	0	0.54
Electricity, gas and water supply	0.02	0.05	0.02	0.06	0.05	0	0.43
Construction	0	0.02	0.02	0.01	0	0	0.15
Wholesale and retail trade; Hotels and restaurants	0.21	0.24	0.06	0.19	0.15	0.01	1.83
Transport and storage, post and telecommunication	0.07	0.25	0.07	0.14	0.06	0	1.68
Financial intermediation	0.06	0.12	0.04	0.05	0.01	0	0.75
Business services	0.07	0.75	0.14	0.51	0.03	0.01	3.81
Other services	0.04	0.06	0.01	0.08	0.02	0.01	0.45

Source: OECD–WTO_Statistics on TiVA

Table 3.15   Shares of China's 2009 Value Added Embodied in Gross Exports by Source Country and Source Industry, Machinery and Equipment nec (%)

	Total	Japan	Korea	East Asia	ASEAN	East and South East Asia	China	China Taipei	United States	Australia	Germany	Russian Federation	OECD
TOTAL	100	5.92	2.94	73.98	2.46	76.44	63.21	1.42	4.34	1.24	3.27	1.09	25.9
Agriculture, hunting, forestry and fishing	2.49	0.02	0	2.22	0.07	2.29	2.19	0	0.04	0.01	0	0.02	0.11
Mining and quarrying	7.87	0.01	0.01	3.1	0.4	3.5	3.07	0.01	0.08	0.46	0.01	0.18	1.53
Food products, beverages and tobacco	0.7	0.02	0	0.62	0.02	0.64	0.6	0	0.01	0	0	0	0.07
Textiles, textile products, leather and footwear	0.61	0.01	0.01	0.54	0.01	0.55	0.51	0.01	0.01	0	0	0	0.06
Wood, paper, paper products, printing and publishing	1.33	0.1	0.05	0.87	0.04	0.91	0.71	0.01	0.11	0.01	0.04	0.02	0.46
Chemicals and non-metallic mineral products	6.39	0.43	0.27	4.65	0.32	4.97	3.78	0.16	0.44	0.03	0.15	0.1	1.78
Basic metals and fabricated metal products	10.71	0.96	0.34	8.26	0.08	8.34	6.82	0.14	0.41	0.2	0.35	0.24	3.08

Machinery and equipment, nec	30.98	0.88	0.35	27.66	0.16	27.83	26.38	0.05	0.68	0.03	1.04	0.16	4.12
Electrical and optical equipment	5.74	0.67	0.72	3.79	0.55	4.34	1.9	0.49	0.44	0	0.3	0.01	2.49
Transport equipment	1.37	0.33	0.11	1.06	0.02	1.08	0.62	0	0.1	0	0.08	0.01	0.71
Manufacturing nec; recycling	2.07	0.27	0.04	1.64	0.02	1.66	1.32	0.01	0.11	0	0.05	0	0.55
Electricity, gas and water supply	2.62	0.16	0.07	2.22	0.03	2.25	1.94	0.04	0.04	0.02	0.07	0.05	0.5
Construction	0.27	0.05	0.01	0.1	0.01	0.11	0.04	0.01	0.02	0.02	0.02	0	0.19
Wholesale and retail trade; Hotels and restaurants	7.44	0.55	0.22	5.49	0.24	5.73	4.44	0.22	0.24	0.06	0.2	0.15	1.95
Transport and storage, post and telecommunication	4.81	0.56	0.21	3.05	0.18	3.23	2.07	0.09	0.33	0.11	0.16	0.07	2.03
Financial intermediation	4.26	0.27	0.09	3.38	0.07	3.45	2.94	0.05	0.19	0.04	0.06	0.01	0.92
Business services	8.39	0.54	0.41	3.91	0.21	4.12	2.64	0.1	1.01	0.21	0.66	0.05	4.83
Other services	1.96	0.09	0.03	1.42	0.02	1.44	1.24	0.05	0.07	0.02	0.09	0.02	0.53

Source: OECD–WTO Statistics on TiVA

Table 3.16 Shares of China's 1995 Value Added Embodied in Gross Exports by Source Country and Source Industry, Basic Metals and Fabricated Metal Products (%)

	Total	Japan	East Asia	ASEAN	East and South East Asia	China	United States	Russian Federation	OECD
TOTAL	100	2.45	91.99	0.92	92.91	87.66	1.57	1.09	7.72
Agriculture, hunting, forestry and fishing	2.27	0	2.08	0.06	2.14	2.06	0.03	0.01	0.09
Mining and quarrying	11.66	0.01	9.98	0.28	10.26	9.95	0.08	0.09	0.57
Food products, beverages and tobacco	0.51	0	0.45	0.01	0.46	0.44	0.01	0	0.03
Textiles, textile products, leather and footwear	1.39	0.06	1.3	0.01	1.31	1.11	0.01	0	0.18
Wood, paper, paper products, printing and publishing	1.2	0.07	0.93	0.06	1	0.81	0.07	0.02	0.26
Chemicals and non-metallic mineral products	8.15	0.24	7.29	0.12	7.41	6.71	0.19	0.16	0.85
Basic metals and fabricated metal products	42.28	0.81	41.09	0.05	41.14	39.84	0.13	0.4	1.64

Machinery and equipment, nec	2.08	0.03	1.93	0	1.94	1.89	0.03	0.04	0.13
Electrical and optical equipment	1.24	0.23	1.03	0.04	1.07	0.67	0.07	0.01	0.41
Transport equipment	0.72	0.03	0.66	0	0.66	0.62	0.01	0.02	0.07
Manufacturing nec; recycling	0.98	0.02	0.95	0	0.95	0.92	0	0	0.04
Electricity, gas and water supply	3.98	0.1	3.79	0.02	3.8	3.62	0.03	0.05	0.23
Construction	0.14	0.02	0.09	0	0.09	0.07	0.02	0	0.07
Wholesale and retail trade; Hotels and restaurants	7.99	0.17	7.39	0.06	7.45	7.08	0.09	0.17	0.5
Transport and storage, post and telecommunication	5.43	0.2	4.78	0.07	4.85	4.43	0.15	0.09	0.7
Financial intermediation	4.71	0.13	4.29	0.06	4.35	4.02	0.09	0	0.46
Business services	4.92	0.28	3.84	0.06	3.9	3.42	0.53	0.01	1.28
Other services	0.36	0.05	0.12	0.01	0.13	0	0.03	0.01	0.2

Source: OECD–WTO_Statistics on TiVA

Table 3.17 Shares of China's 2000 Value Added Embodied in Gross Exports by Source Country and Source Industry, Basic Metals and Fabricated Metal Products (%)

	Total	Japan	Korea	East Asia	ASEAN	East and South East Asia	China	China Taipei	United States	OECD
TOTAL	100	2.81	1.35	88.26	1.23	89.49	82.31	1.55	1.69	10.05
Agriculture, hunting, forestry and fishing	1.84	0.01	0.01	1.62	0.05	1.67	1.6	0	0.02	0.08
Mining and quarrying	10.44	0.01	0.01	7.46	0.42	7.88	7.43	0.02	0.02	0.8
Food products, beverages and tobacco	0.55	0.01	0	0.49	0.01	0.5	0.48	0	0.01	0.04
Textiles, textile products, leather and footwear	0.89	0.03	0.03	0.82	0.01	0.83	0.72	0.03	0.01	0.1
Wood, paper, paper products, printing and publishing	1.35	0.06	0.03	0.98	0.06	1.04	0.87	0.02	0.06	0.29
Chemicals and non-metallic mineral products	7.15	0.27	0.2	6.22	0.17	6.39	5.55	0.16	0.17	0.95
Basic metals and fabricated metal products	38.22	0.89	0.39	36.49	0.1	36.59	34.59	0.61	0.25	2.22

Machinery and equipment, nec	1.96	0.17	0.03	1.51	0.02	1.53	1.27	0.05	0.11	0.48
Electrical and optical equipment	2.55	0.24	0.26	1.96	0.07	2.03	1.38	0.06	0.2	0.97
Transport equipment	0.94	0.03	0.01	0.86	0.01	0.87	0.82	0	0.01	0.09
Manufacturing nec; recycling	0.25	0.03	0	0.22	0	0.22	0.18	0.01	0.01	0.06
Electricity, gas and water supply	6.79	0.12	0.05	6.57	0.03	6.6	6.35	0.05	0.03	0.28
Construction	0.23	0.04	0.01	0.18	0	0.18	0.13	0	0.01	0.08
Wholesale and retail trade; Hotels and restaurants	8.04	0.25	0.09	7.14	0.09	7.23	6.53	0.24	0.1	0.75
Transport and storage, post and telecommunication	6.96	0.21	0.07	6.07	0.07	6.15	5.68	0.08	0.22	0.86
Financial intermediation	7.22	0.18	0.06	6.07	0.08	6.15	5.64	0.13	0.19	0.83
Business services	4.04	0.21	0.09	3.17	0.04	3.21	2.75	0.1	0.24	1
Other services	0.58	0.06	0.01	0.42	0	0.43	0.34	0.01	0.03	0.17

Source: OECD–WTO Statistics on TiVA

Table 3.18   Shares of China's 2005 Value Added Embodied in Gross Exports by Source Country and Source Industry, Basic Metals and Fabricated Metal Products (%)

	Total	Japan	Korea	East Asia	ASEAN	East and South East Asia	China	China Taipei
TOTAL	100	5.42	2.14	70.68	2.11	72.79	61.42	1.38
Agriculture, hunting, forestry and fishing	3.01	0.02	0.03	2.43	0.05	2.48	2.39	0
Mining and quarrying	15.58	0.01	0.01	4.96	0.99	5.95	4.92	0.02
Food products, beverages and tobacco	0.67	0.02	0	0.51	0.01	0.52	0.49	0
Textiles, textile products, leather and footwear	0.57	0.01	0.02	0.42	0.01	0.42	0.38	0.01
Wood, paper, paper products, printing and publishing	1.68	0.1	0.03	0.89	0.05	0.93	0.75	0.01
Chemicals and non-metallic mineral products	6.22	0.45	0.36	4.29	0.29	4.57	3.29	0.15
Basic metals and fabricated metal products	38.18	1.65	0.68	34.46	0.17	34.62	31.66	0.46
Machinery and equipment, nec	2.91	0.3	0.06	1.94	0.04	1.98	1.56	0.02
Electrical and optical equipment	1.6	0.26	0.1	0.91	0.09	0.99	0.45	0.1
Transport equipment	1.07	0.17	0.12	0.83	0.01	0.84	0.54	0.01
Manufacturing nec; recycling	3.49	0.52	0.1	2.12	0.03	2.15	1.46	0.04
Electricity, gas and water supply	4.5	0.17	0.08	3.96	0.04	4	3.66	0.05
Construction	0.2	0.05	0	0.08	0.01	0.09	0.03	0.01
Wholesale and retail trade; Hotels and restaurants	6.17	0.52	0.14	4.16	0.12	4.28	3.18	0.26
Transport and storage, post and telecommunication	4.54	0.51	0.16	2.98	0.09	3.07	2.16	0.07
Financial intermediation	3.86	0.27	0.07	2.81	0.06	2.86	2.37	0.06
Business services	4.26	0.34	0.16	2.03	0.07	2.1	1.41	0.06
Other services	1.47	0.07	0.03	0.92	0.01	0.93	0.73	0.07

	United States	Australia	Germany	India	Russian Federation	Saudi Arabia	OECD
TOTAL	2.57	2.54	1.61	1.41	2.46	2.41	19.98
Agriculture, hunting, forestry and fishing	0.04	0.03	0	0.02	0.03	0	0.15
Mining and quarrying	0.08	1.28	0	0.42	0.77	2.29	2.87
Food products, beverages and tobacco	0.01	0.01	0	0	0	0	0.06
Textiles, textile products, leather and footwear	0.01	0	0	0.01	0	0	0.07
Wood, paper, paper products, printing and publishing	0.08	0.02	0.03	0.01	0.04	0	0.4
Chemicals and non-metallic mineral products	0.3	0.05	0.13	0.07	0.22	0.06	1.72
Basic metals and fabricated metal products	0.39	0.42	0.39	0.12	0.68	0.01	4.31
Machinery and equipment, nec	0.23	0.01	0.24	0.02	0.04	0	1.15
Electrical and optical equipment	0.13	0.01	0.1	0.01	0.01	0	0.79
Transport equipment	0.05	0.01	0.04	0.01	0.01	0	0.47
Manufacturing nec; recycling	0.19	0	0.08	0.3	0	0	1.04
Electricity, gas and water supply	0.05	0.05	0.04	0.03	0.11	0	0.49
Construction	0.01	0.02	0.01	0.01	0	0	0.13
Wholesale and retail trade; Hotels and restaurants	0.17	0.11	0.1	0.14	0.27	0.01	1.48
Transport and storage, post and telecommunication	0.19	0.19	0.1	0.1	0.14	0.01	1.59
Financial intermediation	0.12	0.07	0.03	0.1	0.02	0.01	0.77
Business services	0.47	0.24	0.27	0.04	0.06	0.01	2.19
Other services	0.04	0.03	0.04	0.01	0.04	0.01	0.31

Source: OECD–WTO Statistics on TiVA

Table 3.19 Shares of China's 2008 Value Added Embodied in Gross Exports by Source Country and Source Industry, Basic Metals and Fabricated Metal Products (%)

	Total	Australia	Germany	Japan	Korea	United States	Brazil	China
TOTAL	100	2.86	1.38	3.56	1.2	2.14	1.58	64.16
Agriculture, hunting, forestry and fishing	2.98	0.01	0	0.01	0	0.04	0.04	2.58
Mining and quarrying	21.61	1.85	0.01	0.02	0.01	0.14	0.61	5.59
Food products, beverages and tobacco	0.68	0	0	0.01	0	0.01	0.01	0.59
Textiles, textile products, leather and footwear	0.54	0	0	0.01	0.01	0.01	0	0.45
Wood, paper, paper products, printing and publishing	1.5	0.01	0.03	0.06	0.02	0.07	0.02	0.82
Chemicals and non-metallic mineral products	5.53	0.03	0.09	0.29	0.19	0.26	0.06	3.6
Basic metals and fabricated metal products	36.91	0.21	0.28	1.07	0.41	0.44	0.35	32.39
Machinery and equipment, nec	2.77	0.01	0.23	0.17	0.05	0.11	0.02	1.7
Electrical and optical equipment	1.16	0.01	0.06	0.14	0.08	0.08	0.01	0.51
Transport equipment	0.96	0.01	0.04	0.15	0.04	0.03	0	0.59
Manufacturing nec; recycling	2.76	0	0.1	0.29	0.05	0.15	0	1.6
Electricity, gas and water supply	3.3	0.04	0.04	0.11	0.03	0.04	0.05	2.74
Construction	0.21	0.05	0.01	0.03	0	0.01	0.01	0.03
Wholesale and retail trade; Hotels and restaurants	6.12	0.11	0.1	0.39	0.07	0.14	0.12	3.85
Transport and storage, post and telecommunication	3.96	0.14	0.08	0.35	0.1	0.15	0.1	2.13
Financial intermediation	3.56	0.11	0.02	0.16	0.03	0.08	0.04	2.56
Business services	4.05	0.25	0.23	0.26	0.11	0.36	0.11	1.57
Other services	1.4	0.02	0.05	0.05	0.01	0.03	0.04	0.86

	China Taipei	Russian Federation	Saudi Arabia	OECD	East Asia	ASEAN	East and South East Asia
TOTAL	0.63	1.96	2.96	16.27	69.75	1.63	71.38
Agriculture, hunting, forestry and fishing	0	0.03	0	0.09	2.6	0.05	2.65
Mining and quarrying	0.01	0.45	2.87	3.37	5.62	0.64	6.26
Food products, beverages and tobacco	0	0	0	0.04	0.6	0.02	0.62
Textiles, textile products, leather and footwear	0	0	0	0.04	0.47	0.01	0.47
Wood, paper, paper products, printing and publishing	0	0.05	0	0.29	0.9	0.05	0.95
Chemicals and non-metallic mineral products	0.08	0.19	0.04	1.17	4.16	0.21	4.37
Basic metals and fabricated metal products	0.19	0.51	0	3.12	34.06	0.11	34.16
Machinery and equipment, nec	0.01	0.13	0	0.83	1.93	0.03	1.96
Electrical and optical equipment	0.05	0.01	0	0.45	0.78	0.07	0.85
Transport equipment	0	0.01	0	0.32	0.79	0.01	0.8
Manufacturing nec; recycling	0.02	0	0	0.74	1.96	0.06	2.02
Electricity, gas and water supply	0.01	0.08	0	0.35	2.9	0.02	2.92
Construction	0	0	0	0.14	0.07	0	0.07
Wholesale and retail trade; Hotels and restaurants	0.13	0.26	0.01	1.25	4.48	0.13	4.61
Transport and storage, post and telecommunication	0.03	0.11	0	1.2	2.66	0.1	2.76
Financial intermediation	0.03	0.02	0	0.59	2.8	0.05	2.85
Business services	0.03	0.06	0.01	1.98	2.02	0.07	2.09
Other services	0.03	0.03	0.01	0.3	0.96	0.01	0.98

Source: OECD–WTO_Statistics on TiVA

Table 3.20 Shares of China's 2009 Value Added Embodied in Gross Exports by Source Country and Source Industry, Basic Metals and Fabricated Metal Products (%)

	Total	Japan	Korea	East Asia	ASEAN	East and South East Asia	China	China Taipei
TOTAL	100	3.51	1.45	70.95	1.85	72.8	65.11	0.65
Agriculture, hunting, forestry and fishing	3.06	0.01	0	2.7	0.05	2.75	2.68	0
Mining and quarrying	18.86	0.01	0.01	4.78	0.75	5.54	4.76	0.01
Food products, beverages and tobacco	0.75	0.01	0	0.67	0.02	0.68	0.65	0
Textiles, textile products, leather and footwear	0.69	0.01	0.01	0.63	0.01	0.63	0.6	0
Wood, paper, paper products, printing and publishing	1.62	0.06	0.02	1.03	0.04	1.08	0.94	0
Chemicals and non-metallic mineral products	5.72	0.3	0.16	4.32	0.23	4.55	3.74	0.1
Basic metals and fabricated metal products	36.48	0.92	0.36	33.27	0.1	33.37	31.83	0.15
Machinery and equipment, nec	2.92	0.17	0.1	2.06	0.03	2.09	1.78	0.01
Electrical and optical equipment	1.37	0.15	0.11	0.95	0.11	1.06	0.63	0.06
Transport equipment	1.07	0.18	0.08	0.88	0.01	0.89	0.61	0
Manufacturing nec; recycling	2.87	0.33	0.06	2.23	0.04	2.27	1.82	0.02
Electricity, gas and water supply	3.06	0.12	0.05	2.65	0.02	2.68	2.46	0.02
Construction	0.24	0.03	0	0.08	0.01	0.08	0.03	0
Wholesale and retail trade; Hotels and restaurants	6.54	0.33	0.11	4.93	0.14	5.07	4.32	0.13
Transport and storage, post and telecommunication	4.16	0.36	0.13	2.71	0.13	2.84	2.1	0.05
Financial intermediation	4.11	0.16	0.05	3.33	0.06	3.39	3.08	0.02
Business services	4.76	0.28	0.16	2.48	0.08	2.56	1.93	0.03
Other services	1.72	0.05	0.02	1.25	0.02	1.27	1.14	0.03

	United States	Australia	Brazil	Germany	Russian Federation	Saudi Arabia	OECD
TOTAL	2.24	2.98	1.5	1.42	1.92	2.3	17.19
Agriculture, hunting, forestry and fishing	0.04	0.02	0.04	0	0.03	0	0.11
Mining and quarrying	0.13	1.65	0.26	0.01	0.45	2.19	3.53
Food products, beverages and tobacco	0.01	0.01	0.01	0	0	0	0.05
Textiles, textile products, leather and footwear	0	0	0	0	0	0	0.04
Wood, paper, paper products, printing and publishing	0.07	0.02	0.03	0.02	0.04	0	0.32
Chemicals and non-metallic mineral products	0.29	0.04	0.07	0.08	0.15	0.06	1.19
Basic metals and fabricated metal products	0.33	0.41	0.57	0.29	0.56	0	3.02
Machinery and equipment, nec	0.14	0.01	0.02	0.24	0.08	0	0.94
Electrical and optical equipment	0.09	0	0.01	0.06	0.01	0	0.5
Transport equipment	0.04	0.01	0	0.05	0.01	0	0.41
Manufacturing nec; recycling	0.15	0	0	0.09	0	0	0.75
Electricity, gas and water supply	0.03	0.04	0.04	0.04	0.09	0	0.38
Construction	0.01	0.05	0.01	0.01	0.01	0	0.16
Wholesale and retail trade; Hotels and restaurants	0.13	0.12	0.16	0.1	0.25	0.01	1.2
Transport and storage, post and telecommunication	0.19	0.18	0.1	0.09	0.11	0.01	1.36
Financial intermediation	0.12	0.1	0.05	0.03	0.02	0.01	0.63
Business services	0.42	0.3	0.1	0.27	0.08	0.01	2.27
Other services	0.04	0.03	0.04	0.05	0.03	0.01	0.33

Source: OECD–WTO Statistics on TiVA

intermediates. This helps firms to lower costs, acquire higher-quality inputs, and improve productivity and (export) competitiveness. A number of studies have reported on the positive effect of international sourcing on export performance [Bas and Strauss-Kahn, 2011; Bas, 2012; Feng *et al.*, 2012; Aristei *et al.*, 2013]. Moreover, the effects of offshoring go beyond improved export performance on the firm level; offshoring also matters for countries' export specialization and competitiveness.

The industry-level case studies and their empirical findings suggest that the wood, paper, paper products, printing and publishing industries are best described as the low technology segments of a developing economy. Nevertheless, the existence of value-added linkages provides for the integration of developing economies within the world economy. In the case of the PRC, this sector's upstream connectivity is demonstrated in Tables 3.21–3.26. The developing country participation in China's upstream links starts with Indonesia in 2000 and expands to include Brazil, Saudi Arabia and Russia in 2005 and 2008. Within the developed country participants, China can include Canada, Australia and Germany.

Shifting into the transportation equipment sector, the data demonstrate the interconnectivity of the joint venture operation that China has developed in the post WTO entry period. Tables 3.26–3.30 present the evolution of value added in China's exports within this sector. In the case of China, the development of global production networks goes hand-in-hand with a liberalization of trade in related services. Within the transport sector; Deardorff [2001a, 2001b] identifies several sources of efficiency gains from the cross-border provision of services. Beyond the standard welfare-enhancing forces of comparative advantage, economies of scale and reduced fixed costs, there are gains to be realized from a reduction of border frictions and regulatory costs. These gains are achieved by harmonizing regulations applying to domestic and foreign providers, adopting similar procedures and equipment in different countries.

The largest spillover effect of the upstream linkages that the PRC developed in the transportation sector helped insure that its

Table 3.21 Shares of China's 1995 Value Added Embodied in Gross Exports by Source Country and Source Industry, Wood, Paper, Paper Products, Printing and Publishing (%)

	Total	Japan	Korea	United States	China	China Taipei	OECD	East Asia	ASEAN	East and South East Asia
TOTAL	100	1.73	1.03	2.04	87.98	0.98	7.5	92.08	1.57	93.65
Agriculture, hunting, forestry and fishing	9.36	0	0.03	0.1	8.71	0.01	0.27	8.75	0.28	9.03
Mining and quarrying	7.02	0	0.01	0.07	6.04	0.01	0.39	6.06	0.18	6.24
Food products, beverages and tobacco	0.88	0	0.01	0.02	0.77	0	0.06	0.79	0.02	0.81
Textiles, textile products, leather and footwear	2.64	0.11	0.15	0.02	2.13	0.12	0.34	2.5	0.02	2.52
Wood, paper, paper products, printing and publishing	41.21	0.3	0.21	0.4	39.03	0.19	1.32	39.78	0.45	40.23
Chemicals and non-metallic mineral products	8.84	0.28	0.25	0.32	6.9	0.25	1.19	7.72	0.16	7.88
Basic metals and fabricated metal products	2.37	0.14	0.04	0.05	1.91	0.04	0.34	2.12	0.02	2.14

(Continued)

Table 3.21   (*Continued*)

	Total	Japan	Korea	United States	China	China Taipei	OECD	East Asia	ASEAN	East and South East Asia
Machinery and equipment, nec	1.31	0.02	0.01	0.02	1.18	0	0.1	1.22	0	1.22
Electrical and optical equipment	0.89	0.17	0.02	0.06	0.45	0.05	0.31	0.72	0.03	0.76
Transport equipment	0.57	0.03	0	0.01	0.49	0	0.07	0.52	0	0.53
Manufacturing nec; recycling	1.12	0.02	0.01	0	1.06	0.01	0.04	1.1	0	1.1
Electricity, gas and water supply	2.82	0.05	0.02	0.04	2.52	0.05	0.18	2.65	0.02	2.67
Construction	0.12	0.01	0	0.02	0.05	0	0.06	0.07	0	0.07
Wholesale and retail trade; Hotels and restaurants	9.02	0.11	0.06	0.13	8.13	0.09	0.49	8.42	0.12	8.55
Transport and storage, post and telecommunication	4.01	0.14	0.07	0.15	3.15	0.04	0.59	3.44	0.09	3.53
Financial intermediation	3.24	0.09	0.05	0.08	2.62	0.05	0.38	2.87	0.08	2.95
Business services	4.26	0.22	0.08	0.52	2.85	0.03	1.2	3.24	0.07	3.31
Other services	0.3	0.04	0.01	0.03	0	0.03	0.19	0.1	0.02	0.11

Source: OECD–WTO.Statistics on TiVA

Table 3.22   Shares of China's 2000 Value Added Embodied in Gross Exports by Source Country and Source Industry, Wood, Paper, Paper Products, Printing and Publishing (%)

	Total	Japan	Korea	United States	China	China Taipei	Indonesia	OECD	East Asia	ASEAN	East and South East Asia
TOTAL	100	2.31	1.6	2.45	81.86	1.44	1.19	10.97	87.5	2.51	90.01
Agriculture, hunting, forestry and fishing	7.9	0.01	0.01	0.11	6.73	0.01	0.15	0.43	6.77	0.41	7.18
Mining and quarrying	4.1	0	0	0.02	2.8	0.01	0.11	0.29	2.82	0.22	3.04
Food products, beverages and tobacco	0.88	0.01	0.01	0.02	0.74	0	0.02	0.07	0.77	0.03	0.8
Textiles, textile products, leather and footwear	5	0.16	0.22	0.05	4.18	0.19	0.02	0.52	4.75	0.04	4.78
Wood, paper, paper products, printing and publishing	37.08	0.27	0.3	0.58	33.28	0.16	0.55	2.29	34.03	0.86	34.89
Chemicals and non-metallic mineral products	7.65	0.35	0.28	0.25	5.57	0.24	0.07	1.3	6.49	0.25	6.74
Basic metals and fabricated metal products	3.13	0.23	0.09	0.11	2.19	0.13	0.01	0.67	2.65	0.03	2.69

(Continued)

Table 3.22 (*Continued*)

	Total	Japan	Korea	United States	China	China Taipei	Indonesia	OECD	East Asia	ASEAN	East and South East Asia
Machinery and equipment, nec	1.2	0.12	0.02	0.07	0.77	0.03	0.01	0.33	0.94	0.02	0.96
Electrical and optical equipment	1.99	0.21	0.19	0.19	1.02	0.06	0	0.8	1.49	0.07	1.56
Transport equipment	0.85	0.03	0.01	0.01	0.73	0	0.01	0.09	0.77	0.02	0.78
Manufacturing nec; recycling	0.25	0.04	0	0.01	0.16	0.01	0	0.07	0.22	0	0.22
Electricity, gas and water supply	4	0.08	0.04	0.04	3.58	0.05	0.01	0.26	3.76	0.04	3.8
Construction	0.2	0.02	0	0.01	0.11	0	0	0.07	0.14	0	0.15
Wholesale and retail trade; Hotels and restaurants	10.9	0.21	0.13	0.16	9.24	0.25	0.12	0.84	9.85	0.24	10.09
Transport and storage, post and telecommunication	5.33	0.17	0.08	0.22	4.08	0.08	0.05	0.85	4.46	0.12	4.58
Financial intermediation	4.58	0.14	0.08	0.16	3.45	0.11	0.05	0.68	3.84	0.12	3.95
Business services	4.43	0.2	0.12	0.39	2.96	0.1	0.02	1.2	3.41	0.05	3.45
Other services	0.54	0.05	0.02	0.05	0.26	0.01	0.01	0.21	0.35	0.01	0.36

Source: OECD–WTO_Statistics on TiVA

Table 3.23 Shares of China's 2005 Value Added Embodied in Gross Exports by Source Country and Source Industry, Wood, Paper, Paper Products, Printing and Publishing (%)

	Total	Japan	Korea	East Asia	ASEAN	East and South East Asia	China	China Taipei
TOTAL	100	5.88	2.6	71.45	3.29	74.74	60.88	1.6
Agriculture, hunting, forestry and fishing	11.51	0.04	0.1	7.04	0.54	7.58	6.89	0.01
Mining and quarrying	4.86	0.01	0.01	1.9	0.36	2.25	1.86	0.02
Food products, beverages and tobacco	0.92	0.03	0.01	0.63	0.04	0.67	0.59	0
Textiles, textile products, leather and footwear	0.76	0.03	0.04	0.59	0.02	0.62	0.5	0.02
Wood, paper, paper products, printing and publishing	38.33	0.5	0.29	33.09	0.84	33.93	32.13	0.17
Chemicals and non-metallic mineral products	10.13	1.02	0.8	6.43	0.6	7.04	4.11	0.45
Basic metals and fabricated metal products	2.38	0.3	0.12	1.7	0.03	1.73	1.22	0.06
Machinery and equipment, nec	1.42	0.19	0.04	0.86	0.03	0.89	0.61	0.02
Electrical and optical equipment	1.4	0.27	0.1	0.83	0.09	0.92	0.33	0.13
Transport equipment	0.93	0.21	0.14	0.71	0.02	0.73	0.36	0.01
Manufacturing nec; recycling	3.4	1.04	0.15	2.58	0.04	2.62	1.29	0.1
Electricity, gas and water supply	3.05	0.18	0.07	2.5	0.06	2.56	2.18	0.06
Construction	0.2	0.04	0.01	0.08	0.01	0.09	0.02	0.01
Wholesale and retail trade; Hotels and restaurants	6.32	0.59	0.2	4.22	0.27	4.5	3.09	0.27
Transport and storage, post and telecommunication	4.5	0.6	0.2	2.78	0.14	2.93	1.76	0.09
Financial intermediation	3.47	0.29	0.08	2.48	0.11	2.58	1.99	0.06
Business services	5.1	0.47	0.22	2.24	0.07	2.31	1.36	0.07
Other services	1.3	0.09	0.03	0.78	0.03	0.8	0.59	0.04

(Continued)

Table 3.23 (Continued)

	United States	Australia	Brazil	Canada	Germany	Russian Federation	Saudi Arabia	OECD
TOTAL	6.02	1.3	1.64	1.48	1.78	2.21	1.05	24.55
Agriculture, hunting, forestry and fishing	0.86	0.52	0.55	0.05	0.02	0.58	0	1.83
Mining and quarrying	0.1	0.2	0.08	0.15	0	0.15	0.68	0.81
Food products, beverages and tobacco	0.05	0.01	0.02	0.02	0.01	0.01	0	0.16
Textiles, textile products, leather and footwear	0.03	0	0.01	0	0.01	0	0	0.15
Wood, paper, paper products, printing and publishing	1.06	0.11	0.4	0.59	0.25	0.56	0.01	3.67
Chemicals and non-metallic mineral products	0.88	0.05	0.15	0.12	0.29	0.26	0.25	3.96
Basic metals and fabricated metal products	0.15	0.03	0.04	0.02	0.09	0.06	0	0.91
Machinery and equipment, nec	0.13	0	0.01	0.01	0.15	0.02	0	0.7
Electrical and optical equipment	0.16	0	0.01	0.01	0.08	0.01	0	0.79
Transport equipment	0.04	0.01	0.01	0	0.05	0.01	0	0.51
Manufacturing nec; recycling	0.27	0	0.01	0.01	0.14	0	0	1.79
Electricity, gas and water supply	0.12	0.02	0.05	0.04	0.04	0.08	0.01	0.57
Construction	0.03	0.01	0	0.01	0.01	0	0	0.15
Wholesale and retail trade; Hotels and restaurants	0.37	0.07	0.12	0.11	0.1	0.26	0.02	1.9
Transport and storage, post and telecommunication	0.37	0.1	0.08	0.12	0.11	0.12	0.01	2.03
Financial intermediation	0.25	0.04	0.03	0.06	0.04	0.02	0.01	0.98
Business services	1.03	0.11	0.06	0.12	0.34	0.05	0.03	3.17
Other services	0.12	0.01	0.01	0.04	0.06	0.03	0.03	0.47

Source: OECD–WTO_Statistics on TiVA

Table 3.24 Shares of China's 2008 Value Added Embodied in Gross Exports by Source Country and Source Industry, Wood, Paper, Paper Products, Printing and Publishing (%)

	Total	Japan	Korea	East Asia	ASEAN	East and South East Asia	China	China Taipei	United States
TOTAL	100	4.04	1.66	69.8	2.93	72.73	62.94	0.85	5.85
Agriculture, hunting, forestry and fishing	11.49	0.03	0.01	6.54	0.51	7.04	6.5	0	0.92
Mining and quarrying	5.99	0.01	0.01	2.1	0.32	2.43	2.09	0.01	0.15
Food products, beverages and tobacco	0.96	0.02	0	0.69	0.05	0.74	0.67	0	0.06
Textiles, textile products, leather and footwear	0.78	0.02	0.02	0.64	0.02	0.66	0.59	0.01	0.02
Wood, paper, paper products, printing and publishing	38.83	0.27	0.15	33.63	0.72	34.35	33.15	0.05	1.05
Chemicals and non-metallic mineral products	9.45	0.62	0.62	6.02	0.47	6.49	4.46	0.28	0.9
Basic metals and fabricated metal products	2.26	0.2	0.08	1.61	0.02	1.63	1.3	0.03	0.15
Machinery and equipment, nec	1.34	0.12	0.04	0.83	0.02	0.84	0.67	0.01	0.07
Electrical and optical equipment	1.07	0.16	0.08	0.69	0.07	0.76	0.38	0.06	0.12
Transport equipment	0.83	0.21	0.06	0.65	0.02	0.67	0.39	0	0.02
Manufacturing nec; recycling	3.43	0.74	0.1	2.3	0.07	2.37	1.41	0.04	0.28
Electricity, gas and water supply	2.33	0.12	0.02	1.79	0.04	1.83	1.63	0.02	0.12
Construction	0.21	0.03	0	0.07	0.01	0.07	0.03	0	0.03
Wholesale and retail trade; Hotels and restaurants	6.87	0.45	0.1	4.48	0.26	4.74	3.71	0.17	0.35
Transport and storage, post and telecommunication	4.08	0.41	0.14	2.37	0.16	2.53	1.69	0.05	0.33
Financial intermediation	3.34	0.19	0.04	2.41	0.07	2.48	2.12	0.04	0.22
Business services	5.38	0.38	0.17	2.19	0.08	2.27	1.49	0.05	0.96
Other services	1.38	0.07	0.02	0.8	0.03	0.83	0.68	0.03	0.1

(*Continued*)

Table 3.24   (*Continued*)

	Argentina	Australia	Brazil	Canada	Germany	Indonesia	Russian Federation	Saudi Arabia	OECD
TOTAL	1.29	1.22	2.55	1.52	1.73	1.13	2.65	1.13	21.4
Agriculture, hunting, forestry and fishing	0.95	0.19	1.07	0.12	0.01	0.12	0.6	0	1.45
Mining and quarrying	0.03	0.4	0.11	0.13	0.01	0.17	0.15	0.82	1.02
Food products, beverages and tobacco	0.02	0.01	0.04	0.01	0	0.03	0.02	0	0.14
Textiles, textile products, leather and footwear	0.01	0	0.01	0	0	0	0	0	0.1
Wood, paper, paper products, printing and publishing	0.05	0.06	0.51	0.57	0.16	0.43	0.74	0.01	3
Chemicals and non-metallic mineral products	0.07	0.07	0.15	0.1	0.26	0.14	0.3	0.22	3.26
Basic metals and fabricated metal products	0.01	0.04	0.04	0.02	0.09	0	0.07	0	0.76
Machinery and equipment, nec	0.01	0.01	0.01	0.01	0.15	0	0.05	0	0.57
Electrical and optical equipment	0	0	0.01	0	0.06	0	0.01	0	0.5
Transport equipment	0	0	0.01	0	0.05	0	0.01	0	0.38
Manufacturing nec; recycling	0	0.01	0	0.02	0.24	0.02	0	0	1.67
Electricity, gas and water supply	0.01	0.02	0.04	0.04	0.04	0.01	0.09	0	0.46
Construction	0	0.02	0	0.01	0.01	0	0	0	0.15
Wholesale and retail trade; Hotels and restaurants	0.04	0.07	0.23	0.18	0.13	0.08	0.35	0.02	1.76
Transport and storage, post and telecommunication	0.04	0.1	0.1	0.07	0.1	0.06	0.14	0.01	1.66
Financial intermediation	0.01	0.05	0.05	0.03	0.03	0.01	0.02	0.01	0.77
Business services	0.02	0.16	0.12	0.16	0.33	0.01	0.07	0.02	3.28
Other services	0.01	0.02	0.03	0.06	0.06	0.02	0.04	0.02	0.47

Source: OECD–WTO Statistics on TiVA

Table 3.25 Shares of China's 2009 Value Added Embodied in Gross Exports by Source Country and Source Industry, Wood, Paper, Paper Products, Printing and Publishing (%)

	Total	Japan	Korea	East Asia	ASEAN	East and South East Asia	China
TOTAL	100	3.81	1.66	71.86	2.84	74.7	65.17
Agriculture, hunting, forestry and fishing	11.12	0.02	0.01	6.51	0.49	7	6.48
Mining and quarrying	4.77	0	0.01	1.79	0.31	2.1	1.76
Food products, beverages and tobacco	1.02	0.02	0	0.74	0.05	0.79	0.72
Textiles, textile products, leather and footwear	0.95	0.02	0.03	0.83	0.02	0.85	0.78
Wood, paper, paper products, printing and publishing	39.32	0.24	0.16	34.37	0.59	34.96	33.93
Chemicals and non-metallic mineral products	9.18	0.64	0.4	6	0.48	6.48	4.62
Basic metals and fabricated metal products	2.21	0.18	0.09	1.65	0.02	1.67	1.36
Machinery and equipment, nec	1.36	0.1	0.06	0.86	0.02	0.88	0.69
Electrical and optical equipment	1.23	0.15	0.11	0.82	0.1	0.93	0.49
Transport equipment	0.88	0.21	0.1	0.71	0.02	0.73	0.4
Manufacturing nec; recycling	3.31	0.7	0.11	2.41	0.06	2.47	1.56
Electricity, gas and water supply	2.1	0.12	0.04	1.63	0.04	1.67	1.43
Construction	0.23	0.03	0	0.07	0.01	0.08	0.03
Wholesale and retail trade; Hotels and restaurants	7.11	0.37	0.13	4.87	0.26	5.13	4.17
Transport and storage, post and telecommunication	4.02	0.38	0.15	2.31	0.17	2.48	1.62
Financial intermediation	3.74	0.17	0.05	2.74	0.07	2.81	2.46
Business services	5.85	0.38	0.21	2.54	0.1	2.63	1.78
Other services	1.6	0.06	0.02	1.01	0.03	1.04	0.89

(*Continued*)

Table 3.25   *(Continued)*

	United States	Brazil	Australia	Canada	Germany	Russian Federation	OECD
TOTAL	5.97	2.64	1.12	1.71	1.64	2.02	21.32
Agriculture, hunting, forestry and fishing	1.05	1.15	0.28	0.26	0.01	0.56	1.86
Mining and quarrying	0.1	0.08	0.24	0.13	0.01	0.13	0.79
Food products, beverages and tobacco	0.08	0.03	0.01	0.01	0	0.01	0.17
Textiles, textile products, leather and footwear	0.01	0.01	0	0	0	0	0.09
Wood, paper, paper products, printing and publishing	1.05	0.49	0.07	0.6	0.13	0.46	3.08
Chemicals and non-metallic mineral products	0.86	0.16	0.07	0.06	0.22	0.21	2.92
Basic metals and fabricated metal products	0.11	0.05	0.03	0.02	0.09	0.04	0.68
Machinery and equipment, nec	0.08	0.01	0.01	0.01	0.16	0.03	0.57
Electrical and optical equipment	0.12	0.01	0	0	0.05	0.01	0.52
Transport equipment	0.03	0.01	0	0	0.05	0.01	0.44
Manufacturing nec; recycling	0.22	0	0	0.01	0.21	0	1.46
Electricity, gas and water supply	0.09	0.04	0.02	0.04	0.04	0.07	0.44
Construction	0.04	0	0.02	0.01	0.01	0.01	0.17
Wholesale and retail trade; Hotels and restaurants	0.34	0.27	0.07	0.2	0.11	0.24	1.67
Transport and storage, post and telecommunication	0.35	0.11	0.09	0.08	0.1	0.11	1.68
Financial intermediation	0.31	0.05	0.04	0.04	0.03	0.02	0.86
Business services	1.02	0.12	0.15	0.17	0.35	0.07	3.43
Other services	0.11	0.04	0.02	0.06	0.06	0.03	0.49

Source: OECD–WTO Statistics on TiVA

Table 3.26 Shares of China's 1995 Value Added Embodied in Gross Exports by Source Country and Source Industry, Transport Equipment (%)

	Total	Japan	East Asia	East and South East Asia	China	United States	OECD
TOTAL	100	2.77	92.87	93.62	87.96	1.74	8.16
Agriculture, hunting, forestry and fishing	2.67	0	2.48	2.54	2.45	0.04	0.11
Mining and quarrying	5.01	0.01	4.08	4.23	4.06	0.06	0.35
Food products, beverages and tobacco	0.54	0	0.48	0.49	0.47	0.01	0.04
Textiles, textile products, leather and footwear	2.01	0.08	1.89	1.9	1.62	0.02	0.25
Wood, paper, paper products, printing and publishing	1.43	0.09	1.14	1.2	0.98	0.08	0.31
Chemicals and non-metallic mineral products	10.08	0.32	9.13	9.24	8.33	0.26	1.09
Basic metals and fabricated metal products	9.04	0.51	8.29	8.32	7.51	0.11	1.1
Machinery and equipment, nec	4.51	0.05	4.3	4.31	4.23	0.04	0.2
Electrical and optical equipment	2.28	0.42	1.94	2	1.28	0.12	0.72
Transport equipment	36.29	0.24	35.93	35.94	35.63	0.05	0.49
Manufacturing nec; recycling	0.9	0.02	0.88	0.88	0.85	0	0.04
Electricity, gas and water supply	2.39	0.1	2.23	2.25	2.07	0.03	0.21
Construction	0.14	0.02	0.09	0.09	0.06	0.02	0.06
Wholesale and retail trade; Hotels and restaurants	9.02	0.19	8.46	8.52	8.1	0.11	0.54
Transport and storage, post and telecommunication	4.63	0.19	4.06	4.12	3.73	0.15	0.65
Financial intermediation	4.38	0.13	4	4.05	3.72	0.09	0.46
Business services	4.38	0.35	3.37	3.42	2.87	0.5	1.33
Other services	0.31	0.05	0.11	0.12	0	0.03	0.19

Source: OECD–WTO Statistics on TiVA

Table 3.27   Shares of China's 2000 Value Added Embodied in Gross Exports by Source Country and Source Industry, Transport Equipment (%)

	Total	Japan	Korea	East Asia	ASEAN	East and South East Asia	China	China Taipei	United States	Germany	OECD
TOTAL	100	3.6	1.29	89.59	1.05	90.64	82.92	1.53	2.03	1.06	11.46
Agriculture, hunting, forestry and fishing	1.82	0.01	0.01	1.59	0.05	1.65	1.57	0	0.02	0	0.1
Mining and quarrying	5.47	0.01	0.01	3.81	0.23	4.04	3.78	0.01	0.02	0	0.44
Food products, beverages and tobacco	0.49	0.02	0	0.43	0.01	0.44	0.41	0	0.01	0	0.05
Textiles, textile products, leather and footwear	1.46	0.05	0.06	1.36	0.01	1.37	1.2	0.05	0.02	0	0.16
Wood, paper, paper products, printing and publishing	1.19	0.08	0.03	0.87	0.05	0.92	0.74	0.01	0.07	0.03	0.31
Chemicals and non-metallic mineral products	8.27	0.37	0.22	7.2	0.19	7.39	6.29	0.27	0.24	0.1	1.25
Basic metals and fabricated metal products	8.94	0.63	0.17	7.86	0.07	7.92	6.65	0.39	0.21	0.11	1.54

Machinery and equipment, nec	5.42	0.45	0.04	4.56	0.05	4.6	3.95	0.1	0.26	0.15	1.15
Electrical and optical equipment	3.92	0.33	0.36	3.09	0.1	3.2	2.3	0.08	0.27	0.14	1.37
Transport equipment	36.16	0.34	0.05	35.64	0.01	35.65	35.24	0	0.09	0.17	0.82
Manufacturing nec; recycling	0.25	0.06	0	0.22	0	0.22	0.15	0.01	0.01	0	0.08
Electricity, gas and water supply	4.05	0.12	0.04	3.86	0.02	3.89	3.65	0.05	0.03	0.02	0.28
Construction	0.21	0.04	0	0.16	0	0.16	0.11	0	0.01	0.01	0.08
Wholesale and retail trade; Hotels and restaurants	7.74	0.33	0.1	6.9	0.09	6.99	6.2	0.24	0.14	0.06	0.91
Transport and storage, post and telecommunication	5.43	0.22	0.06	4.69	0.06	4.75	4.3	0.07	0.19	0.05	0.81
Financial intermediation	4.74	0.19	0.06	4.01	0.06	4.07	3.59	0.12	0.14	0.03	0.7
Business services	3.86	0.28	0.09	2.93	0.03	2.96	2.43	0.1	0.27	0.17	1.2
Other services	0.59	0.07	0.01	0.43	0	0.44	0.33	0.01	0.03	0.02	0.2

Source: OECD–WTO Statistics on TiVA

Table 3.28   Shares of China's 2005 Value Added Embodied in Gross Exports by Source Country and Source Industry, Transport Equipment (%)

	Total	Japan	Korea	East Asia	ASEAN	East and South East Asia	China	China Taipei	United States	Germany	OECD
TOTAL	100	8.53	3.55	77.17	1.85	79.02	63.12	1.52	4.59	3.22	27.88
Agriculture, hunting, forestry and fishing	2.41	0.02	0.03	2.09	0.06	2.14	2.04	0	0.04	0	0.15
Mining and quarrying	6.16	0.01	0.01	2.84	0.35	3.19	2.81	0.01	0.06	0	0.96
Food products, beverages and tobacco	0.6	0.03	0	0.49	0.01	0.51	0.46	0	0.01	0	0.07
Textiles, textile products, leather and footwear	0.84	0.03	0.03	0.66	0.02	0.68	0.59	0.02	0.03	0.01	0.14
Wood, paper, paper products, printing and publishing	1.3	0.14	0.04	0.83	0.03	0.87	0.64	0.01	0.1	0.04	0.48
Chemicals and non-metallic mineral products	7.09	0.61	0.49	5.08	0.31	5.39	3.75	0.2	0.45	0.22	2.38
Basic metals and fabricated metal products	9.4	1.06	0.4	7.24	0.09	7.33	5.56	0.21	0.43	0.33	3.04

Machinery and equipment, nec	5.71	0.58	0.12	3.8	0.11	3.91	3.03	0.06	0.51	0.53	2.39
Electrical and optical equipment	4.73	0.7	0.34	3.03	0.33	3.36	1.61	0.37	0.37	0.3	2.26
Transport equipment	33.14	2.27	0.95	30.83	0.09	30.91	27.53	0.08	0.64	0.65	5.33
Manufacturing nec; recycling	1.61	0.25	0.07	1.33	0.01	1.34	1	0.01	0.05	0.03	0.46
Electricity, gas and water supply	3.27	0.21	0.09	2.87	0.03	2.9	2.52	0.04	0.07	0.06	0.56
Construction	0.21	0.06	0.01	0.1	0	0.1	0.03	0	0.02	0.02	0.15
Wholesale and retail trade; Hotels and restaurants	7.44	0.83	0.29	5.7	0.17	5.87	4.26	0.25	0.31	0.16	2.26
Transport and storage, post and telecommunication	4.5	0.69	0.21	3.12	0.1	3.22	2.05	0.07	0.27	0.16	1.94
Financial intermediation	3.7	0.38	0.12	2.92	0.05	2.97	2.32	0.06	0.18	0.06	1.03
Business services	6.5	0.57	0.31	3.25	0.07	3.33	2.12	0.08	0.99	0.58	3.81
Other services	1.41	0.11	0.04	1	0.01	1.01	0.78	0.05	0.07	0.08	0.45

Source: OECD–WTO Statistics on TiVA

Table 3.29   Shares of China's 2008 Value Added Embodied in Gross Exports by Source Country and Source Industry, Transport Equipment (%)

	Total	Japan	Korea	East Asia	ASEAN	East and South East Asia	China	United States	OECD
TOTAL	100	6.91	2.29	76.72	1.69	78.41	66.29	3.89	24.93
Agriculture, hunting, forestry and fishing	2.49	0.02	0	2.19	0.07	2.26	2.17	0.04	0.1
Mining and quarrying	7.57	0.01	0.01	3.16	0.28	3.45	3.14	0.1	1.12
Food products, beverages and tobacco	0.65	0.02	0	0.57	0.02	0.59	0.55	0.01	0.06
Textiles, textile products, leather and footwear	0.9	0.02	0.02	0.73	0.03	0.76	0.68	0.02	0.11
Wood, paper, paper products, printing and publishing	1.24	0.1	0.03	0.83	0.03	0.86	0.7	0.08	0.4
Chemicals and non-metallic mineral products	6.79	0.44	0.33	4.96	0.29	5.25	4.05	0.45	1.97
Basic metals and fabricated metal products	8.96	0.79	0.3	6.88	0.06	6.94	5.68	0.44	2.69
Machinery and equipment, nec	5.56	0.37	0.12	3.75	0.08	3.82	3.23	0.33	2.06
Electrical and optical equipment	3.88	0.46	0.28	2.8	0.27	3.06	1.85	0.27	1.44
Transport equipment	33.39	2.15	0.51	31.27	0.05	31.32	28.57	0.47	4.64
Manufacturing nec; recycling	1.54	0.19	0.05	1.32	0.01	1.33	1.07	0.05	0.37
Electricity, gas and water supply	2.47	0.15	0.03	2.09	0.02	2.12	1.88	0.06	0.46
Construction	0.22	0.05	0	0.09	0	0.09	0.04	0.02	0.16
Wholesale and retail trade; Hotels and restaurants	7.88	0.71	0.15	6.08	0.17	6.24	5.01	0.26	2.11
Transport and storage, post and telecommunication	4.12	0.54	0.13	2.77	0.11	2.88	1.98	0.24	1.69
Financial intermediation	3.57	0.27	0.06	2.89	0.05	2.94	2.5	0.13	0.8
Business services	7.21	0.54	0.24	3.29	0.13	3.43	2.27	0.87	4.25
Other services	1.55	0.1	0.02	1.07	0.01	1.08	0.91	0.06	0.49

Source: OECD–WTO_Statistics on TiVA

Table 3.30 Shares of China's 2009 Value Added Embodied in Gross Exports by Source Country and Source Industry, Transport Equipment (%)

	Total	Japan	Korea	East Asia	ASEAN	East and South East Asia	China	United States	Germany	OECD
TOTAL	100	6.95	2.64	77.38	1.76	79.14	66.52	4	3.28	25.38
Agriculture, hunting, forestry and fishing	2.53	0.02	0	2.25	0.07	2.32	2.23	0.04	0	0.11
Mining and quarrying	6.16	0.01	0.01	2.6	0.29	2.88	2.58	0.07	0.01	1.03
Food products, beverages and tobacco	0.7	0.02	0	0.62	0.02	0.64	0.59	0.01	0	0.06
Textiles, textile products, leather and footwear	1.05	0.02	0.02	0.9	0.02	0.93	0.85	0.01	0	0.1
Wood, paper, paper products, printing and publishing	1.29	0.1	0.03	0.9	0.03	0.93	0.76	0.09	0.03	0.41
Chemicals and non-metallic mineral products	6.67	0.43	0.28	4.96	0.29	5.24	4.1	0.45	0.17	1.82
Basic metals and fabricated metal products	8.1	0.64	0.23	6.33	0.05	6.38	5.38	0.28	0.29	2.18

(*Continued*)

Table 3.30   (*Continued*)

	Total	Japan	Korea	East Asia	ASEAN	East and South East Asia	China	United States	Germany	OECD
Machinery and equipment, nec	5.26	0.28	0.13	3.61	0.07	3.67	3.18	0.36	0.46	1.85
Electrical and optical equipment	4.3	0.42	0.3	3.23	0.29	3.53	2.29	0.26	0.15	1.36
Transport equipment	33.13	2.53	0.76	31.12	0.04	31.16	27.81	0.47	0.74	5.22
Manufacturing nec; recycling	1.61	0.19	0.05	1.4	0.01	1.41	1.16	0.05	0.02	0.35
Electricity, gas and water supply	2.23	0.17	0.06	1.89	0.03	1.91	1.63	0.04	0.07	0.47
Construction	0.24	0.05	0	0.1	0.01	0.1	0.04	0.02	0.02	0.18
Wholesale and retail trade; Hotels and restaurants	8.08	0.61	0.2	6.36	0.17	6.53	5.36	0.21	0.24	1.98
Transport and storage, post and telecommunication	4.2	0.55	0.16	2.71	0.13	2.84	1.86	0.28	0.18	1.82
Financial intermediation	4.02	0.27	0.08	3.29	0.05	3.34	2.88	0.18	0.06	0.87
Business services	8.57	0.56	0.3	3.79	0.19	3.98	2.64	1.12	0.73	5.06
Other services	1.84	0.09	0.03	1.33	0.01	1.35	1.17	0.07	0.1	0.51

Source: OECD–WTO_Statistics on TiVA

domestic auto industry and auto parts sub-sector have a competitive edge over the US and European auto producers. What we observe in this sector is a large amount of both vertical and horizontal value-added linkages. In an industry such as automotive production, with significant vertical integration, German and US transnational corporations engage in both vertical and horizontal investment, especially when they establish assembly plants to produce the same model in different countries under a joint venture. The value added flows that we observe in Table 3.26–3.30 demonstrate the strong developed country linkages between China, Germany and the US. There are very few upstream linkages with developing economies over the same period, nor is there a substitution away from Russia to Germany and the US.

The PRC has over the past twenty years positioned itself both in upstream or downstream in the global value-added chain. This is a function of its specialization and improved competitive position within a very short time frame. Thus far we have seen the data for China's upstream links both in terms of product and country of origin. In most of these cases the upstream suppliers provided China with raw materials and/or knowledge assets at the beginning of the production process (e.g. research, design). The evolution of China's position in the upstream value-added chain has benefited it in terms of R&D and design, process technology and business to business services. The size of China's footprint in international trade has created many opportunities for its neighbors who have participated in its upstream linkages.

With this growth in trade and backward linkages the PRC has benefited from increased productivity. Keller [2004] and Miroudot *et al.* [2009] show that imports of capital goods and intermediate goods increase domestic productivity through embodied technology more than imports of final goods. They find that in industries with a higher proportion of imported intermediate goods display, on average, higher productivity, as foreign inputs embody more productive technology and push the frontier of reallocation of resources towards greater efficiency.

Amiti and Konings [2007] find that companies in Indonesia that participate in these backward value-added linkages by importing foreign inputs are on average 9.2 percent more productive than companies importing no input. Amiti and Freund [2010] show that the skills content of China's exports largely reflects the skills content of the imported intermediates. Branstetter and Lardy [2006] conclude that China can export sophisticated ICT products because it imports the necessary high-value-added parts and components from other countries.

With continuous rounds of trade liberalization, there has been a significant reduction in the prices of imported intermediates relative to final goods accompanied by increased competitiveness of China's neighbors as suppliers of a wide range of imported intermediates [Goldberg *et al.*, 2009]. Grossman and Rossi-Hansberg [2008], Fontagné and Toubal [2010] and Cadot *et al.* [2011] expand on the argument made by Goldberg *et al.* (2009) by noting that imports of intermediates may benefit the competitiveness of domestic firms by lowering prices of intermediates in the domestic economy; increasing variety in the pool of available intermediates; and most importantly increase the productivity effects of access to higher technology embodied inputs and a wider knowledge base. Overall, China which has in the recent past allowed its firms to access technologically advanced inputs, regardless of its country of origin, will, other things being equal, prove to be more productive than those that do not.

As China grows more prosperous, and its wages rise, it will have to shift some of its production offshore to its Asian neighbors. The shift in China's new activities will require workers with higher skills in logistics and B-to-B infrastructure. Trade and production patterns are expected to change in this century much faster than in the past. This dynamics is very appropriate to the integrated PRC firms operation in both upstream and downstream markets. All of these changes will create more value added than simple assembly operations.

3.3. The Value-Added Chain in China's International Trade: Looking Forward

The extent to which China is involved in a vertically fragmented production process has been demonstrated in the country specific linkages noted above. We can summarize China's participation in the global value-added chain by measuring the value of imports contained in China's exports. From Equations (3.12) and (3.14) and Koopman *et al.* [2010], the decomposition of gross exports into *VAS* by source country is restated as:

$$VBE = V(I - A)^{-1}E, \qquad (3.19)$$

where, V is the diagonal of a vector with *VAS* in each country and industry; $(I - A)^{-1}$ is the Leontief inverse and E is the diagonal of a vector of gross exports.

These backward linkages noted as 'VS shares' by Hummels *et al.* [2001] are calculated simply as the elements of the *VBE* matrix excluding the contribution of domestic industries, divided by gross exports in each country. Consequently, VS_{ik} is an element of the vector obtained by summing the columns of the *VBE* matrix corresponding to the import content of exports in country i and industry k.

China's summary backward participation index, VS share, is reported in Table 3.31. Overall China's backward participation is within the OECD norm which is greater than 25 percent. The results clearly show that China's exports are increasingly composed of intermediate inputs that are imported from abroad. Between 1995 and 2009, the import dependency of exports increased in almost all categories. The three major Chinese sectors benefiting from backward linkages, noted above and demonstrated in the summary statistics include, "Textiles and apparel," "Electrical and optical equipment" and "Transportation equipment."

From Gereffi [1994] we know that these inter-firm links are most likely driven by producer-driven value chains, where the lead firms in the respective industries rely on controlling technology and R&D

Table 3.31   China's Participation Index, Backward

	1995	2000	2005	2008	2009
TOTAL	11.87	18.81	36.38	33.27	32.63
Agriculture	0.16	0.10	0.06	0.04	0.03
Mining and quarrying	0.16	0.18	0.20	0.21	0.17
Food products and beverages	0.39	0.30	0.57	0.55	0.54
Textiles, leather and footwear	3.49	3.61	3.41	3.24	3.27
Wood, paper, paper products, printing and publishing	0.12	0.40	0.92	0.85	0.78
Chemicals and non-metallic mineral products	1.33	2.24	4.70	4.37	4.17
Basic metals and fabricated metal products	0.93	1.22	3.37	3.01	2.68
Machinery and equipment nec	0.77	0.45	2.99	2.80	2.87
Electrical and optical equipment	2.07	7.91	15.98	14.30	14.31
Transport equipment	0.30	0.39	1.56	1.42	1.33
Manufacturing nec; recycling	1.06	0.92	1.35	1.29	1.37
Electricity, gas and water supply	0.00	0.02	0.03	0.02	0.02
Construction	0.01	0.01	0.06	0.06	0.05
Wholesale and retail trade; hotels and restaurants	0.15	0.74	0.51	0.51	0.53
Transport and storage; post and telecommunications	0.41	0.31	0.37	0.31	0.24
Financial intermediation	0.03	0.00	0.01	0.01	0.00
Business services	0.48	0.00	0.21	0.19	0.18
Other services	0.02	0.02	0.08	0.08	0.10

Source: OECD–WTO_Statistics on TiVA

with most of the assembly being distributed in different countries. Within the textile and apparel sector a buyer-driven international network involving retailers with branded marketers control the production, which can be totally outsourced. China's "Textile and apparel industry" has been a beneficiary of that international network since its early entry into the global market place.

As China grows more prosperous, wages rise and we see domestic production shifting offshore to other countries. Domestically produced inputs used in third country's exports reflect this 'forward' integration along the global value chain. The latter measured by summing over rows, excluding domestic industries, provides an

Table 3.32 China's Participation Index, Forward

	1995	2000	2005	2008	2009
TOTAL	13.86	13.75	12.25	14.35	13.43
Agriculture	1.06	0.82	0.67	0.72	0.67
Mining and quarrying	1.28	1.41	0.73	0.91	0.65
Food products and beverages	0.24	0.20	0.16	0.20	0.19
Textiles, leather and footwear	0.82	0.61	0.47	0.51	0.55
Wood, paper, paper products, printing and publishing	0.24	0.24	0.31	0.38	0.37
Chemicals and non-metallic mineral products	1.92	1.95	1.56	1.78	1.56
Basic metals and fabricated metal products	1.48	1.15	1.61	1.79	1.45
Machinery and equipment nec	0.44	0.25	0.49	0.58	0.49
Electrical and optical equipment	1.18	2.18	2.15	2.62	2.72
Transport equipment	0.17	0.26	0.25	0.37	0.30
Manufacturing nec; recycling	0.21	0.07	0.24	0.29	0.29
Electricity, gas and water supply	0.36	0.65	0.47	0.40	0.32
Construction	0.02	0.02	0.02	0.02	0.02
Wholesale and retail trade; hotels and restaurants	1.24	1.93	1.39	1.81	1.77
Transport and storage; post and telecommunications	1.21	0.92	0.61	0.65	0.56
Financial intermediation	0.51	0.59	0.45	0.56	0.61
Business services	1.47	0.47	0.53	0.58	0.67
Other services	0.01	0.05	0.15	0.20	0.23

Source: OECD–WTO_Statistics on TiVA

estimate of the contribution of domestically produced intermediates to exports by third countries. Chinese participation in this 'forward' global value chain has grown substantially over the past decade and remains at 13 percent across all categories. These latter summary statistics are presented in Table 3.32. The four major Chinese sectors benefitting from 'forward' linkages include, "Chemicals and other mineral products;" "Basic metals and fabricated metal products;" "Electrical and optical equipment" and "Wholesale and retail trade; hotels and restaurants."

Despite the industry-specific references that we introduce above, it should also be acknowledged that a broader understanding of trade and production patterns in the 21st century reflect trade in "skills" rather than industry specificity. That is, the pattern of Chinese trade that we observe reflects the sub elements of a production function along an international supply chain, such as R&D, procurement, operations, marketing and customer services, etc. China, like other countries that are integrated in the global-production network tend to specialize in specific business functions involving specific tasks rather than specific industries. Despite the fact that the old "trade theories" assume that goods and services are produced domestically and compete with "foreign" products, the reality is that most goods and an increasing number of services are "made in the world" and that countries compete on their specific economic roles within the global-production value chain. With China's accession to the WTO, the role of global-buying syndicates along with global-supply production networks has become the key explanatory factors determining cross-country competitiveness. Focusing on these cross-country linkages helps to identify firms and actors that control and coordinate economic activities in global-production networks.

While information on the degree of backward and forward linkages is an important element to measure the existence of international linkages, it does not provide any information on the number of production stages in these external links. Information on the "length" of these global value-added links would be useful and complementary. Fally [2012] and Antràs *et al.* [2012] provide a useful index which sheds light on the number of stages involved in a specific country's value chain.

Backer and Miroudot [2013], take the Fally [2012] procedure and calculate the inter-industry framework over the OECD Inter-Country Input–Output (ICIO) model, in order to calculate an index of the length of global value-added chain as:

$$N = u(I - A)^{-1}, \qquad (3.20)$$

where N is a column vector with the indexes for all countries i and industries k, u is a column unit vector, I is an identity matrix and A is the matrix of technical coefficients in the ICIO. $(I - A)^{-1}$ is the Leontief inverse.

The distance to final demand presented by Fally [2012] and Antràs *et al.* [2012] is calculated as:

$$D = u(I - G)^{-1}, \qquad (3.21)$$

where D is a column vector with the indexes for all countries i and industries k, u is a column unit vector, I is the identity matrix and G is a matrix of output coefficients, with $(I - G)^{-1}$ being known as the *output inverse* or *Ghosh inverse* in the I–O literature.

The calculated index takes the value of one if there is a single production stage in the final industry, and its value increases when inputs from the same industry or other industries are used, with a weighted average of the length of the production involved in these sectors. If the calculations are made at the firm level, then the index could be interpreted as the actual number of production stages. When calculated at the aggregate level, as they are here, the value is only an index, but still reflects the length of the value chain. The larger the index, the greater fragmentation in production across international partners.

The index of the number of production stages for China in the period 1995–2009 is presented in Table 3.33. The average length of the value chains is presented for both domestic and international components by industry categories. The international length in China has increased and supported the growth of the domestic production length. Continued reductions in trade and transaction costs, coupled with an increase in domestic production costs in China, will in all likelihood, lead to higher levels of fragmentation. The industries with the largest variations in the length of the value chain in China, include "Textiles, leather and footwear;" "Machinery and equipment, nec;" "Electrical and optical equipment" and "Transport equipment." The Chinese service industries such as "Construction" and "Hotels and restaurants," have on average shorter value chains. The "Construction" sector is part of the larger PRC foreign aid effort in Africa and Latin America and will be discussed later as we review the PRC foreign-aid outreach program in Chapter 7.

Fally [2012] and Antràs *et al.* [2012] introduced a measure of "upstreamness" that Backer and Miroudot [2013] referred to as the

Table 3.33   China's Index of the Number of Production Stages in International and Domestic

	International					Domestic				
	1995	2000	2005	2008	2009	1995	2000	2005	2008	2009
TOTAL	0.19	0.27	0.35	0.30	0.25	2.11	2.16	2.21	2.24	2.29
Agriculture	0.12	0.12	0.15	0.13	0.11	1.73	1.88	1.86	1.87	1.90
Mining and quarrying	0.17	0.20	0.30	0.25	0.22	2.03	1.85	2.17	2.19	2.24
Food products and beverages	0.17	0.17	0.25	0.22	0.19	2.32	2.31	2.48	2.51	2.55
Textiles, leather and footwear	0.31	0.37	0.38	0.33	0.27	2.49	2.54	2.89	2.93	3.04
Wood, paper, paper products, printing and publishing	0.26	0.48	0.46	0.40	0.33	2.39	2.28	2.61	2.64	2.73
Chemicals and non-metallic mineral products	0.26	0.38	0.54	0.46	0.40	2.41	2.42	2.56	2.60	2.71
Basic metals and fabricated metal products	0.27	0.39	0.56	0.45	0.38	2.53	2.59	2.73	2.76	2.88
Machinery and equipment nec	0.31	0.40	0.61	0.53	0.44	2.57	2.55	2.73	2.78	2.90
Electrical and optical equipment	0.28	0.60	1.01	0.88	0.76	2.23	2.45	2.41	2.49	2.68
Transport equipment	0.27	0.41	0.65	0.56	0.47	2.64	2.76	2.90	2.95	3.07
Manufacturing nec; recycling	0.28	0.44	0.45	0.39	0.32	2.46	2.45	2.38	2.41	2.51
Electricity, gas and water supply	0.16	0.23	0.34	0.30	0.26	2.10	2.17	2.62	2.60	2.65
Construction	0.22	0.33	0.43	0.36	0.31	2.52	2.58	2.81	2.84	2.92
Wholesale and retail trade; hotels and restaurants	0.16	0.21	0.21	0.18	0.16	1.89	2.11	1.90	1.92	1.95
Transport and storage; post and telecommunications	0.15	0.22	0.29	0.25	0.21	1.82	2.01	2.00	2.03	2.08
Financial intermediation	0.14	0.11	0.15	0.13	0.11	1.81	1.45	1.55	1.57	1.59
Business services	0.20	0.26	0.23	0.19	0.16	2.09	2.02	1.65	1.66	1.70
Other services	0.20	0.23	0.29	0.25	0.21	2.02	2.06	2.04	2.06	2.11

Source: OECD–WTO Statistics on TiVA

"distance to final demand." This index is calculated at the industry level within a given country and measures how many stages of production are left before the goods or services produced by this industry reach final consumers. This index is calculated by the OECD based on the intercountry I–O framework explained by Equation (3.21). The average and industry distance to final demand for China is presented in Table 3.34. It is interesting to note that while the average index for the PRC has increased between 1995 and 2009, the major action is at the industry level. It is at that level that once can see the most significant changes for the PRC, revealing the sector specific expansion in production specialization.

Table 3.34   China's Index of Distance to Final Demand

	1995	2000	2005	2008	2009
TOTAL	2.35	2.42	2.60	2.66	2.67
Agriculture	2.02	2.11	2.84	3.00	3.10
Mining and quarrying	3.98	4.20	4.33	4.37	4.42
Food products and beverages	1.78	1.82	2.28	2.44	2.55
Textiles, leather and footwear	2.23	2.22	2.22	2.31	2.53
Wood, paper, paper products, printing and publishing	3.28	2.98	3.44	3.55	3.64
Chemicals and non-metallic mineral products	3.08	3.13	3.27	3.35	3.41
Basic metals and fabricated metal products	3.20	3.28	3.45	3.49	3.48
Machinery and equipment nec	2.06	2.23	2.25	2.31	2.34
Electrical and optical equipment	1.93	2.29	2.34	2.46	2.55
Transport equipment	2.04	2.39	2.27	2.35	2.34
Manufacturing nec; recycling	2.21	1.77	2.28	2.38	2.53
Electricity, gas and water supply	3.47	3.50	4.11	4.12	4.15
Construction	1.04	1.09	1.05	1.05	1.05
Wholesale and retail trade; hotels and restaurants	2.69	2.69	2.41	2.52	2.59
Transport and storage; post and telecommunications	2.84	2.84	2.83	2.92	2.97
Financial intermediation	2.48	2.85	3.09	3.19	3.27
Business services	1.98	2.08	2.10	2.18	2.24
Other services	1.00	1.12	1.39	1.44	1.51

Source: OECD–WTO Statistics on TiVA

The majority of the PRC single-digit industries contained in the OECD database benefitted from increased specialization. The increase in the measured index by more than 10 percent occurred in: "Agriculture;" "Mining and quarrying;" "Food products and beverages;" "Textiles, leather and footwear;" "Wood, paper, paper products;" Machinery and equipment, nec;" "Electrical and optical equipment;" "Transport equipment;" "Manufacturing nec, recycling;" "Electricity, gas and water supply;" and in services such as "Financial intermediation" and "Other services."

In "Agriculture," the PRC has the highest index of upstreamness, based on the OECD data base. China is involved in much longer agriculture value chain, producing mainly inputs used in the agricultural activities of other countries. In "Transport equipment," China has developed its own domestic automobile industry and its accompanying parts sector which has become a leading world class competitor. The Chinese auto sector, in contrast, is focused more on its domestic market rather than exports. This is expected to change in the next decade as the PRC acquires more Western brands [Ferrarini, 2011].

Given the strong intensity of the PRC's 'backward' and 'forward' linkages in the global value added and production chains, it is difficult to imagine that it or its trade partners would successfully attempt to pursue country-specific independent industrial policies. Country-specific policy discussions, ignoring spillover effects, concerning the strengthening of specific sectors, inducing technologies or promoting areas of economic activity, such as advanced manufacturing, knowledge-intensive business services and/or the "green" economy, become more and more futile [Pelzman, 2003; Schwartz *et al.*, 2008]. The limits imposed by this complicated trade interdependence for the PRC is best observed by noting the very strong linkages between the PRC's value-added exports and its embodiment in the final demands of its major trading partners.

In the next set of tables, we present the data on the PRC's domestic value-added exports as embodied in the total final demand of its various trade partners, aggregated into the standard country subgroups. In Table 3.35, the data for World Total final

Table 3.35 China's Domestic Value Added Embodies in Total Final Demand (Millions US Dollars)

	1995	2000	2005	2008	2009
TOTAL	123,588	215,353	499,031	987,478	838,597
Agriculture, hunting, forestry and fishing	13,855	19,238	45,663	86,436	70,108
Mining and quarrying	6,907	12,589	24,298	51,037	34,361
Food products, beverages and tobacco	3,833	6,181	11,339	23,804	19,808
Textiles, textile products, leather and footwear	17,585	28,698	44,092	88,976	81,279
Wood, paper, paper products, printing and publishing	2,263	4,546	13,940	27,500	24,020
Chemicals and non-metallic mineral products	15,003	26,714	55,025	108,410	88,199
Basic metals and fabricated metal products	8,407	12,228	42,707	81,227	63,917
Machinery and equipment, nec	4,780	4,543	24,835	47,825	37,500
Electrical and optical equipment	9,561	26,854	63,979	131,203	119,732
Transport equipment	1,998	3,984	12,690	24,984	19,816
Manufacturing nec; recycling	4,939	4,047	22,327	43,301	34,440
Electricity, gas and water supply	2,621	8,578	20,127	28,426	20,566
Construction	120	340	591	1,217	973
Wholesale and retail trade; Hotels and restaurants	11,040	26,838	47,365	103,995	94,797
Transport and storage, post and telecommunication	9,175	13,281	22,423	40,561	31,448
Financial intermediation	4,493	8,813	20,621	41,809	40,519
Business services	6,900	6,993	19,469	40,290	39,718
Other services	108	888	7,540	16,479	17,396

Source: OECD–WTO Statistics on TiVA

demand is presented. World demand for China's value-added exports increased substantially from $123.6 billion in 1995 to $838.6 billion in 2009. The foremost PRC sectors accounting for this expansion included "Electrical and optical equipment;" "Wholesale and retail trade, hotels and restaurants;" "Chemicals and non-metallic mineral products;" "Textiles, textile products, leather and footwear" and "Agriculture." The OECD trade data presented in Table 3.35 represent PRC domestic value added and not the existing trade data which includes imported intermediates. Over the 1995–2009 period, the growth of China's value-added exports is nothing short of spectacular, and not concentrated in simple downstream operations.

In Table 3.36, we examine the same OECD trade data for the EU15 as the final group of consumers. In 2009, the EU15 represented approximately 22 percent of China's domestic value-added exports. As in the total product distribution, the main sectors accounting for this traffic included, "Electrical and optical equipment;" "Wholesale and retail trade, hotels and restaurants;" "Chemicals and non-metallic mineral products;" "Textiles, textile products, leather and footwear" and "Agriculture." The level of China's specialization was matched in the EU15 market to that for the total world. Expanding the consumer sample to EU27, in Table 3.37, does not alter the distribution of the results.

In Table 3.38, we shift the focus to US final consumers. The growth in US demand for PRC embodied value added in its final consumption expanded substantially from $33.6 billion in 1995 to $201.2 billion in 2009. The size of the US market in 2009 is larger than the EU15 market. The industry composition of China's value added embodied in US final demand differs slightly from its EU market counterpart. The leading US consumer demand evaluated in terms of their final demand embodying PRC value added are led by "Electrical and optical equipment;" "Chemicals and non-metallic mineral products" and "Textiles, textile products, leather and footwear." The less sizeable PRC industry distribution in the US market is in service sectors represented by "Wholesale and retail trade, hotels and restaurants" and "Agriculture."

The other major country aggregation, representing the 'developed world' is presented in Table 3.39 for the OECD countries. Unmistakably, the majority of China's value-added exports are primarily directed to serving developed country consumers. While this final market has grown from $92.3 billion in 1995 to $588.7 billion in 2009, in percentage terms this translates to a slight

Table 3.36   China's Domestic Value Added Embodies in EU15 Final Demand (Millions US Dollars)

	1995	2000	2005	2008	2009
TOTAL	24,586	43,174	111,493	226,784	187,068
Agriculture, hunting, forestry and fishing	2,522	3,525	9,686	19,605	15,479
Mining and quarrying	1,189	2,137	5,137	11,201	7,253
Food products, beverages and tobacco	628	1,024	2,145	5,014	3,952
Textiles, textile products, leather and footwear	3,265	5,620	10,232	21,404	19,147
Wood, paper, paper products, printing and publishing	456	1,130	3,363	7,036	6,058
Chemicals and non-metallic mineral products	3,008	5,666	12,260	23,808	18,895
Basic metals and fabricated metal products	1,627	2,673	9,405	18,801	14,050
Machinery and equipment, nec	1,137	1,098	6,335	10,777	7,983
Electrical and optical equipment	2,365	5,614	14,298	28,153	24,289
Transport equipment	259	765	2,141	5,456	4,192
Manufacturing nec; recycling	1,089	691	4,357	11,277	8,724
Electricity, gas and water supply	522	1,787	4,637	6,613	4,597
Construction	25	75	208	315	259
Wholesale and retail trade; Hotels and restaurants	2,252	5,571	11,563	25,606	23,523
Transport and storage, post and telecommunication	1,554	2,386	4,769	8,792	6,606
Financial intermediation	849	1,810	4,594	9,467	8,828
Business services	1,826	1,436	4,700	9,702	9,359
Other services	14	167	1,666	3,756	3,875

Source: OECD–WTO_Statistics on TiVA

reduction from 74 percent in 1995 to 70 percent in 2009. If we recalculate the percentages to 2008, in order to take into account the slowdown in developed country economies, we get a slight adjustment to 72 percent. Despite the discussion of the sensitivity of OECD consumers to the macro shocks, which was expected to have a major

Table 3.37   China's Domestic Value Added Embodies in EU27 Final Demand
(Millions US Dollars)

	1995	2000	2005	2008	2009
TOTAL	25,273	46,191	120,996	256,640	211,039
Agriculture, hunting, forestry and fishing	2,610	3,757	10,416	21,769	17,134
Mining and quarrying	1,227	2,286	5,591	12,663	8,174
Food products, beverages and tobacco	652	1,115	2,333	5,619	4,411
Textiles, textile products, leather and footwear	3,350	5,922	10,895	23,473	20,975
Wood, paper, paper products, printing and publishing	468	1,203	3,608	7,804	6,681
Chemicals and non-metallic mineral products	3,096	6,034	13,301	27,005	21,362
Basic metals and fabricated metal products	1,669	2,858	10,264	21,172	15,721
Machinery and equipment, nec	1,160	1,171	6,929	12,588	9,193
Electrical and optical equipment	2,400	6,059	15,779	32,915	28,308
Transport equipment	267	845	2,354	6,046	4,738
Manufacturing nec; recycling	1,113	728	4,666	12,215	9,448
Electricity, gas and water supply	537	1,910	5,038	7,482	5,186
Construction	26	84	242	381	302
Wholesale and retail trade; Hotels and restaurants	2,314	6,007	12,581	29,814	27,281
Transport and storage, post and telecommunication	1,613	2,556	5,137	9,921	7,401
Financial intermediation	874	1,939	4,985	10,727	9,965
Business services	1,883	1,540	5,087	10,838	10,430
Other services	15	179	1,789	4,209	4,329

Source: OECD–WTO Statistics on TiVA

negative outcome for PRC exports, there is very little change in demand for China's value-added exports. The five major industrial sectors involved in these transactions are "Electrical and optical equipment;" "Wholesale and retail trade, hotels and restaurants;"

Table 3.38   China's Domestic Value Added Embodies in US Final Demand
(Millions US Dollars)

	1995	2000	2005	2008	2009
TOTAL	33,618	73,326	159,071	243,746	201,253
Agriculture, hunting, forestry and fishing	3,122	5,429	14,257	21,177	16,871
Mining and quarrying	1,582	3,680	7,443	12,106	7,852
Food products, beverages and tobacco	587	1,270	2,848	5,045	4,044
Textiles, textile products, leather and footwear	5,702	11,451	15,874	24,631	22,157
Wood, paper, paper products, printing and publishing	730	1,578	4,776	7,079	5,785
Chemicals and non-metallic mineral products	4,477	9,582	18,672	28,442	22,408
Basic metals and fabricated metal products	2,126	4,339	13,253	19,618	14,902
Machinery and equipment, nec	1,333	1,513	6,824	9,993	7,234
Electrical and optical equipment	2,583	10,592	21,904	37,801	34,317
Transport equipment	466	1,517	5,330	6,197	5,270
Manufacturing nec; recycling	2,104	2,503	10,996	16,155	11,690
Electricity, gas and water supply	706	3,029	6,646	7,199	5,060
Construction	30	98	83	136	115
Wholesale and retail trade; Hotels and restaurants	2,794	6,572	9,681	16,774	14,494
Transport and storage, post and telecommunication	2,504	4,626	6,122	8,420	6,407
Financial intermediation	1,314	3,042	6,783	10,705	10,246
Business services	1,457	2,265	5,618	9,051	9,007
Other services	4	239	1,960	3,218	3,392

Source: OECD–WTO Statistics on TiVA

"Chemicals and non-metallic mineral products;" "Textiles, textile products, leather and footwear" and "Agriculture."

Switching our focus to Asia, the next few tables emphasize the PRC-Asia downstream linkages. The OECD data on China's

Table 3.39　China's Domestic Value Added Embodies in OECD Final Demand (Millions US Dollars)

	1995	2000	2005	2008	2009
TOTAL	92,336	175,754	399,439	710,288	588,703
Agriculture, hunting, forestry and fishing	10,329	15,702	37,137	63,134	49,959
Mining and quarrying	4,830	9,355	18,979	36,323	23,349
Food products, beverages and tobacco	2,784	4,968	9,081	17,219	13,953
Textiles, textile products, leather and footwear	14,887	25,856	38,194	68,563	61,587
Wood, paper, paper products, printing and publishing	1,709	3,826	11,518	20,659	17,517
Chemicals and non-metallic mineral products	11,145	21,527	43,858	78,112	61,650
Basic metals and fabricated metal products	5,971	9,757	33,231	58,020	43,512
Machinery and equipment, nec	3,457	3,581	18,785	31,712	23,513
Electrical and optical equipment	6,899	21,977	53,364	100,191	89,432
Transport equipment	1,143	3,148	9,853	16,629	13,666
Manufacturing nec; recycling	4,166	3,697	19,286	35,230	26,758
Electricity, gas and water supply	1,924	6,926	16,136	20,503	14,402
Construction	81	264	386	688	552
Wholesale and retail trade; Hotels and restaurants	8,083	21,190	35,669	67,839	61,868
Transport and storage, post and telecommunication	6,559	10,499	16,763	26,505	20,137
Financial intermediation	3,393	7,183	16,597	30,155	28,593
Business services	4,918	5,665	15,014	28,135	27,226
Other services	59	636	5,587	10,671	11,028

Source: OECD–WTO_Statistics on TiVA

domestic value-added exports embodied in ASEAN final demand is presented in Table 3.40. The total size of China's value-added exports expanded from $5.6 billion in 1995 to $40.6 billion in 2009, or an expansion from 4 percent to 5 percent of total value-added exports. The major industrial sectors involved included, "Wholesale

Table 3.40   China's Domestic Value Added Embodies in ASEAN Final Demand
(Millions US Dollars)

	1995	2000	2005	2008	2009
TOTAL	5,580	8,072	21,174	49,072	40,588
Agriculture, hunting, forestry and fishing	691	1,001	1,869	3,970	3,200
Mining and quarrying	365	557	1,148	2,647	1,913
Food products, beverages and tobacco	175	344	450	1,068	904
Textiles, textile products, leather and footwear	315	482	988	2,270	2,196
Wood, paper, paper products, printing and publishing	88	137	508	1,276	1,113
Chemicals and non-metallic mineral products	665	971	2,309	5,375	4,588
Basic metals and fabricated metal products	532	505	2,279	4,555	3,822
Machinery and equipment, nec	268	210	1,474	3,469	2,768
Electrical and optical equipment	464	888	2,424	6,298	5,424
Transport equipment	104	190	710	1,413	1,070
Manufacturing nec; recycling	100	53	516	1,356	1,130
Electricity, gas and water supply	130	325	862	1,432	1,029
Construction	6	15	43	90	98
Wholesale and retail trade; Hotels and restaurants	492	1,243	2,635	6,902	5,122
Transport and storage, post and telecommunication	592	516	986	2,200	1,638
Financial intermediation	196	325	842	2,043	1,910
Business services	398	273	812	1,896	1,840
Other services	1	38	319	811	823

Source: OECD–WTO_Statistics on TiVA

and retail trade, hotels and restaurants;" "Electrical and optical equipment;" "Chemicals and non-metallic mineral products" and "Agriculture."

Table 3.41 presents the OECD data for China's domestic value-added exports embodied in Hong Kong's final demand. Unlike the case for developed-country consumption of China's value-added exports, in the case of Hong Kong, that figure has dropped from 7.8 percent in 1995 to 1.4 percent in 2009. The sectors with more than

Table 3.41   China's Domestic Value Added Embodies in Hong Kong Final Demand (Millions US Dollars)

	1995	2000	2005	2008	2009
TOTAL	9,685	8,194	8,110	12,719	12,839
Agriculture, hunting, forestry and fishing	843	433	459	788	741
Mining and quarrying	497	838	376	740	705
Food products, beverages and tobacco	220	137	133	271	262
Textiles, textile products, leather and footwear	641	407	197	332	346
Wood, paper, paper products, printing and publishing	216	179	255	410	388
Chemicals and non-metallic mineral products	1,160	995	725	1,327	1,332
Basic metals and fabricated metal products	776	618	691	1,039	1,049
Machinery and equipment, nec	466	227	506	820	770
Electrical and optical equipment	1,279	1,508	1,295	1,910	2,086
Transport equipment	501	162	161	285	257
Manufacturing nec; recycling	354	80	191	320	312
Electricity, gas and water supply	217	370	334	414	354
Construction	8	14	16	12	14
Wholesale and retail trade; Hotels and restaurants	757	614	525	1,021	1,103
Transport and storage, post and telecommunication	817	981	914	1,211	1,025
Financial intermediation	347	345	377	616	680
Business services	587	258	806	995	1,163
Other services	0	29	149	208	256

Source: OECD–WTO Statistics on TiVA

$1 billion in China's domestic value in total final demand included "Electrical and optical equipment;" "Chemicals and non-metallic mineral products;" "Basic metals and fabricated metal products;" "Wholesale and retail trade, hotels and restaurants;" "Transport and storage, post and telecommunication" and "Business services."

Table 3.42 presents the data for Japan's final demands. It is surprising that, despite the fact that we can treat Japan as a developed country trade partner, its total demand for China's value added declined substantially, in percentage terms, from 17.9 percent

Table 3.42   China's Domestic Value Added Embodies in Japan's Final Demand
(Millions US Dollars)

	1995	2000	2005	2008	2009
TOTAL	22,156	34,465	56,841	82,875	71,262
Agriculture, hunting, forestry and fishing	3,410	4,272	6,375	9,212	7,338
Mining and quarrying	1,399	2,080	2,710	4,501	2,778
Food products, beverages and tobacco	1,241	1,910	2,378	3,367	2,915
Textiles, textile products, leather and footwear	4,267	5,525	5,774	9,085	8,721
Wood, paper, paper products, printing and publishing	330	621	1,536	2,356	2,159
Chemicals and non-metallic mineral products	2,264	3,320	5,236	8,376	6,567
Basic metals and fabricated metal products	1,300	1,206	3,716	5,129	3,969
Machinery and equipment, nec	516	424	1,754	2,747	1,976
Electrical and optical equipment	1,008	2,802	7,605	11,456	10,527
Transport equipment	294	482	846	1,318	1,051
Manufacturing nec; recycling	587	224	1,385	2,340	1,957
Electricity, gas and water supply	439	1,118	1,934	2,108	1,531
Construction	16	48	29	46	41
Wholesale and retail trade; Hotels and restaurants	1,750	5,829	7,803	9,788	9,770
Transport and storage, post and telecommunication	1,572	2,030	2,632	3,071	2,399
Financial intermediation	802	1,327	2,297	3,388	3,302
Business services	962	1,150	2,078	3,451	3,106
Other services	1	99	755	1,135	1,156

Source: OECD–WTO_Statistics on TiVA

to 8.5 percent of total world demand. The only sectors that showed a substantial increase in final demand for PRC embodied value added were: "Electrical and optical equipment;" "Wholesale and retail trade, hotels and restaurants" and "Textiles, textile products, leather and footwear."

Table 3.43 presents the final demand for Korea. China's domestic value added embodied in Korea's final demand, while small in absolute volume, expanded from less than 1 percent in 1995 to

Table 3.43　China's Domestic Value Added Embodies in Korean Final Demand
(Millions US Dollars)

	1995	2000	2005	2008	2009
TOTAL	3,999	7,002	16,739	33,515	23,218
Agriculture, hunting, forestry and fishing	452	1,038	2,375	3,219	2,192
Mining and quarrying	284	551	1,094	2,345	1,237
Food products, beverages and tobacco	128	339	709	1,159	868
Textiles, textile products, leather and footwear	364	679	1,580	2,576	1,815
Wood, paper, paper products, printing and publishing	53	138	396	810	611
Chemicals and non-metallic mineral products	424	758	1,581	3,326	2,243
Basic metals and fabricated metal products	406	394	1,696	4,104	2,255
Machinery and equipment, nec	94	111	651	1,433	1,033
Electrical and optical equipment	262	824	1,354	3,789	2,656
Transport equipment	37	91	269	755	558
Manufacturing nec; recycling	60	43	411	867	589
Electricity, gas and water supply	89	272	621	947	550
Construction	4	11	11	20	15
Wholesale and retail trade; Hotels and restaurants	602	748	1,266	2,980	2,438
Transport and storage, post and telecommunication	403	488	1,090	1,817	1,280
Financial intermediation	147	255	636	1,368	1,078
Business services	166	221	621	1,387	1,221
Other services	22	44	378	616	579

Source: OECD–WTO_Statistics on TiVA

2.7 percent in 2009. The sectors with more than $2 billion in China's domestic value added in Korean final demand included, "Wholesale and retail trade, hotels and restaurants;" "Electrical and optical equipment;" "Basic metals and fabricated metal products;" "Chemicals and non-metallic mineral products" and "Agriculture."

The trade linkages for Chinese Taipei are presented in Table 3.44. The overall size of these transactions are very small, representing

Table 3.44 China's Domestic Value Added Embodies in Chinese Taipe's Final Demand (Millions US Dollars)

	1995	2000	2005	2008	2009
TOTAL	2,104	3,860	7,264	12,438	10,075
Agriculture, hunting, forestry and fishing	186	269	490	887	643
Mining and quarrying	202	274	522	880	503
Food products, beverages and tobacco	46	76	129	288	209
Textiles, textile products, leather and footwear	64	140	235	445	390
Wood, paper, paper products, printing and publishing	39	89	187	321	277
Chemicals and non-metallic mineral products	206	442	731	1,231	951
Basic metals and fabricated metal products	205	318	913	1,191	782
Machinery and equipment, nec	55	75	357	596	395
Electrical and optical equipment	86	658	942	1,378	1,302
Transport equipment	22	74	199	492	311
Manufacturing nec; recycling	36	57	183	290	239
Electricity, gas and water supply	51	169	280	331	219
Construction	6	7	4	8	7
Wholesale and retail trade; Hotels and restaurants	207	624	923	2,105	2,133
Transport and storage, post and telecommunication	340	270	390	631	463
Financial intermediation	79	163	289	501	460
Business services	275	136	312	515	485
Other services	0	21	178	348	306

Source: OECD–WTO_Statistics on TiVA

1 percent of 2009 value added exports from the PRC. All of the transactions are concentrated in two industries — "Wholesale and retail trade, hotels and restaurants;" and "Electrical and optical equipment."

The trade linkages for Thailand are presented in Table 3.45. Despite the growth in China's domestic value added embodied in Thailand's final demand it is significant in only a single industry — "Wholesale and retail trade, hotels and restaurants."

Table 3.45   China's Domestic Value Added Embodies in Thailand's Final Demand (Millions US Dollars)

	1995	2000	2005	2008	2009
TOTAL	1,162	1,884	5,159	10,746	7,675
Agriculture, hunting, forestry and fishing	90	175	379	783	560
Mining and quarrying	80	95	216	485	304
Food products, beverages and tobacco	31	56	102	253	189
Textiles, textile products, leather and footwear	93	158	271	549	488
Wood, paper, paper products, printing and publishing	18	29	145	310	239
Chemicals and non-metallic mineral products	133	185	454	1,006	792
Basic metals and fabricated metal products	122	87	451	756	626
Machinery and equipment, nec	38	30	210	437	361
Electrical and optical equipment	85	136	559	1,191	865
Transport equipment	13	27	72	188	155
Manufacturing nec; recycling	31	16	146	302	228
Electricity, gas and water supply	27	69	184	276	180
Construction	1	4	4	8	6
Wholesale and retail trade; Hotels and restaurants	155	511	1,247	2,615	1,523
Transport and storage, post and telecommunication	144	142	244	550	333
Financial intermediation	44	83	207	444	360
Business services	57	76	197	432	331
Other services	0	7	72	162	139

Source: OECD–WTO_Statistics on TiVA

Having detailed the micro-components of the value added and production linkages in the International trade of the PRC, we shift the focus in Chapter 4 to a discussion of revealed comparative advantage of the PRC's trade as measured in terms of total trade and that in terms of value-added transactions.

Chapter 4

China's International Trade Competitiveness: An Assessment Based on Revealed Comparative Advantage (RCA) and Constant Market Share (CMS) Indexes

China's relative competitiveness has to be measured in an increasing internationalization of markets for goods and services, financial resources, corporations, industries and technology. While the trade literature points to a wide number of explanatory factors for the increased globalization of world markets, it is convenient to think of three major factors that have facilitated this increased globalization which the PRC has relied on. First, the liberalization of capital movements and deregulation, of financial services in both market and non-market economies, has been a crucial lubricant. Second, the post Uruguay round liberalization of markets to trade and investment, spurred the growth of international competition. Third, as Baldwin [2011] has correctly pointed out, the continued globalization of the world economy and China's role in that globalization could not be accomplished without the pivotal role played by information and communication technologies (ICT) in the PRC and its trade partners.

The PRC is a major beneficiary of this new world economy where distances and national boundaries are far less important than in the period prior to GATT/WTO removal of most obstacles to market access. The production linkages between the PRC, its Asian neighbors and the links to its markets in the OECD countries has changed the dynamics of trade, capital flows and transfer of technology. With the low cost of communication and network technology (ICT), transnational firms are organizing themselves into "transnational networks" in response to intense international competition and the increasing need for strategic interactions.

These changes have altered our concepts of "global competition." In this new environment, competitiveness increasingly depends on the utilization of a broad assortment of specialized industrial, financial, technological, commercial, administrative and cultural skills located in different countries. It is therefore not surprising to find that a growing number of PRC firms are competing in their own markets as well as in foreign ones, with new entrants from around the globe.

This increased dynamics in commercial activities between the PRC and its competitors, places new demands on statistics and indicators designed to assess competitiveness. The traditional economic statistics and indicators were developed largely in an era where most economic activity, with the exception of trade, occurred domestically and trade in intermediate products was rare. Consequently, our discussion of China's relative competitiveness is based on a variety of measures. In the best case scenario, the PRC firm's competitiveness is affected by a number of factors including differentials in productivity, prices, quality of export products and delivery and service schedules. In the absence of analyzing price and non-price determinants of changes in competitiveness, the empirical trade literature has provided a number of statistical measures of trade performance to study the structure and competitiveness of China's foreign trade. Within this class of indicators are indices of trade intensity, the most popular member of this family being the index of "revealed comparative advantage" (RCA). The form of each index and the interpretation given to their values have varied from author to author, but the empirical and theoretical literature appear to agree that a country reveals a comparative advantage (disadvantage) in a commodity if an index's value is greater (less) than one.

The classic RCA index is most often associated with the work of Balassa [1965]. Very simply, the index compares a country's share of world exports in a sector to its share of total exports:

$$\text{RCA}_{ij} = \frac{\dfrac{X_{ij}}{X_{wj}}}{\dfrac{X_{it}}{X_{wt}}}, \tag{4.1}$$

where X_{ij} and X_{wj} are exports of j by country i and the world w and X_{it} and X_{wt} represent the total exports of i and the world (w).

This index in essence, applies a country's *ex post* specialization patterns to infer that a country's actual high specialization in a sector can be viewed as an indication that it has strong comparative advantage in that sector. The term "comparative advantage," as Bowen [1983] correctly points out, is misapplied in this literature since only exports are typically considered whereas comparative advantage is properly a net trade concept. While we use "Revealed Comparative Advantage" in our discussion here for consistency, the reader may wish to consider substituting "Revealed *Competitive* Advantage."

One can restate Balassa's RCA index into two related indices:

$$\text{RCA}_{ij} = \frac{\dfrac{X_{ij}}{X_{wj}}}{\dfrac{X_{it}}{X_{wt}}} = \frac{s_{ij}}{s_i} \tag{4.2}$$

or

$$\text{RCA}_{ij} = \frac{\dfrac{X_{ij}}{X_{wi}}}{\dfrac{X_{jt}}{X_{wt}}} = \frac{c_{ij}}{c_j}, \tag{4.3}$$

where $s_{ij} = \frac{X_{ij}}{X_{wj}}$ represents country i's share in export market j; $s_i = \frac{X_{it}}{X_{wt}}$ represents country i's share in the entire world export market;

$c_{ij} = \frac{X_{ij}}{X_{wi}}$ measures country i's export specialization in product j and $c_j = \frac{X_{jt}}{X_{wt}}$ measures the world export specialization in product j.

From Bowen and Pelzman [1984] we can infer that when $RCA_{ij} > 1$ [Equation (4.2)] country i's competitiveness in product j (measured by s_{ij}) is greater than its average competitiveness (measured by s_i). Furthermore, when $RCA_{ij} > 1$ [Equation (4.3)], country i's export specialization in product j (measured by c_{ij}) is higher than the world average export specialization in the product (measured by c_j). Overall, from both Equations (4.2) and (4.3) when $RCA_{ij} > 1$ it is inferred that country i has strong comparative advantage in product j. If we allow the RCA measure to reflect "competitiveness," than one can argue that trade-policy intervention may have created an outcome that some have incorrectly referred to as "comparative advantage." Furthermore, the concept of competitiveness is more appropriate to firms than to countries [Krugman, 1996]. If a firm is not performing and its business position is unsustainable, i.e. if it is a 'non-performing asset,' it will eventually go bankrupt. It is far less likely that a country that is non-competitive will go bankrupt, although not impossible.

The decomposition of the Balassa RCA measure suggests that an alternative methodology to employ is one that decomposes a country's export growth based on departures from a steady-state world growth. The latter methodology is known as the Constant Market Share (CMS) methodology. The CMS model decomposes the actual growth of a country's exports into four components: world trade, commodity composition, market distribution and (residual) competitiveness. Formally, the CMS identity for a change in total PRC exports can be written as:

$$X^{00} - X^0 \equiv rX^0 + \sum_i (r_i - r)X_i^0 + \sum_i \sum_j (r_{ij} - r_i)X_{ij}^0$$

$$+ \sum_i \sum_j (X_{ij}^{00} - X_i^0 - r_{ij}X_{ij}^0), \tag{4.4}$$

where X is the total PRC exports, X_{ij} is the PRC exports of commodity i to market j, X_j is the total PRC exports of commodity i, r

is the rate of growth of total world exports, r_j is the rate of growth of total world exports of commodity i, r_{ij}) is the rate of growth of world exports of commodity i to market j, 0 is the initial period and 00 is the second period.

The first term in Equation (4.4) is the world-trade component and measures what PRC exports would have been had they grown at the same rate as total world exports. The second term (commodity composition effect) measures whether PRC export composition was skewed toward commodities whose rate of growth either exceeded or fell short of total world export growth. The third term (market distribution effect) measures whether PRC exports were concentrated in markets where demand was growing either faster or slower than total world export demand in those markets. The fourth term (residual competitiveness) measures the difference between the actual increase in PRC exports and the increase that would have occurred had the PRC maintained its export share in each market with respect to each commodity. In theory, an increase (decrease) in competitiveness is indicated by a positive (negative) value of the residual.

The application of the CMS procedure raises a number of questions concerning both measurement and aggregation. For example, what is the appropriate definition of the world market and regional markets in which the PRC competes? What is the appropriate level of commodity aggregation? Also, given a paucity of quantity data, value data are commonly used and thus price changes may hamper interpretation of the CMS estimates, especially if we use PRC data. As Bowen and Pelzman [1984, p. 462] and Richardson [1971a, p. 231] noted, a positive commodity composition effect, normally taken to imply that a country's exports were concentrated in goods for which demand was growing rapidly, may instead be due to a country's exports being concentrated in goods whose (relative) price is rising. Such a price bias also applies to the competitive residual (CR).

When data are in value terms, the CR can be written as:

$$CR = \sum_i \sum_j V_{ij}^0 [(\dot{X}_{ij} - \dot{X}_{ij}^w) + (\dot{P}_{ij} - \dot{P}_{ij}^w)], \qquad (4.5)$$

where V_{ij}^0 is the value of PRC exports of commodity i to market j and a dot over a variable denotes its rate of change. The first term in parentheses is the difference in the rates of growth of PRC and the rest of world's quantity of exports of commodity i to market j. The second term is the difference in the rate of growth of PRC and rest of world export price of commodity i in market j. The first term is the true competitive component, in that failure to maintain market share in quantity terms implies a negative value of this term. But with value data, a negative value of CR could also result from slower growth in PRC export prices relative to the rest of the world's prices. These two forces are essentially in opposition, since a relative decline in PRC export prices would be expected to result in a relative increase in PRC exports. Ultimately, when value data are used, the sign of CR depends not only on differential growth in prices, but also on the elasticity of substitution in each market.

Although an interpretation of the sign of the CR can be confounded by price movements when market shares are measured in value terms, the above does suggest that one can infer a failure to maintain quantity shares if, given a negative value of CR, one observes that a country's export prices increased relative to the export prices of the rest of the world.

In the case of the PRC, with distortionary trade policies and an inconvertible currency, the distinction between value and quantity data for RCA measures may not be as important as the more fundamental flows. For our purposes, the RCA measures we report here are used for the descriptive purpose of identifying in which sectors PRCs exports, measured in value-added terms or gross trade, are more or less than average. The comparison to world exports helps to 'normalize' the trade data for the sizes of sectors and countries, which otherwise might give misleading impressions of the importance of a sector and country in international trade.

We present both RCA and CMS measures as a guide to what causes actual trade patterns, whether these are driven by comparative advantage, strategic trade policy intervention or currency interventions. RCA and CMS indexes could be correlated with additional data on factor endowments and factor intensities to learn whether the Heckscher–Ohlin explanation of trade has significant explanatory power. This is done to a limited extent by analyzing for separate product aggregates classified according to the intensity with which they use unskilled labor, human capital or technology across a group of OECD and non-OECD countries [Richardson, 1971b; Roger, 2008; Saunders, 2006; Schott, 2008; Stone *et al.*, 2011].

To the extent that differences in total factor productivity can be measured, these could be related to RCA and CMS measures to see if a more strictly Ricardian explanation of trade patterns plays an important role.

In addition to the question of PRC trade competitiveness, the question of commodity and country diversification is also addressed. The conventional development literature advocates export diversification as a mechanism by which to generate positive productivity and economic growth. Melitz [2003], Feenstra and Kee [2008] and Feenstra [2010] argue that an increase in export variety — one of the sources of export diversification — can increase productivity given that exporters are more productive than non-exporters. It has also been argued that export diversification can reduce exposure to external shocks, reducing macroeconomic volatility and increasing economic growth. This argument is the reverse of the "Dutch Disease" argument applied to natural resource exporters Lederman and Maloney [2003].

Despite the fact that the theoretical trade discussion is about "trade diversification," the indexes used empirically, most of them borrowed from the income-distribution literature, are about degree of concentration. The most frequently used concentration index is the Herfindahl index listed as Equation (4.6). The Herfindahl index of export concentration (for country (i) can be applied across categories (k) in order to measure product specific-concentration or across countries (n) for a specific commodity classification (k) in order to measure geographic concentration. The index is normalized to range between zero and one, where one implies complete concentration and the reverse to demonstrate complete diversification. For the PRC, we calculate both measures. Our discussion of RCA indexes will use geographic concentration. Our discussion of the CMS measures will present both geographic and product level concentration,

$$H_i^k = \sum_{i=1}^{n} \left(\frac{X_i^k}{\sum_{i=1}^{n} X_i^k} \right)^2. \tag{4.6}$$

4.1. Competitiveness Based on RCA and Herfindahl Indexes

In order to assess China's trade performance and specialization, we begin by exploring the RCA indexes calculated in terms of both China's gross exports and those measured using China's domestic value added embedded in their exports. In retaining both measures, we are able to see the significance of trade in intermediate inputs in the context of China's RCA. For RCA indexes measured using gross exports, the calculations rely on COMTRADE statistics, while new OECD–WTO statistics identifying domestic value added in exports are used for the RCA indexes in value-added terms. The time frame for these indexes are over the period 1995–2009. Despite the short time frame, the changes in the trade environment brought about by the implementation of the Uruguay round and the major liberalization in China in the post-1995 period lead to noteworthy variations across sectors.

Table 4.1 presents the RCA indexes for China for the period 1995–2009 by aggregate manufacturing good categories, estimated for domestic value added embodied in gross exports (in Panel A) and gross exports (in Panel B). These indexes are calculated using the "world" as the target market for China's exports. The OECD value-added data did not allow for bilateral country estimates of RCA indexes for China. Surprisingly, there is a general similarity between RCA indexes calculated in gross terms and value-added terms. China's RCA in textile and textile products in gross terms — an RCA above 1 — is matched in value-added terms and is more

Table 4.1   PRC — Revealed Comparative Advantage Indexes Based on Domestic Value Embodied in Gross Exports and Gross Exports (Manufacturing Goods, to the World)

Industry	(Manufacturing Goods, to the World)									
	Domestic Value Added Embodied in Gross Exports					Gross Exports				
	1995	2000	2005	2008	2009	1995	2000	2005	2008	2009
Food products, beverages and tobacco	0.835	0.772	0.410	0.399	0.345	0.834	0.733	0.387	0.391	0.342
Textiles, textile products, leather and footwear	4.095	3.689	2.922	2.988	2.966	4.076	3.634	2.487	2.671	2.612
Wood, paper, paper products, printing and publishing	0.179	0.432	0.430	0.476	0.473	0.189	0.457	0.487	0.557	0.537
Chemicals and non-metallic mineral products	0.673	0.836	0.575	0.533	0.487	0.655	0.767	0.573	0.528	0.508
Basic metals and fabricated metal products	0.918	0.974	0.950	0.832	0.839	0.907	0.952	0.960	0.837	0.843
Machinery and equipment, nec	0.586	0.313	0.939	0.840	0.776	0.627	0.323	0.953	0.874	0.839
Electrical and optical equipment	0.933	1.164	1.505	1.679	1.769	0.907	1.265	1.708	1.824	1.821
Transport equipment	0.217	0.189	0.316	0.343	0.339	0.215	0.175	0.302	0.330	0.328
Manufacturing nec; recycling	3.498	1.751	2.258	2.010	1.763	3.542	1.766	1.884	1.779	1.591

Source: OECD ITCS and UN COMTRADE Databases

pronounced in value-added terms post Uruguay round when the multi-fiber agreement (MFA) was eliminated. The same RCA pattern was true in electrical and optical equipment and in manufacturing and recycling. In the remaining sectors, there was no difference in RCA indexes where they were measured using gross or value-added exports.

In comparing the RCA indexes over time, the OECD [2011c] has employed a summary measure developed by Geweke *et al.* [1986], Proudman and Redding [2000] and applied by Brasili *et al.* [2000] and Hinloopen and Van Marrewijk [2001], to determine the degree of cross-category mobility.

The mobility indexes are:

$$M_1 = \frac{m - \text{tr}[p]}{m - 1}, \tag{4.7}$$

$$M_2 = \sum_k \pi_k \sum_l p_{kl}|k - l|, \tag{4.8}$$

where m is the number of columns/rows and $\text{tr}(p)$ is the trace of the matrix. High M_1 implies high mobility. M_2 in contrast evaluates the information on the average number of class boundaries crossed by a product originally in state k weighted by the corresponding proportions π of the ergodic distribution. That is, it is the upper bound to which a specialization pattern would tend if we allowed the process to be indefinite. Therefore, a high M_2 implies high mobility.

Estimates of M_1 and M_2 provided by the OECD [2011c, pp. 97–100] point to a relatively low mobility for the PRC as compared to OECD industrial countries. This result is a bit curious. High mobility across sectors tends to be explained by supply-side changes such as rapid increases in a country's factor abundance, due to foreign direct investment; changes in technology, either endogenous or originating from knowledge spillovers or technology transfer; global merger and acquisition causing agglomeration or dispersion of economic activity. There is limited evidence that shifts in comparative advantage can be influenced by targeted policies such as subsidies, trade protection, industrial policy and institutional changes in factor markets and the rule of law.

The dispersion of the RCA indexes for China over the period 1995–2009, using both gross exports and value-added exports, reflects a tendency of continued export specialization in a small number of manufacturing sectors. This observation differs from the general OECD evaluation of China's dispersion of its export specialization. According to the results presented in OECD [2011c], the dispersion of RCAs is expected to fall in time for developed industrialized countries but not for the PRC.

The explanation provided is that developed economies should exhibit greater "polarization" of their export specialization relative to transition economies who are expected to export many products with either high or low RCA. Using COMTRADE data for the period 1990–2007, the OECD [2011c, p. 94] concluded that the PRC's RCA distribution "reflected a high density of products with revealed comparative advantage as well as a high density of products with revealed comparative disadvantage."

The OECD [2011c] concludes that the low estimates of M_1 and M_2 for the PRC are best explained by the country's large size. The report argues that the low mobility result for the PRC suggests that China's "unprecedented trade expansion has not been driven so much by changes in specialization patterns but rather by a general increase in exported volumes across many products."

The COMTRADE data for China's exports based on harmonized system codes (HS) tends to differ from the OECD conclusion noted above. Estimating the RCA index based on HS disaggregation highlights a number of factors. First, there is a limited concentration of comparative advantage for the PRC (RCA > 1). Second, the PRC's indexes of RCA > 1 have changed slightly over the 1996–2009 period. There are limited cases of switching out of products that exhibited RCA > 1. Third, there has been almost no reversal in China's RCA indexes from comparative disadvantage (RCA < 1) to advantage (RCA > 1) over the period 1996–2009.

In Tables 4.2–4.22, we present three related elements of a wider discussion of the PRC's export competitiveness. First, we present the RCA indexes; second, we present the Herfindahl index of geographic concentration and third, the world market shares for

Table 4.2   Competitiveness of PRC Exports RCA Index; World Market Shares and Herfindahl Index of Geographical Concentration Section I — Live Animals — Animal Products Measured by HS Categories

	Live Animals			Meat and Edible Meat Offal			Fish and Crustacean Mollusc and Other Aquatic Invertebrate		
	RCA > 1 Reversing	World Market Shares	HI	RCA < 1	World Market Shares	HI	RCA > 1 Falling	World Market Shares	HI
1996	1.687	4.948	0.788	0.879	2.577	0.279	1.600	4.693	0.294
1997	1.532	5.205	0.793	0.697	2.369	0.279	1.491	5.066	0.272
1998	1.448	4.985	0.808	0.648	2.233	0.313	1.396	4.806	0.229
1999	1.271	4.466	0.801	0.515	1.811	0.397	1.471	5.172	0.250
2000	1.089	4.319	0.804	0.482	1.909	0.361	1.396	5.536	0.226
2001	0.887	3.910	0.793	0.464	2.047	0.226	1.414	6.238	0.216
2002	0.688	3.531	0.788	0.315	1.618	0.190	1.315	6.751	0.227
2003	0.550	3.243	0.797	0.229	1.352	0.166	1.200	7.077	0.185
2004	0.456	2.988	0.737	0.193	1.264	0.208	1.184	7.751	0.179
2005	0.342	2.527	0.703	0.157	1.161	0.221	1.033	7.631	0.163
2006	0.284	2.296	0.649	0.136	1.104	0.247	0.943	7.630	0.143
2007	0.268	2.368	0.664	0.105	0.929	0.349	0.806	7.121	0.129
2008	0.325	2.927	0.706	0.091	0.816	0.427	0.801	7.210	0.116
2009	0.281	2.794	0.705	0.091	0.900	0.475	1.020	10.126	0.101

	Dairy Prod — Birds Eggs — Natural Honey — Edible Prod Nes			Products of Animal Origin Nes or Included		
	RCA < 1	World Market Shares	HI	RCA > 1 Falling	World Market Shares	HI
1996	0.217	0.638	0.180	6.111	17.925	0.110
1997	0.166	0.565	0.192	5.510	18.720	0.110
1998	0.173	0.597	0.166	5.322	18.325	0.116
1999	0.168	0.591	0.156	5.436	19.108	0.120
2000	0.172	0.684	0.172	5.542	21.972	0.132
2001	0.147	0.649	0.171	4.441	19.586	0.129
2002	0.131	0.672	0.230	3.586	18.411	0.133
2003	0.107	0.631	0.202	3.130	18.462	0.124
2004	0.086	0.563	0.221	3.163	20.706	0.131
2005	0.081	0.599	0.192	2.688	19.858	0.121
2006	0.079	0.636	0.171	2.311	18.710	0.119
2007	0.085	0.753	0.095	2.044	18.065	0.111
2008	0.097	0.872	0.114	2.071	18.642	0.101
2009	0.060	0.597	0.158	1.959	19.454	0.095

Source: OECD ITCS and UN COMTRADE Databases

China's exports, all calculated at the HS2 category level. Combining these three indicators, we develop an interesting profile of China's export concentration, or lack thereof in the 14-year period post the Uruguay round reforms and PRC reforms post 2005. Our conclusion differs from that of the OECD. The conventional understanding that the more remote countries tend to have more concentrated exports does not hold for the PRC, which, despite the distance from the USA or Europe, is not 'remote.'

This raises a question regarding the role of human capital accumulation in altering a country's specialization patterns from raw materials to manufactured goods, and finally to services with a larger input of knowledge. The current paradigm would posit that greater availability of specialized human capital at an increasingly lower factor price allow firms to employ a larger amount of human capital for adapting existing goods and technologies for R&D, which would induce export diversification. This is discussed in greater detail in Chapter 8.

Table 4.2 presents the RCA and Herfindahl indexes and world market shares for PRC exports of live animals. Within the HS category for live animals, the PRC exhibited a major reversal in RCA, a decrease in its share of the world market but continued geographic concentration of its exports. In two other categories within this section, there was a reduction in RCA, geographic concentration and importance in world markets. This sector is not a major PRC export category.

The RCA and Herfindahl indexes and world market shares for PRC exports of vegetable products are presented in Table 4.3. Most of the HS categories in this section demonstrate a clear PRC disadvantage (RCA < 1). In the few cases where there was a RCA > 1, it quickly reversed its position and became a disadvantage (RCA < 1). Consequently, it would be a non-debatable issue to mark Sections I and II of the HS code of products as non-comparative advantage export sectors for the PRC. They appear as items on the PRC's demand list for counter-trade in its foreign aid program, discussed in Chapter 7.

Table 4.3 Competitiveness of PRC Exports RCA Index; World Market Shares and Herfindahl Index of Geographical Concentration Section II — Vegetable Products Measured by HS Categories

	Live Tree and Other Plant — Bulb Root — Cut Flowers, etc.			Edible Vegetables and Certain Roots and Tubers			Edible Fruit and Nuts — Peel of Citrus Fruit or Melons		
	RCA < 1	World Market Shares	HI	RCA > 1 Falling	World Market Shares	HI	RCA < 1	World Market Shares	HI
1996	0.119	0.350	0.330	2.536	7.440	0.293	0.530	1.554	0.127
1997	0.115	0.390	0.317	2.216	7.529	0.281	0.456	1.549	0.126
1998	0.104	0.357	0.320	2.055	7.078	0.334	0.422	1.454	0.125
1999	0.100	0.350	0.323	2.052	7.213	0.309	0.409	1.438	0.146
2000	0.094	0.374	0.292	1.950	7.731	0.313	0.372	1.473	0.129
2001	0.092	0.404	0.238	1.789	7.890	0.277	0.341	1.504	0.129
2002	0.088	0.449	0.192	1.575	8.088	0.184	0.349	1.790	0.091
2003	0.071	0.421	0.178	1.330	7.844	0.163	0.340	2.007	0.070
2004	0.076	0.499	0.169	1.260	8.248	0.172	0.327	2.143	0.065
2005	0.077	0.569	0.155	1.246	9.201	0.132	0.295	2.175	0.060
2006	0.084	0.680	0.173	1.194	9.666	0.109	0.300	2.429	0.056
2007	0.087	0.772	0.198	1.018	8.997	0.083	0.301	2.656	0.053
2008	0.089	0.800	0.211	0.954	8.585	0.066	0.328	2.957	0.055
2009	0.120	1.191	0.201	1.076	10.682	0.063	0.370	3.675	0.058

(*Continued*)

Table 4.3 (*Continued*)

	Coffee — Tea — Maté and Spices			Cereals			Prod Mill Indust — Malt — Starches — Inulin — Wheat Gluten		
	RCA > 1 Reversing	World Market Shares	HI	RCA < 1	World Market Shares	HI	RCA < 1	World Market Shares	HI
1996	1.084	3.180	0.122	0.155	0.454	0.177	0.980	2.875	0.253
1997	0.849	2.885	0.089	0.975	3.313	0.205	0.780	2.651	0.242
1998	0.820	2.825	0.063	1.303	4.486	0.157	0.507	1.746	0.242
1999	0.862	3.029	0.087	1.058	3.720	0.100	0.418	1.468	0.274
2000	0.841	3.333	0.100	1.352	5.360	0.195	0.428	1.697	0.164
2001	1.000	4.411	0.112	0.751	3.311	0.183	0.439	1.937	0.169
2002	0.912	4.682	0.084	0.978	5.020	0.220	0.381	1.953	0.161
2003	0.790	4.660	0.074	1.135	6.697	0.183	0.342	2.015	0.128
2004	0.841	5.505	0.082	0.253	1.656	0.205	0.325	2.129	0.115
2005	0.661	4.879	0.078	0.431	3.186	0.344	0.320	2.366	0.114
2006	0.546	4.420	0.062	0.257	2.077	0.173	0.319	2.584	0.094
2007	0.460	4.067	0.055	0.308	2.719	0.219	0.474	4.192	0.070
2008	0.446	4.016	0.048	0.072	0.645	0.068	0.373	3.361	0.070
2009	0.505	5.014	0.045	0.083	0.819	0.114	0.350	3.473	0.066

Year	Oil Seed Oleagi Fruits — Miscell Grain Seed Fruit, etc.			Lac Gums Resins and Other Vegetable Saps and Extracts			Vegetable Plaiting Materials — Vegetable Products Nes		
	RCA > 1 Reversing	World Market Shares	HI	RCA < 1 Reversing	World Market Shares	HI	RCA > 1 Reversing	World Market Shares	HI
1996	1.742	5.109	0.122	0.782	2.295	0.159	3.845	11.278	0.182
1997	1.156	3.927	0.138	0.776	2.635	0.169	3.621	12.301	0.163
1998	1.087	3.743	0.141	0.666	2.292	0.218	3.298	11.359	0.182
1999	1.249	4.391	0.125	0.599	2.106	0.259	2.781	9.773	0.184
2000	1.126	4.463	0.140	0.528	2.092	0.192	2.423	9.607	0.212
2001	1.020	4.498	0.123	0.679	2.994	0.147	2.234	9.853	0.219
2002	0.872	4.478	0.104	0.647	3.322	0.112	2.235	11.474	0.232
2003	0.696	4.106	0.103	0.465	2.740	0.095	1.580	9.320	0.198
2004	0.614	4.018	0.100	0.367	2.401	0.095	1.453	9.510	0.180
2005	0.620	4.580	0.083	0.456	3.369	0.123	1.321	9.754	0.167
2006	0.513	4.154	0.086	0.506	4.096	0.099	1.198	9.697	0.149
2007	0.425	3.758	0.074	0.611	5.403	0.089	1.004	8.871	0.123
2008	0.355	3.197	0.078	1.039	9.358	0.096	1.084	9.764	0.123
2009	0.342	3.396	0.069	1.210	12.021	0.088	0.947	9.404	0.117

Source: OECD ITCS and UN COMTRADE Databases

Table 4.4 Competitiveness of PRC Exports RCA Index; World Market Shares and Herfindahl Index of Geographical Concentration Section III — Animal or Vegetable Fats Measured by HS Categories

	Animal or Veg Fats and Oils and Their Cleavage Products — etc.		
	RCA < 1	World Market Shares	HI
1996	0.490	1.437	0.465
1997	0.684	2.324	0.582
1998	0.314	1.082	0.406
1999	0.154	0.542	0.282
2000	0.153	0.606	0.364
2001	0.129	0.567	0.351
2002	0.080	0.408	0.284
2003	0.066	0.390	0.109
2004	0.065	0.422	0.109
2005	0.097	0.717	0.070
2006	0.107	0.868	0.080
2007	0.058	0.511	0.070
2008	0.072	0.651	0.061
2009	0.051	0.508	0.080

Source: OECD ITCS and UN COMTRADE Databases

Another set of HS products which consistently demonstrate their net-import positions are Section III items composed of animal or vegetable fats. (Table 4.4). This is clearly a net-import sector for the PRC. In Table 4.5, where the RCA estimates are presented for Section IV — prepared foodstuffs, the PRCs net-import position is clearly outlined, as well. There are only two HS categories where RCA > 1. One of these is prepared foodstuffs of meat and fish and prepared foodstuffs of vegetable fruit nuts. In both of these categories, the RCA index while >1 has been consistently declining in the 14-year period between 1996 and 2009. China's exports in these items represents approximately 10 percent of the world market. The degree of country concentration of these exports is very limited.

Table 4.5 Competitiveness of PRC Exports RCA Index; World Market Shares and Herfindahl Index of Geographical Concentration Section IV — Prepared Foodstuffs Measured by HS Categories

	Prep. of Meat Fish or Crustaceans Molluscs etc.			Sugars and Sugar Confectionery			Cocoa and Cocoa Preparations		
	RCA > 1 Falling	World Market Shares	HI	RCA < 1	World Market Shares	HI	RCA < 1	World Market Shares	HI
1996	3.237	9.495	0.594	0.593	1.738	0.166	0.118	0.345	0.462
1997	2.582	8.772	0.529	0.330	1.120	0.162	0.126	0.427	0.671
1998	2.369	8.158	0.577	0.325	1.119	0.200	0.096	0.332	0.419
1999	2.717	9.550	0.596	0.270	0.950	0.125	0.092	0.324	0.478
2000	3.156	12.514	0.563	0.303	1.200	0.123	0.067	0.264	0.420
2001	2.962	13.064	0.518	0.216	0.953	0.095	0.052	0.229	0.280
2002	2.716	13.946	0.509	0.273	1.404	0.090	0.047	0.241	0.095
2003	2.379	14.031	0.416	0.182	1.075	0.091	0.051	0.303	0.114
2004	2.405	15.745	0.410	0.190	1.244	0.091	0.053	0.344	0.136
2005	2.322	17.148	0.354	0.238	1.757	0.081	0.071	0.525	0.168
2006	2.341	18.946	0.292	0.194	1.573	0.060	0.066	0.535	0.176
2007	2.004	17.715	0.266	0.222	1.959	0.066	0.061	0.536	0.124
2008	1.744	15.700	0.205	0.238	2.139	0.065	0.069	0.618	0.156
2009	1.386	13.762	0.251	0.275	2.730	0.065	0.041	0.408	0.070

(*Continued*)

Table 4.5   (Continued)

	Prep. of Cereal Flour Starch — Milk — Pastrycooks Prod			Prep. of Vegetable Fruit Nuts or Other Parts of Plants			Miscellaneous Edible Preparations		
	RCA < 1	World Market Shares	HI	RCA > 1 Falling	World Market Shares	HI	RCA < 1	World Market Shares	HI
1996	0.509	1.494	0.137	1.724	5.056	0.230	0.482	1.414	0.196
1997	0.496	1.685	0.142	1.581	5.370	0.199	0.511	1.737	0.184
1998	0.468	1.613	0.160	1.489	5.128	0.197	0.561	1.931	0.191
1999	0.505	1.777	0.169	1.535	5.397	0.211	0.575	2.022	0.183
2000	0.558	2.211	0.175	1.680	6.659	0.212	0.540	2.142	0.179
2001	0.537	2.367	0.178	1.692	7.463	0.197	0.510	2.249	0.176
2002	0.457	2.347	0.167	1.556	7.986	0.158	0.464	2.383	0.152
2003	0.385	2.271	0.171	1.409	8.312	0.143	0.400	2.360	0.135
2004	0.364	2.383	0.168	1.358	8.889	0.156	0.346	2.264	0.121
2005	0.342	2.523	0.168	1.329	9.820	0.145	0.320	2.367	0.119
2006	0.322	2.604	0.155	1.294	10.476	0.124	0.339	2.746	0.098
2007	0.270	2.385	0.142	1.379	12.185	0.097	0.324	2.863	0.093
2008	0.236	2.126	0.103	1.300	11.704	0.092	0.310	2.786	0.067
2009	0.230	2.285	0.120	1.113	11.050	0.097	0.316	3.136	0.063

	Beverages Spirits and Vinegar			Residues and Waste from the Food Indust — Prepr Ani Fodder			Tobacco and Manufactured Tobacco Substitutes		
	RCA < 1	World Market Shares	HI	RCA < 1	World Market Shares	HI	RCA < 1	World Market Shares	HI
1996	0.391	1.145	0.463	0.508	1.491	0.115	1.309	3.839	0.141
1997	0.392	1.331	0.408	0.341	1.159	0.137	0.749	2.544	0.106
1998	0.373	1.284	0.493	0.277	0.955	0.132	0.695	2.392	0.089
1999	0.356	1.253	0.612	0.337	1.183	0.122	0.429	1.507	0.082
2000	0.351	1.393	0.530	0.329	1.306	0.120	0.353	1.400	0.086
2001	0.352	1.551	0.435	0.317	1.398	0.176	0.414	1.828	0.073
2002	0.285	1.463	0.448	0.363	1.862	0.212	0.402	2.061	0.070
2003	0.217	1.278	0.352	0.264	1.559	0.228	0.383	2.258	0.059
2004	0.206	1.345	0.489	0.267	1.750	0.372	0.332	2.171	0.061
2005	0.164	1.208	0.407	0.222	1.637	0.325	0.290	2.144	0.065
2006	0.198	1.601	0.170	0.198	1.603	0.220	0.265	2.144	0.076
2007	0.116	1.027	0.346	0.284	2.509	0.193	0.242	2.140	0.080
2008	0.106	0.954	0.345	0.342	3.074	0.153	0.243	2.186	0.087
2009	0.109	1.085	0.374	0.367	3.643	0.178	0.279	2.768	0.076

Source: OECD ITCS and UN COMTRADE Databases

The RCA and Herfindahl indexes and world market shares for PRC exports of Mineral products are presented in Table 4.6. These are clear net-import categories that are on the PRC's foreign aid shopping list. PRC exports in these categories are a very small part of their total exposure to the world market with little or no geographic concentration. That shopping list also includes Section VI items — Products of the Chemicals or Allied Industries — listed in Table 4.7. With the exception of "inorganic chemical compounds" that become net imports and "explosives" where the RCA index has been falling, the balance of the category are major items on the PRC foreign aid counter-trade list. PRC exports in these categories are a very small part of their total exposure to the world market with little or no geographic concentration.

The RCA and Herfindahl indexes and world market shares for PRC exports of Section VII — "Plastic and Rubber Articles" products are presented in Table 4.8 and in Section VIII — "Raw Hides and Skins" are presented in Table 4.9. These items contains the list of products where the estimated RCA < 1, the PRCs exposure on the world market is small and then there is no geographic concentration. In only two categories Articles of leather and Furskins and articles thereof — does the PRC maintain an RCA > 1. The explanation for this anomaly is contained in the residual of the MFA on Textile and Apparel exports which expired with the implementation of the Uruguay round. Under the MFA the chief value of the input determined the nature of the final product. For tariff purposes, the PRC had appended leather tags and Furskins to apparel and listed the end product as "leather or furskin goods" rather than apparel. That explains why the world market share for these PRC exports are over 30 percent and 20 percent, respectively.

The RCA and Herfindahl indexes and world market shares for PRC exports of Section IX — "Wood and Articles of Wood" products are presented in Table 4.10. In two of the HS categories the PRC has RCA < 1 with no substantial footprint in the World market and a low level of geographic concentration. In one HS category — "Manufactures of straw" do we have an RCA > 1 and a very substantial footprint in the World market. PRC exports in

Table 4.6 Competitiveness of PRC Exports RCA Index; World Market Shares and Herfindahl Index of Geographical Concentration Section V — Mineral Products Measured by HS Categories

	Salt — Sulphur — Earth and Stone — Plastering Mat — Lime and Cem			Ores Slag and Ash			Mineral Fuels Oils and Product of their Distillation, etc.		
	RCA > 1 Reversing	World Market Shares	HI	RCA < 1	World Market Shares	HI	RCA < 1	World Market Shares	HI
1996	2.667	7.823	0.081	0.101	0.297	0.112	0.480	1.408	0.200
1997	2.478	8.417	0.086	0.149	0.507	0.138	0.479	1.627	0.158
1998	2.177	7.498	0.116	0.105	0.361	0.114	0.456	1.571	0.129
1999	1.914	6.726	0.127	0.106	0.373	0.175	0.307	1.079	0.129
2000	1.942	7.700	0.125	0.083	0.329	0.174	0.279	1.107	0.118
2001	1.876	8.272	0.114	0.088	0.388	0.204	0.299	1.319	0.109
2002	1.375	7.058	0.104	0.147	0.755	0.263	0.277	1.423	0.103
2003	1.185	6.990	0.103	0.147	0.866	0.185	0.255	1.501	0.092
2004	1.006	6.586	0.106	0.195	1.273	0.299	0.219	1.433	0.081
2005	1.131	8.356	0.094	0.216	1.598	0.303	0.167	1.236	0.079
2006	1.109	8.980	0.101	0.120	0.970	0.348	0.127	1.031	0.077
2007	0.917	8.103	0.074	0.090	0.797	0.342	0.121	1.068	0.077
2008	0.907	8.168	0.065	0.072	0.650	0.366	0.126	1.132	0.077
2009	0.689	6.842	0.051	0.019	0.191	0.158	0.123	1.221	0.095

Source: OECD ITCS and UN COMTRADE Databases

Table 4.7 Competitiveness of PRC Exports RCA Index; World Market Shares and Herfindahl Index of Geographical Concentration Section VI — Products of the Chemicals or Allied Industries Measured by HS Categories

	Inorgn Chem — Compds of Prec Met Radioact Elements etc.			Organic Chemicals			Pharmaceutical Products			Fertilizers		
	RCA > 1 Reversing	World Market Shares	HI	RCA < 1	World Market Shares	HI	RCA < 1	World Market Shares	HI	RCA < 1	World Market Shares	HI
1996	1.943	5.699	0.105	0.868	2.545	0.065	0.321	0.941	0.073	0.402	1.178	0.130
1997	1.815	6.165	0.091	0.777	2.640	0.064	0.270	0.918	0.076	0.390	1.325	0.130
1998	1.847	6.359	0.085	0.769	2.648	0.062	0.251	0.864	0.086	0.292	1.005	0.142
1999	1.822	6.402	0.085	0.772	2.712	0.064	0.198	0.696	0.103	0.429	1.508	0.169
2000	1.652	6.548	0.087	0.701	2.778	0.064	0.182	0.720	0.096	0.536	2.123	0.161
2001	1.676	7.389	0.076	0.731	3.222	0.059	0.146	0.645	0.087	0.587	2.587	0.090
2002	1.551	7.963	0.077	0.668	3.430	0.057	0.104	0.533	0.069	0.446	2.288	0.104
2003	1.324	7.808	0.072	0.618	3.643	0.055	0.086	0.507	0.068	0.725	4.276	0.128
2004	1.291	8.448	0.075	0.574	3.759	0.056	0.075	0.492	0.077	0.865	5.662	0.132
2005	1.375	10.157	0.082	0.606	4.478	0.058	0.074	0.547	0.080	0.488	3.606	0.102
2006	1.166	9.440	0.081	0.647	5.234	0.056	0.066	0.533	0.065	0.503	4.075	0.088
2007	1.171	10.353	0.085	0.697	6.161	0.054	0.068	0.601	0.063	1.153	10.190	0.080
2008	1.236	11.127	0.076	0.915	8.240	0.058	0.081	0.726	0.070	0.668	6.013	0.094
2009	0.976	9.694	0.053	0.835	8.288	0.057	0.085	0.839	0.071	0.637	6.324	0.100

| | Tanning–Dyeing Extract — Tannins and Derivs, Pigm etc. | | | Essential Oils and Resinoids — Perf Cosmetic–toilet Prep | | | Soap Organic Surface — Active Agents Washing Prep, etc. | | | Albuminoidal Subs — Modified Starches–glues–enzymes | | |
	RCA < 1	World Market Shares	HI	RCA < 1	World Market Shares	HI	RCA < 1	World Market Shares	HI	RCA < 1	World Market Shares	HI
1996	0.760	2.230	0.106	0.346	1.014	0.173	0.454	1.330	0.132	0.205	0.601	0.145
1997	0.787	2.672	0.086	0.277	0.941	0.163	0.402	1.364	0.114	0.230	0.780	0.140
1998	0.818	2.816	0.077	0.297	1.023	0.157	0.515	1.773	0.123	0.694	2.391	0.544
1999	0.782	2.748	0.066	0.271	0.954	0.119	0.551	1.938	0.096	0.273	0.960	0.147
2000	0.787	3.121	0.060	0.283	1.120	0.114	0.539	2.137	0.086	0.315	1.250	0.111
2001	0.793	3.498	0.058	0.271	1.194	0.115	0.497	2.192	0.095	0.357	1.573	0.104
2002	0.725	3.724	0.057	0.263	1.352	0.135	0.464	2.381	0.106	0.363	1.865	0.087
2003	0.605	3.567	0.055	0.274	1.614	0.151	0.419	2.469	0.084	0.375	2.213	0.072
2004	0.601	3.937	0.053	0.259	1.696	0.130	0.441	2.885	0.078	0.465	3.043	0.065
2005	0.645	4.763	0.050	0.273	2.015	0.133	0.418	3.090	0.049	0.507	3.744	0.067
2006	0.646	5.229	0.045	0.276	2.234	0.117	0.408	3.302	0.040	0.541	4.379	0.062
2007	0.631	5.574	0.044	0.265	2.339	0.113	0.422	3.726	0.036	0.592	5.233	0.048
2008	0.607	5.469	0.042	0.251	2.262	0.091	0.430	3.872	0.032	0.824	7.418	0.046
2009	0.547	5.431	0.038	0.253	2.516	0.092	0.396	3.928	0.034	0.760	7.547	0.045

(*Continued*)

Table 4.7   (Continued)

	Explosives — Pyrotechnic Prod — Matches — Pyrop Alloy, etc.			Photographic or Cinematographic Goods			Miscellaneous Chemical Products		
	RCA > 1 Falling	World Market Shares	HI	RCA < 1	World Market Shares	HI	RCA < 1	World Market Shares	HI
1996	4.803	14.087	0.143	0.184	0.540	0.286	0.530	1.554	0.066
1997	4.356	14.799	0.126	0.205	0.696	0.285	0.518	1.758	0.063
1998	4.964	17.094	0.126	0.239	0.822	0.286	0.482	1.660	0.054
1999	6.165	21.668	0.201	0.371	1.303	0.220	0.536	1.884	0.056
2000	4.436	17.588	0.193	0.572	2.269	0.137	0.524	2.078	0.059
2001	4.293	18.933	0.144	0.570	2.515	0.115	0.544	2.398	0.050
2002	3.803	19.527	0.150	0.586	3.009	0.117	0.481	2.467	0.049
2003	2.943	17.358	0.159	0.648	3.820	0.180	0.454	2.676	0.048
2004	2.592	16.966	0.139	0.678	4.435	0.160	0.515	3.372	0.044
2005	2.420	17.876	0.139	0.701	5.176	0.126	0.539	3.981	0.043
2006	2.284	18.487	0.149	0.464	3.757	0.084	0.495	4.010	0.050
2007	2.214	19.565	0.124	0.427	3.773	0.068	0.560	4.950	0.042
2008	2.002	18.023	0.113	0.534	4.807	0.065	0.646	5.811	0.035
2009	2.153	21.379	0.109	0.488	4.848	0.064	0.542	5.386	0.033

Source: OECD ITCS and UN COMTRADE Databases

Table 4.8   Competitiveness of PRC Exports RCA Index; World Market Shares and Herfindahl Index of Geographical Concentration Section VII — Plastics and Rubber and Articles thereof Measured by HS Categories

	Plastics and Articles Thereof			Rubber and Articles Thereof		
	RCA < 1	World Market Shares	HI	RCA < 1	World Market Shares	HI
1996	0.753	2.208	0.175	0.500	1.465	0.076
1997	0.837	2.845	0.175	0.508	1.725	0.092
1998	0.877	3.021	0.153	0.525	1.809	0.105
1999	0.831	2.922	0.166	0.607	2.132	0.115
2000	0.825	3.269	0.160	0.691	2.741	0.090
2001	0.804	3.543	0.159	0.671	2.960	0.085
2002	0.775	3.979	0.152	0.651	3.342	0.098
2003	0.710	4.190	0.135	0.601	3.544	0.100
2004	0.679	4.446	0.122	0.654	4.284	0.102
2005	0.709	5.233	0.110	0.740	5.464	0.109
2006	0.713	5.769	0.099	0.766	6.204	0.114
2007	0.679	6.005	0.084	0.826	7.304	0.098
2008	0.699	6.292	0.075	0.828	7.451	0.084
2009	0.673	6.681	0.079	0.876	8.703	0.074

Source: OECD ITCS and UN COMTRADE Databases

this HS category represent over 70 percent of the world market. Nevertheless, PRC exports in this category are not concentrated geographically in any one destination.

The RCA and Herfindahl indexes and world market shares for PRC exports of Section X — "Pulp of Wood or Fibrous Cellulosic Material" is presented in Table 4.11. This segment is not on the list of major PRC exportables. There is very little geographic concentration in these exports where the RCA < 1.

Once we move out of the basic commodity portion of PRC exports and turn to the manufacturing sector, we observe an area where the PRC has a RCA. The RCA and Herfindahl indexes and world market shares for PRC exports of Section XI — Textile and Textile Articles" is presented in Table 4.12. In most of these categories, PRC exports have a sizeable world market share. Nevertheless, the geographic concentration index is quite low, reinforcing

Table 4.9   Competitiveness of PRC Exports RCA Index; World Market Shares and Herfindahl Index of Geographical Concentration Section VIII — Raw Hides and Skins Measured by HS Categories

	Raw Hides and Skins (other than furskins) and Leather			Articles of Leather — Saddlery — Harness — Travel Goods, etc.			Furskins and Artificial Fur — Manufactures Thereof		
	RCA < 1	World Market Shares	HI	RCA > 1 Falling	World Market Shares	HI	RCA > 1	World Market Shares	HI
1996	0.472	1.384	0.245	7.399	21.703	0.132	2.519	7.388	0.152
1997	0.488	1.657	0.248	7.447	25.299	0.126	2.072	7.041	0.126
1998	0.556	1.913	0.283	7.302	25.144	0.116	2.128	7.327	0.172
1999	0.577	2.027	0.365	6.962	24.468	0.119	2.529	8.890	0.177
2000	0.656	2.600	0.468	6.835	27.100	0.127	2.609	10.342	0.162
2001	0.915	4.034	0.360	6.481	28.578	0.124	2.776	12.241	0.149
2002	0.859	4.412	0.356	6.233	31.998	0.130	2.464	12.652	0.147
2003	0.808	4.768	0.383	5.727	33.777	0.129	3.006	17.727	0.217
2004	0.810	5.305	0.425	4.890	32.010	0.132	4.471	29.269	0.389
2005	0.802	5.926	0.376	4.373	32.303	0.121	4.523	33.407	0.427
2006	0.748	6.058	0.414	3.984	32.247	0.115	2.025	16.389	0.161
2007	0.426	3.762	0.315	3.681	32.531	0.105	1.622	14.333	0.170
2008	0.154	1.383	0.088	3.820	34.390	0.086	1.388	12.500	0.242
2009	0.117	1.157	0.112	3.617	35.919	0.088	2.275	22.597	0.240

Source: OECD ITCS and UN COMTRADE Databases

Table 4.10 Competitiveness of PRC Exports RCA Index; World Market Shares and Herfindahl Index of Geographical Concentration Section IX — Wood and Articles of Wood Measured by HS Categories

	Wood and Articles of Wood — Wood Charcoal			Cork and Articles of Cork			Manufactures of Straw Esparto-other Plaiting Mat, etc.		
	RCA < 1	World Market Shares	HI	RCA < 1	World Market Shares	HI	RCA > 1 Falling	World Market Shares	HI
1996	0.723	2.119	0.238	0.095	0.279	0.160	17.288	50.710	0.189
1997	0.696	2.365	0.215	0.081	0.275	0.205	15.275	51.896	0.179
1998	0.642	2.209	0.205	0.048	0.166	0.153	14.367	49.475	0.160
1999	0.713	2.505	0.194	0.066	0.232	0.118	13.517	47.509	0.182
2000	0.773	3.065	0.190	0.128	0.506	0.113	12.378	49.077	0.170
2001	0.813	3.585	0.192	0.130	0.573	0.058	11.484	50.643	0.183
2002	0.805	4.135	0.182	0.119	0.612	0.051	10.708	54.974	0.172
2003	0.761	4.489	0.179	0.106	0.623	0.069	9.832	57.993	0.151
2004	0.809	5.295	0.153	0.114	0.749	0.091	9.225	60.389	0.137
2005	0.860	6.351	0.137	0.124	0.917	0.170	8.308	61.362	0.123
2006	0.957	7.749	0.128	0.152	1.229	0.193	7.825	63.339	0.107
2007	0.897	7.926	0.101	0.111	0.982	0.154	7.703	68.081	0.088
2008	0.885	7.969	0.088	0.108	0.972	0.151	8.292	74.653	0.083
2009	0.866	8.602	0.096	0.104	1.033	0.126	7.283	72.327	0.091

Source: OECD ITCS and UN COMTRADE Databases

Table 4.11 Competitiveness of PRC Exports RCA Index; World Market Shares and Herfindahl Index of Geographical Concentration Section X — Pulp of Wood or of other Fibrous Cellulosic Material Measured by HS Categories

	Pulp of Wood — of Other Fibrous Cellulosic Mat — Waste, etc.			Paper and Paperboard — Art of Paper Pulp Paper — Paperboard			Printed Books Newspapers Pictures and Other Product, etc.		
	RCA < 1	World Market Shares	HI	RCA < 1	World Market Shares	HI	RCA < 1	World Market Shares	HI
1996	0.022	0.066	0.021	0.290	0.851	0.228	0.290	0.851	0.225
1997	0.020	0.067	0.112	0.315	1.071	0.249	0.383	1.300	0.217
1998	0.017	0.059	0.080	0.299	1.031	0.202	0.401	1.382	0.191
1999	0.005	0.019	0.131	0.272	0.957	0.178	0.418	1.469	0.233
2000	0.011	0.044	0.222	0.344	1.363	0.151	0.436	1.730	0.302
2001	0.010	0.044	0.087	0.337	1.485	0.154	0.435	1.917	0.289
2002	0.016	0.083	0.097	0.322	1.651	0.167	0.452	2.322	0.274
2003	0.017	0.098	0.093	0.334	1.970	0.153	0.394	2.324	0.311
2004	0.010	0.066	0.102	0.332	2.175	0.145	0.421	2.758	0.277
2005	0.019	0.137	0.088	0.389	2.872	0.119	0.423	3.124	0.251
2006	0.024	0.195	0.165	0.450	3.645	0.092	0.458	3.710	0.230
2007	0.028	0.251	0.167	0.490	4.328	0.073	0.511	4.512	0.199
2008	0.027	0.242	0.092	0.489	4.400	0.073	0.584	5.258	0.177
2009	0.030	0.299	0.103	0.514	5.108	0.073	0.567	5.632	0.171

Source: OECD ITCS and UN COMTRADE Databases

Table 4.12 Competitiveness of PRC Exports RCA Index; World Market Shares and Herfindahl Index of Geographical Concentration Section XI — Textile and Textile Articles Measured by HS Categories

	Silk			Wool Fine-coarse Animal Hair Horsehair Yarn and Fabric			Cotton			Other Vegetable Textile Fibers — Paper Yarn and Woven Fab		
	RCA > 1 Falling	World Market Shares	HI	RCA > 1	World Market Shares	HI	RCA > 1	World Market Shares	HI	RCA > 1 Falling	World Market Shares	HI
1996	10.211	29.950	0.184	1.864	5.468	0.225	3.009	8.825	0.296	4.992	14.643	0.390
1997	9.451	32.108	0.175	1.923	6.534	0.218	2.555	8.680	0.289	4.614	15.675	0.455
1998	9.462	32.583	0.151	1.795	6.183	0.217	2.397	8.256	0.285	4.128	14.216	0.429
1999	10.059	35.355	0.130	2.453	8.622	0.153	2.936	10.319	0.219	3.940	13.849	0.314
2000	9.419	37.345	0.100	2.530	10.030	0.151	2.787	11.050	0.211	4.259	16.886	0.279
2001	8.329	36.731	0.111	2.120	9.350	0.169	2.458	10.837	0.226	3.763	16.593	0.318
2002	7.202	36.977	0.134	1.847	9.481	0.136	2.727	14.001	0.201	3.378	17.343	0.382
2003	6.266	36.955	0.133	1.898	11.196	0.124	2.450	14.453	0.189	2.649	15.627	0.366
2004	5.759	37.700	0.151	1.950	12.768	0.118	2.087	13.661	0.181	2.250	14.730	0.258
2005	5.625	41.546	0.133	1.900	14.035	0.107	2.143	15.830	0.155	2.301	16.999	0.135
2006	5.233	42.358	0.100	1.827	14.792	0.085	2.154	17.433	0.148	2.213	17.917	0.120
2007	4.834	42.728	0.123	1.620	14.317	0.082	2.055	18.160	0.125	1.927	17.029	0.095
2008	4.560	41.058	0.099	1.662	14.963	0.096	2.275	20.479	0.098	1.919	17.277	0.064
2009	4.663	46.309	0.130	1.590	15.792	0.111	2.313	22.972	0.091	2.215	21.995	0.071

(*Continued*)

Table 4.12   (*Continued*)

	Man-made Filaments			Man-made Staple Fibers			Wadding Felt and Non-woven — Yarns — Twine Cordage, etc.			Carpets and Other Textile Floor Coverings		
	RCA > 1 Increasing	World Market Shares	HI	RCA > 1	World Market Shares	HI	RCA > 1 Increasing	World Market Shares	HI	RCA > 1	World Market Shares	HI
1996	0.578	1.696	0.252	2.820	8.273	0.158	0.796	2.335	0.177	1.702	4.992	0.433
1997	0.779	2.646	0.214	2.948	10.016	0.147	0.910	3.091	0.222	1.474	5.009	0.206
1998	0.826	2.845	0.155	2.782	9.580	0.119	0.880	3.030	0.209	1.477	5.085	0.223
1999	0.778	2.735	0.121	2.781	9.775	0.108	0.774	2.721	0.122	1.378	4.842	0.241
2000	1.018	4.034	0.068	2.832	11.229	0.087	0.802	3.179	0.092	1.418	5.622	0.237
2001	1.245	5.489	0.044	2.742	12.093	0.079	0.802	3.535	0.088	1.425	6.284	0.239
2002	1.564	8.032	0.046	2.218	11.387	0.078	0.721	3.703	0.074	1.342	6.890	0.256
2003	1.891	11.151	0.043	1.982	11.688	0.073	0.670	3.949	0.054	1.151	6.789	0.237
2004	2.085	13.650	0.037	1.992	13.039	0.063	0.702	4.596	0.049	1.122	7.342	0.194
2005	2.124	15.686	0.033	2.143	15.826	0.053	0.810	5.983	0.044	1.108	8.186	0.179
2006	2.089	16.907	0.032	2.346	18.994	0.042	0.845	6.844	0.040	1.060	8.583	0.167
2007	2.106	18.616	0.029	2.301	20.338	0.034	0.892	7.884	0.040	1.072	9.475	0.130
2008	2.295	20.665	0.026	2.457	22.117	0.030	1.099	9.895	0.040	1.226	11.042	0.099
2009	2.194	21.790	0.027	2.377	23.606	0.030	1.180	11.720	0.042	1.276	12.673	0.092

	Special Woven Fab — Tufted Tex Fab — Lace — Tapestries etc.			Impregnated Coated Cover-laminated Textile Fabric etc.			Knitted or Crocheted Fabrics		
	RCA > 1	World Market Shares	HI	RCA > 1 Increasing	World Market Shares	HI	RCA > 1 Increasing	World Market Shares	HI
1996	2.997	8.791	0.223	0.480	1.408	0.272	2.108	6.182	0.608
1997	3.560	12.093	0.230	0.645	2.191	0.280	1.771	6.016	0.529
1998	3.051	10.505	0.163	0.510	1.756	0.174	1.848	6.363	0.423
1999	2.346	8.247	0.118	0.595	2.091	0.150	1.922	6.754	0.422
2000	2.255	8.940	0.116	0.765	3.034	0.124	2.069	8.202	0.426
2001	2.290	10.100	0.116	0.815	3.592	0.095	2.090	9.214	0.477
2002	2.537	13.024	0.093	0.934	4.794	0.085	2.449	12.574	0.411
2003	2.729	16.097	0.089	0.986	5.818	0.081	2.401	14.164	0.349
2004	2.844	18.613	0.069	1.192	7.805	0.072	2.348	15.368	0.302
2005	3.175	23.453	0.057	1.443	10.661	0.074	2.486	18.364	0.258
2006	3.348	27.101	0.052	1.515	12.260	0.063	2.629	21.279	0.219
2007	3.883	34.317	0.052	1.651	14.587	0.054	2.683	23.709	0.165
2008	4.167	37.514	0.045	2.026	18.238	0.049	2.844	25.606	0.120
2009	3.405	33.818	0.039	2.259	22.432	0.046	2.975	29.544	0.095

(*Continued*)

Table 4.12   (*Continued*)

	Art of Apparel and Clothing Access Knitted or Crocheted			Art of Apparel and Clothing Access Not Knitted–crocheted			Other Made Up Textile Articles — Sets — Worn Clothing etc.		
	RCA > 1 Falling	World Market Shares	HI	RCA > 1 Falling	World Market Shares	HI	RCA > 1 Falling	World Market Shares	HI
1996	4.130	12.114	0.231	5.450	15.986	0.217	5.754	16.877	0.149
1997	4.888	16.607	0.300	5.230	17.768	0.206	5.150	17.496	0.132
1998	4.546	15.654	0.231	4.591	15.808	0.180	4.888	16.831	0.137
1999	4.369	15.356	0.183	4.568	16.055	0.181	4.987	17.526	0.146
2000	4.166	16.517	0.168	4.579	18.155	0.178	5.003	19.834	0.148
2001	3.784	16.686	0.160	4.221	18.612	0.180	4.764	21.009	0.145
2002	3.633	18.654	0.129	3.737	19.187	0.149	4.458	22.885	0.143
2003	3.471	20.471	0.114	3.507	20.687	0.124	4.133	24.378	0.141
2004	3.454	22.610	0.110	3.305	21.633	0.113	4.070	26.641	0.137
2005	3.374	24.921	0.092	3.262	24.095	0.102	4.152	30.669	0.138
2006	3.844	31.120	0.071	3.434	27.797	0.086	4.066	32.917	0.139
2007	4.067	35.947	0.061	3.178	28.087	0.084	3.801	33.592	0.126
2008	3.817	34.365	0.056	3.228	29.068	0.074	4.173	37.573	0.105
2009	3.566	35.414	0.069	3.127	31.058	0.089	4.101	40.727	0.105

Source: OECD ITCS and UN COMTRADE Databases

the general conclusion that the PRC has sufficiently diversified its exports in this area to withstand major demand side fluctuations. The RCA indexes in this section demonstrate the continued and historic revealed comparative and competitive advantage. An in depth discussion of this sector will be presented in Chapter 5. It is, nevertheless, important to recognize that the RCA measures for this HS section are consistently greater than 1. The variation in the RCA measures are symptoms of the continued global competition in this set of products with many suppliers being added post the Uruguay round, where the MFA was eliminated.

The other manufacturing sector with a long history of PRC comparative advantage is HS Section XII — "Footwear." The RCA and Herfindahl indexes and world market shares for PRC exports in Section XII are presented in Table 4.13. As in the case of textiles and apparel, PRC's world market share in these HS categories is substantial. Complementing these results is the fact that the in all of the categories, the estimated RCA measure is greater than 1. Increased competition from neighboring lower-cost Asian countries is eating at the PRC's competitiveness in this sector. As Pelzman and Shoham [2009] demonstrate, Vietnam is the first clear beneficiary of China's increased labor costs in the footwear sector.

An interesting area where the PRC shows a positive RCA over the 14-year period, 1996–2009 includes Section XIII — "Articles of Stones." The RCA and Herfindahl indexes and world market shares for PRC exports in Section XIII are presented in Table 4.14. The PRC performance in this area reflects their diversification into light manufactures. PRC's world market shares in this sector has been consistently rising since 1996. Its geographic market concentration is very low reflecting a healthy expansion across the entire world market.

The RCA and Herfindahl indexes and world market shares for PRC exports in Section XIV — "Natural or Cultured Pearls" is presented in Table 4.15. In this sector the PRC does not have a comparative advantage. Its exports represent a very small part of world footprint with no meaningful geographic concentration.

Table 4.13   Competitiveness of PRC Exports RCA Index; World Market Shares and Herfindahl Index of Geographical Concentration Section XII — Footwear Measured by HS Categories

	Footwear Gaiters and the Like — Parts of Such Articles			Headgear and Parts Thereof			Umbrellas Walking-sticks Seat-sticks, Whips etc.			Prepr Feathers and Down — Arti Flower — Articles Human Hair		
	RCA > 1 Falling	World Market Shares	HI	RCA > 1 Falling	World Market Shares	HI	RCA > 1 Falling	World Market Shares	HI	RCA > 1 Falling	World Market Shares	HI
1996	5.027	14.747	0.257	5.384	15.792	0.065	9.568	28.064	0.107	9.451	27.722	0.253
1997	5.203	17.678	0.274	5.184	17.614	0.063	9.483	32.218	0.105	8.963	30.451	0.257
1998	5.427	18.690	0.282	5.497	18.928	0.069	11.404	39.272	0.117	9.633	33.172	0.309
1999	5.616	19.739	0.270	5.447	19.143	0.077	11.583	40.711	0.121	9.749	34.263	0.320
2000	5.363	21.261	0.262	5.220	20.696	0.081	10.728	42.535	0.113	9.105	36.101	0.334
2001	4.856	21.414	0.265	4.876	21.501	0.088	10.201	44.983	0.104	8.628	38.049	0.355
2002	4.454	22.868	0.223	4.731	24.291	0.103	9.466	48.596	0.088	7.603	39.034	0.342
2003	4.063	23.965	0.186	4.582	27.027	0.121	8.507	50.172	0.087	6.941	40.936	0.306
2004	3.878	25.385	0.171	4.401	28.812	0.117	8.300	54.330	0.070	6.623	43.352	0.282
2005	3.894	28.760	0.145	4.510	33.312	0.125	7.965	58.831	0.065	6.227	45.997	0.246
2006	3.692	29.891	0.140	4.420	35.778	0.125	7.712	62.427	0.058	6.186	50.076	0.249
2007	3.513	31.048	0.125	4.237	37.450	0.114	7.372	65.154	0.052	6.120	54.091	0.215
2008	3.642	32.793	0.117	4.522	40.712	0.101	7.420	66.805	0.051	6.388	57.516	0.160
2009	3.581	35.559	0.116	4.376	43.460	0.099	7.098	70.490	0.046	6.372	63.276	0.166

Source: OECD ITCS and UN COMTRADE Databases

Table 4.14   Competitiveness of PRC Exports RCA Index; World Market Shares and Herfindahl Index of Geographical Concentration Section XIII — Articles of Stones Measured by HS Categories

	Art of Stone Plaster Cement Asbestos Mica-sim Mat			Ceramic Products			Glass and Glassware		
	RCA > 1	World Market Shares	HI	RCA > 1	World Market Shares	HI	RCA > 1 Increasing	World Market Shares	HI
1996	1.590	4.664	0.442	2.109	6.186	0.110	0.763	2.237	0.101
1997	1.535	5.216	0.348	2.403	8.164	0.098	0.752	2.554	0.109
1998	1.361	4.685	0.332	2.406	8.286	0.109	0.783	2.696	0.115
1999	1.401	4.924	0.317	2.450	8.612	0.096	0.865	3.041	0.112
2000	1.436	5.692	0.286	2.360	9.356	0.086	0.954	3.781	0.107
2001	1.521	6.705	0.260	2.027	8.941	0.094	0.978	4.311	0.114
2002	1.453	7.457	0.216	2.158	11.081	0.093	1.080	5.543	0.103
2003	1.344	7.925	0.166	2.064	12.174	0.079	1.065	6.282	0.090
2004	1.254	8.209	0.129	2.084	13.642	0.064	1.178	7.709	0.078
2005	1.330	9.826	0.099	2.262	16.706	0.054	1.291	9.537	0.070
2006	1.368	11.071	0.078	2.285	18.494	0.052	1.325	10.726	0.064
2007	1.342	11.858	0.070	1.958	17.303	0.045	1.376	12.165	0.049
2008	1.416	12.744	0.060	2.163	19.476	0.039	1.564	14.081	0.038
2009	1.530	15.195	0.062	2.427	24.104	0.036	1.466	14.561	0.038

Source: OECD ITCS and UN COMTRADE Databases

Table 4.15   Competitiveness of PRC Exports RCA Index; World Market Shares and Herfindahl Index of Geographical Concentration Section XIV — Natural or Cultured Pearls Measured by HS Categories

	Natural-cultured Pearls Prec Stones and Metals Coin, etc.		
	RCA < 1	World Market Shares	HI
1996	0.441	1.295	0.387
1997	0.525	1.784	0.403
1998	0.584	2.010	0.470
1999	0.696	2.447	0.479
2000	0.551	2.185	0.413
2001	0.481	2.121	0.335
2002	0.452	2.323	0.342
2003	0.388	2.289	0.318
2004	0.391	2.559	0.315
2005	0.382	2.822	0.302
2006	0.351	2.841	0.315
2007	0.319	2.819	0.341
2008	0.270	2.426	0.314
2009	0.238	2.360	0.296

Source: OECD ITCS and UN COMTRADE Databases

Shifting the discussion from manufactures to basic products one can see the mixed results for PRC RCA. The RCA and Herfindahl indexes and world market shares for PRC exports in Section XV — "Basic Metals" are presented in Table 4.16. In some of the HS categories in this section, e.g. "Iron and Steel" the PRC does not demonstrate any comparative advantage. Yet, in "Articles of Iron or Steel" it does have an estimated RCA > 1, with a world market share in excess of 15 percent and a completely diversified export pattern. Likewise in "Articles" of Lead, Zinc Tin and Other Base metals, it does have an estimated RCA > 1, with a growing global footprint in terms of market shares and a completely diversified export pattern. Overall, it is in the "manufacturing" stage that the PRC has an estimated RCA > 1. Our results differ substantially from the observations made by the OECD.

Table 4.16 Competitiveness of PRC Exports RCA Index; World Market Shares and Herfindahl Index of Geographical Concentration Section XV — Base Metals Measured by HS Categories

	Iron and Steel			Articles of Iron or Steel			Copper and Articles Thereof			Nickel and Articles Thereof		
	RCA < 1	World Market Shares	HI	RCA > 1 Increasing	World Market Shares	HI	RCA < 1	World Market Shares	HI	RCA < 1	World Market Shares	HI
1996	0.867	2.543	0.139	1.249	3.664	0.083	0.451	1.323	0.248	0.046	0.134	0.225
1997	0.902	3.066	0.153	1.276	4.333	0.086	0.481	1.635	0.232	0.192	0.651	0.356
1998	0.596	2.053	0.077	1.340	4.614	0.091	0.544	1.873	0.213	0.424	1.461	0.404
1999	0.534	1.875	0.092	1.461	5.136	0.105	0.525	1.844	0.224	0.364	1.278	0.348
2000	0.718	2.846	0.090	1.561	6.191	0.109	0.516	2.044	0.259	0.243	0.963	0.578
2001	0.452	1.991	0.086	1.513	6.671	0.106	0.394	1.736	0.255	0.155	0.681	0.466
2002	0.361	1.852	0.085	1.470	7.546	0.112	0.418	2.145	0.222	0.117	0.602	0.277
2003	0.355	2.094	0.096	1.438	8.484	0.109	0.400	2.357	0.214	0.199	1.173	0.330
2004	0.701	4.591	0.082	1.462	9.568	0.115	0.528	3.457	0.163	0.224	1.466	0.311
2005	0.723	5.341	0.093	1.502	11.096	0.106	0.537	3.969	0.160	0.214	1.579	0.294
2006	0.943	7.636	0.061	1.585	12.828	0.099	0.534	4.320	0.110	0.219	1.770	0.291
2007	1.069	9.452	0.057	1.632	14.421	0.074	0.400	3.537	0.104	0.174	1.537	0.271
2008	1.147	10.331	0.083	1.767	15.909	0.065	0.418	3.766	0.084	0.109	0.982	0.199
2009	0.463	4.593	0.098	1.517	15.062	0.043	0.344	3.413	0.095	0.355	3.526	0.177

(*Continued*)

Table 4.16 (*Continued*)

	Aluminium and Articles Thereof			Lead and Articles Thereof			Zinc and Articles Thereof			Tin and Articles Thereof		
	RCA < 1	World Market Shares	HI	RCA > 1 Reversing	World Market Shares	HI	RCA > 1 Reversing	World Market Shares	HI	RCA > 1 Reversing	World Market Shares	HI
1996	0.325	0.953	0.259	3.459	10.147	0.163	1.718	5.040	0.129	4.093	12.006	0.286
1997	0.447	1.519	0.208	2.144	7.284	0.179	3.195	10.854	0.220	3.796	12.898	0.320
1998	0.503	1.734	0.194	2.553	8.793	0.142	2.303	7.931	0.179	5.078	17.486	0.285
1999	0.403	1.418	0.155	4.072	14.310	0.109	2.869	10.082	0.124	5.973	20.991	0.366
2000	0.399	1.580	0.152	3.507	13.904	0.110	2.785	11.042	0.118	6.225	24.681	0.331
2001	0.526	2.317	0.125	3.548	15.647	0.107	2.586	11.403	0.149	4.645	20.483	0.329
2002	0.677	3.473	0.132	2.915	14.968	0.096	1.861	9.555	0.159	2.208	11.335	0.278
2003	0.763	4.499	0.142	2.428	14.318	0.098	1.547	9.124	0.148	1.865	10.997	0.187
2004	0.864	5.655	0.113	2.510	16.433	0.085	0.894	5.850	0.157	1.607	10.523	0.173
2005	0.796	5.878	0.096	2.079	15.356	0.110	0.593	4.381	0.117	0.902	6.664	0.208
2006	0.847	6.855	0.093	2.144	17.359	0.091	0.915	7.408	0.089	0.791	6.402	0.223
2007	0.837	7.394	0.060	1.119	9.892	0.115	0.752	6.643	0.052	0.966	8.541	0.149
2008	0.969	8.727	0.053	0.467	4.205	0.073	0.331	2.978	0.044	0.381	3.426	0.208
2009	0.859	8.527	0.068	0.245	2.435	0.061	0.240	2.388	0.058	0.157	1.560	0.141

	Other Base Metals — Cermet's — Articles Thereof			Tool Implement Cutlery Spoon and Fork of Base Met etc.			Miscellaneous Articles of Base Metal		
	RCA > 1 Falling	World Market Shares	HI	RCA > 1	World Market Shares	HI	RCA > 1	World Market Shares	HI
1996	2.170	6.365	0.170	1.850	5.425	0.090	1.603	4.702	0.126
1997	2.020	6.864	0.163	1.888	6.416	0.086	1.679	5.704	0.112
1998	2.224	7.659	0.145	1.970	6.785	0.100	1.704	5.868	0.118
1999	2.600	9.137	0.138	1.883	6.617	0.107	1.664	5.850	0.118
2000	2.410	9.554	0.127	2.015	7.988	0.104	1.609	6.380	0.121
2001	2.440	10.760	0.113	1.913	8.436	0.110	1.621	7.148	0.134
2002	2.066	10.606	0.108	1.892	9.715	0.119	1.681	8.630	0.143
2003	2.474	14.593	0.113	1.860	10.971	0.111	1.541	9.088	0.131
2004	2.737	17.920	0.124	1.848	12.095	0.102	1.667	10.914	0.112
2005	2.430	17.946	0.131	1.841	13.596	0.099	1.757	12.980	0.105
2006	2.241	18.141	0.103	1.741	14.094	0.092	1.868	15.123	0.113
2007	2.291	20.252	0.111	1.709	15.105	0.085	1.840	16.265	0.094
2008	2.518	22.671	0.105	1.581	14.231	0.074	1.808	16.276	0.075
2009	1.674	16.623	0.092	1.597	15.863	0.073	1.767	17.551	0.076

Source: OECD ITCS and UN COMTRADE Databases

Table 4.17   Competitiveness of PRC Exports RCA Index; World Market Shares and Herfindahl Index of Geographical Concentration Section XVI — Machinery and Mechanical Appliances Measured by HS Categories

	Nuclear Reactors Boilers Mchy and Mech Appliance — Parts			Electrical Mchy Equip Parts Thereof — Sound Recorder, etc.		
	RCA < 1 Reversing	World Market Shares	HI	RCA > 1 Increasing	World Market Shares	HI
1996	0.479	1.404	0.110	1.021	2.995	0.146
1997	0.495	1.683	0.121	1.003	3.408	0.137
1998	0.583	2.008	0.121	1.069	3.682	0.128
1999	0.639	2.246	0.115	1.154	4.056	0.129
2000	0.726	2.877	0.116	1.170	4.640	0.123
2001	0.851	3.754	0.114	1.336	5.892	0.118
2002	1.052	5.402	0.128	1.444	7.413	0.120
2003	1.318	7.775	0.127	1.501	8.851	0.115
2004	1.405	9.199	0.119	1.603	10.491	0.114
2005	1.455	10.746	0.111	1.664	12.290	0.123
2006	1.463	11.846	0.110	1.721	13.929	0.122
2007	1.525	13.481	0.098	1.827	16.148	0.114
2008	1.598	14.388	0.080	1.954	17.590	0.101
2009	1.625	16.134	0.085	1.882	18.690	0.107

Source: OECD ITCS and UN COMTRADE Databases

The same concentration in favor of manufacturing goods is observed in Section XVI — "Machinery and Mechanical Appliances" whose estimated RCA indexes and Herfindahl indexes and world market shares for PRC exports are presented in Table 4.17. In both of these HS categories the PRC has experienced not only an RCA index >1, but also one that has increased over the 14 years with a growing export footprint and a complete diversified exposure.

The RCA and Herfindahl indexes and world market shares for PRC exports in Section XVII — "Vehicles, Aircraft and Vessels" are presented in Table 4.18. While for "rail" and "ships" the PRC has an increasing footprint in world markets, it is not concentrated in any one country and has an estimated RCA index greater than one. In the PRC autos where production is exclusively targeting the growing domestic market, the calculated RCA index, based on 1996–2009

Table 4.18 Competitiveness of PRC Exports RCA Index; World Market Shares and Herfindahl Index of Geographical Concentration Section XVII — Vehicles, Aircraft and Vessels Measured by HS Categories

	Railw-tramw Locom Rolling-stock and Parts Thereof, etc.			Vehicles o-t Railw-tramw Roll-stock Pts and Accessories			Aircraft Spacecraft and Parts Thereof			Ships Boats and Floating Structures		
	RCA > 1	World Market Shares	HI	RCA < 1	World Market Shares	HI	RCA < 1	World Market Shares	HI	RCA > 1 Increasing	World Market Shares	HI
1996	3.834	11.247	0.286	0.123	0.361	0.114	0.076	0.223	0.204	1.022	2.998	0.094
1997	3.334	11.326	0.270	0.123	0.417	0.127	0.092	0.312	0.186	1.278	4.342	0.105
1998	4.103	14.129	0.158	0.126	0.433	0.145	0.112	0.387	0.151	1.258	4.331	0.087
1999	3.918	13.769	0.158	0.143	0.501	0.155	0.144	0.505	0.161	1.137	3.997	0.100
2000	5.420	21.490	0.133	0.202	0.800	0.104	0.121	0.481	0.171	1.016	4.028	0.070
2001	4.375	19.291	0.140	0.193	0.851	0.104	0.076	0.336	0.174	0.974	4.297	0.076
2002	3.825	19.640	0.121	0.182	0.936	0.120	0.072	0.369	0.297	0.796	4.089	0.077
2003	3.966	23.390	0.156	0.190	1.121	0.117	0.062	0.368	0.149	0.952	5.616	0.080
2004	3.768	24.668	0.137	0.213	1.396	0.120	0.060	0.391	0.160	0.754	4.934	0.072
2005	3.666	27.081	0.134	0.246	1.820	0.101	0.072	0.534	0.182	0.900	6.650	0.065
2006	3.170	25.660	0.117	0.272	2.199	0.085	0.091	0.739	0.159	1.144	9.262	0.071
2007	3.357	29.675	0.107	0.306	2.705	0.061	0.087	0.772	0.148	1.310	11.576	0.088
2008	3.022	27.208	0.103	0.354	3.188	0.047	0.093	0.834	0.130	1.532	13.792	0.094
2009	1.105	10.972	0.085	0.332	3.293	0.052	0.075	0.746	0.151	2.021	20.068	0.080

Source: OECD ITCS and UN COMTRADE Databases

data completely misses the reality of this sector. Despite the fact that currently the RCA index points to the non-existence of a RCA, the next decade will prove that the PRC does in fact a positive RCA index as it begins to export to the developed markets and compete with Japan and Korea.

The RCA and Herfindahl indexes and world market shares for PRC exports for Section XVIII — "Optical, Photographic And Cinematographic" equipment are presented in Table 4.19. Apart from "clocks and watches" were the PRC has concentrated in cheap spinoffs, and has established a sizeable global footprint, with complete geographic diversification, the other HS categories in this section have demonstrated a learning-by-doing process where there has been an increase in the RCA index above one, since the Chinese reforms in 2005. It is the latter reforms that facilitated the increased use of merger and acquisition by non-PRC firms. It was these reforms that altered the Chinese automobile and auto-parts industry by facilitating joint-venture activity with foreign firms.

The RCA and Herfindahl indexes and world market shares for PRC exports in Section XIX — "Arms and Ammunition" are presented in Table 4.20. The trade data that is available point to a lack of RCA for the PRC in this area. Furthermore, it points to a very limited exposure in the world market, but with a high level of geographic concentration. The key destination for Chinese arms is the USA. It is possible that this result is driven by the lack of the complete export data in this category (HS93).

The RCA and Herfindahl indexes and world market shares for PRC exports in Section XX — "Miscellaneous Manufactured Articles" are presented in Table 4.21. In all of the HS categories reviewed in this section, the PRC enjoyed a RCA index greater than 1, had a substantial footprint in the world market and a complete geographic diversification of its exports. In Toys, PRC exports represent over 32 percent of the world market. In bedding mattresses, its market share in 2009 was over 27 percent. Clearly manufacturing is the PRC competitive advantage.

The RCA and Herfindahl indexes and world market shares for PRC exports in Section XXI — "Works of Art" are presented in

Table 4.19 Competitiveness of PRC Exports RCA Index; World Market Shares and Herfindahl Index of Geographical Concentration Section XVIII — Optical, Photographic, Cinematographic Measured by HS Categories

	Optical Photo Cinemas Checking Precision etc			Clocks and Watches and Parts Thereof			Musical Instruments — Parts and Access of Such Articles		
	RCA <1 Reversing	World Market Shares	HI	RCA >1 Reversing	World Market Shares	HI	RCA > 1	World Market Shares	HI
1996	0.706	2.071	0.147	3.040	8.918	0.229	2.175	6.379	0.135
1997	0.756	2.567	0.152	2.810	9.546	0.219	2.309	7.844	0.147
1998	0.783	2.697	0.146	2.825	9.728	0.207	2.464	8.484	0.173
1999	0.779	2.737	0.155	2.682	9.427	0.198	2.795	9.823	0.176
2000	0.817	3.239	0.154	2.316	9.182	0.218	2.574	10.204	0.180
2001	0.755	3.329	0.144	1.934	8.528	0.225	2.595	11.441	0.158
2002	0.736	3.780	0.128	1.669	8.566	0.254	2.649	13.601	0.197
2003	0.772	4.555	0.137	1.531	9.031	0.256	2.578	15.205	0.182
2004	0.858	5.618	0.155	1.308	8.560	0.264	2.670	17.476	0.187
2005	1.058	7.811	0.159	1.071	7.914	0.259	2.569	18.978	0.162
2006	1.085	8.780	0.133	0.906	7.331	0.250	2.451	19.838	0.129
2007	1.059	9.363	0.140	0.886	7.827	0.250	2.457	21.718	0.118
2008	1.099	9.894	0.118	0.854	7.686	0.286	2.701	24.321	0.123
2009	1.008	10.009	0.119	0.854	8.477	0.218	2.396	23.799	0.096

Source: OECD ITCS and UN COMTRADE Databases

Table 4.20   Competitiveness of PRC Exports RCA Index; World Market Shares and Herfindahl Index of Geographical Concentration Section XIX — Arms and Ammunition Measured by HS Categories

	Arms and Ammunition — Parts and Accessories Thereof		
	RCA < 1	World Market Shares	HI
1996	0.127	0.373	0.147
1997	0.094	0.319	0.127
1998	1.073	3.693	0.114
1999	0.070	0.244	0.148
2000	0.043	0.170	0.137
2001	0.063	0.279	0.125
2002	0.055	0.281	0.167
2003	0.041	0.240	0.140
2004	0.053	0.344	0.236
2005	0.054	0.402	0.255
2006	0.065	0.524	0.497
2007	0.087	0.769	0.412
2008	0.101	0.906	0.380
2009	0.074	0.736	0.397

Source: OECD ITCS and UN COMTRADE Databases

Table 4.22. Here we have a clear non-competitive sector. Despite the uniqueness of Chinese art, it has not become a substantial component of its export sector. Clearly this is not one of the areas that the PRC is currently focusing its exports. Historically, the colonial powers in the 19th Century looked at Chinese art and porcelain as the treasured imports from China.

Overall the HS-based RCA indexes, the geographical Herfindahl indexes and the calculated world-market shares point to a small list of manufacturing items where the PRC has maintained a RCA.

4.2. Competitiveness Based on Constant Market Share Decompositions

The Constant Market Share (CMS) decomposition of PRC export growth stresses the importance of the competitiveness effect as the predominant explanation behind the changes in PRC exports over the period 2005–2013. Table 4.23 presents the estimates of the source

Table 4.21 Competitiveness of PRC Exports RCA Index; World Market Shares and Herfindahl Index of Geographical Concentration Section XX — Miscellaneous Manufactured Articles Measured by HS Categories

	Furniture — Bedding Mattress Matt Support Cushion etc			Toys Games and Sports Requisites — Parts and Access Thereof			Miscellaneous Manufactured Articles		
	RCA > 1 Increasing	World Market Shares	HI	RCA > 1 Falling	World Market Shares	HI	RCA > 1 Increasing	World Market Shares	HI
1996	1.664	4.882	0.196	4.969	14.575	0.240	2.747	8.058	0.110
1997	1.735	5.893	0.192	5.099	17.323	0.258	2.850	9.682	0.110
1998	1.827	6.293	0.227	5.303	18.262	0.288	2.912	10.026	0.107
1999	2.109	7.414	0.254	4.987	17.527	0.286	2.763	9.712	0.099
2000	2.271	9.004	0.247	5.068	20.093	0.265	2.713	10.758	0.083
2001	2.223	9.805	0.233	4.752	20.955	0.252	2.753	12.142	0.084
2002	2.319	11.906	0.248	4.835	24.825	0.253	2.585	13.273	0.083
2003	2.277	13.430	0.230	4.508	26.589	0.221	2.490	14.684	0.078
2004	2.337	15.298	0.219	4.229	27.684	0.221	2.632	17.230	0.078
2005	2.448	18.082	0.202	4.192	30.965	0.199	2.724	20.118	0.076
2006	2.512	20.335	0.190	4.085	33.064	0.193	2.687	21.753	0.072
2007	2.520	22.269	0.163	3.688	32.593	0.193	2.866	25.331	0.068
2008	2.706	24.360	0.131	3.752	33.776	0.178	3.251	29.267	0.059
2009	2.755	27.362	0.123	3.295	32.717	0.164	3.090	30.686	0.060

Source: OECD ITCS and UN COMTRADE Databases

Table 4.22   Competitiveness of PRC Exports RCA Index; World Market Shares and Herfindahl Index of Geographical Concentration Section XXI — Works of Art Measured by HS Categories

	Works of Art Collectors Pieces and Antiques		
	RCA < 1	World Market Shares	HI
1996	0.281	0.825	0.245
1997	0.303	1.028	0.255
1998	0.208	0.717	0.268
1999	0.153	0.537	0.259
2000	0.058	0.231	0.213
2001	0.046	0.203	0.163
2002	0.047	0.243	0.173
2003	0.036	0.210	0.189
2004	0.036	0.237	0.193
2005	0.041	0.306	0.139
2006	0.047	0.382	0.123
2007	0.041	0.366	0.091
2008	0.040	0.356	0.070
2009	0.034	0.335	0.072

Source: OECD ITCS and UN COMTRADE Databases

of growth in PRC exports calculated at the six digit HS classification and presented for the aggregate HS categories in each of the five sub periods, 2005–2009, 2006–2010, 2007–2011, 2008–2012 and 2009–2013. The first column represents the overall percentage change in PRC exports to the world market, measured in terms of their changes in market share. With the exception of 'Minerals' the PRC enjoyed a positive global performance in all other sectors in all time bands. The percentage change in the first column is calculated as:

$$\left(\frac{X_{ik}^{t_n}}{X_{wk}^{t_n}}\right) - \left(\frac{X_{ik}^{t_o}}{X_{wk}^{t_o}}\right) = \sum_j \left[\left(\frac{X_{ik}^{t_n}}{X_{jk}^{t_n}}\right)\left(\frac{X_{jk}^{t_n}}{X_{wk}^{t_n}}\right) - \left(\frac{X_{ik}^{t_o}}{X_{jk}^{t_o}}\right)\left(\frac{X_{jk}^{t_o}}{X_{wk}^{t_o}}\right)\right],$$
(4.9)

where

t_o = first period considered; t_n = end period considered; i = the PRC; k = the HS sector; w = are the world exports and j = importers.

Table 4.23 Decomposition of Changes in PRC Exports into CMS Components (Various Years and Percent)

Sectors	2005–2009					2006–2010				
	Relative Change of World Market Share	Competitiveness Effect (a)	Initial Geographic Specialization (b)	Initial Product Specialization (c)	Adaptation Effect (d)	Relative Change of World Market Share	Competitiveness Effect (a)	Initial Geographic Specialization (b)	Initial Product Specialization (c)	Adaptation Effect (d)
Fresh food	0.002	-0.002	0.001	0.000	0.003	0.028	0.008	0.008	0.009	0.003
Processed food	-0.001	0.015	-0.017	-0.008	0.008	0.005	0.009	-0.004	-0.012	0.011
Wood products	0.085	0.076	-0.022	0.023	0.009	0.048	0.041	-0.013	0.002	0.017
Textiles	0.085	0.049	0.012	0.009	0.015	0.074	0.040	0.015	0.005	0.014
Chemicals	0.073	0.084	0.003	-0.003	-0.011	0.091	0.074	0.015	0.012	-0.010
Leather products	0.038	0.002	0.002	0.022	0.011	0.048	0.005	0.006	0.025	0.011
Basic manufactures	0.049	0.021	-0.001	0.003	0.027	0.036	0.007	0.005	0.002	0.023
Non-electronic machinery	0.204	0.132	0.008	0.003	0.060	0.175	0.107	0.013	0.002	0.053
IT & Consumer electronics	0.101	0.049	0.012	-0.010	0.050	0.093	0.038	0.016	-0.005	0.044
Electronic components	0.120	0.049	0.001	-0.013	0.083	0.103	0.024	0.002	-0.013	0.090
Transport equipment	0.227	0.100	0.025	0.033	0.069	0.224	0.090	0.043	0.035	0.056
Clothing	0.042	0.031	0.000	0.001	0.010	0.030	0.012	-0.007	0.002	0.024
Miscellaneous manufacturing	0.063	0.047	-0.010	0.016	0.009	0.072	0.048	-0.003	0.013	0.015
Minerals	-0.022	-0.023	0.010	-0.014	0.005	0.017	-0.006	0.024	0.006	-0.008

(*Continued*)

Table 4.23   (*Continued*)

Sectors	2007–2011					2008–2012				
	Relative Change of World Market Share	Competitiveness Effect (a)	Initial Geographic Specialization (b)	Initial Product Specialization (c)	Adaptation Effect (d)	Relative Change of World Market Share	Competitiveness Effect (a)	Initial Geographic Specialization (b)	Initial Product Specialization (c)	Adaptation Effect (d)
Fresh food	0.025	0.005	0.015	0.006	−0.001	0.056	0.017	0.014	0.014	0.011
Processed food	0.012	0.002	0.009	−0.004	0.006	0.044	0.010	0.022	0.003	0.009
Wood products	0.061	0.044	0.001	0.011	0.005	0.111	0.057	0.008	0.015	0.031
Textiles	0.073	0.038	0.016	0.006	0.013	0.058	0.024	0.014	0.005	0.015
Chemicals	0.085	0.060	0.020	0.018	−0.012	0.056	0.050	0.014	−0.001	−0.008
Leather products	0.050	0.006	0.007	0.027	0.011	0.051	0.008	0.013	0.019	0.011
Basic manufactures	0.031	−0.006	0.007	0.001	0.028	0.032	−0.009	0.005	0.006	0.029
Non-electronic machinery	0.091	0.069	0.007	0.013	0.002	0.054	0.031	0.010	−0.007	0.020
IT & Consumer electronics	0.051	0.023	0.011	0.007	0.010	0.060	0.028	0.016	0.010	0.006
Electronic components	0.079	0.033	0.004	0.030	0.012	0.069	0.037	0.012	0.013	0.008
Transport equipment	0.166	0.055	0.033	0.044	0.034	0.101	0.048	0.025	0.017	0.011
Clothing	0.015	−0.001	−0.004	0.000	0.020	0.033	0.000	0.012	0.005	0.016
Miscellaneous manufacturing	0.058	0.039	0.006	0.000	0.012	0.084	0.041	0.023	−0.005	0.025
Minerals	−0.014	−0.015	0.022	0.010	−0.031	−0.035	−0.041	0.042	−0.037	0.000

2009–2013

Sectors	Relative Change of World Market Share	Competitiveness Effect (a)	Initial Geographic Specialization (b)	Initial Product Specialization (c)	Adaptation Effect (d)
Fresh food	0.024	0.010	0.010	0.000	0.005
Processed food	0.051	0.017	0.013	0.015	0.006
Wood products	0.095	0.061	0.011	0.004	0.019
Textiles	0.046	0.018	0.009	0.008	0.011
Chemicals	0.081	0.068	0.011	0.011	−0.009
Leather products	0.027	0.005	0.010	0.004	0.009
Basic manufactures	0.083	0.043	0.006	0.015	0.019
Non-electronic machinery	0.063	0.054	0.006	0.001	0.002
IT & Consumer electronics	0.041	0.017	0.011	0.006	0.008
Electronic components	0.089	0.051	0.015	0.002	0.021
Transport equipment	0.024	0.024	−0.004	−0.010	0.014
Clothing	0.029	−0.002	0.016	0.009	0.006
Miscellaneous manufacturing	0.096	0.039	0.023	0.008	0.025
Minerals	−0.002	−0.015	0.037	−0.009	−0.015

Source: COMTRADE and ITC

Consequently, $\left(\dfrac{X_{ik}^{tn}}{X_{jk}^{tn}}\right)$ is the PRC market share on all import markets

for end period t_n; $\left(\dfrac{X_{jk}^{tn}}{X_{wk}^{tn}}\right)$ is the share of import markets in world

imports in t_n; $\left(\dfrac{X_{ik}^{to}}{X_{jk}^{to}}\right)$ is the PRC market share on all import markets

for the initial period t_o; $\left(\dfrac{X_{jk}^{to}}{X_{wk}^{to}}\right)$ is the share of import markets in

world imports in t_o;

The second column, marked as column (a) is labeled the competitiveness effect. It is expressed in percent and represents a residual hypothetical gain (or loss) of the PRC's aggregate market share that would occur if changes were only due to variations in the country's market share in import markets (demand side), regardless of the structure of China exports. The percentage change in column (a) is calculated as:

$$\sum_{j}\left(\frac{X_{ijk}^{tn}}{X_{jk}^{tn}} - \frac{X_{ijk}^{to}}{X_{jk}^{to}}\right)\left(\frac{X_{jk}^{to}}{X_{wk}^{to}}\right), \qquad (4.10)$$

where

$\left(\dfrac{X_{ijk}^{tn}}{X_{jk}^{tn}} - \dfrac{X_{ijk}^{to}}{X_{jk}^{to}}\right)$ is the variations in the PRC's market share in its

import markets; $\left(\dfrac{X_{jk}^{to}}{X_{wk}^{to}}\right)$ is the initial share of world markets in world
imports.

The data show that the competitiveness effect was the major explanatory factor, across all periods, in China's exports of 'chemicals'; 'non-electrical equipment' and 'transport equipment.' These results are in addition to the standard positive competitiveness already observed in 'textiles' and 'clothing.'

The third column, marked as column (b) is labeled as the initial geographic specialization effect. It represents the degree to which the initial country distribution of PRC exports were helpful to PRC export growth. As was noted above, when we were discussing the Herfindahl index for PRC geographic concentration, the exports of the PRC showed no geographic concentration. The PRC's export pattern was more characteristic of developed country exporters than developing or transition economy exporters. The percentage change in column (b) is calculated as:

$$\sum_j \left(\frac{X_{ijk}^{to}}{X_{jk}^{to}} \right) \left(\frac{X_{jk}^{tn}}{X_{wk}^{tn}} - \frac{X_{jk}^{to}}{X_{wk}^{to}} \right), \tag{4.11}$$

where

$\left(\frac{X_{ijk}^{to}}{X_{jk}^{to}} \right)$ is the PRC's initial export share in the partner country's imports; $\left(\frac{X_{jk}^{tn}}{X_{wk}^{tn}} - \frac{X_{jk}^{to}}{X_{wk}^{to}} \right)$ is the geographic variation in PRCs export destination.

With no trade impact coming from geographic distribution, we turn to the fourth column, marked as column (c) which is labeled as the initial product specialization effect. This calculation reflects trade impact of commodity concentration. Were PRC exports in those commodities where there was 'dynamic demand.?' In majority of HS categories, over the various five year time bands, PRC exports were concentrated in those areas where there was 'dynamic demand.' The percentage change in column (c) is calculated as:

$$\sum_j \left(\frac{X_{ijk}^{to}}{X_{jk}^{to}} - \frac{X_{ij}^{to}}{X_{j}^{to}} \right) \left(\frac{X_{jk}^{tn}}{X_{w}^{tn}} - \frac{X_{jk}^{to}}{X_{w}^{to}} \right), \tag{4.12}$$

where

$\left(\frac{X_{ijk}^{to}}{X_{jk}^{to}} - \frac{X_{ij}^{to}}{X_{j}^{to}} \right)$ is the difference between the PRC's initial market share in import markets and the PRC's initial market share in the partner country's total imports. $\left(\frac{X_{jk}^{tn}}{X_{w}^{tn}} - \frac{X_{jk}^{to}}{X_{w}^{to}} \right)$ is the shift in product specialization.

Overall, PRC exports are most positively affected by the "competitiveness" factors rather than geographic or product concentration. That leaves the last components in the CMS decomposition. We turn to the fifth column, marked as column (d) which is labeled as the adaptation effect. This calculation reflects the PRC's ability to respond to shifts in world demand. The largest shifts appeared in 'non-electronic machinery;' and 'electronic components;' in the period prior to 2010. In the three subperiods until 2013, the hypothetical adaptation effect became insignificant. The percentage change in column (d) is calculated as:

$$\sum_j \left(\frac{X_{ijk}^{tn}}{X_{jk}^{tn}} - \frac{X_{ijk}^{to}}{X_{jk}^{to}} \right) \left(\frac{X_{jk}^{tn}}{X_w^{tn}} - \frac{X_{jk}^{to}}{X_w^{to}} \right), \qquad (4.13)$$

where

$\left(\frac{X_{ijk}^{tn}}{X_{jk}^{tn}} - \frac{X_{ijk}^{to}}{X_{jk}^{to}} \right)$ is the variation in the PRC's market share in import

markets. $\left(\frac{X_{jk}^{tn}}{X_w^{tn}} - \frac{X_{jk}^{to}}{X_w^{to}} \right)$ is the variation in the share of import market in world imports.

The CMS decomposition suggest that during all the subperiods between 2005 and 2013, the major factor accounting for increases in PRC exports was the competitiveness effect. While the general increase in world trade, the commodity and geographic concentrations were also factors they were not the principal factor. One should observe, however, that a wide range of economic aspects affect the competitiveness of PRC exports in the world market. A change in competitiveness reflects changes in non-tariff barriers, shifts in competing sources and tastes and changes in technology of both exporting and consuming industries. The most noteworthy factor, however, is the change in relative prices. The fact that the Chinese currency was and continues to be non-convertible may explain the latitude that PRC exporters have to "price to market" with much higher degrees of freedom than market economy exporters. This suggests that a comparison of the relative growth of export and export unit values in a single sector is warranted. In order to accomplish this, we focus in the next chapter on the adjustments of PRC Textile and Apparel exports to the US, during the post-2008 adjustment period, as it responded to the elimination of the longest living and highly distortionary quota system — the MFA.

Chapter 5

Evolution of China's International Trade Competitiveness in Textiles and Apparel Exports to the USA — Pre- and Post-MFA

International trade in textiles and apparel, governed by the very intricate Multi-Fiber Arrangement (MFA) for textile and apparel trade was liberalized with respect to the PRC in 2008, three years after the MFA expired for the rest of the world [OECD, 2011d; Pelzman, 1983, 1984, 1988a, 1988b]. This liberalization raised many uncertainties about the impact of the elimination of the quota system on PRC textile and apparel exports in general, and on its displacement of smaller exporter competitors in the developing countries of Asia, Latin America and the Caribbean. Some of these concerns have proven to be correct. Despite the increase in cost of production in the PRC, it remains the major global exporter of textile apparel products in the post-liberalization period. Table 5.1 summarizes the PRCs share of the world market for both textile and apparel products for the period 2001–2013. Regardless of one's priors, the PRC is currently the clear competitive winner in exports of HS 50 — Silk; HS 53 — Vegetable Fibers; HS 54 — Man-made Fibers; HS 55 — Man-made Staple Fibers; HS 58 — Special Woven Fabric; HS 59 — Coated Fabric and HS 61, 62 and 63 — Apparel. Whereas the US was once the clear-cut competitive leader in the textile and fiber segment of this industry, it has relinquished that position to the PRC. The enormity of the PRC footprint in these sectors cannot be underestimated.

Table 5.1 PRC Exports to the World of Textiles and Apparel Products
(Percentage Share by HS Category)

	2001	2002	2003	2004	2005	2006	2007	2008	2009	2010	2011	2012	2013
HS 50 Silk	36.8	37.2	37.2	37.8	41.5	42.5	42.6	40.8	46.3	50.2	51.9	54.7	53.9
HS 51 Wool, animal hair, horsehair yarn and fabric thereof	9.3	9.5	11.2	12.8	13.9	14.7	14.2	15.0	15.7	18.6	18.2	17.9	18.6
HS 52 Cotton	10.1	13.1	14.4	13.5	15.7	17.4	18.0	20.5	22.5	22.4	21.9	22.2	25.8
HS 53 Vegetable textile fibers nes, paper yarn, woven fabric	16.6	17.3	15.6	14.7	17.0	17.9	16.7	18.0	21.3	22.7	26.0	27.8	31.4
HS 54 Manmade filaments	5.6	8.2	11.4	13.9	15.7	17.1	18.2	20.4	21.9	24.5	28.3	30.9	33.7
HS 55 Manmade staple fibers	11.8	11.0	11.6	13.1	15.8	18.8	19.4	21.1	22.3	23.5	26.7	27.3	28.6
HS 56 Wadding, felt, non-wovens, yarns, twine, cordage, etc.	3.5	3.7	3.9	4.6	6.0	6.8	7.7	9.7	11.4	13.3	14.8	15.8	17.4
HS 57 Carpets and other textile floor coverings	6.1	6.7	6.8	7.3	8.1	8.6	9.6	11.5	12.7	13.9	15.0	16.3	16.1

HS 58 Special woven or tufted fabric, lace, tapestry etc.	10.3	13.3	16.3	18.7	23.4	27.2	34.3	38.1	33.1	32.6	35.4	36.8	38.8
HS 59 Impregnated, coated or laminated textile fabric	3.6	4.8	5.8	7.8	10.6	12.2	14.5	18.2	21.9	25.1	28.2	28.1	29.6
HS 60 Knitted or crocheted fabric	9.2	12.6	14.2	15.2	18.3	21.3	23.6	25.5	29.3	32.9	34.8	37.1	41.8
HS 61 Articles of apparel, accessories, knit or crochet	16.4	18.4	20.5	22.5	24.8	31.0	35.8	33.9	33.8	37.3	38.4	41.0	43.3
HS 62 Articles of apparel, accessories, not knit or crochet	18.4	19.0	20.6	21.6	24.1	27.6	27.8	28.7	29.8	32.3	31.8	31.8	33.8
HS 63 Other made textile articles, sets, worn clothing etc.	19.6	21.3	24.5	26.7	30.6	32.9	33.4	37.1	39.6	40.8	40.5	42.8	43.3

Source: COMTRADE

The country distribution in terms of the top 5 import markets for the PRC are listed in Table 5.2 by two-digit HS categories. As we noted in Chapter 4, PRC exports in this sector are not concentrated geographically to a very small group of countries, so we cannot argue that, currently, the US or the EU represent its exclusive destination market. While that may have been true in the 1980s and 1990s, the PRC has managed to diversify its textile and apparel exports both pre- and post-MFA. Furthermore, the PRC's post-MFA export performance has included its neighboring developing countries in a production network which includes joint production in a large global value-added chain. The countries excluded from this PRC network are in Latin America and the Caribbean. The latter are still part of the US-dominated production network which is primarily offshore.

The successful PRC experience in this sector, post liberalization, cannot be relegated to a simple crowding-out theory. Rather, it is a story of upgrading, diversification and the development of value-added production chains within the Asia market. In large part, the joint production in this sector is driven by the fact that PRC's textile and apparel industry has adjusted to lower costs in transportation, higher efficiency in its ICT support industry and continued rationalization of the industry. The constraints imposed by the complicated and intricate MFA system with its fiber-based categories and rules of origin have, ex-post, provided the clear-cut rationalization of the industry across East Asia, including countries like the Philippines, India and Vietnam who now represent the low-cost components of the industry [Pelzman, 1993; Pelzman and Rees, 1999].

In what follows, we discuss the evolution of the industry in the PRC as it responded to the elimination of a "certain degree" of market certainty, dictated by the MFA, to a decentralized non-regulated trading environment, surrounded by a larger set of competitors like India and Vietnam. On the demand side, we estimate whether or not PRC, Indian and Vietnamese textile and apparel items, formally under quota control, were substitutes or complements in the US market. On the supply side, we focus on institutional differences

Table 5.2 PRC Exports of Textiles and Apparel Products — Top Five Import Markets
(million US Dollars by HS Category)

	2001	2002	2003	2004	2005	2006	2007	2008	2009	2010	2011	2012	2013
HS 50 Silk													
World	826.6	767.3	824.2	1,062.3	1,336.3	1,423.8	1,396.9	1,434.0	1,287.7	1,642.0	1,745.5	1,706.5	1,630.0
India	181.0	219.5	239.3	358.6	425.2	354.2	414.2	372.0	411.8	492.0	420.3	364.2	303.5
Italy	113.3	103.2	105.7	128.8	172.5	213.8	185.2	224.9	141.1	232.7	262.4	232.9	247.4
Pakistan	2.4	5.6	9.7	16.6	50.5	84.3	74.2	73.4	120.9	166.1	192.5	250.5	226.2
Japan	98.9	92.6	103.8	89.9	125.4	132.6	93.2	98.8	72.1	101.5	121.5	123.4	125.9
Hong Kong, China	136.4	107.1	111.8	137.3	121.4	142.5	169.3	162.9	97.5	112.7	118.6	120.7	100.0
HS 51 Wool, Animal Hair, Horsehair Yarn and Fabric thereof													
World	1,082.5	1,068.5	1,316.5	1,715.4	1,845.1	1,996.7	2,124.6	2,087.5	1,625.9	2,361.7	2,959.0	2,583.9	2,619.2
Hong Kong, China	363.4	312.3	372.0	496.6	515.9	436.6	454.1	538.5	484.6	701.2	526.4	519.8	513.1
Italy	111.6	145.6	157.5	200.4	238.7	261.0	301.9	265.9	205.7	350.3	501.2	351.8	394.4
Japan	229.5	198.8	225.1	244.7	218.2	259.3	245.8	228.3	134.7	176.2	276.1	297.2	262.2
Korea, Republic of	76.1	103.1	118.3	138.6	152.2	192.9	225.4	179.5	134.4	196.5	288.5	179.7	176.2
Germany	43.3	40.6	58.5	86.4	86.3	133.9	154.7	133.0	79.7	142.4	230.6	180.4	155.4
HS 52 Cotton													
World	3,658.1	4,894.2	6,220.1	6,587.2	7,437.9	8,877.1	9,359.6	10,690.5	9,600.9	13,066.6	15,497.5	14,838.9	17,546.7
Hong Kong, China	1,688.0	2,124.6	2,610.0	2,702.6	2,774.9	3,215.9	3,033.1	2,867.7	2,414.4	2,703.8	2,478.9	2,429.3	2,813.3
Vietnam	22.5	74.3	119.0	146.9	210.1	268.7	371.4	445.5	634.1	1,167.2	1,561.1	1,459.2	2,496.6
Bangladesh	196.2	247.8	357.3	399.1	544.2	687.1	749.8	975.2	890.0	1,330.4	1,787.6	1,828.7	2,164.2
Benin	82.8	142.0	221.9	196.6	305.9	422.6	642.1	987.6	803.6	850.4	850.1	591.7	915.6
Philippines	44.1	59.8	68.8	88.3	99.3	106.7	103.7	103.4	142.1	171.7	284.0	489.9	795.4

(Continued)

Table 5.2   (*Continued*)

	2001	2002	2003	2004	2005	2006	2007	2008	2009	2010	2011	2012	2013
HS 53 Vegetable Textile Fibers Nes, Paper Yarn, Woven Fabric													
World	454.0	501.6	525.7	552.7	618.0	660.6	615.9	594.6	592.8	869.6	1,131.3	1,068.3	1,285.3
Hong Kong, China	241.0	304.0	314.1	272.8	213.7	207.3	160.8	115.4	89.6	114.0	94.0	108.9	337.2
Korea, Republic of	77.8	50.3	37.8	52.1	45.7	59.9	58.8	46.4	96.9	155.7	160.6	132.3	179.2
India	6.6	9.8	12.9	18.2	28.8	45.5	50.3	43.2	46.5	71.0	117.4	127.3	155.6
Bangladesh	24.7	15.0	10.8	7.6	8.0	9.6	12.4	23.3	29.4	47.0	86.9	88.0	93.2
Italy	4.1	5.4	10.0	14.2	71.3	59.4	59.1	66.9	48.4	79.1	92.1	68.0	61.8
HS 54 Manmade Filaments													
World	1,623.8	2,426.2	3,751.6	5,155.9	5,890.4	6,598.6	7,801.0	8,769.9	7,494.1	10,085.6	13,815.3	14,300.7	16,014.3
Vietnam	11.2	21.5	44.6	73.8	113.6	158.9	239.4	312.1	273.9	443.7	663.8	780.1	971.1
United Arab Emirates	134.6	273.8	451.7	564.8	529.9	526.8	525.8	551.7	454.3	491.8	885.2	874.7	966.3
Pakistan	12.9	22.4	52.9	144.6	224.2	379.0	443.1	425.1	580.6	688.2	754.6	779.0	964.4
Brazil	11.5	41.1	103.7	217.4	213.6	216.8	301.1	372.4	306.0	448.8	630.4	697.5	804.1
Indonesia	31.4	34.6	59.1	95.4	137.2	143.5	151.4	200.3	178.9	304.9	499.4	620.6	636.6
HS 55 Manmade Staple Fibers													
World	2,659.2	2,523.4	2,787.0	3,554.5	4,387.2	5,532.5	6,367.6	6,886.7	6,060.9	7,956.7	11,176.0	10,624.4	11,211.4
Vietnam	23.3	38.1	54.8	81.5	138.4	199.8	303.8	416.6	355.2	419.4	620.3	733.7	1,069.6
Bangladesh	123.7	113.3	154.0	216.5	244.8	296.6	284.0	384.6	351.2	525.3	737.6	651.8	722.3
Pakistan	1.2	11.7	9.3	8.9	29.1	41.5	106.5	128.1	148.4	252.2	371.2	398.6	632.5
Hong Kong, China	571.2	550.9	611.9	732.8	781.9	816.3	699.0	610.1	532.1	618.2	969.2	735.1	532.1
United States of America	64.6	76.4	76.6	92.2	261.0	354.9	363.1	389.7	321.1	426.2	537.1	505.8	497.1

HS 56 Wadding, Felt, Non-wovens, Yarns, Twine, Cordage, etc.

World	329.9	364.6	468.8	594.7	860.3	1,100.0	1,377.5	1,916.2	1,962.2	2,683.3	3,457.6	3,540.5	4,125.3
United States of America	5.5	10.0	20.2	37.7	80.5	110.6	138.7	229.0	251.6	369.9	463.8	451.7	497.7
Japan	39.8	42.1	50.3	65.1	90.1	102.1	124.9	178.8	197.5	244.3	321.8	331.4	320.1
Korea, Republic of	26.8	31.6	35.6	37.7	56.3	76.1	102.3	125.0	115.5	162.5	189.1	195.6	220.9
Hong Kong, China	81.9	78.0	75.6	83.9	87.1	95.3	109.7	109.1	96.8	96.8	101.6	111.6	206.3
Vietnam	1.9	4.7	7.0	9.6	13.3	25.9	44.3	56.9	82.6	133.3	140.9	135.5	188.3

HS 57 Carpets and Other Textile Floor Coverings

World	490.7	557.0	637.5	773.3	932.2	1,068.6	1,320.0	1,618.5	1,491.3	1,954.9	2,323.7	2,403.7	2,505.5
United States of America	208.4	250.5	276.1	281.1	314.2	337.2	361.9	361.5	281.6	332.0	448.1	469.1	440.4
Japan	109.1	120.8	130.2	177.6	221.1	259.2	279.5	316.8	315.6	381.4	423.6	455.8	411.4
Australia	6.7	8.9	11.3	15.6	16.2	25.1	44.1	56.2	53.2	67.5	85.1	96.4	108.6
Malaysia	2.4	3.2	8.9	12.1	10.8	13.5	21.6	27.1	31.7	51.0	74.9	87.4	99.8
Hong Kong, China	15.1	14.3	17.7	25.6	32.2	32.1	34.8	45.4	39.1	51.0	66.1	80.5	82.1

HS 58 Special Woven or Tufted Fabric, Lace, Tapestry, etc.

World	786.4	1,155.1	1,554.7	1,975.3	2,709.1	3,366.5	4,691.0	5,360.8	3,529.8	3,804.7	4,569.9	4,637.7	4,874.9
Hong Kong, China	245.1	314.9	413.3	443.7	518.0	567.2	795.3	770.8	418.5	455.0	477.7	501.8	617.3
United States of America	31.2	62.6	72.7	96.9	194.1	244.6	297.4	317.7	244.0	296.0	369.7	375.0	384.7
United Arab Emirates	47.1	63.5	76.2	91.4	132.9	225.3	356.7	373.4	246.5	252.1	337.8	323.9	366.1
Vietnam	7.8	18.0	26.3	33.6	43.1	52.0	68.0	89.2	72.0	116.0	166.5	196.8	229.9
Bangladesh	31.9	44.7	70.8	97.1	105.2	121.7	126.8	156.6	137.5	161.5	184.7	201.7	217.6

(Continued)

Table 5.2 (*Continued*)

	2001	2002	2003	2004	2005	2006	2007	2008	2009	2010	2011	2012	2013
HS 59 Impregnated, Coated or Laminated Textile Fabric													
World	448.4	624.1	825.7	1,235.1	1,755.0	2,132.3	2,841.1	3,864.3	3,965.4	5,626.1	7,254.4	6,848.8	7,375.9
India	41.8	71.9	125.5	179.9	313.9	338.8	440.5	569.0	571.6	733.9	854.7	716.3	719.1
Vietnam	10.5	11.1	13.3	22.8	46.1	62.9	98.0	136.3	164.2	470.8	554.7	466.7	595.5
Hong Kong, China	119.0	147.6	174.2	231.7	285.7	313.2	340.0	389.3	352.0	400.3	417.7	384.5	586.1
United States of America	23.9	37.4	42.8	74.1	123.3	130.7	159.3	214.1	222.6	343.3	425.9	456.9	460.6
Indonesia	13.7	19.1	27.9	47.0	65.1	81.8	119.0	183.5	170.0	229.0	344.2	366.5	370.1
HS 60 Knitted or Crocheted Fabric													
World	1,361.0	2,006.4	2,508.3	2,993.7	3,652.2	4,640.0	5,738.1	6,367.2	6,422.5	8,666.5	10,697.6	11,219.3	12,900.4
Hong Kong, China	935.6	1,279.5	1,467.8	1,625.8	1,825.6	2,123.1	2,235.8	2,045.3	1,781.0	1,932.0	2,043.7	1,997.7	1,998.8
Vietnam	7.0	32.8	71.4	101.2	133.9	205.8	342.8	434.6	471.9	740.8	958.3	1,136.5	1,542.5
Cambodia	30.4	44.4	70.9	86.0	123.5	207.7	252.2	287.7	268.5	402.1	594.8	647.9	878.0
United States of America	3.0	20.6	39.7	42.2	135.4	113.7	124.2	135.5	281.8	452.7	555.1	579.3	665.1
Indonesia	11.8	15.4	21.9	33.6	62.6	99.8	140.0	227.2	235.8	364.3	462.9	517.8	540.0
HS 61 Articles of Apparel, Accessories, Knit or Crochet													
World	13,455.9	15,983.7	20,678.1	25,802.6	30,870.8	44,900.4	61,509.4	60,877.5	53,763.0	66,710.9	80,164.6	87,045.0	96,792.7
United States of America	1,241.8	1,415.9	1,835.5	2,408.7	5,118.8	6,303.0	7,826.9	7,295.4	8,484.0	11,250.6	13,218.5	13,674.4	14,810.2
Japan	4,557.1	4,404.4	5,145.2	6,058.7	6,544.3	7,103.7	7,866.2	8,629.7	8,703.9	9,350.9	10,937.0	11,151.5	11,236.6
Hong Kong, China	2,327.6	3,033.3	3,906.1	5,004.6	3,154.8	4,742.4	5,083.6	4,283.8	4,182.1	4,147.0	4,306.2	5,408.3	7,120.9
Vietnam	8.2	48.5	61.0	56.8	44.2	39.0	115.1	289.6	643.4	785.9	1,529.6	3,689.3	4,769.2
United Kingdom	155.9	214.8	263.5	326.9	681.2	1,000.9	1,213.8	2,106.7	1,862.4	2,340.9	2,917.7	3,283.2	3,948.7

HS 62 Articles of Apparel, Accessories, Not Knit or Crochet

World	18,952.1	20,582.5	25,079.0	28,980.9	35,030.8	43,720.3	47,371.8	52,490.1	46,716.3	54,361.5	63,073.9	61,224.4	68,251.9
United States of America	2,132.5	2,306.5	2,856.1	3,475.7	6,603.8	7,884.4	8,893.7	9,104.6	9,582.7	11,643.6	12,256.4	12,527.8	13,399.9
Japan	6,902.1	6,389.3	6,938.7	7,546.3	7,610.7	8,066.0	8,052.0	8,395.6	8,096.6	8,391.1	10,283.5	10,254.7	10,033.3
Germany	429.0	550.7	816.1	1,017.2	1,732.1	2,076.9	2,725.9	3,313.0	3,087.5	3,783.5	4,600.8	3,694.3	3,933.0
United Kingdom	292.9	369.1	519.4	639.4	1,250.1	1,565.5	2,030.4	2,810.4	2,447.6	2,717.3	3,057.8	2,874.4	3,416.2
Russian Federation	449.4	447.0	791.1	1,025.5	1,587.5	1,492.0	1,846.5	1,631.1	1,239.4	1,812.1	2,103.1	2,121.9	3,387.8

HS 63 Other Made Textile Articles, Sets, Worn Clothing, etc.

World	3,700.2	4,394.8	6,169.0	7,783.7	10,336.1	12,076.4	13,591.4	16,776.1	16,816.8	19,744.2	22,673.3	24,015.9	26,825.2
United States of America	684.4	1,075.6	1,779.4	2,338.0	3,296.3	3,946.6	4,245.2	4,663.7	4,471.9	5,672.3	5,950.5	6,274.5	6,874.1
Japan	1,162.7	1,178.3	1,342.1	1,465.4	1,638.1	1,798.4	1,822.7	2,106.1	2,589.2	2,333.8	2,945.4	2,939.0	2,917.7
Russian Federation	77.5	58.7	195.9	290.0	556.2	447.4	577.7	683.6	413.8	549.1	719.9	1,242.1	1,623.2
Germany	155.6	143.5	211.5	262.8	385.3	441.0	514.9	709.9	718.8	870.4	1,009.9	933.9	1,008.3
United Kingdom	112.4	163.8	235.6	337.1	409.0	510.4	589.4	724.9	721.4	861.0	900.8	891.1	922.4

Source: COMTRADE

between each country's textile and apparel sectors and the different domestic government policies that have contributed to their growth post-MFA.

The specific textile and apparel items to be compared are based on the pre-2005 quota limits where India, Vietnam and the PRC were constrained. The full list of the PRC products under quota control included 77 three-digit textile and apparel categories divided by fiber between fabric, textiles and apparel. The full set of Indian products under quota control, which intersects with the PRC product list, included 57 three-digit categories. Since Vietnam was a relatively new start-up in the textile and apparel sector, there were only 20 three-digit categories which intersected with those of the PRC. The full list of textile and apparel categories under MFA control for India and Vietnam are listed in Table 5.3.

Table 5.3   Textile Categories Under MFA Quota for the PRC, Vietnam and India

CAT	Description	Unit
	Vietnam	
237	Playsuits, sun suits, etc.	Doz
331	Cotton gloves and mittens	DPR
334	Other M/B coats, cotton	Doz
335	W/G cotton coats	Doz
336	Cotton dresses	Doz
340	M/B cotton shirts, not-knit	Doz
341	W/G cotton shirts/blouses, not-knit	Doz
342	Cotton skirts	Doz
347	M/B cotton trousers/breeches/shorts	Doz
348	W/G cotton trousers/slacks/shorts	Doz
635	W/G MMF coats	Doz
636	MMF dresses	Doz
638	M/B MMF knit shirts	Doz
639	W/G MMF knit shirts/blouses	Doz
640	M/B not-knit MMF shirts	Doz
641	W/G not-knit MMF shirts/blouses	Doz
644	W/G MMF suits	Doz
648	W/G MMF slacks/breeches/shorts	Doz
651	MMF nightwear/pajamas	Doz
652	MMF underwear	Doz

(*Continued*)

Table 5.3 (*Continued*)

CAT	Description	Unit
	India	
218	Fabrics of yarns of diff. colors	M2
219	Duck fabric	M2
220	Fabric of special weave	M2
222	Knit fabric	KG
224	Pile/tufted fabrics	M2
225	Blue denim fabric	M2
226	Cheesecloth, batistes, lawns/voile	M2
227	Oxford cloth	M2
237	Playsuits, sun suits, etc.	Doz
300	Carded cotton yarn	KG
301	Combed cotton yarn	KG
313	Cotton sheeting fabric	M2
314	Cotton poplin/broadcloth fabric	M2
315	Cotton print cloth fabric	M2
317	Cotton twill fabric	M2
326	Cotton sateen fabric	M2
331	Cotton gloves and mittens	DPR
333	M/B suit-type coats, cotton	Doz
334	Other M/B coats, cotton	Doz
335	W/G cotton coats	Doz
336	Cotton dresses	Doz
340	M/B cotton shirts, not-knit	Doz
341	W/G cotton shirts/blouses, not-knit	Doz
342	Cotton skirts	Doz
345	Cotton sweaters	Doz
347	M/B cotton trousers/breeches/shorts	Doz
348	W/G cotton trousers/slacks/shorts	Doz
351	Cotton nightwear/pajamas	Doz
352	Cotton underwear	Doz
360	Cotton pillowcases	Doz
361	Cotton sheets	Doz
363	Cotton terry/other pile towels	No
613	MMF sheeting fabric	M2
614	MMF poplin/broadcloth fabric	M2
615	MMF printcloth fabric	M2
617	MMF twill and sateen fabric	M2
619	Polyester filament fabric, light-weight	M2
620	Other synthetic filament fabric	M2
625	MMF poplin/broadcloth stap/fil	M2

(*Continued*)

Table 5.3   (*Continued*)

CAT	Description	Unit
628	MMF twills/sateens stap/fil	M2
629	Other MMF fabrics of stap/fil	M2
634	Other M/B MMF coats	Doz
635	W/G MMF coats	Doz
636	MMF dresses	Doz
638	M/B MMF knit shirts	Doz
639	W/G MMF knit shirts/blouses	Doz
640	M/B not-knit MMF shirts	Doz
641	W/G not-knit MMF shirts/blouses	Doz
642	MMF skirts	Doz
643	M/B MMF suits	Doz
644	W/G MMF suits	Doz
645	M/B MMF sweaters	Doz
646	W/G MMF sweaters	Doz
647	M/B MMF trousers/breeches/shorts	Doz
648	W/G MMF slacks/breeches/shorts	Doz
651	MMF nightwear/pajamas	Doz
652	MMF underwear	Doz

Source: The US Department of Commerce, Office of Textiles and Apparel

5.1. The Control of Textile and Apparel Trade: The Early Years

In the United States, the protection of the domestic textile and apparel industry began in 1956, when Congress enacted §204 of the Agricultural Act authorizing the President, among other things, to negotiate textile-restraint agreements to provide the U.S. textile and apparel industry with "temporary" relief.[3] The first of these multilateral agreements was the Short-Term Arrangement Regarding International Trade in Cotton Textiles (STA), initiated in 1961.[4] This was followed by the Long-Term Arrangement Regarding

---

[3] See Pub. L. No. 540, §204, 70 Stat. 188, 200 (1956) (codified at 7 U.S.C. §1854 (1982)).

[4] Interim Arrangements Regarding International Trade in Cotton Textiles, July 21, 1961, 12 U.S.T. 1674, T.I.A.S. No. 4884 [hereinafter STA].

International Trade in Cotton Textiles (LTA) in 1962,[5] and by the MFA in 1974,[6] designed to be in effect until 1991.[7]

In 1961, the United States convened a conference between exporters and importers of textiles and apparel in order to devise a mechanism by which LDC exports of textiles and apparel could increase under a set of mutually acceptable controls. The STA, which was the outcome of this conference, outlined three goals: (1) to increase significantly LDC access to markets that were then restricted; (2) to maintain orderly access to markets that were relatively open and (3) to secure a measure of restraint on the part of exporting countries to avoid disruption. This agreement was to last for a year, beginning in October 1961, while a Provisional Cotton Textile Committee was established to work out the text of a Long-Term Arrangement Regarding International Trade in Cotton Textiles (LTA). The initial LTA came into force in October 1962 for a period of five years. It was then extended twice through 1973.

LTA notwithstanding, the developing country exporters diversified the fiber content of their exports towards man-made apparel. In large part, this diversification was encouraged by the US fiber manufacturers that joined textile machinery manufacturers [Pelzman, 1977]. In 1971, the United States reached bilateral agreements with its principal suppliers — Japan, Hong Kong, Taiwan and Korea, to control the flow of wool and man-made textile and apparel products. These restrictions were not included in the LTA, but subsequently the United States focused on amending the LTA to cover textile and apparel products of all three fibers.

---

[5]Long-Term Arrangements Regarding International Trade in Cotton Textiles, February 9, 1962, 13 U.S.T. 2672, T.I.A.S. No. 5240, 471 U.N.T.S. 296 [hereinafter LTA].

[6]Arrangement Regarding International Trade in Textiles, December 20, 1973, 25 U.S.T. 1001, T.I.A.S. No. 7840 [hereinafter MFA]. Since 1974, the MFA was renewed on six occasions.

[7]A history of the early agreements is provided in USITC [1978], and in Keesing and Wolf [1980]. A discussion of MFA III and IV is provided in Pelzman [1987a, 1987b and 1987c]. The texts of the STA, LTA and MFA are reprinted in USITC.

A comprehensive agreement to cover all fibers was reached on December 20, 1973, the Arrangement Regarding International Trade in Textiles or, more commonly, the MFA.[8] It became the "statement of principle and policy" regarding international textile trade. The heart of the MFA is contained in Articles 3 and 4, which outline permissible restrictions. Article 3 covers situations of actual market disruption, and permits the imposition of unilateral import restrictions. Article 4 covers situations involving a "real risk" of market disruption and therefore is the primary instrument sanctioning bilateral agreements.

As with all other trade agreements concerning textile and apparel, the initial MFA was considered a "temporary" measure, despite the fact that it was extended three times. Its basic objective was clearly spelled out in Article 1, where the MFA is designed to insure both that developed countries' textile and apparel industries are not adversely affected by developing country exports, and to allow for the regulated growth of developing country textile and apparel exports. Article 1 further encourages the industrialized countries to shift resources out of non-competitive segments of their textile and apparel industries.

The importing countries interpreted the major objective of the MFA as a device to limit the growth of imports. The protection afforded the domestic industry was furthermore interpreted as a commitment to guarantee it a share of the domestic market. A guarantee of this nature would justify the dollar cost of "restructuring" the domestic textile and apparel industries. In fact, the United States, the EC and the other industrialized countries have pursued policies promoting and encouraging investment in textiles and apparel. Large segments of the textile and apparel industries are now far more capital intensive than was considered possible [Pelzman, 1989].

Articles 3 and 4 and Annex B of the MFA prescribe that annual import growth not be lower than 6 percent. Lower growth rates are allowed, but must be implemented only under "exceptional circumstances." Under flexibility provisions in Annex B, exporting

---

[8]MFA, supra note 6.

countries are allowed to transfer unused quotas among categories and between the previous or subsequent year and the current year.

At the expiration of the first MFA (December, 1977) the European Community's (EC) member states, who had not negotiated comprehensive bilateral agreements during this period, asked for major modifications. To satisfy EC concerns, the extension protocol renewing the MFA contained an amendment that allowed "jointly-agreed reasonable departures" from the 6 percent growth rate in quotas and from the agreement's "flexibility provisions." This not only allowed growth at less than 6 percent, but also zero or negative growth in those products considered sensitive by importing countries.

Under MFA II, the EC negotiated a series of five-year bilateral agreements which used this clause to establish "global" quotas for a number of products it considered to be "sensitive." The United States never formally invoked the "reasonable departures" clause, but it did reduce some of the flexibility in existing agreements and target major exporters. The United States, in fact, reopened bilateral agreements with Hong Kong, Taiwan and Korea to amend them and reduce the flexibility provisions [Keesing and Wolf, 1980, p. 77].

MFA III eliminated the "reasonable departures" clause of the earlier Protocol. Yet it also impeded "flexibility" provisions of Annex B, and reaffirmed the right of industrial countries to negotiate bilateral agreements with lower than 6 percent, annual import growth rates.

Although the U.S. had been successful in negotiating an MFA that would permit highly restrictive agreements, the U.S. textile and apparel industry continued to demand highly protectionist unilateral action on the fringes of the MFA.

The extension of the MFA beyond 1986 was agreed to after intensive negotiations over a period of several months. In general, the United States and most other industrialized importing countries favored extending the MFA with added control features, whereas many developing exporting countries favored more liberal provisions and a schedule to phase out the agreement and return textile trade to operations under GATT rules. Indicated U.S. objectives in the negotiations included: (1) provision for controls on products made of fibers not covered in the existing MFA (silk and non-cotton vegetable fibers); (2) prevention of "surges" in imports and (3) lower growth rates for major suppliers. These objectives were accomplished to a large degree. Some U.S. textile interests in industry and, in the Congress, had proposed more stringent measures such as limiting total imports of textiles and apparel to a growth rate equal to growth in the domestic market, allowing reductions or "roll-backs" of imports from predominant suppliers, and to allow strong unilateral action against countries that circumvent quotas.

Even while the negotiations on extension of the MFA were being conducted, the United States was engaged in discussions with its major suppliers regarding renegotiation of their bilateral agreements and suggesting a three-year "freeze" on import levels.

MFA IV expanded the product coverage of the MFA to include silk, linen, ramie and jute, and further expanded the right of importing countries to restrict imports. With the inclusion of silk and vegetable fibers, the developed countries temporarily eliminated the possibility of having trade diverted into non-MFA fibers. MFA IV also included an authorization to allow importing countries the right to extend a 12-month quota imposed under Article 3 for an additional 12-month period. In contrast to the original MFA, the importing country no longer has to reach agreement with the exporting country before extending the original quota.

The MFA as set out in the original agreement is straightforward in principle. Its restrictiveness in practice arises from individual country implementation. The United States has negotiated very comprehensive bilateral agreements under the authority of Article 4. These agreements restrain textile and apparel imports under a variety of quota instruments, classified by degree of restrictiveness. That is, specific limits specifying upper bound constraints, and designated consultation levels specifying when the Department of Commerce would issue a request for a consultation. The latter also included minimum consultation levels, agreed limits, restraint limits, "export" type restraints applicable only to Hong Kong, Taiwan and S. Korea, consultation provisions and other miscellaneous limits. Over time, the U.S. bilateral agreements involved more specific limits and fewer consultation provisions. That is, the US attempted to stop any "water" in their bilateral quota agreements [Pelzman, 1987c].

5.2. Moving Away from the MFA: The Agreement on Textiles and Clothing

The Agreement on Textiles and Clothing (ATC),[9] like the original MFA, attempted to meet both the objectives of the developing country exporters and the developed country importers. As such, it inherited the same conflicting goals and implementation difficulties as were found in the first MFA. For the exporters, the ATC was designed to eliminate quotas, thereby providing increased market access for textile and apparel exports during the phase-out period, and integration of textile and apparel trade into the WTO regime, by the year 2005.[10] From the importers' perspective, the ATC was designed to provide stronger means for enforcing quotas during the 10-year phase-out period, and to establish transitional safeguard measures for the temporary protection of domestic industries from increased imports. The implementing group established by the ATC to oversee implementation of the agreement was the quasi-judicial body Textiles Monitoring Body (TMB). The track record of the TMB has been mixed. In fact, given the harsh criticism it has suffered from both exporting and importing countries, one could argue that it has been very successful.[11]

With the adoption of the ATC, it was expected that textile and apparel trade would be progressively integrated into GATT. The mechanism adopted to ensure this transfer included: (1) eliminating

---

[9]ATC, April 15, 1994, Marrakesh Agreement Establishing the World Trade Organization, Annex 1A: Multilateral Agreements on Trade in Goods, The Results of the Uruguay Round of Multilateral Trade Negotiations: The Legal Texts, 85 (GATT Secretariat ed., 1994) [hereinafter ATC].

[10]While there was a commitment to eliminate quotas, the ATC did not make a commitment to reduce the extremely high tariffs in existence for both textiles and apparel.

[11]A review of a number of the US calls through 1998 is presented in Pelzman and Rees [1998].

quotas on selected products in four stages over a 10-year period, culminating in 2005 and (2) increasing quota growth rates on remaining products at each of the first three stages.[12] The elimination of the MFA quotas was to take a number of stages, beginning with the first stage which became effective on January 1, 1995, with the removal of quotas on imports accounting for 16 percent of 1990 textile and apparel imports. In stage 2, implemented on January 1, 1998, an additional 17 percent of 1990 imports was eliminated, followed by another 18 percent scheduled for integration on January 1, 2002. The balance of quantitative restrictions, predominantly in the apparel area, (potentially up to 49 percent) was scheduled to be removed by January 1, 2005.[13] Despite what appeared to be a replacement of the MFA with the ATC, the MFA persisted during the phase-out process established by the ATC, because restrictions pursuant to the MFA framework continued until each product was integrated into the GATT [Wolf *et al.*, 1984].

The heart of the ATC was contained in Article 2, which established the time frame for the 10-year integration cycle by which quotas will be removed on 51 percent of textile and apparel products, listed in the Annex of the ATC, maintaining for the tenth year the integration of the balance — 49 percent.[14] Products that were not integrated into the WTO during this 10-year phase out period, and were subject to quotas, were to have annual quota growth rates accelerated.[15] After the 10-year phase-out period is completed there were no planned extensions of the ATC.[16]

In order to take into account the concerns of the developed country importers, Article 6 of the ATC provided a "transitional

---

[12] ATC, Art. 2.

[13] ATC, Art. 2. The ATC explicitly provided that there shall be no extension of the agreement. ATC, Art. 9.

[14] ATC, Art. 2, ¶¶ 6, 8.

[15] ATC, Art. 2, ¶¶ 13, 14 and 18. In the first 36 months from date of entry of the WTO, the increase in quota growth rate was set at 0.16 percent. Thereafter, it would be 0.25 percent from the 37th month till the end of the 84 month, and 0.27 percent for the balance of the period.

[16] ATC, Art. 9.

safeguard" mechanism which allowed a country to take action to protect its textile and apparel industries if there was "serious damage" or the "actual threat thereof," due to increased imports. This provision of the ATC was intended to be used "as sparingly as possible," and was not to be applied if the "particular product" to be restrained was already under restraint or if it fell in the integration procedure prescribed by the ATC.[17]

Based on the US experience with requests for safeguards, there appeared to be no bright line standard for the complaints of either "serious damage" or "actual threat thereof." The evidence presented in the cases specified a whole list of factors, such as changes in domestic output of the competing good, productivity, utilization of capacity, inventories, market share, exports, wages, employment, domestic prices, profits and investment. According to Article 6, in order to invoke a transitional safeguard, the importing country must show that the damage to the industry was caused by "increased quantities in total imports of that product." The latter has to be targeted to a specific exporter. Damage due to changes in

---

[17]ATC, Art. 6, ¶ 1. The ATC called for transitional quotas to be applied on a Country-by-Country basis, id. Art. 7, ¶ 4. Furthermore, the ATC allowed a safeguard to be placed on unfairly traded goods without requiring compensation to the restricted party, which was the practice under the earlier GATT rules. Unfairly traded goods are those tainted by dumping, government subsidies, or sellers' evasion of legitimate regulations regarding the environment, fair competition, intellectual property protection, etc. Additionally, the TMB had primary responsibility of supervising transitional safeguard measures, ATC, Art. 8, ¶ 1. In the United States, the Committee for the Implementation of Textile Agreements (CITA), a committee with members from the Departments of Labor, Commerce, Treasury and State, as well as the Office of the U.S. Trade Representative (USTR), was responsible for making the United States' initial determination of serious damage. A serious damage determination by CITA leads to a notification or "call" on the relevant country, which informs the country that rising imports are damaging the U.S. industry and that the United States intends to put import restraints in place. When a country is called on a particular category, the United States presents a "Statement of Serious Damage" which describes the economic facts underlying the serious damage determination. Id. Art. 6, ¶¶ 1 and 4.

technology or consumer preference was not actionable under this provision.[18]

In the spirit of enlarging the market for both new entrants and the least developed countries, Article 6 encouraged the differential treatment for this latter group when an importing country applied the transitional safeguards. Similarly, exporters whose total exports were small relative to the total volume of exports of others, and who accounted for only a small percentage of total imports of that product into a particular importing market, were afforded "deferential and more favorable" treatment in the application of safeguards. In addition, developing country exporters of wool products were provided deference and "special consideration" when establishing quota levels, growth rates and flexibility, if they could demonstrate that their economy was (1) dependent on the wool sector; (2) textile and clothing exports consisted almost exclusively of wool products and (3) exports to the importing market were small relative to total imports in that market. Safeguards were not to be used at all on exports of "handloom fabrics of the cottage industry . . . or traditional folklore handicraft," products traded in "commercially significant quantities prior to 1982," and products made of pure silk.[19]

Apart from the special provisions listed, importing countries had significant control over the use of safeguards in that they could choose when to issue a "call" and could apply a unilateral restraint if consultations did not produce an agreement. The process usually began when an importing country requesting a safeguard

---

[18]See Art. 6, ¶¶ 1–4. The ATC specified that a safeguard may be applied when "it is demonstrated" that serious damage exists and is "demonstrably" caused by imports. Furthermore, the evidence to be provided must be such as to show that there exists a "sharp and substantial increase in imports, actual or imminent" from a given exporter and "the level of imports as compared with imports from other sources, market share, and import and domestic prices at a comparable stage of commercial transaction." An "imminent increase" must be measurable and based on more than mere allegation, conjecture, or possibility.

[19]See Art. 6, ¶¶ 6(a)–6(d). The ATC does not specify what constitutes "significantly more favorable" treatment, nor does it define developing or least developed nations. Likewise, the ATC does not specify what it means by "commercially significant."

determination presented its case to both the exporting country and the TMB. If the consultations produced an agreement on a restraint level, then a quota was fixed at not less than the level of imports over the 12 months ending two months before the notification was issued. If there was no agreement within 60 days of the request for consultations, the initiating country had the right to apply a unilateral restraint. Safeguard measures could be maintained for up to three years without extension, or until the product was integrated into the WTO. If the restraint was in place for more than one year, it had to be increased at an annual rate of at least 6 percent, unless otherwise justified to the TMB.[20]

The unilateral power of developed country importers to set safeguard quotas was designed to be checked by the TMB. It is the TMB which was empowered to review all safeguard actions. Even in cases where both sides concluded a bilateral agreement, the TMB was empowered to determine whether the agreement was justified by the ATC. In cases where a safeguard was unilaterally imposed, the TMB was to "promptly conduct an examination of the matter" and "make appropriate recommendations...within 30 days." If one or both of the parties did not accept the recommendations, the parties involved were to provide the TMB with its reasons within one month of receiving the recommendations. Following consideration of the reasons given, the TMB was to issue further recommendations. If the matter remained unresolved, either party had the right to refer it to the Dispute Settlement Body (DSB) and invoke Article XXIII of GATT and the Dispute Settlement Understanding (DSU).[21]

The US was the primary country to invoke the ATC safeguard clause. The United States issued 25 calls on WTO Members during the first 20 months of the ATC. The TMB did not disturb any bilateral settlements[22] of the six cases decided by the TMB. It decided

---

[20]See Art. 6, ¶¶ 7, 8, 10–13.
[21]See Art. 6, ¶¶ 9–11, and Art. 8 ¶¶ 5–7, 9 and 10.
[22]See World Trade Organization: *Hearing Before the House Ways and Means Comm.*, 104th Cong., 2d Sess. (1996). Between 9 and 10 cases were referred to the TMB.

in favor of the exporting country in two cases; in favor of the United States in one case; and reached no decision in three other cases.

5.3. Review of Transition TMB Decisions: The First 20 Months

A review of the six "calls" brought to the TMB during this transition period demonstrates the degree to which there was no agreed standard for either "series damage" or the "actual threat thereof." While it was understandable that an exit strategy for the MFA needed to provide protection to the vested interest groups in the developed markets, transparency would have dictated that a clear standard would be developed. In order to ensure predictability in the trading system, the TMB, in its decision process, should have developed an understanding of a "bright-line" rule which exporters could rely on. The cases briefly reviewed here demonstrate that the TMB was far from this goal.

5.3.1. *Category 352/652 (Cotton and Man-made Fiber Underwear)*

The U.S. called five WTO countries on "Underwear" exports: the Dominican Republic, Costa Rica, Honduras, Thailand and Turkey.[23] Bilateral agreements were reached with the Dominican Republic and Turkey. The safeguard action against Thailand was withdrawn.

The evidence provided by the US to support its claim of "serious damage" to the U.S. domestic-underwear industry was based on the following factors: (1) a decline in domestic production of 3.8 percent in 1993 and 3.5 percent in the first nine months of 1994; (2) the domestic producers' share of the domestic market declined from 73 percent in 1992 to 65 percent in 1994; (3) an increase in underwear imports into the United States between calendar year 1992 and 1994 by 48.7 percent; (4) a decline in domestic employment, during the same period, by 2,321 jobs, or approximately 5 percent of

---

[23]CITA, Statement of Serious Damage: Category 352/652 (Cotton and Manmade Fiber Underwear) (1995), available at the US Department of Commerce, Trade Reference Room.

category jobs and (5) an increase in imported goods as a percentage of total domestic production from 37 percent in 1992 to 54 percent by September 1994.

At the country level, the US argued that Costa Rica accounted for 15 percent of total underwear exports in 1994 and experienced a 61 percent increase in exports between 1992 and 1994. Honduras represented 6.7 percent of U.S. imports in 1994, and saw a 182 percent increase in exports between 1992 and 1994.

The TMB formally reviewed the unilateral quotas imposed by the U.S. against Costa Rica and Honduras. It found that neither country's underwear was causing serious damage to the U.S. industry; however, the TMB could not reach a consensus on whether the imports constituted a "threat of serious damage." Consequently, the TMB recommended that the parties resume consultations. Barring a TMB recommendation of a rescission of the safeguard, the quota remained in place during additional consultations. The dispute with Honduras was eventually settled in an agreement that also involved nightwear and women's and girls' wool coats.

Despite consultations advised by the TMB, the U.S. and Costa Rica failed to reach an agreement. Upon examination of reports from the two countries, the TMB affirmed its earlier findings. Costa Rica requested additional consultations under Article XXIII of the GATT and Article 4 of the WTO DSU. No agreement was reached, and on February 22, 1996, Costa Rica requested panel review under the DSU. In November of 1996, the DSB panel found that the United States had not demonstrated the existence of "serious damage."

5.3.2. *Category 351/651 (Cotton and Man-made Fiber Pajamas and Other Nightwear)*

The U.S. called four countries — Costa Rica, El Salvador, Honduras, and Jamaica — on "Cotton and Man-made Fiber Pajamas and Other Nightwear" imports.[24] Bilateral agreements were reached with

---

[24]CITA, Statement of Serious Damage: Category 351/651 Updated to Include Costa Rica (Cotton and Man-made Fiber Pajamas and Other Nightwear), (June 1995), on file in the US Department of Commerce, Trade Reference Room.

Jamaica and El Salvador. Unilateral limits were imposed on Costa Rica, but were later rescinded. Unilateral limits were imposed on Honduras, and the TMB conducted a formal review of the Honduran quota.

The U.S. alleged "serious damage" based on a 14.1 percent decrease in domestic manufacturers market share and a corresponding 10.7 percent decrease in U.S. production between 1992 and 1994. During this time period, the US experienced a loss of 807 jobs in the nightwear industry, or 5.4 percent of industry jobs. The US argued that a 22 percent increase in total category imports during that period was sufficient to cause a decline in domestic industry output. According to the CITA report, imports as a percentage of domestic production in these categories rose from 80 percent in 1992 to 110 percent in the first nine months of 1994. Honduran exports increased by 71 percent in 1994 and expanded by 722 percent between 1992 and 1994. What CITA ignored in its allegations, is that this expansion in trade originated from a very small supplier. In the 12-month period ending in March 1995, it accounted for only 1.5 percent of U.S. nightwear imports.

The TMB found that "Nightwear" imports from Honduras were not causing "serious damage" to the U.S. industry and that there was not a "threat of such damage." The TMB accordingly recommended that the U.S. rescind the unilateral quotas it had imposed. The U.S. ultimately rescinded the safeguard on Honduran "Nightwear" in an agreement that also covered outstanding disputes over underwear and women's and girls' wool coats.

5.3.3. *Category 434 (Men's and Boy's Wool Coats Other Than Suit Type)*

The U.S. called two countries — Brazil and India — in "Men's Coats."[25] The US imposed a unilateral safeguard on India's products in this category, alleging "serious damage" to its domestic industry.

---

[25]CITA, Statement of Serious Damage: Category 434 (Men's and Boy's Wool Coats Other Than Suit Type) (1995), on file in the US Department of Commerce, Trade Reference Room.

The U.S. position was that a 4.2 percent decline in production and a 14.3 percent decline in market share in this category, during the nine-month period ending September 1994, constituted "serious damage." Between 1993 and 1994, 275 jobs — 4.8 percent of total category jobs — were lost. The causality between additional imports and domestic industry damage was never established. However, the US argued that an increase in total category imports by 40.2 percent in the year ending January 1995 was the primary factor for the domestic industry's difficulties. Imported items as a percentage of domestic production increased from 85 percent in 1992 to 111 percent during the nine-month period ending September 1994. Imports from India rose by 105 percent and accounted for 24 percent of total U.S. imports in the year ending January 1995. In both 1993 and 1994, India was the leading exporter of coats to the U.S. The TMB found no serious damage or threat thereof and recommended that the US rescind its safeguard.[26]

5.3.4. *Category 435 (Women's and Girl's Wool Coats)*

In Women's Coats, the U.S. called two countries — India and Honduras.[27] Barring a bilateral agreement the US imposed a unilateral quota against India. The U.S. alleged that decline in domestic production of 1.0 percent during the nine-month period ending September 1994 and 1.8 percent during the 12-month period ending September 1994 was due to "serious damage." Furthermore, the U.S. producers' market share declined by 6.8 percent in the first nine months of 1994 and was down by 4.4 percent for the 12-month period ending September 1994. According to the US argument, the causality between imports and the domestic market was reflected in the fact that imports rose by 9 percent during the year ending January 1995

---

[26]Notices, Cancellation of a Limit on Certain Wool Textile Products Produced or Manufactured in India, 60 Fed. Reg. 56,985 (Comm. for the Implementation of Textile Agreements 1996).

[27]CITA, Statement of Serious Damage: Category 435 (Women's and Girl's Wool Coats) (April 1995), on file in the US Department of Commerce, Trade Reference Room.

and captured 59 percent of the U.S. market. During this period, Indian exports surged by 402 percent to capture 3.1 percent of the US market.

Although the TMB found that there was no "serious damage," it could not reach a consensus on whether there was a "threat of serious damage." Since the TMB did not recommend rescission of the safeguard, it remained in place. India requested that a WTO trade-dispute panel be set up to hear this matter, as well as a dispute regarding woven wool shirts and blouses. In March of 1996, the United States turned down India's request for dispute panels. However, pursuant to the terms of the WTO's dispute-settlement procedures the DSB agreed to set up dispute panels at its next meeting in April 1996. Subsequently, the US withdrew the safeguard on "Women's and Girls' Wool Coats," leaving only the dispute over "Woven Wool Shirts and Blouses" (summarized below), a matter in which the TMB unanimously agreed there was a threat of serious damage, to be heard by a dispute panel.

5.3.5. *Category 440 (Woven Wool Shirts and Blouses)*

The U.S. called two countries — India and Hong Kong — on imports of "Woven Blouses."[28] No bilateral agreements were reached and the TMB heard cases from both countries. The Hong Kong case was resolved in favor of Hong Kong. The TMB determined that, since the Hong Kong products were subject to a group limit, the US could not apply a specific limit to the category.

In its allegations, the U.S. argued that "serious damage" to its domestic industry was evidenced by a decline of 7.58 percent during the nine-month period ending September 1994 and 12.5 percent for the 12-month period ending September 1994. During these periods, the U.S. manufacturers' market share declined by 34.4 percent and 36.1 percent respectively. In 1994, a total of 2,125 jobs were lost, representing 6.2 percent of all category jobs. The US argued that

---

[28]CITA, Statement of Serious Damage: Category 440 (Woven Wool Shirts and Blouses) (April 1995), on file in the US Department of Commerce, Trade Reference Room.

the causality between domestic impact and imports was based on the 94 percent increase in total imports in the year ending January 1995. Imports held 60.1 percent of the domestic market in the nine-month period ending September 1994. Imports from India expanded by 414 percent and accounted for 54 percent of total imports during the year ending January 1995.

The U.S. applied a quota on the Indian goods, and the TMB, after reviewing the case determined that a "threat of serious damage" existed. India asked the TMB to reconsider its decision, and in December of 1995, the TMB affirmed its earlier findings. India sought the establishment of a dispute-settlement panel. However, it was blocked by the US in March 1996. Nonetheless, the DSB, at its meeting the following month, automatically agreed to establish the panel. To date, the panel has not issued a report on the matter.

The TMB decisions summarized above could not find a case of "serious damage." Consequently, it was not clear where the trigger existed for these determinations. Only in the case of "Woven Blouses" did the TMB find an "actual threat of serious damage." It was in this case that the U.S. argued that, based on the decline in U.S. production of 12.5 percent, a decline in market share to 36.1 percent, and a loss of 6.2 percent of those employed in this category within the most recent 12-month period, there was "serious damage." Furthermore, the U.S. argued that total imports rose by 95.8 percent and well exceeded the amount of domestic production for the most recent 12 months. India, the largest exporter of these goods, increased its exports by 414 percent. A finding of "serious damage," given these results, would require a more dramatic decline in domestic production, a large increase in imports and a significant job loss, or some equivalent combination of economic facts. Notwithstanding these factors, the TMB did not calculate the marginal impact of additional imports on the domestic industry as part of its impact analysis.

It is obvious from these cases that the TMB had to take the lead to define the "serious damage" standard by providing reasoned opinions for its decisions. Such a standard would have created a predictor of future TMB decisions. The opinions should have stated the significant facts as the TMB found them, set forth the applicable legal principles, and explained why those facts did or did not indicate "serious damage" or "a threat thereof." Increased certainty and transparency would have promoted more efficient decision-making and reduced the temptation for discretionary safeguard measures.

In addition to providing reasoned opinions for its decisions, the TMB hearings should have been open to interested persons, and the final briefs of both parties should have been made available to the public. Making these documents publicly available would not only lead to a public review, but would also minimize the conflicting political influences on decision-making. Scrutiny and outside criticism would have been good for the decision-making process by the TMB.

5.4. The ACT and the PRC

The ATC, as noted above, was primarily designed to eliminate the MFA quotas system by the year 2005 and to integrate textiles and apparel trade into the WTO regime. The governing paradigm was that, immediately after the removal of the MFA quota system, PRC textile and apparel exports would be uncontrollable and grow exponentially. The U.S. was determined to control PRC exports. The U.S. total textile and apparel imports from the PRC increased from 18.3 million square meter equivalents (SMEs) in 1995 to 22.9 million SMEs in 1997. The single largest quota-constrained country remained the PRC, whose 1997 imports represented 9 percent of all MFA fibers, 8 percent of all apparel imports and 10 percent of all non-apparel imports. The combined 1997 imports from the PRC, Hong Kong, Taiwan and Korea represented 21.7 percent of total MFA fiber imports, 23 percent of all apparel imports, and 20.6 percent of all non-apparel imports fibers.

The U.S. was determined to use its power under the ATC to force a substitution of the U.S. imports of textiles and apparel from the PRC, in favor of Mexico, Canada and the Caribbean. In 1997, imports from Mexico represented 13.3 percent of all MFA fibers, 13.7 percent of all apparel imports and 12.9 percent of all non-apparel imports. While total exports of textile and apparel products increased by an average of 8.4 percent, Mexican exports increased by 32.1 percent. Similarly, imports from the Caribbean represented 13 percent of all MFA fibers, 25 percent of all apparel imports and only 1 percent of all non-apparel imports. In 1997, imports from Canada represented 9 percent of all MFA fibers, 1.6 percent of all apparel imports and 16.4 percent of all non-apparel imports.

When the PRC acceded to the WTO, they had to sign a separate bilateral "Memorandum of Understanding (MOU)." This MOU assured the U.S. of a unique bilateral consultation mechanism to remain in effect for four additional years beyond the end of quotas for the rest of the WTO countries (through December 31, 2008).[29] These more extensive "safeguard" measures between the U.S. and the PRC provided the U.S. with rights to re-impose quotas under specified circumstances.[30]

The first PRC category in 2003 to have restraints returned to it was Category 222 — Knit Fabric. The United States established at 12-month limit on PRC-origin knit fabric not to exceed 9,664,477 kilograms. The reasons cited in this case became the benchmark

---

[29]The Memorandum of Understanding regarding PRC's accession to the WTO was signed on February 1, 1997. Listed under paragraph 242 of the Report of the Working Party on the Accession of China to the World Trade Organization (Accession Agreement), the United States (and any other WTO member country) is offered the right to institute a safeguard measure on textiles and apparel of Chinese origin that, due to a market disruptions, are threatening to impede the orderly development of trade. Thereafter in the Memorandum of Understanding Between The Governments Of The United States of America and The People's Republic Of China Concerning Trade in Textile and Apparel Products [2005], the PRC agreed to hold its shipments to a level no greater than 7.5 percent (6 percent for wool categories) above the amount entered during the first 12 months of the most recent 14 months preceding the request for consultations.

[30]This safeguard mechanism allowed the U.S. to seek to extend quotas with the PRC for specific goods where the elimination of such restrictions would result in "...market disruption, threatening to impede the orderly development of trade between the two countries." USITC [1999].

for all subsequent cases that came before the Court of International Trade (CIT). The elements that the U.S. showed were as follows:

(a) The U.S. imports from the PRC were increasing in absolute terms;
(b) The U.S. imports from the PRC were increasing rapidly relative to other imports;
(c) The PRC average unit values were well below values from other countries;
(d) The U.S. imports from the PRC were likely to increase greatly and that
(e) The U.S.-knit fabric industry was vulnerable to any increase in imports.

The cases brought against the PRC in the period 2004 to the end of 2008 used the same logic.

5.5.   Estimating the Impact of Quota Removal: Methodological Considerations

How will the volume and composition of PRC, Indian and Vietnamese textile and apparel exports to the United States change as a result of complete market liberalization, post-MFA and post-ACT? The conventional wisdom was that the PRC would dominate the market and the U.S. would litigate under the guise of market disruption. The OECD [2004] predicted that the PRC would increase its share of the U.S. textile market from 11 percent to 18 percent after quotas were eliminated, and would boost its apparel market share from 16 percent to 50 percent. The predictions for India and Vietnam were not as upbeat. In order to get a reasonably accurate estimate of the impact of complete removal of the quota restrictions in this industry, one must begin by estimating the impact of the distortions in terms of tariff equivalents.

The textile and apparel trade environment, as it evolved over the past 50 years, is so complex that its modeling requires the separation of the country-specific import market, at a minimum, into at least three markets. The first market, composed of less developed country (LDC) suppliers, constitutes those suppliers under bilateral restraint. The second market, composed predominantly of developed country suppliers, constitutes those suppliers free of bilateral constraint. The third market is the domestic producers who are affected by the activities of both constrained and unconstrained suppliers.

In order to determine the price effects attributable to these bilateral constraints, one needs to model both constrained and unconstrained markets, such that for every actual price-quantity combination observed in the presence of these quotas, a non-quota bound price-quantity combination can be simulated. A likely scenario for the three markets would be as follows: a shortage generated in the quota-bound market, holding all other things equal, creates an increase in both non-quota bound imports as well as domestic output. The supply response from the unconstrained suppliers is tempered, however, by the possibility that a too-enthusiastic response could make them subject to quota limits in the future. The domestic supply response also may be tempered by expectations of greater future foreign competition from unconstrained suppliers.

Given the nature of this market, ordinary least squares (OLS) regression of import demand on prices and other explanatory variables is inappropriate. Estimation of the demand and supply responses in the unconstrained market must account for changes in prices in the constrained market. In the constrained market, the supply curve is truncated, and the import quantities demanded (M^D) and quota upper bound (S^Q) are not necessarily equal to each other; they are related to actual observed imports (M^A) by the equation:

$$M^A = \min(M^D, S^Q). \tag{5.1}$$

The price in this controlled market will affect the equilibrium in both the uncontrolled import market and the domestic market for comparable domestic product. Adjustments in the quota bound imports as these countries borrow across categories and time are already incorporated in the quota upper bound (S^Q).

A complete disequilibrium model applicable to the textile and apparel industry would consist of the following set of structural equations:

Import demand:

$$M_t^D = \alpha_1 P_1 + \alpha_2 X_t + \mu_{1t}. \tag{5.2}$$

Import supply:

$$M_t^S = Q_t^S \tag{5.3}$$

Or

$$M_t^S = \beta_1 P_t + \beta_2 Y_t + \mu_{2t}. \tag{5.4}$$

A Walrasian price adjustment mechanism[31]:

$$P_t = P_{t-1} + \gamma_1 \left(M_t^D - S_t^Q \right) + \gamma_2 X_t + \mu_{3t}. \tag{5.5}$$

Market clearing mechanism:

$$M_t^A = \min \left(M_t^D, S_t^Q \right), \tag{5.6}$$

where

M_t^A = observed import transaction at time t,

M_t^D = unobserved import demand at time t,

M_t^S = quantity of imports supplied at time t,

S_t^Q = quantity of imports constrained due to bilateral agreement,

P_t = set of prices,

X_t and Y_t = set of exogenous explanatory variables and

α_i = demand elasticities,

β_i = supply elasticities,

γ_i = adjustment coefficients and

t = time.

---

[31] In effect, this assumption claims that, *ceteris paribus*, prices change in proportion to the current excess demand.

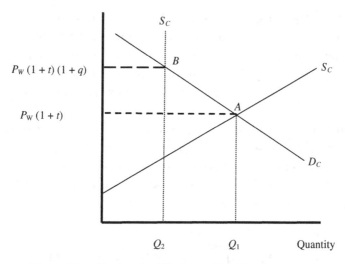

Figure 5.1   Market Equilibrium with a Binding Quota

The controlled markets for a specific T&A category can be seen in Figure 5.1. The introduction of a quota limit turns the supply curve to a perfectly inelastic portion. The quota-free equilibrium occurs at point A, where the import price is tariff inclusive. While S^Q is observed, M and the true P_t (quota inclusive) are unobserved. Since P_t is not independent of μ_{1t}, it is not appropriate to estimate α by substituting M of Equation (5.2) and S^Q into Equation (5.5) and applying the Tobit method.[32] Furthermore, since the true M is not observed we cannot estimate γ of Equation (5.5) directly. Equilibrium at point B is after the imposition of the quota. The price gap is the effective quota rent that will be removed with the demise of the MFA. Tariffs are unaffected by the new trading regime. With all other things held constant, an elimination of the quotas on textile and apparel imports from the PRC, India and Vietnam would cause the U.S. imports to increase as the U.S. buyers substitute the now lower-priced uncontrolled foreign goods for the U.S. substitutes (trade creation) or the U.S. imports from other countries (trade diversion). The total expansion of the U.S. imports

---

[32]See Maddala [1983a and 1983b].

from either the PRC or India or Vietnam would be the sum of the trade creation and trade diversion effects. Since our concern, on the demand side, lies in determining changes in Indian or PRC or Vietnam dollar earnings resulting from expanded exports to the United States, total trade expansion (or gross trade creation) will be measured.

Equations (5.2)–(5.5) and condition (5.6) can be utilized to define the conditional joint-density functions $g_1(\cdot)$ of M and P_t, given that M is on the demand function and $g_2(\cdot)$ when it is on the supply function. The unconditional joint density of the observed endogenous variables M and P_t is given by:

$$f(M, P_t \mid X_t, Y_t) = \int_{M^A}^{\infty} g\big(M_t^A, M_t^S, P_t \mid X_t, Y_t\big) dM_t^S$$

$$+ \int_{M^A}^{\infty} g\big(M_t^A, M_t^D, P_t \mid X_t, Y_t\big) dM_t^D. \quad (5.7)$$

The maximum likelihood (ML) estimates of the parameters (α and β) and the variance-covariance matrix Σ are obtained by maximizing the log likelihood function corresponding to the above joint density function. This procedure is, however, a full information ML procedure which is inappropriate in the MFA case where M is not directly observed.

In order to measure the difference between the unobserved equilibrium price with no quotas and the observed transaction price with quotas, the reduced form of M must be substituted into Equation (5.6) where consistent estimators of the reduced form parameters can be obtained by Tobit analysis. Predictions of the unobserved variable M^{33} can then be substituted into Equation (5.5) to directly estimate γ along with the predicted prices without the

---

[33] As Hartley [1976] points out, these predicted values are only for the cases where we are on the vertical segment of the supply curve. In all other cases we are already on the demand curve.

quota. It is this price differential which measures the value of the MFA quotas.[34]

The structural model outlined in Equations (5.1) through (5.6) is estimated as follows:

5.5.1. *Import Demand*

The import demand equation for the two markets (controlled and uncontrolled) is specified as a function of its specific market price, the price of a similar product from the alternative market, the domestic price of a competing good, and a real activity variable, or

$$M_{ij,t}^D = \alpha_0 + \alpha_1 P_{Cj,t} + \alpha_2 P_{Uj,t} + \alpha_3 P_{Dj,t} + \alpha_4 E_t + \mu, \qquad (5.8)$$

where M = import demand for commodity j from i (controlled or uncontrolled suppliers) at time period t; $P_{Cj,t}$ = import price from controlled market at time period t; $P_{Uj,t}$ = import price from uncontrolled market at time period t; $P_{Dj,t}$ = domestic price of the competing product at time t; E_t = real activity variable at time t and μ = random error term. Since there are two differentiated regions, there are two import demand equations that depend on all three prices over time.

This Armington [1969] specification of the import demand equations requires the following set of assumptions. First, it is necessary for these import demand equations to be weakly separable between textile and apparel products and other products which enter the consumer's utility function. In effect, each of our products is treated as a distinct good with imperfect substitutes differentiated by country of origin. Second, Armington's two-step process assumes that the marginal rate of substitution for any two products (differentiated by source) are independent of the quantities demanded of third goods entering the consumer's utility function. This assumption of a zero income compensated cross price effect between textile and apparel

---

[34]The tariff equivalent of the MFA quotas can be measured inclusive or exclusive of the existing tariffs. In this paper we estimate the non-tariff inclusive quota differential. In this case, if the tariff equivalent of the MFA quotas is higher then the tariff, the MFA quota dominates and the tariff is redundant.

goods and third goods. It means that a change in the price of this third good will have an impact on the demand for textile and apparel imports, but only when it has an impact on real expenditures. The restrictive nature of this assumption, if violated, may result in a misspecification bias in our estimated import demand equations.[35]

While Armington's assumptions may be reasonable for textile and apparel end products, they may present a problem for some of the intermediate textile products. In the case of intermediate imports, such as yarn and fabric, the import demand equations noted by Equation (5.8) are, in fact, derived demand functions. The assumption of independence between the marginal rates of substitution of different classes of intermediate inputs, such as man-made fibers for cotton or vegetable fibers for both may represent a problem. In these latter cases, the import demand equations will include the prices of all possible substitutes. Omission of these prices clearly will cause the import demand equations for the intermediate textile imports to be misspecified.

5.5.2. *Import Supply*

The specification for the textile and apparel import supply functions must take into account that there are two markets, one controlled and the other uncontrolled. These markets are related in that the price of the controlled product affects the equilibrium price in the uncontrolled market. This uncontrolled market would be characterized by a demand curve given by Equation (5.8) and by the following supply and equilibrium conditions:

$$M_{ij,t}^S = \beta_0 + \beta_1 P_{Uj,t} + \varepsilon, \tag{5.9}$$

$$M_{ij,t}^D = M_{ij,t}^S, \tag{5.10}$$

where ε is normally distributed.

It is assumed that the supply equation for uncontrolled countries (Equation (5.9)) is a function of its product and time specific export

---

[35]For a discussion of the theoretical implications of the weak separability assumption see Winters [1984].

price. The solution of an equilibrium price and quantity, however, must take into account the price of substitutes from domestic and controlled suppliers.

The distortionary impact of the quota system is captured in Equations (5.3) and (5.5). The reduced form estimating equations consist of import demand Equation (5.8) and supply Equations (5.11) and/or (5.12). The market clearing condition noted earlier as Equation (5.10) can be replaced by conditions (5.13) or (5.14). The added equations for the controlled country scenario are:

$$M_{ij,t}^S = \lambda_0 + \lambda_1 P_{Cj,t} + \nu, \tag{5.11}$$

$$M_{ij,t}^S = S_{ij,t}^Q, \tag{5.12}$$

$$M_{ij,t}^A = M_{ij,t}^D = M_{ij,t}^S \quad \text{if } M_{ij,t}^A < S_{ij,t}^Q, \tag{5.13}$$

$$M_{ij,t}^A = S_{ij,t}^Q \quad \text{if otherwise,} \tag{5.14}$$

where S is the import quota limit.

As noted above, the controlled market has two possible sets of price and quantity equilibria. In the first case,

$$M_{ij,t}^A < S_{ij,t}^Q,$$

we have a simultaneous equation model where both the quantity transacted and the price are observed endogenous variables. In this case, the price and quantity of imports is determined by the intersection of import demand and supply.

The second case,

$$M_{ij,t}^A = S_{ij,t}^Q$$

yields an unobserved excess demand situation where the controlled quantity S is an exogenous variable. In this case, the price is an element of the supply constraint, not the demand curve.

The market effects of the MFA can be analyzed by treating the problem as a standard disequilibrium Tobit model.[36] The simplest

---

[36] See Maddala and Nelson [1974], Hartley [1976] and Maddala [1983a].

disequilibrium model, noted above as Equations (5.13) and (5.14), can be restated as Equation (5.6):

$$M_t^A = \min \left(M_t^D, S_t^Q \right)$$

implying that the actual quantity of imports sold is the minimum of supply and demand. This latter disequilibrium term can be substituted for Equations (5.13) and (5.14) above. Furthermore, this disequilibrium caused by the MFA creates an inequality between the actual observed price and the *ex-ante* market equilibrium price. Thus, a Walrasian price-adjustment equation suggested in Fair and Jaffee [1972] can to be added. The price-adjustment equation can take the following simple form:

$$\phi P_{Cj,t} = \phi_0 \left(D_{ij,t}^M - S_{ij,t}^M \right) + \phi_1 P_{Uj,t} + \phi_2 P_{Dj,t} + \phi_3 E_t + \varepsilon,$$

where

$$\phi P_{Cj,t} = P_{Cj,t} - P_{Cj,t-1}.$$

The two-stage estimation procedure suggested by Maddala [1983a] and outlined above requires that Equation (5.8) be estimated in its constrained form, as:

$$Z_{ij,t}^* = \alpha_0 S_{ij,t}^Q + \alpha_1 P_{Cj,t} + \alpha_2 P_{Uj,t} + \alpha_3 P_{Dj,t} + \alpha_4 E_t + \nu, \quad (5.15)$$

where

$$Z_{ij,t}^* = \left(M_{ij,t}^D - S_{ij,t}^Q \right)$$

and[37]

$$Z_{ij,t} = M_{ij,t}^D - S_{ij,t}^Q \ (= Z_{ij,t}^*) \quad \text{if } Z_{ij,t}^* < 0,$$
$$Z_{ij,t} = 0 \quad \text{if otherwise.}$$

The estimated values of $P_{Cj,t}$ are then substituted into the demand and supply equations in both controlled and uncontrolled

---

[37]Note that Z is the truncated variable so that $Z_{ij,t} = Z$ if $Z < 0$ and $= 0$ otherwise.

markets in order to estimate the relative price and income elasticities absent the quota distortions. The result of this empirical model consists of a set of *ad valorem* tariff equivalents of the MFA quotas, along with a consistent set of unconstrained demand elasticities for both controlled and uncontrolled markets. All are estimated at the textile category level used to monitor the U.S. textile program.

Once the tariff equivalents of the MFA quota system are estimated we move to the second step of estimating the changes in demand as these quota margins are removed. The methodology applied is best described by the following system of demand and supply equations for the both controlled and uncontrolled countries and the United States. Let the United States be denoted as country i and the three beneficiary countries as j, where $j = 1, 2, 3$. Then a series of equations for trade in k three-digit categories $(k = 1, \ldots, K)$ can be described as follows:

$$M_{ik} = f(P_{ik}^D), \tag{5.16}$$

$$P_{ik}^D = t_{ik}\delta_{ik}P_{jk}^W, \tag{5.17}$$

$$X_{jk} = g(P_{jk}^W), \tag{5.18}$$

$$M_{ik} = X_{jk}, \tag{5.19}$$

$$R_{jk} = P_{jk}^W X_{jk}, \tag{5.20}$$

where M is the quantity of the U.S. imports, X is the quantity of beneficiary country exports, P_{ik}^D is the domestic U.S. price for commodity k, P_{jk}^W is the world market price assumed to be the price at which India, Vietnam and the PRC export to the United States, t is one plus the *ad valorem* MFN duty rate (t) applied by the United States, δ is one plus the *ad valorem* tariff equivalent of the quota estimated by the price gap in Figure 5.1, and R is the beneficiary country's export revenue on products exported into the United States.

Totally differentiating Equations (5.16) through (5.20) and solving for the proportional changes in imports, export prices and revenues yields:

$$\hat{M}_{ik} = \left[\frac{\eta_{ik}}{\frac{1-\eta_{ik}}{e_{ik}}}\right]\hat{\delta}_{ik}, \qquad (5.21)$$

$$\hat{P}_{jk}^{W} = -\left[\frac{\eta_{ik}}{(\eta_{ik} - e_{jk})}\right]\hat{\delta}_{ik}, \qquad (5.22)$$

$$\hat{R}_{jk} = \eta_{ik}\left[\frac{(1 + e_{jk})}{(e_{jk} - \eta_{ik})}\right]\hat{\delta}_{ik}, \qquad (5.23)$$

where η is the relative price elasticity of import demand, e is the export supply elasticity and ^ denotes percent change.

Within this partial equilibrium framework, export flows, import flows and export revenues are each a function of the percentage change in relative prices due to the elimination of quotas and the elasticities of import demand and export supply. From the perspective of India, Vietnam and the PRC, as long as the U.S. import demand is elastic, each country will gain if their products are sufficiently differentiated and their export supply elasticity is infinite. In the event that their supply elasticity was zero, each exporting country suppliers would simply receive the amount of the quota rent as added profit.

In order to derive empirical estimates of the effects of MFA elimination on these two beneficiary country exporters using the model described above, several things would be needed. To determine the responsiveness of the U.S. buyers and Indian and PRC sellers to removal of the quota premiums on goods imported from these countries, reliable estimates of the U.S. import demand and Indian and PRC export supply elasticities would be required. In addition, it would be necessary to make assumptions about the potential price response by Indian and PRC exporters to a change in the U.S. import quota-equivalent duties. If the individual country suppliers perceive the market as being less than competitive, then they may pass through all, some or none of the duty equivalent reduction to the U.S. buyers by maintaining export prices unchanged, raising them by a fraction of the tariff equivalent of the quota elimination, or raising them by the full amount of the quota rent. In sum, an estimate of the total trade expansion will depend on the U.S. import-demand elasticity, the export-supply elasticity and pricing strategy of the two beneficiaries, the magnitude of the change in the U.S. tariffs equivalents of the quota, and the current volume of the U.S. imports from the region.

The relative sensitivity of Equations (5.21)–(5.23) to the estimated demand and supply elasticities employed can be seen from the following scenarios of changes in exporters' revenues that might occur for different magnitudes of the demand and supply elasticities:

	Supply Elasticities (e)				
Demand Elasticity (η)	0	0.5	1	2	∞
-0.5	$-\hat{\delta}$	$-\dfrac{3}{4}\hat{\delta}$	$-\dfrac{2}{3}\hat{\delta}$	$-\dfrac{3}{5}\hat{\delta}$	$-\dfrac{1}{2}\hat{\delta}$
-1	$-\hat{\delta}$	$-\hat{\delta}$	$-\hat{\delta}$	$-\hat{\delta}$	$-\hat{\delta}$
-2	$-\hat{\delta}$	$-\dfrac{6}{5}\hat{\delta}$	$-\dfrac{4}{3}\hat{\delta}$	$-\dfrac{3}{2}\hat{\delta}$	$-2\hat{\delta}$

It should be clear, therefore, that a slight modification in the elasticities will bring about a major change in the estimated results.

5.6. Predicted Estimates of the Post-MFA PRC–India and PRC–Vietnam Competition Outcome

In order to address the post-MFA competition between the PRC and India and the PRC and Vietnam we estimate an import demand equation for each of the three-digit Textile and Apparel categories where each of the PRC competitors share an items under MFA control. Each of the demand equations is specified as a function of its specific relative market price, the relative price of an identical three digital category from the alternative market, the relative rest-of-the world (ROW) uncontrolled market price, and a real activity variable or

$$M_{ij}^k = \alpha_0 + \alpha_1 \frac{P_k^{PRC}}{P_k^{US}} + \alpha_2 \frac{P_k^{V,I}}{P_k^{US}} + \alpha_3 \frac{P_k^{ROW}}{P_k^{US}} + \alpha_4 Y_i + \mu, \quad (5.24)$$

where M_{ij}^k = quantity of the US import demand (i) for commodity (k) from j (PRC, India or Vietnam); P_k^{PRC} = import price from the PRC for commodity k; P_k^V = import price from India or Vietnam for commodity k; P_k^{ROW} = average ROW market price of commodity k; P_k^{US} = domestic price of the competing product; Y = real activity variable; and μ = random error term. This equation is estimated in log form for both the US imports from the PRC and Vietnam.[38]

While Armington's assumptions may be reasonable for textile and apparel end products, they may present a problem for some of the intermediate textile products. In the case of intermediate imports, such as yarn and fabric, the import demand equations noted by Equation (5.24) are, in fact, derived demand functions. The assumption of independence between the marginal rates of substitution of different classes of intermediate inputs, such as man-made fibers for cotton or vegetable fibers for both may represent a problem. In these latter cases, the import demand equations will include the prices of all possible substitutes. Omission of these prices

---

[38]This Armington [1969] specification of the import demand equations requires the following set of assumptions. First, it is necessary for these import demand equations to be weakly separable between textile and apparel products and other products which enter the consumer's utility function. In effect, each of our products is treated as a distinct good with imperfect substitutes differentiated by country of origin. Second, Armington's two-step process assumes that the marginal rate of substitution for any two products (differentiated by source) is independent of the quantities demanded of third goods entering the consumer's utility function. This assumption of a zero income compensated cross price effect between textile and apparel goods and third goods. It means that a change in the price of this third good will have an impact on the demand for textile and apparel imports, but only when it has an impact on real expenditures. The restrictive nature of this assumption, if violated, may result in a misspecification bias in our estimated import demand equations. For a discussion of the theoretical implications of the weak separability assumption, see [Winters, 1984].

clearly will cause the import demand equations for the intermediate textile imports to be misspecified.

Table 5.4 presents the OLS estimates for the U.S. import demand from Vietnam. The overall conclusion that one can draw from these results is that out of a total of 20 three-digit categories where competition is possible, there are only five categories where the cross price elasticity of a change in PRC's prices on US imports from Vietnam is significantly different from zero. In category 635, "Women and Girl MMF Coats," for every 1 percent decrease in the U.S. import prices from Vietnam, imports from the PRC competitor would decline by 3.5 percent. In category 640, "Men and Boys' non-knit MMF Shirts," for every percent decrease in the U.S. import prices from Vietnam, the PRC competitor would decrease its sales by 5.0 percent. A similar decline in sales would occur in category 641, "Women and Girls' not-knit MMF Shirts and Blouses." In category 648, "Women and Girl MMF Slacks, Breeches and Shorts," a 1 percent decline in the U.S. import prices from Vietnam, leads to the PRC competitor to lose 3.0 of sales. In category 651, "MMF Nightwear and Pajamas," a 1 percent decline in prices from Vietnam leads to a decline in PRC sales of 6.5 percent. For every 1 percent decrease in the U.S. import prices from Vietnam, in category 652, "MMF Underwear," sales from the PRC would decline by 4.6 percent. In all of these categories, Vietnam and the PRC proved to be competitors in the U.S. market.

When we re-run the demand equations from the point of view of the U.S. imports from the PRC with Vietnam as the competitor (see Table 5.5), the cross-price elasticity is significant in only two categories. In category 237, "Playsuits and Sunsuits," a decline in US import prices for PRC sourced imports leads to an increase in Vietnam sales by 0.53 percent. In category 347, "Men and Boys' Cotton Trousers and Shorts," a 1 percent decline in the U.S. prices from the PRC, will lead to a 1.76 percent increase in imports from the PRC and 0.716 percent from Vietnam. In both categories we have two categories that are complements rather than substitutes.

Overall, these results confirm the hypothesis found in the industry that PRC and Vietnam had a very limited area for direct

Table 5.4   OLS Estimates of the US Import Demand from the Vietnam with the PRC as the Presumed Competition

(By T&A Category, 1995–2008)

CAT	Description	$\dfrac{P_k^{PRC}}{P_k^{US}}$	$\dfrac{P_k^{V}}{P_k^{US}}$	$\dfrac{P_k^{ROW}}{P_k^{US}}$	Y_i	C	
237	Playsuits, sunsuits, etc.	5.073332	0.7976299	−11.96701	3.116805	−20.05524	Adj R-squared = 0.7506
		5.085089	0.6533758	8.369811	2.438482	12.02279	$F(4,9) = 10.78$
		0.344	0.253	0.187	0.233	0.13	
331	Cotton gloves and mittens	−0.3644664	−4.139699***	−0.757925	−8.375363	36.60786	Adj R-squared = 0.9593
		1.359223	0.8275211	5.291946	7.60178	28.1968	$F(4,9) = 77.68$
		0.795	0.001	0.889	0.299	0.226	
334	Other M/B coats, cotton	2.09271	−1.019121	−14.57472	5.769863	−27.25657	Adj R-squared = 0.7778
		3.25401	0.7291014	18.51931	17.69427	107.4719	$F(4,9) = 12.37$
		0.536	0.196	0.452	0.752	0.805	
335	W/G cotton coats	2.413634	−1.194918	13.60321	39.39014***	−228.8181***	Adj R-squared = 0.8258
		1.914375	0.9390353	10.85738	13.21337	79.012	$F(4,9) = 16.40$
		0.239	0.235	0.242	0.015	0.018	
336	Cotton dresses	−0.714335	−4.07791***	−5.980759	8.855261	−51.82321	Adj R-squared = 0.8850
		1.752876	1.540294	5.668082	6.359675	35.2278	$F(4,9) = 26.01$
		0.693	0.027	0.319	0.197	0.175	

340 M/B Cotton shirts, not-knit	−0.1980501 0.7020926 0.784	1.135281** 0.4060898 0.021	4.130511 3.855533 0.312	3.41098*** 0.8406581 0.003	−11.91945** 4.804672 0.035	Adj R-squared = 0.9420 F(4,9) = 53.82
341 W/G Cotton shirts/blouses, not-knit	3.11852 2.247127 0.199	1.000043 3.866529 0.802	−2.49287 15.16099 0.873	16.38149*** 3.30527 0.001	−90.8595*** 18.39223 0.001	Adj R-squared = 0.8099 F(4,9) = 14.85
342 Cotton skirts	3.002873 3.211092 0.374	0.1833263 1.910101 0.926	−19.07048 23.35357 0.435	11.70097 6.908165 0.125	−71.00574* 33.15593 0.061	Adj R-squared = 0.6740 F(4,9) = 7.72
347 M/B Cotton trousers/breeches/shorts	1.023909 1.479346 0.506	2.960699*** 0.5624377 0.001	−3.730118 6.9008 0.602	5.122446** 1.850163 0.022	−22.07958* 10.58693 0.067	Adj R-squared = 0.9471 F(4,9) = 59.24
348 W/G cotton trousers/slacks/shorts	2.227438 1.673146 0.216	1.13785* 0.5792787 0.081	3.009041 7.103905 0.682	16.92671*** 1.87913 0	−90.55069*** 10.31144 0	Adj R-squared = 0.9029 F(4,9) = 31.24

(*Continued*)

Table 5.4 (*Continued*)

CAT	Description	$\frac{P_k^{PRC}}{P_k^{US}}$	$\frac{P_k^V}{P_k^{US}}$	$\frac{P_k^{ROW}}{P_k^{US}}$	Y_i	C	
635	W/G MMF coats	3.565148***	3.008037***	−17.41815*	12.06539**	−61.87215*	Adj R-squared = 0.9464
		0.9480565	0.6284561	7.903696	5.127145	32.62715	$F(4, 9) = 58.41$
		0.004	0.001	0.055	0.043	0.09	
636	MMF dresses	1.199308	1.915316	0.389792	16.91561***	−94.21578***	Adj R-squared = 0.8925
		0.8183637	1.238126	4.35705	3.529172	21.37214	$F(4, 9) = 27.98$
		0.177	0.156	0.931	0.001	0.002	
638	M/B MMF knit shirts	2.562597	0.9329983	−5.22662	13.52084***	−76.53501***	Adj R-squared = 0.8996
		1.777653	0.7905236	6.439921	2.692183	16.5175	$F(4, 9) = 30.11$
		0.183	0.268	0.438	0.001	0.001	
639	W/G MMF knit shirts/blouses	0.967875	1.813806**	−1.608916	13.64569***	−73.45303***	Adj R-squared = 0.9037
		2.097742	0.7380851	8.799649	1.768048	10.77896	$F(4, 9) = 31.49$
		0.655	0.036	0.859	0	0	
640	M/B not-knit MMF shirts	5.060037*	−0.2488792	−30.98901***	8.321235***	−52.44523***	Adj R-squared = 0.9490
		2.580509	0.9624141	5.89648	2.537981	15.31303	$F(4, 9) = 61.52$
		0.082	0.802	0.001	0.01	0.008	

641 W/G not-knit MMF shirts/blouses	5.429534* 3.028319 0.107	−0.0649266 1.084654 0.954	−8.361039 12.70456 0.527	14.67283 10.27712 0.187	−83.01183 55.68477 0.17	Adj R-squared = 0.8909 F(4, 9) = 27.54
644 W/G MMF suits	−13.61159 12.60742 0.308	−0.1348965 1.28563 0.919	3.243524 47.66163 0.947	8.144428 69.47413 0.909	−56.67573 335.242 0.869	Adj R-squared = 0.2389 F(4, 9) = 2.02
648 W/G MMF slacks/breeches/ shorts	3.058323** 1.246856 0.037	−0.4259334 1.392736 0.767	−16.04271* 8.673729 0.097	13.79055*** 1.446277 0	−79.12143*** 10.64255 0	Adj R-squared = 0.9406 F(4, 9) = 52.44
651 MMF nightwear/ pajamas	6.511342*** 1.612799 0.003	−0.5156593 0.6071717 0.418	−18.65969 11.21052 0.13	11.1278 6.548355 0.123	−70.9572** 31.133 0.049	Adj R-squared = 0.9538 F(4, 9) = 68.03
652 MMF underwear	4.643861** 1.810436 0.03	−0.1177987 0.4560599 0.802	−0.598533 7.601652 0.939	17.29288*** 2.21421 0	−88.89001*** 23.92544 0.005	Adj R-squared = 0.9016 F(4, 9) = 30.79

The results are listed on the first line, followed by the standard errors, followed by the probability that the coefficient is greater than zero.
*Denotes significance at 10 percent; **denotes significance at 5 percent; ***denotes significance at 1 percent. All parameters are estimated in logs.

Table 5.5 OLS Estimates of the US Import Demand from the PRC with Vietnam as the Presumed Competitor

(By T&A Category, 1995–2008)

CAT	Description	$\dfrac{P_k^{PRC}}{P_k^{US}}$	$\dfrac{P_k^{V}}{P_k^{US}}$	$\dfrac{P_k^{ROW}}{P_k^{US}}$	Y_i	C	
237	Playsuits, sunsuits, etc.	1.111307	−0.5353333***	−5.368849***	−4.638792***	30.04953***	Adj R-squared = 0.8474
		1.257695	0.1615995	2.070106	0.6031098	2.973597	$F(4,9) = 19.05$
		0.4	0.009	0.029	0	0	
331	Cotton gloves and mittens	−2.358496***	−0.1162613	3.748393***	3.644298**	−6.790447	Adj R-squared = 0.9769
		0.2463461	0.1499803	0.959147	1.37775	5.110399	$F(4,9) = 138.71$
		0	0.458	0.004	0.027	0.217	
334	Other M/B coats, cotton	−4.2787***	−0.114502	9.288934***	8.083305***	−40.7016**	Adj R-squared = 0.9510
		0.4977118	0.1115185	2.832591	2.706398	16.43819	$F(4,9) = 64.10$
		0	0.331	0.01	0.015	0.035	
335	W/G cotton coats	−3.053732***	0.2335518	5.094066**	7.458172***	−35.87369**	Adj R-squared = 0.9609
		0.3398363	0.1666959	1.927382	2.345613	14.02607	$F(4,9) = 80.81$
		0	0.195	0.027	0.011	0.031	
336	Cotton dresses	−2.256698***	−0.0282577	5.166661***	6.181665***	−27.67101***	Adj R-squared = 0.9641
		0.408429	0.3588965	1.320692	1.481837	8.208259	$F(4,9) = 88.28$
		0	0.939	0.004	0.002	0.008	

340 M/B cotton shirts, not-knit	-1.718825 1.705481 0.34	-0.384921 0.9864491 0.705	3.418412 9.365629 0.724	3.86094* 2.042076 0.091	-15.07503 11.67122 0.229	Adj R-squared = 0.5800 $F_{(4,9)}$ = 5.49
341 W/G cotton shirts/blouses, not-knit	-3.53921*** 0.314471 0	-0.7044008 0.541096 0.225	6.466969*** 2.121683 0.014	3.277312*** 0.4625513 0	-9.979663*** 2.573875 0.004	Adj R-squared = 0.9710 $F_{(4,9)}$ = 109.91
342 Cotton skirts	-2.754313*** 0.3529175 0	0.2043122 0.209931 0.356	-1.482831 2.566692 0.578	3.806012*** 0.7592471 0.001	-16.01031*** 3.644027 0.002	Adj R-squared = 0.9737 $F_{(4,9)}$ = 121.40
347 M/B cotton trousers/ breeches/shorts	-1.76476*** 0.4674805 0.004	-0.7165907*** 0.177733 0.003	-4.196266* 2.180686 0.086	3.056094*** 0.5846603 0.001	-10.88569*** 3.345521 0.01	Adj R-squared = 0.9304 $F_{(4,9)}$ = 44.43
348 W/G cotton trousers/slacks/ shorts	-2.085162*** 0.2475499 0	0.1207164 0.085707 0.193	-3.156543*** 1.051056 0.015	3.174566*** 0.2780261 0	-10.78772*** 1.525627 0	Adj R-squared = 0.9814 $F_{(4,9)}$ = 172.62

(Continued)

Table 5.5   (*Continued*)

CAT	Description	$\frac{P_k^{PRC}}{P_k^{US}}$	$\frac{P_k^V}{P_k^{US}}$	$\frac{P_k^{ROW}}{P_k^{US}}$	Y_i	C	
635	W/G MMF coats	-2.11186***	-0.0817073	3.128647*	3.025585*	-9.589169	Adj R-squared = 0.9746
		0.1952795	0.1294486	1.627994	1.056083	6.7205	$F(4, 9) = 125.78$
		0	0.544	0.087	0.019	0.187	
636	MMF dresses	-1.59173***	-0.0465674	-1.559836***	0.5612214*	5.874571***	Adj R-squared = 0.9953
		0.0717291	0.108521	0.381893	0.3093299	1.873256	$F(4, 9) = 696.46$
		0	0.678	0.003	0.103	0.012	
638	M/B MMF knit shirts	-2.579069***	0.3920608	4.629072	-0.6421592	13.89039*	Adj R-squared = 0.5359
		0.7340955	0.3264528	2.659415	1.111758	6.82103	$F(4, 9) = 4.75$
		0.007	0.26	0.116	0.578	0.072	
639	W/G MMF knit shirts/blouses	-2.187683***	-0.2627354	1.345358	2.566302***	-6.579542	Adj R-squared = 0.8748
		0.6980194	0.2455963	2.928065	0.5883143	3.586676	$F(4, 9) = 23.71$
		0.012	0.313	0.657	0.002	0.1	
640	M/B not-knit MMF shirts	-1.803215***	-0.0022253	0.2345746	-0.1704376	7.631584**	Adj R-squared = 0.6435
		0.4916812	0.183375	1.123495	0.4835781	2.917692	$F(4, 9) = 6.87$
		0.005	0.991	0.839	0.733	0.028	

641 W/G not-knit MMF shirts/blouses	-4.293999*** 0.4496708 0	0.2783592 0.1610588 0.118	3.608244* 1.886482 0.088	0.1313159 1.526036 0.933	7.879923 8.268553 0.365	Adj R-squared = 0.9666 $F(4, 9)$ = 95.01
644 W/G MMF suits	-0.9767618 0.6600472 0.173	-0.026547 0.0673077 0.702	-0.6787117 2.495271 0.792	0.3248181 3.63724 0.931	4.241173 17.55122 0.814	Adj R-squared = 0.7972 $F(4, 9)$ = 13.78
648 W/G MMF slacks/ breeches/shorts	-1.66902*** 0.3281091 0.001	-0.0906994 0.3664972 0.81	2.630068 2.282484 0.279	1.690558*** 0.3805864 0.002	-1.458321 2.800577 0.615	Adj R-squared = 0.9212 $F(4, 9)$ = 38.99
651 MMF nightwear/ pajamas	-3.554701*** 0.4826817 0	0.1047401 0.1817156 0.578	5.980654* 3.355106 0.108	3.196406 1.959805 0.137	-8.38021 9.31755 0.392	Adj R-squared = 0.9548 $F(4, 9)$ = 69.66
652 MMF underwear	-1.199353*** 0.2855615 0.002	0.110163 0.0719347 0.16	-1.709024 1.199014 0.188	2.151907*** 0.349249 0	-8.64884** 3.773778 0.048	Adj R-squared = 0.9149 $F(4, 9)$ = 35.95

The results are listed on the first line, followed by the standard errors, followed by the probability that the coefficient is greater than zero.
*Denotes significance at 10 percent; **denotes significance at 5 percent; ***denotes significance at 1 percent. All parameters are estimated in logs.

competition when the MFA quotas were removed. When one digs deeper into the trade and price data, one observes that the U.S. imports from the PRC tend to be more expensive than comparable three-digit textile and apparel categories from Vietnam. The key question is the long term impact of continued liberalization in Vietnam as it affects the textile and apparel sector.

Table 5.6 presents the OLS estimates for the U.S. import demand of textile and apparel products from the PRC, and Table 5.7 presents the results for India. The overall conclusion that one can draw from these results is that out of a total of 57 three-digit categories where competition is possible, there are only five categories where the cross price elasticity of a change in India's prices on the U.S. imports from the PRC is significantly different from zero. In category 237, "Playsuits, Sunsuits, etc.," for every 1 percent increase in India's price the U.S. imports from the PRC would rise by 0.86 percent, a substitute product; in category 300, "Carded Cotton Yarn," for every 1 percent increase in India's price the U.S. imports from the PRC would fall by 0.63 percent, suggesting complementarity; in category 336, "Cotton Dresses," for every 1 percent increase in India's price the U.S. imports from the PRC would fall by 0.95 percent, suggesting complementarity; in category 345, "Cotton Sweaters," for every 1 percent increase in India's price the U.S. imports from the PRC would fall by 1.30 percent, suggesting complementarity; and in category 642, "MMF Skirts," for every 1 percent increase in India's price the U.S. imports from the PRC would fall by 0.61 percent, suggesting complementarity. In the other 52 product categories, there was no statistically significant cross price elasticity between a movement in India's prices and the U.S. import demand from the PRC.

When we estimate the U.S. import demand from India and ask what would be the partial equilibrium impact of an increase in PRC prices, we get almost the same results. Out of the 57 total possible cases where there can be some competition on the demand side, there are only three cases where the cross-price elasticity is significantly different from zero. In category 218, "Fabrics of Yarns of Different Colors," for every 1 percent increase in PRC's price the U.S. imports from India would fall by 1.41 percent, suggesting complementarity;

Table 5.6   OLS Estimates of the US Import Demand from the PRC with India as the Presumed Competitor

(By T&A Category, 1995–2008)

CAT	Description	$\dfrac{P_k^{PRC}}{P_k^{US}}$	$\dfrac{P_k^V}{P_k^{US}}$	$\dfrac{P_k^{ROW}}{P_k^{US}}$	Y_i	C	
222	Knit fabric	−3.875877**	−1.241403	−5.374053	41.28253	−248.6314	Adj R-squared = 0.7050
		−2.69	−0.72	−0.75	1.61	−1.53	$F(5,4) = 5.30$
		0.055	0.514	0.495	0.182	0.201	
224	Pile/tufted fabrics	−3.025923*	0.1977838	−1.675879	18.8556**	−95.00168*	Adj R-squared = 0.7433
		1.34	0.56	2.27	6.36	40.71	$F(5,4) = 6.21$
		0.087	0.742	0.502	0.041	0.08	
225	Blue denim fabric	7.243525*	8.156986	−6.377531	−20.86227	123.6565	Adj R-squared = 0.7538
		3.15	4.76	3.71	13.19	76.47	$F(5,4) = 6.51$
		0.083	0.162	0.161	0.189	0.181	
237	Playsuits, sunsuits, etc.	−2.122574***	0.8634586*	2.91586**	12.23223***	−67.55352***	Adj R-squared = 0.9086
		0.28	0.34	0.79	1.81	12.51	$F(5,4) = 18.90$
		0.002	0.064	0.021	0.003	0.006	
300	Carded cotton yarn	−4.352694***	−0.6387913***	0.5669832	27.87685***	−140.4872***	Adj R-squared = 0.9211
		0.73	0.18	1.54	6.72	38.44	$F(5,4) = 22.03$
		0.004	0.024	0.731	0.014	0.022	
301	Combed cotton yarn	0.6679575***	0.0223051	0.2194674	−28.99227	120.0916	Adj R-squared = 0.8976
		0.17	0.52	3.89	18.77	102.78	$F(5,4) = 16.78$
		0.016	0.968	0.958	0.197	0.308	

(Continued)

Table 5.6   (Continued)

CAT	Description	$\frac{P_k^{PRC}}{P_k^{US}}$	$\frac{P_k^V}{P_k^{US}}$	$\frac{P_k^{ROW}}{P_k^{US}}$	Y_i	C	
326	Cotton sateen fabric	-2.33183	-10.11545	-15.9849*	40.74594	-187.8302	Adj R-squared = 0.8504
		1.31	8.65	7.46	24.45	138.86	$F(5,4) = 11.23$
		0.15	0.307	0.099	0.171	0.248	
331	Cotton gloves and mittens	-2.136754***	-0.2242898	0.3586604	6.39402**	-15.01707	Adj R-squared = 0.9774
		0.34	0.19	0.93	1.99	15.94	$F(5,4) = 79.01$
		0.003	0.306	0.72	0.032	0.4	
333	M/B suit-type coats, cotton	-1.892198*	0.2368104	0.4133095	-33.55848*	158.377	Adj R-squared = 0.8625
		0.78	0.21	0.82	12.79	63.15	$F(5,4) = 12.29$
		0.073	0.332	0.642	0.059	0.066	
336	Cotton dresses	-1.68011***	-0.9569597**	2.591622***	9.307612*	-48.38924	Adj R-squared = 0.9379
		0.31	0.34	0.73	4.16	18.68	$F(5,4) = 28.17$
		0.006	0.049	0.023	0.089	0.061	
342	Cotton skirts	-2.320549***	0.5165068	-2.924723	4.792254	-9.299892	Adj R-squared = 0.6502
		0.54	0.85	1.85	10.21	40.91	$F(5,4) = 4.35$
		0.012	0.576	0.19	0.663	0.831	
345	Cotton sweaters	-0.865751**	-1.304801*	-0.9627516	21.85527***	-66.85775***	Adj R-squared = 0.8537
		0.24	0.59	1.07	4.40	14.27	$F(5,4) = 11.50$
		0.023	0.091	0.418	0.008	0.009	

347	M/B cotton trousers/breeches/ shorts	-3.23364 1.70 0.131	0.8525099 0.62 0.244	2.338036 3.00 0.479	26.23118* 12.53 0.104	-118.032 61.41 0.127	Adj R-squared = 0.7412 $F(5,4) = 6.16$
360	Cotton pillowcases	-0.6676893 0.35 0.127	-0.0536734 0.21 0.809	0.2995284 0.40 0.496	2.830358 7.56 0.727	-18.38864 37.17 0.647	Adj R-squared = 0.7668 $F(5,4) = 6.92$
361	Cotton sheets	-1.548013** 0.55 0.049	0.5629188 0.56 0.371	-2.34639 1.26 0.135	29.78556* 13.45 0.091	-142.6323 63.43 0.088	Adj R-squared = 0.6090 $F(5,4) = 3.80$
363	Cotton terry/other pile towels	-1.434402** 0.49 0.043	0.0754208 0.46 0.878	1.231656 1.39 0.424	-1.390698 9.61 0.892	0.8442091 49.21 0.987	Adj R-squared = 0.6268 $F(5,4) = 4.02$
613	MMF sheeting fabric	-1.443622 1.07 0.249	-0.1449588 0.63 0.828	0.1129485 0.45 0.814	-39.46159 24.91 0.188	164.9838 120.24 0.242	Adj R-squared = 0.6617 $F(5,4) = 4.52$
620	Other synthetic filament fabric	-1.12421 0.99 0.318	-1.843806 1.37 0.249	2.856102 2.91 0.381	40.10514 22.18 0.145	-225.3108 104.76 0.098	Adj R-squared = 0.8718 $F(5,4) = 13.25$

(*Continued*)

Table 5.6   (*Continued*)

CAT	Description	$\dfrac{P_k^{PRC}}{P_k^{US}}$	$\dfrac{P_k^{V}}{P_k^{US}}$	$\dfrac{P_k^{ROW}}{P_k^{US}}$	Y_i	C	
625	MMF poplin/broadclth stap/fil	3.481294** 1.23 0.047	−0.5962748 0.30 0.114	2.195255** 0.71 0.036	−130.6343* 52.14 0.066	553.4632 238.37 0.081	Adj R-squared = 0.8040 $F(5,4) = 8.38$
628	MMF twills/sateens stap/fil	1.17888 2.28 0.632	0.636764 0.61 0.356	−2.097183 1.16 0.145	66.47859 34.26 0.124	−315.7992 155.24 0.112	Adj R-squared = 0.7305 $F(5,4) = 5.88$
629	Other MMF fabrics of stap/fil	0.2984143 0.83 0.738	−0.3590447 0.61 0.589	−0.7427493 2.86 0.808	28.21403 31.60 0.422	−202.6021 157.96 0.269	Adj R-squared = 0.9530 $F(5,4) = 37.51$
634	Other M/B MMF coats	−1.43561 0.85 0.167	−0.1407266 0.50 0.793	1.534907 0.96 0.184	14.13656 8.42 0.168	−67.36927 42.84 0.191	Adj R-squared = 0.6642 $F(5,4) = 4.56$
636	MMF dresses	−1.62126*** 0.20 0.001	−0.0003535 0.29 0.999	0.9753294 0.69 0.23	6.318372* 2.70 0.08	−29.20432* 12.59 0.081	Adj R-squared = 0.9532 $F(5,4) = 37.62$
638	M/B MMF knit shirts	−0.1318519 0.96 0.897	0.0951106 1.51 0.953	0.4179813 1.50 0.794	−3.153502 17.09 0.863	32.33153 79.19 0.704	Adj R-squared = 0.6600 $F(5,4) = 4.49$

639 W/G MMF knit shirts/blouses	3.153522* 1.49 0.102	−0.3321236 0.44 0.491	−1.706177 1.00 0.163	−31.8609 18.89 0.167	149.9112 90.75 0.174	Adj R-squared = 0.6138 F(5, 4) = 3.86
642 MMF skirts	−1.297682*** 0.27 0.008	−0.6059406* 0.28 0.097	−1.564651 1.18 0.255	−3.298886 4.65 0.517	33.56944 19.50 0.16	Adj R-squared = 0.8713 F(5, 4) = 13.19
645 M/B MMF sweaters	1.547335* 0.59 0.06	0.0909935 0.18 0.64	−1.842223** 0.48 0.019	−55.55793** 18.08 0.037	273.0552** 81.89 0.029	Adj R-squared = 0.8164 F(5, 4) = 9.00
647 M/B MMF trousers/ breeches/shorts	−2.618607** 0.70 0.02	0.3989706 0.29 0.235	1.936152 1.09 0.149	17.60475 8.91 0.119	−90.15216* 43.15 0.105	Adj R-squared = 0.6091 F(5, 4) = 3.80

The results are listed on the first line, followed by the standard errors, followed by the probability that the coefficient is greater than zero.
*Denotes significance at 10 percent; ** denotes significance at 5 percent; *** denotes significance at 1 percent. All parameters are estimated in logs.

Table 5.7   OLS Estimates of the US Import Demand from India with the PRC as the Presumed Competitor
(By T&A Category, 1995–2008)

CAT	Description	$\dfrac{P_k^{PRC}}{P_k^{US}}$	$\dfrac{P_k^{V}}{P_k^{US}}$	$\dfrac{P_k^{ROW}}{P_k^{US}}$	Y_i	C	
218	Fabrics of yarns of diff. colors	−1.408258**	−0.6603098	−2.206125**	2.747523	−29.93459	Adj R-squared = 0.6565
		0.36	0.32	0.57	0.94	13.98	$F(5,4) = 4.44$
		0.018	0.111	0.018	0.043	0.099	
220	Fabric of special weave	1.39707	−2.507868**	−1.598857	−0.5068979	23.02346	Adj R-squared = 0.8204
		1.48	0.64	0.93	2.03	34.78	$F(5,4) = 9.22$
		0.398	0.017	0.162	0.815	0.544	
222	Knit fabric	−1.443665	−0.5274845	5.10466	17.78799*	−106.5029	Adj R-squared = 0.8924
		0.85	1.03	4.24	6.50	96.30	$F(5,4) = 15.93$
		0.165	0.635	0.295	0.052	0.331	
224	Pile/tufted fabrics	−1.713317	0.0053338	−9.681732	15.21918	−285.5483*	Adj R-squared = 0.9191
		3.81	1.59	6.45	9.14	115.58	$F(5,4) = 21.44$
		0.676	0.997	0.208	0.171	0.069	
225	Blue denim fabric	−1.545386	−8.829323**	3.802108	−16.88863***	101.6002*	Adj R-squared = 0.9535
		1.81	2.73	2.13	3.67	43.90	$F(5,4) = 37.94$
		0.441	0.032	0.149	0.01	0.082	
226	Cheesecloth, batistes, lawns/ voile	0.0782644	−2.808852**	0.8378266	−3.325044	53.05885	Adj R-squared = 0.8319
		1.66	0.66	1.56	4.35	86.26	$F(5,4) = 9.91$
		0.965	0.013	0.62	0.487	0.572	

Code	Item						Statistics
227	Oxford cloth	0.0632893	-9.716022	2.982143	-9.589094	33.46967	Adj R-squared $= 0.8032$
		0.19	5.17	2.44	6.21	108.85	$F(5, 4) = 8.35$
		0.755	0.133	0.289	0.197	0.774	
237	Playsuits, sunsuits, etc.	0.5793793	-0.8470404	-0.1399445	-4.598864^{**}	59.27044	Adj R-squared $= 0.8454$
		0.83	1.02	2.38	1.40	37.64	$F(5, 4) = 10.84$
		0.525	0.454	0.956	0.03	0.19	
301	Combed cotton yarn	0.0462192	-2.13407^{**}	2.933361	-9.404056^{**}	107.7222	Adj R-squared $= 0.9440$
		0.09	0.42	2.43	2.84	52.44	$F(5, 3) = 27.97$
		0.631	0.015	0.314	0.046	0.132	
313	Cotton sheeting fabric	1.035812	1.936859	3.505628^{**}	-3.764625^{**}	63.92302	Adj R-squared $= 0.7390$
		0.93	1.31	0.93	1.14	31.74	$F(5, 4) = 6.10$
		0.328	0.213	0.02	0.03	0.114	
334	Other M/B coats, cotton	2.428064	-1.842912	2.614513	5.165002^{**}	159.0756^{**}	Adj R-squared $= 0.8081$
		1.29	1.09	1.98	1.70	57.00	$F(5, 4) = 8.58$
		0.133	0.166	0.256	0.038	0.049	
335	W/G cotton coats	1.279299	-0.8627212	0.8093013	4.096595^{**}	-55.19256	Adj R-squared $= 0.8459$
		0.86	1.04	0.73	1.33	54.45	$F(5, 4) = 10.88$
		0.21	0.452	0.329	0.037	0.368	

(*Continued*)

Table 5.7   (Continued)

CAT	Description	$\frac{P_k^{PRC}}{P_k^{US}}$	$\frac{P_k^V}{P_k^{US}}$	$\frac{P_k^{ROW}}{P_k^{US}}$	Y_i	C	
336	Cotton dresses	0.1324514 0.56 0.825	−0.9654765 0.62 0.194	1.141825 1.31 0.432	2.139325 1.91 0.326	−7.127961 33.64 0.843	Adj R-squared = 0.9148 $F(5,4) = 20.32$
340	M/B cotton shirts, not-knit	1.067907 0.95 0.322	−0.6306513 0.50 0.276	0.5503387 1.78 0.773	1.362609* 0.60 0.087	54.46825 36.91 0.214	Adj R-squared = 0.8078 $F(5,4) = 8.57$
341	W/G cotton shirts/ blouses, not-knit	0.7230001 0.57 0.27	−0.9697436 0.67 0.219	−0.3149558 0.91 0.748	0.8199792 0.41 0.117	10.9076 32.16 0.752	Adj R-squared = 0.7616 $F(5,4) = 6.75$
342	Cotton skirts	0.0817701 0.41 0.853	0.8259492 0.66 0.276	−2.39468 1.43 0.17	1.665868** 0.61 0.053	65.7025* 31.59 0.106	Adj R-squared = 0.9323 $F(5,4) = 25.78$
345	Cotton sweaters	−0.0269084 0.66 0.97	−3.800196 1.61 0.077	−7.575201* 2.91 0.06	−12.86657* 5.26 0.071	−77.16694 38.94 0.119	Adj R-squared = 0.7913 $F(5,4) = 7.83$
347	M/B cotton trousers/breeches/ shorts	1.000544 2.93 0.75	−0.9429211 1.07 0.429	−1.588924 5.15 0.773	2.784272 2.19 0.273	33.55144 105.54 0.766	Adj R-squared = 0.7700 $F(5,4) = 7.02$

348 W/G cotton trousers/slacks/shorts	2.121549** 0.76 0.049	−0.9866618 0.49 0.112	−2.236553 1.27 0.153	1.41613 0.88 0.184	85.22404* 32.29 0.058	Adj R-squared = 0.9591 $F(5,4)$ = 43.26
351 Cotton nightwear/pajamas	0.0647249 0.70 0.931	−0.8632778 0.59 0.219	0.1426507 1.35 0.921	1.759351 1.70 0.36	−0.7847724 57.56 0.99	Adj R-squared = 0.8930 $F(5,4)$ = 16.02
352 Cotton underwear	2.020725 1.74 0.309	−2.751125*** 0.62 0.012	−2.056526 3.99 0.633	1.236705 3.66 0.752	−237.6314 173.48 0.243	Adj R-squared = 0.8850 $F(5,4)$ = 14.86
360 Cotton pillowcases	0.0092369 0.92 0.992	−1.763004** 0.55 0.032	−1.457952 1.06 0.241	9.005541*** 1.82 0.008	−81.03298 98.31 0.456	Adj R-squared = 0.9869 $F(5,4)$ = 136.40
361 Cotton sheets	−0.7943184 1.26 0.562	−2.367808 1.28 0.137	0.1381333 2.87 0.964	12.98116*** 1.97 0.003	−32.52393 144.77 0.833	Adj R-squared = 0.9776 $F(5,4)$ = 79.48
363 Cotton terry/other pile towels	−0.4432382 0.42 0.355	−0.5921327 0.40 0.212	−1.265317 1.20 0.351	3.992891** 1.28 0.036	45.22948 42.59 0.348	Adj R-squared = 0.9578 $F(5,4)$ = 41.83

(Continued)

Table 5.7   (*Continued*)

CAT	Description	$\frac{P_k^{PRC}}{P_k^{US}}$	$\frac{P_k^V}{P_k^{US}}$	$\frac{P_k^{ROW}}{P_k^{US}}$	Y_i	C	
629	Other MMF fabrics of stap/fil	0.3142834	−2.163715*	8.024332	18.7998***	−442.1825	Adj R-squared = 0.8816
		1.40	1.03	4.81	3.80	265.73	$F(5,4) = 14.40$
		0.834	0.103	0.171	0.008	0.171	
635	W/G MMF coats	1.289963	0.0612929	−1.031021	1.067721	14.93464	Adj R-squared = 0.8992
		0.63	1.13	1.11	1.49	52.44	$F(5,4) = 17.06$
		0.112	0.959	0.406	0.512	0.79	
638	M/B MMF knit shirts	1.219204	1.822266	−5.226054	9.77842**	−123.2566	Adj R-squared = 0.9361
		1.73	2.73	2.71	2.93	143.37	$F(5,4) = 27.38$
		0.52	0.542	0.126	0.029	0.438	
639	W/G MMF knit shirts/blouses	−1.348755	−1.930937**	1.614132	5.227401***	−139.8347	Adj R-squared = 0.9389
		1.85	0.55	1.24	0.69	112.74	$F(5,4) = 28.66$
		0.507	0.024	0.263	0.002	0.283	
640	M/B not-knit MMF shirts	11.32782*	−1.657179	−20.37964**	−2.354697	−510.6767**	Adj R-squared = 0.9352
		4.94	0.81	6.03	2.45	131.34	$F(5,4) = 26.99$
		0.083	0.11	0.028	0.39	0.018	

642 MMF skirts	1.218348**	−0.0511972	1.320319	−1.628094	−31.09228	Adj R-squared = 0.8483
	0.31	0.32	1.36	1.48	22.50	$F(5,4) = 11.06$
	0.017	0.882	0.387	0.334	0.239	
645 M/B MMF sweaters	0.2964078	−3.597614**	0.3609161	−0.9543702	−365.3091*	Adj R-squared = 0.9318
	0.90	0.67	0.78	1.37	146.30	$F(5,3) = 22.85$
	0.762	0.013	0.677	0.537	0.088	
647 M/B MMF trousers/breeches/ shorts	3.3145	0.7457215	−9.293988*	5.365626	16.58102	Adj R-squared = 0.9519
	2.69	1.11	4.20	2.94	166.89	$F(5,4) = 36.60$
	0.286	0.537	0.092	0.142	0.926	
652 MMF underwear	2.685645	−0.3838418	−1.58167	5.01552	−97.78327	Adj R-squared = 0.8356
	2.33	0.71	8.20	2.65	807.86	$F(5,3) = 9.13$
	0.332	0.628	0.859	0.154	0.911	

The results are listed on the first line, followed by the standard errors, followed by the probability that the coefficient is greater than zero.

*Denotes significance at 10 percent; **denotes significance at 5 percent; ***denotes significance at 1 percent. All parameters are estimated in logs.

in category 348, "W/G Cotton trousers/slacks/shorts," for every 1 percent increase in PRC's price the U.S. imports from India would rise by 2.12 percent, suggesting a substitute product; and in category 642, "MMF Skirts," for every 1 percent increase in PRC's price the U.S. imports from India would rise by 1.22 percent, suggesting a substitute product.

Overall, these results confirm the hypothesis found in the industry that the PRC and India compete in apples and oranges. When one digs deeper into the trade and price data, one observes that the U.S. imports from the PRC tend to be more expensive than comparable three-digit T&A categories from India. Given that there is no head-to-head competition between these two suppliers what changes has the PRC undertaken on the supply side to maintain its world leadership in this industry?

5.7. The Supply Side Response

During the long history of the MFA, the search for low wage producers was a key explanatory variable for the world's distribution of quotas. In the past decade, this has changed drastically. The primary ingredient for a successful textile and apparel sector is quick turnaround time for apparel and economies of scale for textiles. In the apparel segment of the industry, which is considered by many to be fashion-oriented, time sensitivity is even more crucial. While the low-wage sewing provides some competitive advantages to developing countries, it is only applicable to the assembly process of low-end garments and does not necessarily lead to the development of a sophisticated textile and apparel sector. The PRC, which represents the higher end textile and apparel industry, has managed to combine its export-led strategy in textile and apparel with the development of higher value-added segments of the supply chain. This was achieved by integrating scale economies with diversification of its labor pool, upgrading domestic skills in local design, material sourcing, quality control, logistics and retail distribution.

In describing the supply side responses of the PRC resulting from the elimination of quotas, one needs to appreciate the fact that what is called the textile and apparel sector is composed of a chain of separable activities. This linear chain of production functions starts with agriculture where we have the initial fiber stage.

5.7.1. *Cotton Fiber*

Textiles are produced by both natural and man-made fibers. In the natural fiber side, a country's potential comparative advantage is affected by the traditional factor endowment availabilities, e.g. land, climate and by domestic internal subsidy programs, e.g. cotton. In the synthetic fiber area, the industry is a derivate of chemical producers. Economies of scale in this sector have traditionally benefited the developed countries.

In the case of the PRC, cotton is regarded as a "strategic" commodity.[39] Consequently, every aspect of cotton from production, internal and external sales, and firm consumption are part of a complex set of State interventions. Despite the PRC's openness with respect to international trade, the central government had until 1998, determined cotton's procurement prices and resale prices and established a State monopsony/monopoly (the Supply and Marketing Cooperatives (SMCs)) as the sole agent for purchasing cotton from the rural sector. From 1985 to 1998, cotton farmers where obligated under a production "contract" to supply the SMC with a certain quantity of cotton at the planned procurement price; they could also sell any above-quota quantity of cotton to the SMC. The introduction of market reform, decentralized purchases and direct links between producers and consumers of cotton did not begin in earnest till the late 1990s.

Beginning in 1996, SMCs were allowed to trade cotton directly with local textile mills. This decentralized linkage system still had a local constraint in that the tradable quantities were still bound by assigned quotas for importing and exporting regions. Furthermore, the definition of a market price actually meant that the two parties

---

[39]For a detailed discussion of the PRC's domestic and international policies with respect to Cotton, see OECD [2005].

to a trade were allowed to decide the terms of trade within a very limited price band of ±4 percent of the state-set cotton allocation price.

As of September 1999, cotton prices in the PRC are determined by market forces, while the government issues a minimum price. These minimum prices serve as purchase prices for the SMCs, who as of 1999 no longer have exclusive rights to purchase cotton from producers, but do purchase stocks of cotton for special reserve holdings by the State. These reserves along with rules for international purchases of cotton are designed to stabilize local cotton prices, the major input into the textile industry.

The role of the State is very much part of the PRC's external arrangement with respect to cotton, as well. Trade in cotton, despite the PRC's accession to the WTO is still dominated by a State-Owned Enterprise (SOE) — China National Textiles Import and Export Company (Chinatex). As part of the WTO accession process the PRC introduced a tariff rate quota system where there was an in-quota tariff of 3 percent and an over-quota tariff of 90 percent. This distortion combined with the role of SOEs as purchasing agents guarantees a limited role for international market prices to affect the local cotton industry. This may change as the PRC fights to reduce the role of SOEs to a minimum of the volume of trade. The PRC is a master in using price and trade controls to encourage the development of a large scale cotton industry in regions as far away as Xinjiang.

5.7.2. *Textiles*

The textile mill products sector of the textile industry includes all operations that are involved in converting fiber to finished fabric and the production of many non-apparel consumer products. Technological innovations have greatly increased the speed of operations and resulted in huge productivity gains. Traditionally the developed countries have innovated more in this segment of the industry. The PRC has not lagged far behind. However, non-clothing applications of textiles — the so-called "technical textiles" — are now more important than clothing applications and account for the fastest-growing segment of total textile production in developed countries.

It is generally understood that in markets like the United States, the textiles sector makes fabric in three steps that are often made by different factories. The first step is spinning fibers into thread or yarn, the second is weaving or knitting thread or yarn into fabrics and the third is chemical processing to finish the fabric. In addition, there are non-woven fabrics that are produced by mechanically, thermally or chemically bonding or interlocking fibers, filaments or yarns. These processes in the United States are highly capital-intensive and are subject to economies of scale.[40] Having said that, we still have in many developing countries, textile industries that are utilizing very simple technology within the household or in micro-enterprises. In the new quota free world, these latter small-scale producers are destined to expire.

After the PRC received MFN status in the US in 1979, a whole set of domestic reforms were initiated to induce domestic PRC producers to enter the global market. These incentives were not only important for the success of the PRC in the textile industry it also introduced new forms of corporate governance which has enabled the PRC to compete in the Textile sector with developed countries like the United States. The primary institutional shift was a set of reforms that allowed the rural companies to form alliances with the SOEs, enabling the new corporate form to take advantage of a merger of cheap rural labor with high investments in new technology in the textile industry SOEs.

According to the OECD, the PRC textile and apparel sector continue to receive a sizeable share of total state subsidies from the central government. It is estimated that the percentage of the total subsidies that the central government granted to textile SOEs rose from 1.61 percent in 1990 to 20.57 percent in 1998. The PRC's central government intervention in the Textile industry does not

---

[40]See Pelzman and Martin [1981] where estimates of textile and apparel production functions are presented.

depend only on price incentives. It also involves setting performance targets. In order to appreciate the importance of Central Planning to the development of this industry, one need only review the goals established for textiles in the Tenth Five-Year Plan (2000–2005) seeking to upgrade the value added of textiles.

The following goals were contained in the Tenth Five-Year Plan for 2000–2005[41]:

- Increasing the value added of the sector from 267.8 billion Yuan in 2000 to 430 billion Yuan in 2005, or an increase of 60.6 percent;
- Increasing the production volume of textile fiber from 12.1 million tons in 2000 to 14.25 million tons in 2005;
- Increasing the apparent consumption per person from 6.6 kgs to 7.4 kgs for the same period;
- Increasing exports from 52 billion dollars in 2000 to between 70 and 75 billion dollars in 2005;
- Increasing labor productivity from 25,000 Yuan per worker in 2000 to 35,000 Yuan in 2005.
- Reducing energy consumption for every 10,000 Yuan of production by 15 percent; and
- Using recycled water in production for 30 percent of 1999 consumption by 2005; in the prints sector, reducing water consumption for every 100 meters from 3.6 tons to 3.0 tons.

In order to reach the goals that it had set, the PRC government provided a stable area for growing cotton. It guaranteed the textile industry that it would supply 4.5 million tons of cotton annually. It provided incentives for technological progress by encouraging alliances between companies and research centers and established development centers for the large SOEs.

According to the USITC [2004], the PRC Textile industry in 2000, had 18,900 SOEs with a sales volume higher than 5 million yuan; with total assets of 977,300 million yuan, which generated

---

[41]See USITC [2004].

tax revenue of 267,800 million yuan in value-added taxes and which represented 11.9 percent; 8.3 percent; and 11.3 percent, respectively, of the entire manufacturing industry. Employment in Textiles was around 13 million.[42]

Since the mid 1990s the PRC accounted for more than 25 percent of the global spinning machines.[43] This share has increased substantially in the past 10 years. Furthermore, the industry created both forward and backward linkages integrating a large number of production segments namely, cotton and other fibers; accessories; thread, yam and textile manufacturing; and the processing of these products into garments, rugs and industrial textiles [USITC, 2004]. The PRC now has the national and global supply and input companies necessary to make almost all products.

The current textile market requires rapid turnaround. During the past two decades, the PRC developed a highly competitive maritime transportation system, ensuring that its products arrive on the East Coast of the United States between 12 and 18 days from boarding, while its competitors from Asia may take three times as long to arrive [USITC, 2004].

The PRC has a centralized government with market orientation. It can transfer long-term views to its public without having to meet short-term demands from competing constituencies. The latter can therefore focus better on export-led growth policies with an expectation that welfare improvements will eventually confirm this economic direction. In the case of the PRC, the end result has justified the 30-year investment in export led growth.

---

[42] *Ibid.*, The total workers in Textiles and Apparel has been estimated by the ILO to be 19 million or approximately 22 percent of all manufacturing sector employment. According to the ILO another 80 million people are directly linked to this combined sector. The number of Apparel companies are estimated to be 40,000 of which only 6 percent are SOEs. We do not have current estimates of apparel sector employment.

[43] *Ibid.*, In 2002 China had around 22.8 percent of all spinning machines and had acquired more than 50 percent of them during 2000–2002.

5.7.3. *Apparel*

The global apparel industry has evolved substantially from its earliest form where the industry in the developing countries acted like subcontractors, where garment were sewn from imported inputs ready for assembly. In the current market, these operations are still found in simple non-competitive producers of homogenous apparel items. Slightly more sophisticated is a subcontracting process most commonly as original equipment manufacturing (OEM). The characteristics of this outsourcing operation include the supplying firm making a product according to a design specified by the buyer; the product is sold under the buyer's brand name; the supplier and buyer are separate firms; and the buyer lacks control over distribution. The most sophisticated upgrading of this outsourcing process is commonly referred to as Original brand name manufacturing (OBM) where the developing country apparel manufacturer begins to design their own end product and then sell it under their own brand name.

The critical element in the apparel chain is therefore the retailer. In the United States at the beginning of the 1990s, the five largest retail chains represented 45 percent of the apparel market. By 1995, these five largest retailers — Walmart, Sears, Kmart, Dayton Hudson Corporation and JC Penney — accounted for 68 percent of all apparel sales. The next top 24 retailers represented an additional 30 percent of these sales. The two top discount giants, Walmart and Kmart, controlled one quarter of all apparel (in terms of unit sold) in the United States.

By 2000, only 10 percent of the apparel sold by these chains was of U.S. origin. These retailers' overseas operations are not primarily handling a middle-man function of just facilitating the transfer of apparel to the U.S. market, they are actively engaged in product design, fabric selection and procurement, and monitoring contracted sewing as well as other production functions handled by offshore manufacturers. Another new development is the growth of private-label goods, which have been estimated to cover up to 25 percent of the United States apparel market in 2000.

As a result of these linkages and the new practice in the U.S. of reducing inventory costs, time factors play a far more crucial role in determining international competitiveness. With the removal of the quota system, low-wage countries like India that had depended on being an offshore assembly center relying on their quota allocations found itself vulnerable because of the inherent cost disadvantage of their business model based on production fragmentation. Time factors can be an important trade barrier for intermediary inputs involved in an internationally fragmented production process.

The emergence of more competitive and integrated suppliers in the PRC, who increased their sales in a quota free world, will exert considerable pressure on fragmented suppliers like India.[44] The comparative advantage of India in the assembly process, i.e. in low-wage sewing, does not necessarily translate into a comparative advantage in the management of the entire supply chain when all services-related dimensions are taken into consideration. Efficiency in managing the entire supply chain is required, including in design, fabric procurement, and logistical skills in transport, quality control, export financing and clearing of trade formalities. The latter has become more of the PRC model.[45]

---

[44] As wages in the PRC keep rising they are taking advantage of their upscale production and marketing skills and have implemented a number of preferential policies in order to encourage its T&A manufacturers to invest more in other developing countries. These measures include preferential loans, simplified administrative procedures and enhanced information and intelligence support. The PRC appears to be entering this new market in order to subcontract its apparel production. The PRC's current focus is on Africa where they have started discussions with Morocco and in Asia with Bangladesh.

[45] The PRC has made great strides in the Apparel sector. Output in the sector rose by 37 percent from 1995 to 1999, while industry employment fell by 27 percent. See UN [2002]. The PRC's increase in its apparel quality and productivity comes at the same time that it has accepted the necessity to import its better quality textiles from abroad. Eighty percent of Japan's import apparel is currently of PRC country of origin. Achieving such a high penetration rate is proof that PRC Apparel can compete at the highest quality end. The PRC is the benchmark that India will have to measure itself to.

Chapter 6

China's 10-Year WTO Experience: Applying Market Solutions to a Non-Market Player

On December 11, 2001 [WTO, 2001], the day the PRC became a member of the WTO, the *People's Daily* anticipated the following outcome for the PRC [USGAO, 1995]:

> "*We should actively spur foreign capital to flow into high and new technological industries and encourage transnational corporations to come to China to set up R&D centers and regional headquarters.*"

This expectation is understandable given the history of the unique PRC-specific growth model that we refer to as "State-Supervised-Capitalism" (SSC) — rather than the official Chinese rendering that paints their brand of development as "Socialism with Chinese characteristics" [World Bank and Development Research Center of the State Council, the People's Republic of China, 2013].

In terms of GDP growth rates, the PRC economy achieved double-digit growth rates post accession in 2002. This rapid growth started in the 1980s and 1990s as the PRC expanded its participation in the world community. Accession to the WTO further strengthened domestic incentives for local reforms, as the leadership could point to the success of its unique SSC growth model. In the 20-year period after the US granted the PRC MFN status, their footprint — measured in terms of world output on a purchasing power parity (PPP) basis, increased from 2 percent to over 14 percent.

The major driver for this unprecedented growth was local market structural reforms under the rubric of SSC. These reforms facilitated the opening of the State-owned enterprises (SOEs) and deregulated inward FDI and local municipal supervision and control. They also facilitated the expansion and growth of the export sector, which in 2013 accounted for over 12 percent of global exports. This, in turn, increased international integration, as discussed in Chapters 2 and 3 above. Together with sustained vigorous domestic growth this converted the PRC into a large-country actor and creditor that was able to influence the growth of the world economy. Between 2009 and 2013, the absolute increase in PRC GDP constituted more than 45 percent of the absolute increase in output in the rest of the world. The role of the WTO, in terms of the long accession negotiations and the 10-plus years of post — WTO accession litigation, was crucial in securing the unique PRC domestic reforms we refer to as SSC [Sally, 2009; Scissor, 2011; Szamosszegi and Kyle, 2011; OECD, 2011].

In joining the WTO, the PRC, despite its non-market-economy (NME) status, committed to bring its trade laws and practices into compliance with WTO rules and other market-economy-opening measures. In doing so, it departed from other NME players like Russia, and took a major step in integrating its trading system with the rest of the world. Those commitments included [Church *et al.*, 2001]:

- *Most-favored nation treatment (MFN)*: non-discriminatory treatment of imports of goods and services;
- *National treatment*: imports of goods and services are treated no less favorably than like goods and certain services produced domestically;
- *Transparency*: ensuring transparency when implementing domestic trade measures;
- *Lowering trade barriers through negotiations*: reducing tariffs and binding tariff levels via multilateral negotiations. Prior

to WTO accession, the PRC reduced its tariffs by 50 percent. With accession, those tariffs were reduced by another 50 percent (Table 6.1). Chinese tariffs in 2011, on average, across all products was less than 6.0 percent, down from 32 percent in 1992. Tariffs on consumer goods, which was over 63.8 percent in 1992, was down to 11.1 percent in 2011.

- *Reliance on tariffs to protect sensitive sectors*: a commitment to use tariffs and avoid using quotas or other non-tariff measures when restricting imports to counter the effects of unfairly — traded imports or surges in fairly — traded imports. With accession, the PRC committed to eliminate non-tariff measures both on their import and export sides in agriculture to tariff measures. It has committed to restrict its subsidies for agricultural production to 8.5 percent of the value of farm output [OECD, 2005, 2011b].
- *Dispute resolution*: a commitment to accept WTO dispute settlement procedures [OECD, 2005, 2010].

China's integration with the world at large also involved negotiating hundreds of bilateral preferential agreements.[1] China concluded Free Trade Agreements (FTAs) with ASEAN, Chile, Costa Rica, Iceland, Pakistan, Peru, Singapore, Switzerland and New Zealand. It has also concluded separate customs area agreements with Hong Kong and Macau. The PRC is also party to the Asia-Pacific Trade Agreement, which includes a number of states not covered in its other agreements, including Bangladesh, Brunei, India, Korea and Sri Lanka. FTA negotiations are currently underway with Australia, the Gulf Cooperative Council, Norway, South Korea, a trilateral FTA with Korea and Japan, Sri Lanka and with the Regional Comprehensive Economic Partnership, (RCEP). The PRC is considering FTA agreements with Columbia, India, and the Maldives.

In 2004 and 2005, the PRC expanded its reforms beyond the trade sector. In 2004, a large number of domestic regulations were standardized as the Party reinforced the importance of the

---

[1]http://fta.mofcom.gov.cn/english/fta_qianshu.shtml.

Table 6.1 China's Tariffs on Agricultural and Manufactured Products MFN Weighted Average (%)

Product Group	1992	1993	1994	1996	1997	1998	1999	2000	2001	2003	2004	2005	2006	2007	2008	2009	2010	2011
All Products	32.2	30.3	27.9	19.8	15.8	15.5	14.5	14.7	14.1	6.5	6.0	4.9	4.4	5.1	4.5	4.0	4.7	5.5
Capital goods	26.7	25.5	23.3	15.1	12.6	12.9	12.2	12.1	11.7	4.6	4.2	3.9	3.2	4.8	4.6	3.4	4.8	7.2
Consumer goods	63.8	62.8	56.5	29.2	19.4	22.8	19.1	18.9	18.9	14.3	12.4	10.0	9.7	10.1	9.6	10.1	11.4	11.1
Intermediate goods	33.6	28.9	28.6	20.0	16.5	15.7	14.6	13.5	12.7	8.1	7.5	6.5	5.9	6.0	5.4	5.1	5.2	5.2
Raw materials	8.6	8.4	8.9	26.4	22.4	17.9	20.8	27.9	27.1	4.0	5.1	2.6	3.0	2.4	1.5	1.4	1.5	1.2
Animal	38.3	36.4	34.7	32.9	19.6	19.3	19.3	20.5	19.2	12.0	10.5	9.3	10.2	9.9	8.6	9.2	9.7	9.9
Chemicals	17.2	20.0	17.9	11.1	9.8	13.1	10.5	11.1	10.3	8.0	7.5	6.5	6.2	6.1	5.4	5.6	5.5	5.3
Food Products	42.1	53.9	29.7	24.6	15.3	14.2	18.5	22.8	32.5	17.5	16.1	12.0	15.4	13.9	11.5	12.1	13.1	16.0
Footwear	77.6	71.6	65.9	40.2	24.1	24.3	24.9	25.2	24.3	17.7	16.0	15.6	15.6	15.7	15.6	15.7	15.7	15.5
Fuels	7.8	8.3	8.0	5.5	8.3	4.9	8.1	8.0	8.2	2.1	1.9	1.6	1.3	1.5	1.1	0.9	1.0	0.8
Hides and Skins	36.2	33.4	29.1	17.9	10.5	10.5	10.6	10.5	10.0	7.7	7.6	7.5	7.4	7.5	7.6	7.8	8.0	8.1
Mach and Elec	26.9	26.2	23.4	15.6	13.0	13.3	12.4	12.1	11.8	4.0	3.5	3.2	2.6	4.2	4.1	2.6	4.3	7.2
Metals	16.1	13.9	15.4	11.0	9.7	9.6	9.1	8.4	7.9	5.0	4.8	4.7	4.4	4.4	3.9	3.1	3.0	2.9
Minerals	1.7	2.4	2.4	0.6	0.4	0.5	0.7	0.7	0.7	0.6	0.3	0.3	0.1	0.2	0.0	0.0	0.1	0.1
Miscellaneous	42.0	35.6	32.5	24.4	14.7	14.3	13.9	13.6	12.5	7.6	7.5	7.5	6.6	7.7	7.2	7.4	7.4	7.2
Plastic or Rubber	32.6	30.8	27.0	19.9	16.4	16.3	16.0	18.6	18.1	11.0	9.9	9.3	7.7	8.4	7.6	7.5	7.7	7.1
Stone and Glass	38.8	39.3	35.0	23.1	15.9	11.6	13.3	12.5	11.9	8.9	8.7	8.0	6.9	7.7	7.3	7.6	7.5	7.9
Textiles and Clothing	61.6	61.1	50.1	28.1	23.4	24.7	24.1	22.3	20.4	15.9	16.8	11.9	16.3	15.4	15.6	10.6	10.0	12.0
Transportation	63.7	70.4	58.1	21.4	15.1	16.2	16.9	23.5	19.6	18.3	16.0	13.5	10.8	11.9	13.2	12.8	15.0	16.1
Vegetable	9.4	12.4	13.3	91.8	81.6	73.7	66.3	75.4	79.6	13.5	20.0	8.1	7.5	6.7	5.4	6.0	6.4	7.0
Wood	22.4	22.1	20.1	15.2	10.5	10.7	8.7	8.4	7.7	3.1	2.2	1.9	1.7	1.4	1.3	1.3	1.2	1.0

Source: UN Trains accessed through the World Integrated Trade Solution

private sector within its SSC development model. In 2005, the Party eliminated regulations that had prevented private sector participation in a wide range of areas including financial services, infrastructure and utilities. The end result was a large inflow of investment in the automobile industry. In 2008, the introduction of a new Anti-Monopoly Law represented another important milestone in integrating the Chinese SSC model with that of international best practices [OECD, 2009]. The new law provided a comprehensive legal basis for combating a wide range of anti-competitive practices, including abuses by dominant firms, and corporate mergers. This new law has been applied to both foreign firms as well as state-owned telecom companies that were accused of restricting competition.

In addition to cementing internal reforms within the PRC, WTO membership has had an additional and significant spillover effect. That is, it has subjected the PRC to a wide variety of foreign trade litigations. This is not surprising since there is a normal correlation between increased volume of trade and increased trade litigation. The more interesting question is the degree to which membership within the WTO has disciplined PRC firms and the government from discontinuing actions that are perceived as violating accepted WTO norms. Surprisingly, the PRC — along with India — have expanded their own anti-dumping (AD) litigation displacing the EU and the United States as the lead litigants in this area. As Pelzman and Shoham [2007, 2009b] demonstrate, the PRC's use of these litigations in order to discipline foreign "unfair" traders is desirable, and representative of their understanding of WTO law.

Despite the major systemic changes that the PRC undertook post accession, there has been widespread use of AD litigations against the PRC. AD trade policy is at the heart of the WTO attempt to assure organized "contingent protection" rights to its members. Its use is warranted on the grounds of eliminating deleterious dumping by foreign firms and re-establishing conditions of "fair" trade. Given the size of China's footprint in international trade, it is not surprising to find that it is among the leading targets on a worldwide basis, accounting for over 20 percent of AD cases reported by the WTO. What is not clear is whether China would have faced the same number of "contingent protection" cases if it were not a member of the WTO. Most economists are of the opinion that AD has little to do with "unfair" trade and that litigation against China is driven by local protectionist forces [Takacs, 1981; Grilli, 1988; Knetter and Prusa, 2003; Feinberg, 2005; Rose, 2012; Bown and Crowley, 2013a, 2013b].

Having said that, one should keep in mind that China's WTO accession protocol includes special provisions on AD and safeguards that its trading partners may use against Chinese exports. These include continuing use of "non-market economy" status in AD investigations for 15 years and use of a special "transitional product-specific safeguard" provision for 12 years. These "contingent protection" provisions have clearly been exercised. Moreover, the PRC itself has exercised its own contingent protection.

The accepted international trade paradigm is that trade contingency measures are a necessary part of any trade agreement [Bagwell and Staiger, 1999, 2002, 2003a, 2003b, 2004, 2005, 2006]. This paradigm posits that greater liberalization commitments are possible because the AD instruments allow these countries to exercise short-term relief from competitive pressure. In the absence of such measures, countries might not even contemplate signing new trade agreements or entering into new rounds of negotiations.

A statistical summary of the post — WTO AD litigations is presented in the next section. The obvious questions are the following: What is the relationship between China's export penetrations in a country and its AD action against it? Is there a correlation between the import market share and the resulting AD litigation? Is China targeted as a precautionary step and, if so, is it targeted unfairly?

6.1. The Overall Reliance on AD Measures

Modern AD law starts with the 1947 GATT agreement, resulting in the 1994 agreement establishing the WTO. The agreement defines dumping as the practice whereby the "products of one country are introduced into the commerce of another country at less than the normal value of the products." Exceptions to the international rules of bound tariffs and the MFN principle are permitted in the form of AD duties if such action is proved to cause "material injury" to a domestic industry. AD is just one form of "contingent protection" now permitted under WTO rules and employed by importing countries to provide remedies against unfair trade or sudden surges in imports, which can harm domestic industries.

These exceptions to the fundamental principles of the WTO are based on the rationale of providing a 'free and fair trading environment' in global markets. When it comes to unfair trade, GATT Article VI (5) states that no one product from any one country can be subject to both AD and countervailing duties (CVD). Complainants therefore need to make a choice about which course to follow. Of the two, AD has been by far the most popular, constituting around 90 percent of protection measures consistently between 1995 and 2014. Between 1995 and 2014, a total of 3407 contingent protection measures were initiated worldwide — 3058 of which were AD measures; while just 202 were CVD duties and 147 were safeguard measures [Tables 6.2 to 6.4].

During the 1995–2014 period, a complex picture emerges from the implantation of contingent protection measures by members of the WTO. It is no longer true that worldwide AD enforcement, the primary contingent protection instrument, is predominantly concentrated in the developed countries. It is true, however, that China was the most frequent subject of new investigations. An examination of the record of AD, CVD and safeguard measures in force over the 1995–2014 period outlined in Tables 6.2 to 6.4 demonstrate a number of important evolutionary changes in the implementation of AD measures.

First, in the pre-2002 period, the predominant AD users enforcing the majority of the AD measures, were the developed economies who represented 70 percent of world GDP and 50 percent of the world trade. This changed drastically as the major new intensive AD and safeguard users are developing economies (Argentina, Brazil, India, Mexico, South Africa and Turkey), and they have surpassed the four major traditional users. These new developing — country users implemented close to 50 percent of the AD measures in force in 2014,

Table 6.2 Anti-Dumping Measures Imposed as Reported by WTO Members 1995–2014

Reporting Member	1995	1996	1997	1998	1999	2000	2001	2002	2003	2004	2005	2006	2007	2008	2009	2010	2011	2012	2013	2014	Total
Developed Countries																					
Australia	1	1	1	20	6	5	11	9	10	4	3	5	1	3	2	2	5	10	9	14	122
Canada	7		7	10	10	14	19		5	8	4		3	3	2	3	1	10	7	6	119
European Union	15	23	23	28	18	41	13	25	2	10	20	12	12	15	9	5	11	3	12	1	298
United States	33	12	20	16	24	31	33	27	12	14	18	5	5	23	15	17	4	7	7	22	345
Share of Total	0.47	0.39	0.4	0.4	0.31	0.38	0.45	0.28	0.13	0.23	0.33	0.15	0.2	0.31	0.2	0.2	0.21	0.25	0.22	0.27	0.29
Developing Countries																					
Argentina	13	20	11	12	9	16	14	22	19	1	8	4	8	5	16	15	8	9	9	9	228
Brazil	3	6	2	14	5	9	13	5	2	5	3	5	9	11	16	5	13	14	30	32	197
India	7	2	8	22	23	55	38	64	52	29	18	16	24	31	30	32	26	30	12	15	534
Mexico	16	4	7	7	7	6	6	4	1	7	8	5	1	3	1	2	1	4	2	8	99
South Africa		8	18	13	36	13	5	15	1	4	7	7	1	3	3	1	2	1	4	1	132
Turkey	11				1	8	2	11	28	16	9	21	6	11	9	10	2	1	8	9	163
Share of Total	0.42	0.43	0.36	0.37	0.43	0.45	0.44	0.56	0.49	0.4	0.33	0.37	0.45	0.43	0.52	0.49	0.51	0.49	0.39	0.47	0.44
China				3	2	5		5	33	14	16	24	12	4	12	15	6	5	8	12	176
Share of Total				0.02	0.01	0.02		0.02	0.15	0.09	0.12	0.17	0.11	0.03	0.08	0.11	0.06	0.04	0.05	0.08	0.06
Other WTO Members	14	16	30	40	49	35	18	31	52	42	31	43	25	33	28	27	22	26	55	28	645
Share of Total	0.12	0.17	0.24	0.22	0.26	0.15	0.11	0.14	0.23	0.27	0.22	0.3	0.24	0.23	0.2	0.2	0.22	0.22	0.34	0.18	0.21
Total	120	92	127	185	190	238	169	218	223	154	138	142	106	142	143	134	99	120	161	157	3058

Source: Author's computations based on the WTO Report (2015) of the Committee on Anti-Dumping Practices, (Adopted October 28, 2015) and earlier years. AD measures by reporting member: https://www.wto.org/english/tratop_e/adp_e/adp_e.htm

Table 6.3   Countervailing Measures Imposed as Reported by WTO Members 1995–2014

Reporting Member	1995	1996	1997	1998	1999	2000	2001	2002	2003	2004	2005	2006	2007	2008	2009	2010	2011	2012	2013	2014	Total
Developed Countries																					
Australia													1	1		1	1	2	3		9
Canada			1	2	3	5	1							3	1	1	1	4	3	—	24
European Union			1	2	3	10		2	3	2	1			3	3	3	2		3	2	35
United States	5	2		1	11	10	10	10	2	2	2	2	1	7	6	10	3	2	4	7	86
Share of Total	0.32	0.4	0.33	0.5	1	0.86	0.79	0.86	0.83	0.63	0.75	0.67	1	0.91	0.89	0.79	0.78	0.8	1	0.75	0.76
Developing Countries																					
Argentina		2		2																	4
Brazil		2								1				1							7
Mexico						2	2	2		1	1							2		1	11
South Africa					1																5
Turkey															1						1
Share of Total	0.63	0.4	0.33	0.33	0	0.05	0.14	0.14	0	0.13	0.25	0	0	0.09	0.11	0	0	0.2	0.08	0.14	0.14
China	0	0	0	0	0	0	0	0	0	0	0	0	0	0	0	2	2	0	2	2	6
Share of Total	0	0	0	0	0	0	0	0	0	0	0	0	0	0	0	0.11	0.22	0	0.17	0.17	0.03

(*Continued*)

Table 6.3   (*Continued*)

Reporting Member	1995	1996	1997	1998	1999	2000	2001	2002	2003	2004	2005	2006	2007	2008	2009	2010	2011	2012	2013	2014	Total
Other WTO Members																					
Chile						2															2
Costa Rica										1											1
Japan												1									1
New Zealand		1	2	1																	4
Peru	1						1		1	1						2					5
Venezuela										1											1
Share of Total	0.05	0.2	0.67	0.17	0	0.1	0.07	0	0.17	0.25	0	0.33	0	0	0	0.11	0	0	0	0	0.07
Total	19	5	3	6	14	21	14	14	6	8	4	3	2	11	9	19	10	9	13	12	202

Source: Author's computations based on the WTO Report (2015) of the Committee on Subsidies and Countervailing Measures, (Adopted October 27, 2015) and earlier years. CV measures by reporting member. https://www.wto.org/english/tratop_e/scm_e/scm_e.htm

Table 6.4   Safeguard Measures Imposed as Reported by WTO Members 1995–2014

Reporting Member	1995	1996	1997	1998	1999	2000	2001	2002	2003	2004	2005	2006	2007	2008	2009	2010	2011	2012	2013	2014	Total
Developed Countries																					
European Union	0	0	0	0	0	0	0	0	1	1	1	0	0	0	0	0	0	0	0	0	3
United States	1	0	1	1	2	0	1	0	0	0	0	0	0	0	0	0	0	0	0	0	6
Share of Total	1	0	0.2	0.2	0.29	0	0.14	0	0.17	0.17	0	0	0	0	0	0	0	0	0	0	0.06
Developing Countries																					
Argentina	0	1	0	0	0	2	0	0	0	0	0	1	0	0	0	0	0	0	0	0	4
Brazil	0	1	0	0	0	0	1	0	0	0	0	0	0	0	0	0	0	0	0	0	2
India	0	0	4	1	1	0	2	0	0	1	0	0	0	3	0	1	2	0	4	0	19
South Africa	0	0	0	0	0	0	0	0	0	0	0	1	0	0	0	0	0	0	1	0	2
Turkey	0	0	0	0	0	0	0	0	0	2	4	1	4	1	0	1	0	0	1	0	14
Share of Total	0	0.67	0.8	0.2	0.14	0.22	0.21	0	0	0.5	0.57	0.6	0.67	0.4	0	0.18	0.33	0	0.43	0	0.28
China	0	0	0	0	0	0	1	0	0	0	0	0	0	0	0	0	0	0	0	0	1
Share of Total	0	0	0	0	0	0	0.07	0	0	0	0	0	0	0	0	0	0	0	0	0	0.01
Other WTO Members	0	1	0	3	4	7	8	15	5	2	3	2	2	6	4	9	4	8	8	5	96
Share of Total	0	0.33	0	0.6	0.57	0.78	0.57	1	0.83	0.33	0.43	0.4	0.33	0.6	1	0.82	0.67	1	0.57	1	0.65
Total	1	3	5	5	7	9	14	15	6	6	7	5	6	10	4	11	6	8	14	5	147

Source: Author's computations based on the WTO Report (2015) of the Committee on Safeguards, (Adopted October 26, 2015) and earlier years. Safeguards measures by reporting member. https://www.wto.org/english/tratop_e/safeg_e/safeg_e.htm

up from 40 percent in 1995. Meanwhile, the share of measures of the four traditional users declined from 47 percent to 27 percent of the total number of AD measures in force during the period. Likewise for safeguard actions, the developed countries are no longer the primary litigants.

Second, it has always been the accepted paradigm that contingent protection measures are correlated with trade. Between 2001 and 2014, the value of world exports has increased by an average of 5.0 percent per annum. This is substantially larger than the annual rate of growth of AD initiations over the same period. The rate of expansion of world trade was also substantially higher than the annual growth in global AD measures. In fact, the number of measures per dollar of trade actually declined over the same period. However, this conclusion obscures the fact that trade — contingency measures are not targeted evenly against countries. As noted above, a number of developing Asian countries and especially the PRC have been subjected to a significant share of AD actions.

Having said that, one must keep in mind that the number of measures does not indicate what dumping margin was found and whether the duty that the authorities levy corresponds to the full dumping margin or only a part of it. Furthermore, AD measures are targeted at products, not countries. Consequently, the product subject to a trade contingency measure may differ in economic importance, depending on its volume and value, which country is applying the measure, and who the supplier is. Simply counting the number of safeguard investigations and measures would tend to underestimate the number of countries they impact, since such actions will apply in a non-discriminatory manner. With respect to AD and CVD, each country/product combination counts as a separate investigation and measure.

The continued spread of the use of AD measures to the smaller developing economies, raises the global share of AD measures in force during the observation period from 12 percent to 18 percent. There could be any number of reasons for the increase in the application of these trade contingency measures. Many countries did not have laws covering these measure but have enacted legislation on trade remedies in recent years. This may be a partial explanation for the preponderance of contingent protection measures coming from developing countries. Furthermore, the reduction in tariffs worldwide from bilateral, regional, plurilateral and multilateral initiatives have made smaller developing countries more open and more sensitive to disruptions arising from foreign trade. With this expanded trade comes expanded opportunities for investigating more imports for trade — contingency measures.

Examination of the stock of anti-dumping measures in force by targeted country (Table 6.5) shows a discernable asymmetry between AD users and targets. The top 10 users are the targets of less than 20 percent of all those targeted in the 1995–2014 period. A clear conclusion is that AD as a contingent protection instrument is an instrument enforced by a few developed and developing countries against the more successful exporting economies of the rest of the world. It is therefore not difficult to understand that there is little pressure to restrain their actions. In fact, the pressure is on each country to create its own anti-dumping investigating units.

This suggests that the domestic interests that are hurt by foreign AD measures are smaller than the interests that benefit from AD protection. This reflects the well-known economic proposition contained in the literature on contingent protection that views protection more as a conflict between domestic export interests and import-competing interests than as a conflict between countries.

To capture this aspect, the number of foreign AD measures adopted against the PRC over the 1995–2014 period are listed in Table 6.6, along with data on PRC exports to the litigant, as well as the litigant's exports to the PRC. Using this data, we wish to measure the competing pressures imposed by the import competing sector and the export sector on the drive to impose AD measures against the PRC.

The testable hypothesis is that:

$$AD_A = \alpha PRC_L^X + \beta PRC_L^M, \tag{6.1}$$

where AD_A represents the adopted AD measures. China's average exports to the litigant over the 1995–2014 period is represented by

Table 6.5   Top 10 Anti-Dumping Targets, 1995–2014 (number of measures in force)

Reporting Member	1995	1996	1997	1998	1999	2000	2001	2002	2003	2004	2005	2006	2007	2008	2009	2010	2011	2012	2013	2014	Total
Developed Countries																					
Australia	1		2	2	3	4	1	3	2			1	2	2	1		1	1	1		26
Canada	2	1	3	4			7	5	4	2	1	1	2	2	2	2		1	2	8	41
European Union	1	1	2	4	7	9	9	10	10	3	5	3	2	4	6	9	3	5	8	8	108
United States	12	21	15	16	14	13	15	11	21	14	12	11	7	8	14	19	10	9	13	11	266
Share of Total	0.1	0.1	0.09	0.1	0.07	0.09	0.09	0.09	0.16	0.09	0.09	0.08	0.08	0.07	0.1	0.17	0.09	0.07	0.08	0.08	0.09
Developing Countries																					
Argentina	1			1	4	2	5	3	1	3	4	3	1	2	2	2	1	2	5	2	44
Brazil	8	10	5	6	13	9	13	3	3	10	4	7	2	3	12	3	3	2	6	2	122
India	3	11	8	13	13	10	12	16	14	8	14	6	4	6	7	5	7	10	11	15	192
Mexico	3	5	2	9	4	6	4	1	4	3	2	2	2	3	1	1	3	3	6	3	66
South Africa	2	6	4	5	4	6	9	10	4	4	2	2	1	1	1	1	3	2	3	2	68
Turkey	2	3	1	2	6	7	5	4	4	1	2	2	3	4	2	4	4	5	5	8	72
Share of Total	0.12	0.15	0.08	0.14	0.12	0.12	0.13	0.13	0.13	0.11	0.13	0.11	0.08	0.08	0.13	0.11	0.12	0.12	0.13	0.13	0.12
China	20	43	33	27	43	43	55	50	53	49	53	73	61	78	78	44	51	60	75	63	1052
Share of Total		0.1		0.1	0.12	0.15	0.16	0.16	0.23	0.22	0.27	0.36	0.37	0.36	0.36	0.25	0.31	0.29	0.26	0.27	0.22
Other WTO Members	79	96	129	136	213	164	199	172	113	99	88	72	98	78	64	72	100	133	110		2312
Share of Total	0.5	0.42	0.52	0.52	0.59	0.55	0.53	0.55	0.41	0.51	0.5	0.43	0.44	0.45	0.36	0.37	0.44	0.48	0.46	0.47	0.49
Total	157	226	246	264	359	296	372	311	234	220	200	203	165	218	217	173	165	208	287	236	4757

Source: Author's computations based on the WTO Report (2015) of the Committee on Anti-Dumping Practices, (Adopted October 28, 2015) and earlier years. AD measures by reporting member: https://www.wto.org/english/tratop_e/adp_e/adp_e.htm

Table 6.6   Countries Targeting China for Anti-Dumping Measures, 1995–2014

Reporter	Number of Measures	China's Exports to AD Imposing Country Average 2001–2014 (Million $)	China's Exports as a Share of its Total Exports	China's Exports as a Share of Litigants Total Imports	Litigants Exports to China (Million $)
Argentina	91	4,031	0.003	0.093	4,012
Australia	45	20,312	0.016	0.129	35,777
Brazil	83	16,121	0.013	0.119	19,994
Canada	36	17,306	0.014	0.049	10,142
Chile	1	5,940	0.005	0.125	10,129
Colombia	39	3,026	0.002	0.087	1,521
Egypt	18	4,627	0.004	0.121	346
European Union	119	222,809	0.180	0.047	112,666
Guatemala	1	826	0.001	0.068	37
India	169	26,033	0.021	0.101	9,488
Indonesia	21	17,205	0.014	0.168	11,559
Israel	7	3,905	0.003	0.073	1,462
Jamaica	1	281	0.000	0.054	66
Japan	2	102,760	0.083	0.166	102,071
Korea, Republic of	26	55,037	0.045	0.157	85,343
Malaysia	8	20,416	0.017	0.145	17,248
Mexico	46	13,981	0.011	0.051	2,842
Morocco	1	1,909	0.002	0.063	151
New Zealand	9	2,277	0.002	0.079	2,939
Pakistan	11	5,740	0.005	0.169	1,207
Peru	22	2,514	0.002	0.107	3,753
Philippines	2	9,468	0.008	0.176	4,458
Poland	2	6,786	0.005	0.047	1,134
Russian Federation	11	24,669	0.020	0.136	19,692
South Africa	39	8,027	0.007	0.114	5,153
Taipei, Chinese	10	23,554	0.019	0.115	53,574
Thailand	17	15,510	0.013	0.102	15,373
Trinidad and Tobago	3	212	0.000	0.035	14
Turkey	68	9,130	0.007	0.058	1,479
Ukraine	9	4,246	0.003	0.083	1,237
United States	124	224,565	0.182	0.121	68,550
Uruguay	1	1,032	0.001	0.152	391
Venezuela	9	3,171	0.003	0.097	252
Vietnam	1	19,030	0.015	0.266	5,652
Total	1052	1,234,520			

Source: Author's computations based on the WTO Report (2015) of the Committee on Anti-Dumping Practices (Adopted October 28, 2015), and earlier years. AD measures by reporting member: https://www.wto.org/english/tratop_e/adp_e/adp_e.htm

PRC_L^X and the litigants average exports to the PRC over the same period is noted as PRC_L^M. It is expected that China's exports to the litigant will have a larger impact on probability of the litigant's desire to move for an AD measure. That is, $\alpha > 0$ and $\beta < 0$.

Applying a generalized linear estimator for this cross-section data, we have the following results, which fall within the expected hypothesis.

	Constant	PRC_L^X	PRC_L^M
Coefficient	33.92142	0.0006195	−0.0005727
Std. Error	7.824198	0.0001821	0.0002435
z	4.34	3.40	−2.35
$P > |z|$	0.000	0.001	0.019
Wald chi$^2(2)$ = 12.71			
Prob > chi^2 = 0.0017			

The import — competing sector has a larger say in the litigation decision with respect to the PRC than do the export interests of the litigant.

The PRC, which experienced its own litany of AD measures, (as shown in Table 6.6) has joined the other AD users, expanding its use of these measures from less than 1 percent at its entry into the WTO to 8 percent in 2014. Table 6.7 summarizes China's AD actions against other WTO members.

6.2. The Sectoral Pattern of AD Measures, CVDs and Safeguards

The evidence shows that AD measures, are concentrated in certain sectors: metals and metal products, chemical products, plastic and rubber products, machinery and electrical appliances and textiles and textile articles (see Figure 6.1). Base metals and articles (30 percent of all AD measures) and chemical and allied industries (20.9 percent of all AD measures) accounted for more than half of all AD measures over the last 20 years (1995–2014).

Table 6.7   Countries Against Whom China is
Imposing Anti-Dumping Measures, 1995–2014

Exporter	Number of Measures
Belgium	1
Brazil	1
Canada	2
European Union	20
France	2
Germany	4
India	7
Indonesia	3
Iran	1
Italy	1
Japan	29
Kazakhstan	1
Korea, Republic of	27
Malaysia	3
Mexico	1
Netherlands	2
New Zealand	1
Russian Federation	9
Saudi Arabia	1
Singapore	5
Taipei, Chinese	14
Thailand	4
Ukraine	1
United Kingdom	3
United States	33
Total	176

One conceivable explanation for this sectoral distribution is that it is due to a sector's relative importance in world trade. This explanation does not hold any credibility. The frequency of AD measures is not related to that sectors' share of world trade. For example, in the case of base metals and articles and products from chemical and allied industries, their share of world trade was below 10 percent, during the 1995–2014 period.

It is far more likely that the explanatory factors that account for their prominent role in the AD measures is due to industry — specific characteristics like the presence of economies of scale, predisposition

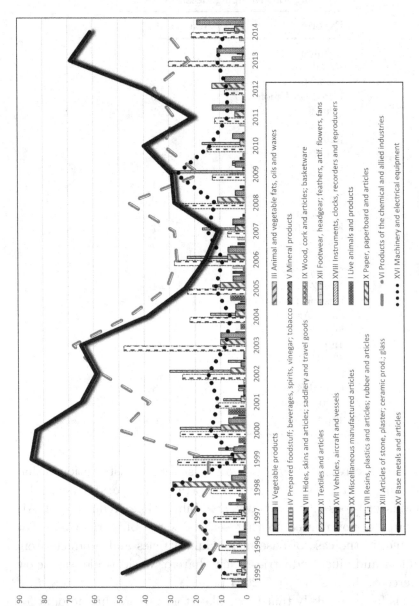

Figure 6.1   AD Measures, by HS Sector and Year

to cyclical downturns, capital intensity of the industry, exposure to trade (both on the import and export side) and the political importance of the sector as measured by the size of employment and spillover effects.

For safeguard measures (Figure 6.2) and CVD measures (Figure 6.3), the general commodity composition of the protected sectors is identical to that for AD measures. For the most part, the data on AD, CVD and safeguard measures are consistent with the notion that some contingency measures are used as tools of flexibility. Whether these are related to macroeconomic downturns is simply conjecture. The increased use of AD actions, CVDs and safeguards seems to be linked to the increased participation of developing countries.

Overall, when we shift our focus to the commodity composition of China's use of AD measures, it should not be surprising that over the past 15 years, there has been the most extensive AD action in the chemicals and metals sectors and industrial component parts comprised of semi-transformed raw materials (see Table 6.8). For HS — VI and VII, China reported that these products represented 28 percent of AD measures imposed on it. Similarly, these products represented 74 percent of AD measures that China imposed on others.

Lower input costs in China place these industries at a distinct advantage vis-à-vis the US and EU with regard to production levels and pricing, thus inviting accusations of price undercutting in AD actions. China's own litigation in the same sectors points to the costs differentials between China and other Asian developing countries. Whatever the reason, the trends in sector targeting over the past 15 years are a clear indicator that a high proportion of AD investigations have been concentrated in sectors where production has shifted to other countries and the standard US and EU pattern of competitive advantage is in decline. The Chinese litigation in the same broad sectors highlights its own cost sensitivity.

The discussion of the sectoral specificity of AD, CVD and safeguard actions verify the often — cited view that these actions are specific to the country, product and time in question. As the various

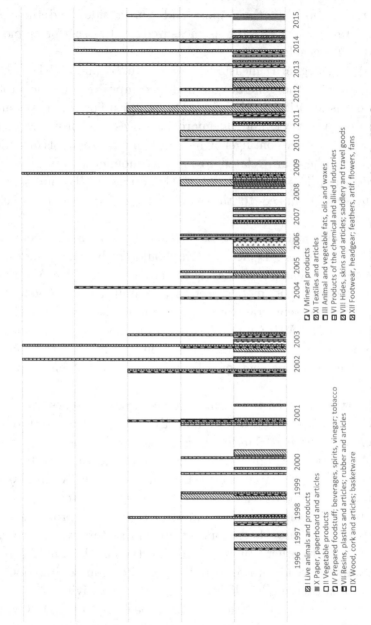

Figure 6.2   Safeguard Measures by HS Sector and Year, Reported by the WTO

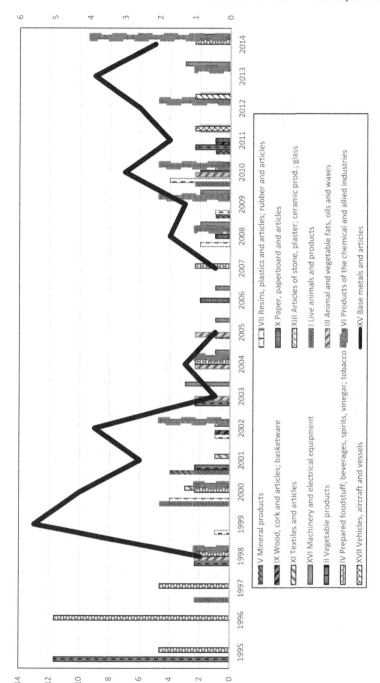

Figure 6.3   Countervailing Measures by HS Sector and Year

Table 6.8   Commodity Composition of China's CV and AD Measures, 1995–2014

HS Section Name	Countervailing Measures		AD Measures	
	China Exporter	China Reporter	China Exporter	China Reporter
I Live animals and products	6	1	3	1
II Vegetable products	1	1	11	1
III Animal and vegetable fats, oils and waxes				
IV Prepared foodstuff; beverages, spirits, vinegar; tobacco	2		4	4
V Mineral products	3		8	
VI Products of the chemical and allied industries	2	2	159	95
VII Resins, plastics and articles; rubber and articles			57	36
VIII Hides, skins and articles; saddlery and travel goods			2	
IX Wood, cork and articles; basketware	3		15	
X Paper, paperboard and articles			14	13
XI Textiles and articles	31		70	3
XII Footwear, headgear; feathers, artif. flowers, fans			16	
XIII Articles of stone, plaster; ceramic prod.; glass	7		48	
XIV Natural or cultured pearls, stones, precious metals, articles thereof				

XV	Base metals and articles	1	1	202	15
XVI	Machinery and electrical equipment			85	1
XVII	Vehicles, aircraft and vessels		1	12	2
XVIII	Instruments, clocks, recorders and reproducers			13	5
XIX	Arms and ammunition; parts and accessories thereof				
XX	Miscellaneous manufactured articles			40	
Total		56	6	759	176

Source: Author's computations based on the WTO Report (2015) of the Committee on Anti-Dumping Practices (Adopted October 28, 2015), and earlier years. AD measures by reporting member: https://www.wto.org/english/tratop_e/adp_e/adp_e.htm and on the WTO Report (2015) of the Committee on Subsidies and Countervailing Measures, (Adopted October 27, 2015) and earlier years. CV measures by reporting member. https://www.wto.org/english/tratop_e/scm_e/scm_e.htm.

sources of external competition have shifted over the past 15 years, so too have the focal points of these protective measures. As Finger [1996] has pointed out, these measures are "legalized backsliding" from the liberalization of multilateral trade negotiations. Industries that are confronted with global competition and reduced barriers to trade are constantly looking for creative methods to protect themselves. The PRC is a part of this new game.

6.3. US Measures Against the PRC as a Non-Market Economy

Under US jurisprudence, AD law considers dumping to have occurred when a foreign manufacturer charges a price that is "less than the fair market value" (LTFMV) for its product.[2] For allegations to market based economies, the Department of Commerce (DOC) employs a standard methodology for determining a product's fair — market value. First, the DOC determines whether a foreign manufacturer's goods were sold in the United States for LTFMV by comparing the U.S. price of the product with the fair market value of similar merchandise in the firm's domestic market. If the product is not sold or offered for sale in the foreign firm's domestic market, the DOC identifies the price at which the product is sold or offered for sale in countries other than the US. Finally, if there are no sales in the home market or to third countries, the statute authorizes the DOC to utilize a "constructed value."

If the DOC finds that dumping has occurred, it establishes the "dumping margin" by calculating the average amount by which the product's fair market value exceeds the price of the product in the United States. The finding of dumping and establishing the "dumping margin" is the first of the two prongs required to impose an AD duty. The final step in imposing an AD duty is an affirmative determination that the dumping has caused, or threatens to cause, a material injury to a U.S. industry. The latter injury determination is

---

[2]The US law is contained in 19 U.S.C. § 1677 (2000). Constructed value is contained in 19 U.S.C. § 1677b(a)2 (2000). The methodology to calculate the latter is contained in 19 U.S.C. § 1677b(e)(1) (2000).

made by the International Trade Commission (ITC), an independent agency.[3]

The difficulty here is that the PRC was considered a NME during the period after its accession to the WTO. NMEs do not allocate resources according to traditional market concepts of supply and demand, and do not adhere to the concept of prices being determined by demand and supply — ala market forces. Consequently, it is impossible to determine "fair market value" in the case of the PRC. Given this problem, the US practice was to use administrative agency action rather than a statute.[4]

In the 1960s, the US Treasury Department, which was at the time, the agency with responsibility over domestic trade remedy laws, developed and began using what was known as the "surrogate country" approach for applying AD law to NMEs. Under this approach, comparable prices and costs from similarly situated third countries were substituted for the NME to determine fair market value. This approach was adopted and codified by Congress in the Trade Act of 1974. The "surrogate country" methodology has a multitude of problems in finding a "similarly situated third country" and was ultimately withdrawn as a sanctioned practice when there was no available "surrogate country."

An alternative methodology adopted in 1975, known as the "factors of production" approach, required that the amount of each factor input be taken from a market economy country considered to be at a "comparable stage of economic development."[5] Congress expressly adopted this approach in the Trade Agreements Act of

---

[3]Under 19 U.S.C. § 1677(7)(A)(2000) the term 'material injury' means 'harm which is not inconsequential, immaterial, or unimportant'. In the event that the issue is 'threatened injuries' 19 U.S.C. § 1677(7)(F)(ii) (2000) requires that the ITC support its findings by evidence that 'the threat of material injury is real and that actual injury is imminent' and 'not merely based on conjecture or supposition.'

[4]This US action existed in the period between the US Antidumping Act of 1921, ch. 14 § 205, 42 Stat. 9, 13 (1921) and the US Trade Act of 1974, P.L. 93-6 18, § 32 1, 88 Stat. 1978, 2074 (1974).

[5]The famous case where this was applied was the Electric Golf Cars from Poland, 40 FED. REG. 5,497 (1975).

1979. This did not solve many of the problems found in investigating a NME.

In the Omnibus Trade and Competitiveness Act of 1988 (OTCA), Congress enacted numerous reforms to the AD laws, starting with a definition of a NME as well as a set of standards that the DOC was to take into consideration when determining whether a specific country is a NME. According to the OTCA, a NME is a country that "does not operate on market principles of cost or pricing structures, so that sales of merchandise in such country do not reflect the fair value of the merchandise." The factors the DOC must take into consideration when making a determination regarding a country's status as a NME include:

> (i) the extent to which the currency of the foreign country is convertible into the currency of other countries; (ii) the extent to which wage rates in the foreign country are determined by free bargaining between labor and management; (iii) the extent to which joint ventures or other investments by firms of other foreign countries are permitted in the foreign country; (iv) the extent of government ownership or control of the means of production; (v) the extent of government control over the allocation of resources and over the price and output decisions of enterprises and (vi) such other factors as the administering authority considers appropriate.

The most import change is that the DOC was given significant administrative discretion in determining when a foreign country is a NME. According to the statute, the determination of NME status may be made with respect to any foreign country at any time, and remains effective until expressly revoked by the DOC. Moreover, the DOC's determinations are not subject to judicial review in any AD investigation [Pelzman, 2003].

Along with AD statues, the US CVD laws are designed and intended to provide relief to domestic industries that have been, or are threatened with the adverse impact from imported goods sold in the U.S. market that have been subsidized by a foreign government or other public entity. Specifically, the relief provided takes the form of an additional import duty on the subsidized imports. The duty levied is to be equal to the estimated amount of the government or other public entities' subsidization. Similar to AD law, for an industry to obtain relief, both the ITC and the DOC must make conclusive determinations. The DOC must find that the targeted imports have been subsidized, and ITC must find that the domestic industry has been materially injured or threatened with material injury due to the subsidized imports.

Unlike the AD laws, however, U.S. CVD laws have not been traditionally applied to NMEs. This is largely as a result of a 1984 determination by the DOC that there is no adequate way to measure market distortions caused by subsidies in a NME. The first determination by the DOC regarding the application of CVD law to NMEs involved carbon steel wire rods manufactured in Czechoslovakia and Poland, both of which were NMEs. At the time of the DOC's decision, the United States had two separate CVD statutes. The first, § 303 of the Tariff Act of 1930, applied

> [w]henever any country, dependency, colony, province or other political subdivision of government, person, partnership, association, cartel or corporation, shall pay or bestow, directly or indirectly, any bounty or grant upon the manufacture or production or export of any article or merchandise manufactured or produced in such country, dependency, colony, province or other political subdivision of government.[6]

The second CVD statute, section 701(b) of the Tariff Act of 1930, was enacted as part of the Trade Agreements Act of 1979 and intended to bring the United States into compliance with the Agreement on the Interpretation and Application of Articles VI, XVI and XXIII of the GATT (Subsidies Code). This section of the CVD law to "country under the Agreement" required that the United States first make a determination that the subsidized imports either caused, or threatened to cause, material injury to an industry in the United States, or caused the establishment of an industry in the United States to be materially retarded.

After a number of cases involving NMEs were brought before the DOC, it concluded that CVD laws do not apply to NMEs. Despite this decision, and the decision of the US Court of International Trade (USCIT) ordering the DOC to reconsider its decision, the Court of

---

[6]Tariff Act of 1930, ch. 479, § 303 (1930).

Appeals for the Federal Circuit reversed the USCIT decision and reinstated the DOC conclusion not to apply CVD law to NMEs. The Court interpreted Congressional action as its intention to deal with imports from NMEs under AD laws, not CVD laws.

Questions concerning CVD action against NMEs reappeared in 1991. That year, the DOC did have occasion to examine a petition alleging the subsidization of ceiling and oscillating fans imported from China.[7] Although China was considered a NME, the petition was based on the theory that this particular industry was sufficiently market-oriented that the DOC could reliably use the economic data provided by the industry itself, consistent with the standards utilized for CVD investigations in market economies.

The overriding question remained how to evaluate an industry within a NME to be a market player. The DOC, in its discretion, utilized a three-part test which has been subject to many objections. First, "there must be virtually no government involvement in setting prices or amounts to be produced." Second, the industry "should be characterized by private or collective ownership." There may be SOEs in the industry, but substantial state ownership would weigh heavily against finding a market-oriented industry. Finally, "[m]arket-determined prices must be paid for all significant inputs, whether material or non-material (e.g. labor and overhead), and for an all-but-insignificant proportion of all the inputs accounting for the total value of the merchandise under investigation." After completing its investigation in this case, the DOC concluded that CVD law did not apply to the Chinese ceiling and oscillating fan industry. With that ruling, the DOC did not receive another CVD petition against a NME until 2006.

The various CVD cases brought against the PRC after 2006 sparked a legal debate in the US and the WTO. In order to quench this debate, the US Administration pushed new legislation authorizing the DOC to impose CVDs on NME products. This

---

[7]Department of Commerce, Final Negative Countervailing Duty Determinations: *Oscillating and Ceiling Fans from the People's Republic of China*, 57 FED. REG. 4,018 (June 5, 1992).

Table 6.9 US Antidumping and Countervailing Duty Orders in Place (1977–2009/2015)

Country	AD	CVD	Grand Total	Percent of Total
China	98	31	129	39.7
India	15	8	23	7.1
Taiwan	21	1	22	6.8
Korea	14	3	17	5.2
Japan	15		15	4.6
Vietnam	9	3	12	3.7
Indonesia	8	3	11	3.4
Mexico	10		10	3.1
Brazil	7	2	9	2.8
Thailand	7	1	8	2.5
Turkey	4	4	8	2.5
Italy	6	1	7	2.2
Russia	6		6	1.8
Ukraine	5		5	1.5
South Africa	3	1	4	1.2
Germany	4		4	1.2
Malaysia	4		4	1.2
Iran	1	2	3	0.9
Spain	3		3	0.9
United Arab Emirates	2		2	0.6
France	2		2	0.6
Moldova	2		2	0.6
Canada	2		2	0.6
Sweden	1		1	0.3
Ukraine	1		1	0.3
Chile	1		1	0.3
Poland	1		1	0.3
Venezuela	1		1	0.3
Romania	1		1	0.3
Philippines	1		1	0.3
Australia	1		1	0.3
Belarus	1		1	0.3
India		1	1	0.3
Netherlands	1		1	0.3
Belgium	1		1	0.3
Kazakhstan	1		1	0.3
Argentina	1		1	0.3
Oman	1		1	0.3

(*Continued*)

Table 6.9   (*Continued*)

Country	AD	CVD	Grand Total	Percent of Total
Latvia	1		1	0.3
Trinidad and Tobago	1		1	0.3
Grand Total	264	61	325	100.0

Source: USITC, Antidumping and Countervailing Duty Orders in Place, as of September 29, 2015

Table 6.10   USITC, Antidumping and Countervailing Duty Orders Against China, in Place, as of September 29, 2015 (1984–2015)

Order Date	AD/ CVD	Product Group	Product	Fed Reg
01/31/1984	A	CH	Potassium permanganate	75 FR 65448
03/22/1984	A	CH	Chloropicrin	80 FR 57149
10/17/1984	A	CH	Barium chloride	75 FR 36629
05/09/1986	A	ISO	Iron construction castings	75 FR 70900
08/28/1986	A	MSC	Petroleum wax candles	76 FR 773
12/02/1986	A	MSC	Porcelain-on-steel cooking ware	76 FR 13602
06/15/1987	A	ISO	Tapered roller bearings	77 FR 52682
02/19/1991	A	MSC	Heavy forged hand tools-Axes & adzes	
02/19/1991	A	MSC	Heavy forged hand tools-Bars & wedges	76 FR 52313
02/19/1991	A	MSC	Heavy forged hand tools-Hammers and sledges	
02/19/1991	A	MSC	Heavy forged hand tools-Picks and mattocks	
06/10/1991	A	MM	Silicon metal	77 FR 23660
07/06/1992	A	ISO	Carbon steel butt-weld pipe fittings	76 FR 21331
08/19/1992	A	CH	Sulfanilic acid	76 FR 66039
10/19/1993	A	MSC	Helical spring lock washers	76 FR 75873
11/16/1994	A	AG	Fresh garlic	77 FR 28355
11/25/1994	A	MSC	Paper clips	76 FR 44575
12/22/1994	A	MM	Silicomanganese	7 FR 66956
12/28/1994	A	MSC	Cased pencils	76 FR 40880
03/29/1995	A	CH	Glycine	76 FR 57951
05/12/1995	A	MM	Pure magnesium (ingot)	76 FR 72172
06/21/1995	A	CH	Furfuryl alcohol	77 FR 9203
07/07/1997	A	CH	Persulfates	79 FR 17506

(*Continued*)

Table 6.10 (*Continued*)

Order Date	AD/ CVD	Product Group	Product	Fed Reg
09/15/1997	A	AG	Crawfish tail meat	79 FR 24482
10/24/1997	A	ISM	Carbon steel plate	74 FR 57994
02/19/1999	A	AG	Preserved mushrooms	80 FR 53104
09/07/2001	A	ISM	Steel concrete reinforcing bar	78 FR 43858
09/17/2001	A	MM	Foundry coke	77 FR 66956
11/19/2001	A	MM	Pure magnesium (granular)	7 FR 63787
11/29/2001	A	ISM	Hot-rolled carbon steel flat products	79 FR 7425
12/10/2001	A	AG	Honey	77 FR 74173
01/08/2002	A	MSC	Folding gift boxes	78 FR 14269
01/28/2003	A	MM	Ferrovanadium	80 FR 8607
04/07/2003	A	ISO	Non-malleable cast iron pipe fittings	79 FR 8437
10/01/2003	A	CH	Barium carbonate	80 FR 8286
10/01/2003	A	CH	Polyvinyl alcohol	80 FR 30208
11/19/2003	A	CH	Refined brown aluminum oxide	79 FR 61606
12/12/2003	A	ISO	Malleable iron pipe fittings	79 FR 47089
08/06/2004	A	MSC	Ironing tables	75 FR 36629
08/06/2004	A	CH	Tetrahydrofurfuryl alcohol	80 FR 20470
08/09/2004	A	PRSG	Polyethylene retail carrier bags	75 FR 38978
12/02/2004	A	MSC	Hand trucks	80 FR 50266
12/29/2004	A	CH	Carbazole Violet Pigment 23	75 FR 29718
01/04/2005	A	MSC	Wooden bedroom furniture	75 FR 82373
01/25/2005	A	MSC	Crepe paper	80 FR 57149
02/01/2005	A	AG	Frozen warm-water shrimp and prawns	76 FR 23972
03/30/2005	A	MSC	Tissue paper	75 FR 42067
04/15/2005	A	MM	Magnesium	76 FR 13356
06/24/2005	A	CH	Chlorinated Isocyanurates	75 FR 62764
06/01/2006	A	MSC	Certain artist canvas	76 FR 69704
09/28/2006	A	MSC	Certain lined paper	77 FR 53172
04/27/2007	A	CH	Certain activated carbon	78 FR 16654
06/01/2007	A	CH	Certain polyester staple fiber	77 FR 62217
03/19/2008	A	CH	Sodium Hexametaphosphate	78 FR 42754
07/22/2008	A	ISP	Circular welded carbon quality steel pipe	78 FR 72863
07/22/2008	C	ISP	Circular welded carbon quality steel pipe	78 FR 72863

(*Continued*)

Table 6.10   (*Continued*)

Order Date	AD/ CVD	Product Group	Product	Fed Reg
08/01/2008	A	ISO	Steel nails	79 FR 1830
08/05/2008	A	ISP	Light-walled rectangular pipe and tube	79 FR 35522
08/05/2008	C	ISP	Light-walled rectangular pipe and tube	79 FR 35522
08/07/2008	A	MSC	Laminated woven sacks	79 FR 16770
08/07/2008	C	MSC	Laminated woven sacks	79 FR 17134
08/27/2008	A	CH	Sodium nitrite	79 FR 8438
08/27/2008	C	CH	Sodium nitrite	79 FR 53016
09/04/2008	A	PRSG	New Pneumatic Off-the-Road Tires	79 FR 6539
09/04/2008	C	PRSG	New Pneumatic Off-the-Road Tires	79 FR 6539
09/17/2008	A	MSC	Raw flexible magnets	79 FR 6886
09/17/2008	C	MSC	Raw flexible magnets	79 FR 6886
10/06/2008	A	ISO	Steel wire garment hangers	79 FR 13613
10/07/2008	A	MM	Electrolytic manganese dioxide	73 FR 58537
11/10/2008	A	PRSG	Polyethylene terephthalate film, sheet, and strip	80 FR 6689
11/24/2008	A	MSC	Lightweight thermal paper	80 FR 5083
11/24/2008	C	MSC	Lightweight thermal paper	80 FR 5083
12/11/2008	A	MSC	Uncovered innerspring units	79 FR 22624
01/23/2009	C	ISP	Circular welded carbon quality steel line pipe	79 FR 28894
01/23/2009	C	ISP	Circular welded carbon quality steel line pipe	74 FR 4136
02/19/2009	A	MSC	Uncovered innerspring units	79 FR 22624
02/26/2009	A	MSC	Small diameter graphite electrodes	79 FR 35523
03/17/2009	A	ISP	Circular welded austenitic stainless pressure pipe	79 FR 42760
3/19/2009	C	ISP	Circular welded austenitic stainless pressure pipe	79 FR 47089
4/14/2009	A	ISO	Steel threaded rod	79 FR 49050
5/13/2009	A	ISP	Circular welded carbon quality steel line pipe	79 FR 28894
5/13/2009	A	ISP	Circular welded carbon quality steel line pipe	74 FR 22515
5/29/2009	A	CH	Citric acid and certain citrate	80 FR 36318
5/29/2009	C	CH	Citric acid and certain citrate	80 FR 36318
8/3/2009	A	MSC	Tow Behind Lawn Groomer	80 FR 6049

(*Continued*)

Table 6.10 (*Continued*)

Order Date	AD/ CVD	Product Group	Product	Fed Reg
9/14/2009	A	MSC	Kitchen Appliance Shelving and Racks	80 FR 12983
9/14/2009	C	MSC	Kitchen Appliance Shelving and Racks	80 FR 12983
1/20/2010	C	ISP	Oil Country Tubular Goods	80 FR 28224
5/21/2010	A	ISP	Oil Country Tubular Goods	80 FR 28224
6/29/2010	A	ISO	Prestressed Concrete Steel Wire Strand	75 FR 37382
7/7/2010	C	ISO	Prestressed Concrete Steel Wire Strand	75 FR 38977
7/22/2010	A	CH	Potassium Phosphate Salts	75 FR 42683
7/22/2010	C	CH	Potassium Phosphate Salts	75 FR 42682
7/23/2010	A	ISO	Steel Grating	75 FR 43143
7/23/2010	C	ISO	Steel Grating	75 FR 43144
9/1/2010	A	TX	Narrow Woven Ribbons With Woven Selvedge	75 FR 53632
9/1/2010	C	TX	Narrow Woven Ribbons With Woven Selvedge	75 FR 53642
9/20/2010	A	MSC	Certain Magnesia Carbon Bricks	75 FR 57257
9/21/2010	C	MSC	Certain Magnesia Carbon Bricks	75 FR 57442
11/10/2010	A	ISP	Seamless Carbon and Alloy Steel Standard, Line, and Pressure Pipe	75 FR 69052
11/10/2010	C	ISP	Seamless Carbon and Alloy Steel Standard, Line, and Pressure Pipe	75 FR 69050
11/17/2010	A	MSC	Coated Paper Suitable for High-Quality Print Graphics Using Sheet-Fed Presses	75 FR 70203
11/17/2010	C	MSC	Coated Paper Suitable for High-Quality Print Graphics Using Sheet-Fed Presses	75 FR 70201
11/22/2010	A	MSC	Seamless Refined Copper Pipe and Tube	75 FR 71070
05/26/2011	A	MM	Aluminum Extrusions	76 FR 30650
05/26/2011	C	MM	Aluminum Extrusions	76 FR 30653
12/08/2011	A	MSC	Multilayered Wood Flooring	76 FR 76690
12/08/2011	C	MSC	Multilayered Wood Flooring	76 FR 76693

(*Continued*)

Table 6.10   (*Continued*)

Order Date	AD/ CVD	Product Group	Product	Fed Reg
05/10/2012	A	CH	Stilbenic Optical Brightening Agent	77 FR 27423
06/21/2012	A	ISO	High Pressure Steel Cylinders	77 FR 37377
06/21/2012	C	ISO	High Pressure Steel Cylinders	77 FR 37384
12/07/2012	A	MSC	Crystalline Silicon Photovoltaic Cells	77 FR 73018
12/07/2012	C	MSC	Crystalline Silicon Photovoltaic Cells	77 FR 73017
02/15/2013	A	ISO	Utility Scale Wind Towers	78 FR 11146
02/15/2013	C	ISO	Utility Scale Wind Towers	78 FR 11152
4/11/2013	A	ISO	Drawn Stainless Steel Sinks	78 FR 21592
4/11/2013	C	ISO	Drawn Stainless Steel Sinks	78 FR 21596
07/19/2013	A	CH	Xanthan Gum	78 FR 43143
06/24/2014	A	ISO	Prestressed Concrete Steel Rail Tie Wire	79 FR 35727
11/13/2014	C	CH	Chlorinated Isocyanurates	79 FR 67424
11/26/2014	A	CH	Monosodium Glutamate	79 FR 70505
12/03/2014	A	ISM	Non-Oriented Electrical Steel	79 FR 71741
12/03/2014	C	ISM	Non-Oriented Electrical Steel	79 FR 71749
1/8/2015	A	ISM	Carbon and Certain Alloy Steel Wire	80 FR 1015
1/8/2015	C	ISM	Carbon and Certain Alloy Steel Wire	80 FR 1018
01/30/2015	A	CH	Calcium Hypochlorite	80 FR 5085
01/30/2015	C	CH	Calcium Hypochlorite	80 FR 5082
02/18/2015	A	ME	Crystalline Silicon Photovoltaic Products	80 FR 8592
02/18/2015	C	ME	Crystalline Silicon Photovoltaic Products	80 FR 8592

AA = Antidumping Act of 1921
A = Section 731 of the Tariff Act of 1930
    (antidumping)
C = Section 701 of the Tariff Act of 1930
    (countervailing duty)
C4 = Section 104 of the Trade Agreements Act of 1979
    (countervailing duty)
C-None = No Commission investigation (countervailing duty)
AG = Agricultural, forest and processed food products
CH = Chemicals and pharmaceuticals

(*Continued*)

Table 6.10 (*Continued*)

Order Date	AD/ CVD	Product Group	Product	Fed Reg
ISM = Iron & steel: Mill products				
ISO = Iron & steel: Other products & castings				
ISP = Iron & steel: Pipe products				
ME = Machinery and electronic/scientific equipment				

Source: USITC, Antidumping and Countervailing Duty Orders in Place, as of September 29, 2015

legislation was introduced in February 20, 2012, quickly enacted by Congress and signed by the President in March 13, 2012. This legislation was made effective as of November 20, 2006. Many believe that a retroactive date for the new CVD authority was unconstitutional. The USCIT upheld the constitutionality of this law with its retroactive date.

The USITC data listed in Table 6.9 clearly reveal that the focus of AD and CVD action has been predominantly on the PRC. Between 1984 and 2015, 40 percent of AD and CVD orders were against the PRC. The product categories affected are listed in Table 6.10. As we noted above, the choice of products under investigation are those where the US has lost competitiveness. Out of the total of 325 tariff lines, 49 percent were iron and steel mill products (ISM), other products and castings (ISO) and Pipe products (ISP). The other major subgroup consisted of miscellaneous manufactured products (MSC), making up 17.5 percent of the tariff lines under AD or CVD orders. Overall, one can reasonably conclude that the PRC was subjected to the market principle of "creative protectionism" above and beyond other defendants.

Chapter 7

Quantifying and Modeling PRC Foreign Aid — A Search for Markets, Infrastructure and Service Contracts and Resources

In the past 15 years, the PRC's involvement in the economies of Latin America, Africa and Southeast Asia has caused concern in the US. Unlike the US and the former Soviet Union, the PRC has bolstered its economic presence in Latin America, Africa and Southeast Asia through its offers of financing or concessional loans for infrastructure projects, large economic investments and the signing of trade agreements. To many in these recipient countries, the PRC's aid activity is viewed as filling a major unmet development need, particularly in countries that have been relatively neglected by major aid donors.

The nature of the PRC's foreign aid is a major avenue for its "spillover effects" in Africa, Latin America and Southeast Asia. It is common to see roads, ports and rail transport being built by PRC engineers and construction teams. It is also common to see telecom services being provided by PRC companies. Consequently the PRC's aid activity represents a major challenge to the US aid program, which has traditionally relied on politically — motivated "tied aid" rather than on concessional loans, service contracts and infrastructure development. This chapter builds and tests a behavioral model of the PRC's foreign assistance. In order to accomplish this task, we first address the basic question of identifying statistically the components of what we refer to as PRC foreign aid.

7.1. Measuring PRC Foreign Aid

The PRC's foreign assistance is sufficiently different from the conventional norm that it is critical to first measure what it is. This task is made difficult because there is no PRC "budget line" designation called "foreign assistance." The current view of the PRC's aid activity is defined as simply "*ad hoc*" project funding [Lancaster, 2007]. The current paradigm of developed — country aid programs, when used to analyze the PRC's foreign aid, emphasizes the US — aid model as its benchmark and therefore misses the unique commercial PRC approach to foreign assistance. The point of departure for reviewing the PRC's aid flows must be done in an environment where the State is not centralized, but rather working under a "State Supervised Capitalism" (SSC) economy model, where economic objectives dominate the quantity of foreign aid and its location. Consequently, we look for project funding in infrastructure, telecom and energy.

In that context, it is no surprise to observe that the PRC's foreign assistance will encompass largely concessional or low-interest loans, as well as government-backed and subsidized investments in infrastructure and natural — resource extraction. With that new paradigm, it is not surprising that a very small portion of the PRC's aid would include what typically is characterized as "Official Development Assistance" (ODA) by other aid donors.[1] Few PRC foreign — aid activities fit the Organisation for Economic Co-operation and Development's (OECD) definition of ODA, as "flows of official financing to developing countries provided by official agencies which have a clear development or anti-poverty purpose and are at least partially concessional in nature," with a grant element of at least 25 percent.

---

[1]The focus of mainstream donors is on development grants, humanitarian assistance, social welfare programs and food aid. The PRC provided limited aid packages that fit this old mind set.

The starting point for quantifying the PRC's foreign aid is to understand that the objective function of its foreign assistance is its own development needs. In that context, the PRC's industrial development requires first and foremost access to host country raw materials at a reasonable price and a clear unencumbered path facilitating the export of the PRC's machinery and services. By contrast, the foreign aid programs of the US, Europe and most other major aid donors are not directly linked to their own country's development programs. Moreover, the other major DAC donors link their aid packages to non-economic objectives, such as political development and democratic reform. Among OECD countries, only Japan's history of ODA, with its relatively large loan component (from 60 percent in the mid-1990s to roughly 25 percent a decade later), emphasis on infrastructure projects, and links to its own economy, may come closest to providing a model for the PRC's foreign assistance [CRS, 2009; OECD, 2008a, 2008b; Japan Ministry of Foreign Affairs, 2007].

In the past few years, the PRC has taken some tentative steps toward making its foreign aid process more transparent, coordinating its programs with other aid providers, and offering more development-oriented assistance. The PRC has begun sending abroad "youth volunteers," similar to U.S. Peace Corps volunteers, engaged in teaching and training in such subjects as Chinese language and medicine, computer skills, agricultural technologies and sports.

Many of the PRCs economic activities in developing countries are supported by the PRC government, and provide benefits to recipient countries that otherwise may not be available, such as low or subsidized loans. Furthermore, many of the PRC's economic investments abroad can be counted as aid rather than as foreign direct investment (FDI) because they are secured by official bilateral agreements, do not impose real financial risks upon the PRC companies involved, or do not result in PRC ownership of foreign assets.

In Table 7.1, we present the official PRC aid flows to Africa, Latin America and Southeast Asia for the period 2000–2012, calculated by Aid Data on a project basis. This data includes ODA-like data that

Table 7.1   PRC Aid Commitments by Recipient (2000–2012)

(Thousand US$ 2009)

Recipient_name	2000	2001	2002	2003	2004	2005	2006	2007	2008	2009	2010	2011	2012
Afghanistan	849	8,895	289,580	27,939	32,247	0	14,849	14,404	16,399	77,288	23,133	22,560	20,516
Angola	0	54,479	2,982	18,205	0	136,750	269	8,157	0	0	8,239	257	0
Argentina	0	0	0	0	527,403	0	0	0	0	0	0	0	0
Bangladesh	82,041	0	221,520	15,572	1,425	56,056	299,132	4,236	8,804	893,688	5,493	76,975	19,945
Burundi	0	80,046	0	5,839	0	0	16,892	62,781	12,949	0	5,493	20,404	1,298
Benin	0	0	0	0	0	0	0	4,706	34,786	0	0	0	0
Brunei	0	0	0	0	0	0	0	0	0	0	14	0	0
Bolivia	0	0	0	48	0	0	0	0	524	830	99,475	49,737	23,786
Brazil	0	0	0	0	0	0	0	0	0	0	0	83	0
Botswana	1,025	0	0	38,929	61,736	5,255	12,682	1,569	163	4,403	5,493	200	0
Congo, Dem. Rep.	0	0	0	5,061	10,923	2,368	14,800	0	0	586	9	6,415	0
Central African Rep.	0	0	0	36,355	9,945	0	14,194	0	0	0	0	32,500	0
Congo, Rep.	0	131,516	0	12,474	0	8,311	19,867	0	677	33,475	75,698	7,108	1,038,758
Cote D'Ivoire	0	0	59,918	0	3,641	0	1,858	105,547	120,665	24,638	0	7,909	577,662
Chile	0	0	0	0	0	0	0	0	0	0	2,817	0	0
Cameroon	0	40,782	171	554	0	0	0	8,535	0	2,387	20,509	14,304	23,644
Colombia	0	0	0	0	0	0	1	0	354	293	186	0	0
Cape Verde	0	0	0	0	0	22,657	9,300	0	0	0	0	0	52,950
Djibouti	0	4,007	0	1,092	5,110	1,752	0	78	2,503	11,128	0	0	8,405
Algeria	0	0	4,959	973	0	0	0	0	0	0	0	0	0
Ecuador	0	0	71,085	4,028	0	0	1,884	0	0	58,600	0	0	0
Egypt	0	0	5,992	0	5,462	0	0	784	12,432	76	0	8,526	610,305
Eritrea	16,972	9,977	3,968	3,222	2,731	0	0	9	0	0	5,578	0	0
Ethiopia	380	229,568	41,445	24,070	0	61,829	1,109,806	25,512	10,302	459,002	520,828	675,760	118,692
Gabon	0	0	11,984	0	16,576	0	0	0	151,112	0	0	109,048	0
Ghana	50,103	64,061	101,668	157,267	34,984	5,255	80,412	233,577	9,090	170,817	1,016,183	13,375	207,558

Recipient_name													
Guinea	0	0	0	0	64,595	3,006	64,440	10,111	0	0	0	41,463	0
Equatorial Guinea	0	0	10,332	0	0	3,365	89,656	5,909	0	0	137	0	0
Guinea-Bissau	0	9,644	0	28,999	1,607	0	35,800	101	10,370	13,275	0	0	0
Guyana	0	0	0	10,247	46,221	0	0	44	0	34,891	0	3,849	0
Indonesia	68	8,036	10,152	32	284,558	951,082	345,938	9,982	1,892	550	1,401	110,250	267,273
Kenya	183,303	22,614	6,718	120	212,932	11,207	0	119,112	18,668	130,009	123,466	0	273,719
Cambodia	25,422	28,801	366,182	48,430	71,792	60,688	64,017	62,417	361,046	552,366	325,814	0	606,530
Kiribati	0	0	9,092	0	0	0	0	0	0	0	0	0	0
Comoros	0	0	0	13,886	0	0	0	0	4,303	9,125	0	0	193
Laos	0	0	66	4,588	124	0	2,153	202	973	44	0	36	358
Sri Lanka	0	10,043	0	11,204	45,863	79,532	6,497	0	200,928	465,331	1,283	0	214,070
Liberia	0	0	0	16,111	8,967	13,899	6,067	0	17,507	16,552	34,155	0	53,128
Lesotho	0	8,692	3,764	4,292	6,721	12,392	3,459	0	34,254	465	12,829	0	18,559
Libya	4,792	0	0	0	0	0	0	0	0	0	2,566	0	0
Morocco	0	0	6,152	910	10,118	0	50,120	0	4,070	0	1,061	0	0
Madagascar	0	56,416	6,613	5,839	29	0	75,589	10,570	22,730	2,746	63,217	0	66,566
Mali	0	83,930	0	340,996	15,191	50,120	72,793	21,055	8,208	0	0	0	10,259
Myanmar	29,958	0	119,026	0	813	40,593	16,274	291,028	9,222	0	6,415	0	0
Mauritania	0	0	0	30,281	195,220	3,365	15,335	0	280,488	2	7,461	0	7,262
Mauritius	29,096	8,036	23,967	0	7,829	160,818	4,172	4,752	0	0	0	0	13,296
Maldives	2,050	0	0	0	6,338	0	0	0	0	0	0	0	0
Malaysia	0	0	0	0	287	954,696	0	0	0	0	0	143	0
Malawi	0	0	0	11,301	0	0	0	70,779	47,764	0	0	0	2,626
Mozambique	339	36,831	198	8,700	16,508	94,233	277,364	3,033	50,750	6,674	565,013	0	72,029
Namibia	0	3,863	8,626	18,618	106,719	3,376	94,302	2,910	17,668	1,911	4,237	0	108,560
Niger	0	19,954	8,310	51	5,663	5,823	7,210	218	7,612	1,655	2,635	0	23,347
Nigeria	0	0	15,077	9,891	7,054	1,357,456	119,996	0	0	0	0	0	863,173
Nepal	10,251	119,024	0	1,557	21,948	36,942	9,573	15,238	439	41,138	79,375	0	673,869
Peru	0	0	1,984	1,933	1,688	0	358	101	0	0	0	0	3,989
Philippines	169,725	0	0	0	602,821	2,760,309	0	0	439	41,138	79,375	0	25

(Continued)

Table 7.1   (Continued)

Recipient_name	2000	2001	2002	2003	2004	2005	2006	2007	2008	2009	2010	2011	2012
Pakistan	9,801	99,727	0	322,618	75	23,148	3,634	477,725	314,907	24,005	1,898,773	11,842	0
Rwanda	8,201	39,259	9,092	0	0	77	20,078	193,274	1,506	37,983	15,076	0	153,147
Seychelles	424	0	0	0	0	72	1,688	18,270	3,539	5,928	5,493	50,679	0
Sudan	4,294	73,762	10,125	0	910	1,752	0	102,356	11,641	0	6,866	16,934	39,889
Singapore	0	0	0	0	0	0	0	0	0	0	0	0	0
Sierra Leone	424	0	0	403	0	0	0	26,253	16,785	0	0	170,195	8,538
Senegal	0	0	0	0	0	0	77,670	36,113	0	34,711	18,280	8,980	0
Somalia	0	0	0	0	208	13,066	0	1,948	0	146	0	13,263	0
Suriname	0	8,314	0	8,619	0	0	0	0	142,063	0	0	3,316	42,051
South Sudan	0	0	0	0	0	0	0	0	0	0	0	26,288	0
Chad	0	0	0	0	0	0	25,234	39,838	0	0	0	0	9,245
Togo	0	0	0	0	100	144	6,901	4,243	14,664	12,495	45,475	7,027	13,095
Thailand	51	0	0	0	150	20,165	9,421	478,585	0	117	1,373	2,155	0
Timor-Leste	10,251	0	0	0	1,055	0	0	549	578	4,391	5,578	0	0
Tunisia	0	0	0	0	65,541	388	0	0	4,365	0	2,754	11,432	35,883
Tanzania	95,606	100,547	3,862	15,894	0	0	16,131	0	1,525	28,179	9,511	66,896	1,469,277
Uganda	5,431	221,520	8,437	8,594	18,160	0	33,687	62,688	17,859	11,565	3,602	302,962	15,650
Uruguay	0	0	0	0	912	0	0	60	0	2,500	0	6,632	0
Venezuela	91,091	0	145,338	0	217	56,707	8,439	0	0	60,000	9,612,224	0	0
Vietnam	0	50	0	0	0	0	0	0	0	0	56	29	8
South Africa	44,266	0	0	0	0	0	3,376	0	0	0	0	0	0
Zambia	205	78,793	17,881	22,652	6,027	12,867	315,304	19,242	0	82,400	59,587	150,028	18,743
Zimbabwe	5,550	7,670	11,464	551,665	1,175,674	8,759	20,209	18,949	7,781	7,160	535,930	104,300	889,765
Total	881,970	1,668,859	1,617,728	1,810,037	2,933,273	2,215,692	7,167,845	3,953,255	1,553,427	3,141,151	15,287,401	3,383,427	8,677,641
Africa, regional	1,697,246	19,922	0	0	0	57	276,562	126,492	607	39,900	0	455,923	55,556

Source: Open Data for International Development

represent flows of official financing, administered with the promotion of the economic development and welfare of developing countries as the main objective. These financing flows are perceived to be concessional in character with a grant element of at least 25 percent (using a fixed 10 percent rate of discount), and OOF-like data that the OECD defines as "official sector transactions which do not meet the ODA criteria, e.g.:

  (i) Grants to developing countries for representational or essentially commercial purposes.

 (ii) Official bilateral transactions intended to promote development but having a grant element of less than 25 percent.

(iii) Official bilateral transactions, whatever their grant element, that are primarily export-facilitating in purpose. This category includes by definition export credits extended directly to an aid recipient by an official agency or institution ("official direct export credits").

(iv) The net acquisition by governments and central monetary institutions of securities issued by multilateral development banks at market terms.

 (v) Subsidies (grants) to the private sector to soften its credits to developing countries.

(vi) Funds in support of private investment.

"OOF-like" data includes grants with a representational or commercial purpose (i.e. grants that do not have a primary objective of promoting economic development or welfare in the recipient country), loans from a government institution that do not have any apparent grant element (commercial loans based on LIBOR or LIBOR plus a margin) or a grant element lower than 25 percent, and export credits from a government institution to a recipient institution [Brautigam, 2011]. OOF activities also include "short-term credits to exporters (export sellers' credits) to help them finance foreign sales, and ... longer-term credits to foreign buyers to assist in the export of goods and services" [Brautigam, 2011a]. OOF also includes lines of credit that a government provides to a donor enterprise (state-owned or not-state-owned) to do business overseas.[2] These projects may include any type of donor intent, such as for development, commercial, representational or mixed purposes.

Finally the data includes Vague (OF) data on official financing that are either ODA or OOF, but for which *Aid Data* cannot assign to either category. These projects may have "development" or "mixed (some development)" intent.

Overall, the total bundle of the PRC's aid grew from $881 million in 2000 to $8.7 billion in 2012. Despite the polemics, the PRC's aid to Latin America dropped from $1.7 billion in 2000 to $55.5 million in 2012. The data strongly indicate that the PRC has been providing significant and growing amounts of economic assistance, including ODA-like, OOF-like and Vague (OF), to developing countries. However, the estimated totals should be interpreted with caution. Some reported values may be inflated. Some loans represent offers or pledges that may not have been fulfilled. Some projects may have been cancelled, while others involving several parts or taking several years to complete may have been counted more than once. Furthermore, some reported PRC investments included in the *Aid Data* database may, in fact, qualify as FDI. Moreover, these data may also be underestimate of the value of PRC economic assistance, if the PRC does disclose the projects or if the reported values of the project do not include data on PRC materials and labor.

The PRC's foreign aid, despite its size, has a much larger impact factor than the larger DAC aid flows. The primary reasons given are that:

(i) The PRC's aid flows in the form of subsidized FDI are offered with limited bureaucratic pushback and without the political, economic, social and environmental conditions and safeguards

---

[2]In Ethiopia, ZTE was able to offer financing for the Ethiopian Government's Millennium Telecoms project, securing a US$1.5 billion deal for which the interest rate was LIBOR plus 150 basis points. Huawei offered a Brazilian firm financing at LIBOR plus 200 basis points, with a two-year grace period. As with the other forms of non-concessional official finance, these strategic lines of credit are clearly not ODA [Brautigam, 2011a].

that major OECD aid donors, multilateral financial institutions and multinational corporations typically impose.

(ii) The PRC targets developing countries that DAC countries have avoided because they are not financially viable.

(iii) The PRC, like the former Soviet Union, uses public works such as national cultural centers, stadiums, and highways, as a sign of PRC-LDC bonds. The announcement of these projects are done with great fanfare and noted as PRC "assistance" and not "foreign aid."

A review of the projects supported by PRC's economic "assistance" supports the argument that the PRC is driven primarily by the need for natural resources, export market, market for its services and by diplomatic objectives, such as bonds with the non-aligned movement. The PRC's economic assistance consists largely of concessional loans administered by the Ministry of Commerce through its Department of Aid to Foreign Countries. The PRC's government-backed investments made up over 65 percent of reported economic assistance activity, concessional loans constituted 30 percent, and grants and debt cancellations accounted for the remaining 5 percent during the 2000–2012 period. Approximately 50 percent of the PRC's economic "assistance" was directed at the natural resources and agricultural sectors, with the balance supporting infrastructure development.

7.2. A Behavioral Model of PRC Foreign Aid

One of the major foci of researchers on PRC foreign aid policies has been the exploration of the motivations for aid giving. The literature on the PRC's foreign aid to less-developed countries proposes several motivations for its extension of economic aid including: strategic benefits, economic returns and political gains. It also advances propositions concerning why there have been changes in aid patterns over time. Despite the fact that these explanations are often presented as hypotheses, they are all too often accepted as fact without systematic testing. More often than not, these studies are limited to a single continent, and hypotheses are often based on single-country studies. In addition, there have been minor attempts made at time-series analysis, but no extensive use has been made of this method.

In this chapter, we construct an economic behavioral model using time-series, multi-country, multi-continent data. This model integrates hypotheses or propositions extracted from the literature on the PRC's foreign aid and tests the reliability of these propositions. The basic question we address is: what determines the supply of the PRC's foreign economic aid to less-developed countries (LDCs)?

The basic assumption behind our model is that foreign aid is not given as a grant, but rather is given with the expectation that there will be some reciprocal flows. The return flow from this investment may take many forms, including:

(i) some displacement of the United States' influence in a region or country;
(ii) access to or possession of air and/or naval facilities; protection/security of PRC borders;
(iii) an increase in trade or access to raw materials;
(iv) political favors (i.e. support for actions in the United Nations).

The first two expectations listed above represent the strategic concerns that come into aid calculations. Strategic importance is often cited as the primary impetus for the PRC's aid to LDCs. However, the definition of what strategic importance means is somewhat vague. Four elements have been identified in the literature as contributing to a country's strategic importance. First is the opportunity to enhance the PRC's strategic position on a global basis or, in other words, to increase its strategic maneuverability around the world.

The second reason for a country's strategic importance is its proximity to the US. PRC decision-makers seem to want to increase their security by using aid to establish good relations around the entire globe and not just in areas closest to their border.

A third explanation for a country being of potential strategic importance is the possibility of the weakening of U.S. influence in that country and the surrounding area. Anywhere the American position can be eroded enhances the PRC's security, or at least enhances the sense of security, of the PRC.

The final reason for considering a country strategically important is to gain access to strategic raw materials. However, this criteria also overlaps with economic benefits. Since it is very hard in many cases to extract this particular element from other types of economic dealings, and since strategic raw materials are most likely to be acquired through economic aid or general trade agreements, this particular element will be included in the analysis of economic benefits.

Economic benefits include access not only to raw materials, but also to markets for end products and demand for the PRC's experts and services. Given the preference of LDCs for Western-made goods, it is necessary for the PRC to initially provide subsidized economic project funding that would finance the purchase of PRC goods, infrastructure and end products. In general, the PRC has a track record of providing long-term, low interest loans for infrastructure projects that provide local country development needs and allow the PRC to acquire raw materials necessary for its own consumption. A spillover effect of this aid package is the lock-in factor both for spare parts for PRC equipment and service personal.

The final explanation for the extension of economic aid is political or ideological affinity. Although there seems to be some inconsistency in the PRC's foreign aid activity, they do seem to have a policy of providing subsidized loans and infrastructure projects to countries that have not received assistance from the DAC countries.

The basic hypotheses for PRC — aid decisions are as follows:

(i) The PRC provides subsidized infrastructure projects in return for access to local markets.
(ii) The PRC provides these aid flows in countries not well served by the DAC countries.
(iii) The PRC provides assistance and informally promotes internal political conditions in a recipient country that fit their ideological predispositions.

(iv) The PRC gets access to a treasure of natural resources in exchange for its aid packages.

(v) The PRC gets a market for its exports and services.

7.3. A Model of PRC Supply of Foreign Aid

In modeling the supply of the PRC's foreign aid to recipients in Latin America, Africa and Southeast Asia based on our conceptual material outlined above, we begin by assuming that the PRC's decision-makers maximize their utility function (U)

$$U = \phi(D, R), \tag{7.1}$$

where D is the consumption of non-aid related goods and R is the consumption of goods and services originating from the aid recipients. This reciprocal flow of goods and services originating from the recipient is assumed to be a function of:

$$R = \sum_{j=1}^{n} R\left(A_j^{\text{PRC}}, Y_j, X_j^{\text{PRC}}, M_j, A_j^{\text{DAC}}, A_j^{\text{US}}, Z_j\right), \tag{7.2}$$

where

A_j^{PRC} = foreign aid received by country j from the PRC;

$\quad Y_j$ = GNP of country j;

$\quad X_j$ = exports from the PRC to country j;

$\quad M_j$ = exports from country j to the PRC;

A_j^{DAC} = foreign aid received by country j from DAC countries;

$\quad A_j^{\text{US}}$ = foreign aid received by country j from the US;

$\quad Z_j$ = vector of binary political variables describing political links between the PRC and country j.

If we assume that the PRC has a fixed income to allocate between non-aid related consumption and aid to country j, then its budget constraint can be expressed as:

$$Y = D + \sum_{j=1}^{n} A_j^{\text{PRC}}, \tag{7.3}$$

where

Y = GNP of the PRC;
A_j^{PRC} = the amount of foreign aid granted to country j by the PRC.

The quantity of goods and services originating from the recipient may be considered an increasing function of the economic aid it receives from the PRC in the form of loan repayment, the quantity of trade between donor and recipient and positive political ties, and a decreasing function of the recipient's GNP, and foreign assistance received from other donors:

$$\frac{\partial R}{\partial Y_j} < 0 \qquad \frac{\partial R}{\partial A_j^{\text{PRC}}} > 0 \qquad \frac{\partial R}{\partial A_j^{\text{DAC}}} < 0 \qquad \frac{\partial R}{\partial X_j} > 0$$

$$\frac{\partial R}{\partial A_j^{\text{US}}} < 0 \qquad \frac{\partial R}{\partial M_J} > 0 \qquad \frac{\partial R}{\partial Z_j} > 0.$$

Equation (7.2) can be rewritten in the following form:

$$R_j = \frac{\left(A_j^{\text{PRC}}\right)^{\alpha_1} X_j^{\alpha_2} M_j^{\alpha_3} Z_j^{\alpha_4}}{Y_j^{\alpha_5} \left(A_j^{\text{DAC}}\right)^{\alpha_6} \left(A_j^{\text{US}}\right)^{\alpha_7}}. \tag{7.2'}$$

Maximization of Equation (7.1) subject to (7.2) and (7.3) yields the following first-order conditions:

$$\frac{\phi_{R_j}}{\phi_D} = \alpha_1 \left(A_j^{\text{PRC}}\right)^{\frac{\alpha_1 - 1}{\alpha_1}} \cdot \frac{X_j^{\alpha_2} M_j^{\alpha_3} Z_j^{\alpha_4}}{Y_j^{\alpha_5} \left(A_j^{\text{DAC}}\right)^{\alpha_6} \left(A_j^{\text{US}}\right)^{\alpha_7}}, \tag{7.4}$$

where ϕ_{R_j} and ϕ_D are the first-order partial derivatives of U with respect to R_j and D and the right-hand side of Equation (7.4) represents the relative price of non-aid related goods to aid related goods. This equation can be solved to obtain the amount of foreign aid which the PRC will give to country j.

$$A_j^{\text{PRC}} = \left[\frac{\alpha_1 X_j^{\alpha_2} M_j^{\alpha_3} Z_j^{\alpha_4}}{k Y_j^{\alpha_5} \left(A_j^{\text{DAC}}\right)^{\alpha_6} \left(A_j^{\text{US}}\right)^{\alpha_7}}\right]^{\frac{-\alpha_1}{\alpha_1 - 1}}, \tag{7.5}$$

where k represents the marginal rate of substitution between non-aid related goods to aid related goods. In equilibrium this marginal rate of substitution should be identical across recipients. Furthermore, given that

$$\frac{\partial R}{\partial A_j^{\text{PRC}}} > 0$$

and

$$\frac{\partial^2 R}{\partial A_j^{\text{PRC}^2}} < 0 \quad 0 < \alpha_1 < 1.$$

In order to determine to what extent these explanatory variables determine the amount of aid to be given, Equation (7.5) is estimated in its natural log form:

$$\log A_j^{\text{PRC}} = \delta_0 + \delta_1 \log X_j + \delta_2 \log M_j + \delta_3 \log Z_j$$
$$+ \delta_4 \log Y_j + \delta_5 \log_j^{\text{DAC}} + \delta_6 \log_j^{\text{US}} + \mu, \qquad (7.6)$$

where

$$\delta_0 = \frac{\ln -\alpha_1^2}{k(\alpha_1 - 1)}; \quad \delta_1 = \frac{-\alpha_1\alpha_2}{(\alpha_1 - 1)}; \quad \delta_2 = \frac{-\alpha_1\alpha_3}{(\alpha_1 - 1)}; \quad \delta_3 = \frac{-\alpha_1\alpha_4}{(\alpha_1 - 1)};$$

$$\delta_4 = \frac{-\alpha_1\alpha_5}{(\alpha_1 - 1)}; \quad \delta_5 = \frac{-\alpha_1\alpha_6}{(\alpha_1 - 1)}; \quad \delta_6 = \frac{-\alpha_1\alpha_7}{(\alpha_1 - 1)}$$

and μ is a log normal distribution error term. Equation (7.6) is estimated using generalized linear model (GLM).

7.4. Statistical Results

In order to determine the applicability of the various explanations for PRC's foreign aid as expressed by Equation (7.6), we use the PRC's aid commitments for the period 2000–2012. Over that period, there was a total of 78 aid recipients that received aid commitments from the PRC at least once over the entire sample period. What portion of those commitments was actually a multi-year package is unknown.

Optimally, the use of this entire period should provide information on both the key determinants of the supply of the PRC's foreign aid, as well as possible paradigm changes that would alter these determinants. The nature of the PRC's aid commitments does not allow for a full econometric test of these questions. The lack of consistency in the time series across countries is a major problem. In Table 7.2, we present a summary of the PRC Aid data. First, very few countries receive annual assistance from the PRC. Out of a total of 78 recipients only four countries received annual PRC assistance over the entire 13-year period.

Table 7.2   Summary Characteristics of the PRC Aid Data

Recipient	Number of Positive PRC Aid Commitments Over the Period 2000–2012	Total Value of PRC Aid Over the Period 2000–2012 (Thousand US$ 2009)
Afghanistan	12	548,658
Angola	9	229,339
Argentina	1	527,403
Bangladesh	12	1,684,886
Burundi	8	205,703
Benin	2	39,491
Brunei	1	14
Bolivia	6	174,400
Brazil	1	83
Botswana	9	130,429
Congo, Dem. Rep.	8	41,187
Central African Rep.	4	92,993
Congo, Rep.	11	1,327,885
Cote D'Ivoire	8	901,839
Chile	1	2,817
Cameroon	8	110,886
Colombia	3	833
Cape Verde	3	84,908
Djibouti	8	34,076
Algeria	2	5,933
Ecuador	4	135,597
Egypt	7	643,577
Eritrea	7	42,457
Ethiopia	12	3,277,193
Gabon	4	288,719
Ghana	13	2,144,349
Guinea	5	183,615
Equatorial Guinea	5	109,399

(*Continued*)

Table 7.2 (*Continued*)

Recipient	Number of Positive PRC Aid Commitments Over the Period 2000–2012	Total Value of PRC Aid Over the Period 2000–2012 (Thousand US$ 2009)
Guinea-Bissau	8	110,043
Guyana	4	85,005
Indonesia	13	1,991,213
Kenya	12	1,102,001
Cambodia	13	2,573,946
Kiribati	1	9,092
Comoros	5	27,574
Laos	8	8,479
Sri Lanka	8	955,219
Liberia	10	251,343
Lesotho	11	149,776
Libya	2	7,358
Morocco	5	22,160
Madagascar	7	123,718
Mali	8	340,540
Myanmar	10	570,979
Mauritania	6	578,042
Mauritius	11	575,206
Maldives	6	45,944
Malaysia	2	954,983
Malawi	5	132,613
Mozambique	12	1,131,673
Namibia	12	377,788
Niger	11	82,478
Nigeria	7	2,376,039
Nepal	11	1,009,354
Peru	6	10,053
Philippines	4	3,532,880
Pakistan	11	3,186,257
Rwanda	10	477,693
Seychelles	6	78,477
Sudan	12	276,145
Singapore	0	0
Sierra Leone	6	222,598
Senegal	5	175,754
Somalia	5	28,631
Suriname	5	204,363

(*Continued*)

Table 7.2 (*Continued*)

Recipient	Number of Positive PRC Aid Commitments Over the Period 2000–2012	Total Value of PRC Aid Over the Period 2000–2012 (Thousand US$ 2009)
South Sudan	1	26,288
Chad	2	49,084
Togo	9	122,475
Thailand	8	509,496
Timor-Leste	7	31,823
Tunisia	5	119,975
Tanzania	11	1,807,816
Uganda	12	710,155
Uruguay	3	9,191
Venezuela	3	9,673,135
Viet Nam	9	301,936
South Africa	2	47,642
Zambia	12	783,729
Zimbabwe	13	3,344,876
Total		54,291,708

Given this major data problem, the appropriate econometric methodology used was a "GLM" estimator over the entire sample, excluding the political dummy variables.

Our first attempt was to estimate Equation (7.6) on an annual basis for the full sample excluding political variables. The rationale was the focus in the literature on economic rather than political explanations for PRC aid. As a proxy for political variables, the competition from US and DAC aid is considered more reliable. The results presented in Table 7.3 are not as satisfactory as one would expect, yet they represent our most credible annual results. There is some credible tie between PRC assistance and reciprocal trade. Likewise, there is some degree of competition between PRC, US and DAC country assistance.

Our next set of estimates are based on a cross-section–time-series pooling procedure for the entire period using a generalized least squares estimator (GLS). The results in this case are far more promising. These results are presented in Table 7.4. The variables

Table 7.3   GLM Estimates of PRC AID by Year

(All variables estimated in natural logs)

Year	Explanatory Variables	Coef.	Std. Err.	z	P > |z|	[95% Conf. Interval]	
2000	LUSAAID	0.032851	0.140549	0.23	0.815	−0.24262	0.308322
	LDACAID	0.139877	0.171814	0.81	0.416	−0.19687	0.476627
	LGNI	−0.12792	0.221472	−0.58	0.564	−0.562	0.306158
	LPRCIMP	0.021229	0.085415	0.25	0.804	−0.14618	0.188639
	LPRCEXP	0.093094	0.131852	0.71	0.48	−0.16533	0.351519
	_cons	0.382343	1.706519	0.22	0.823	−2.96237	3.727059
2001	LUSAAID	0.213106	0.142851	1.49	0.136	−0.06688	0.493088
	LDACAID	0.069159	0.179471	0.39	0.7	−0.2826	0.420915
	LGNI	−0.63483	0.244176	−2.6	0.009	−1.11341	−0.15626
	LPRCIMP	0.137214	0.091864	1.49	0.135	−0.04284	0.317265
	LPRCEXP	−0.18527	0.134801	−1.37	0.169	−0.44948	0.078931
	_cons	5.06849	1.853198	2.73	0.006	1.436288	8.700692
2002	LUSAAID	−0.06086	0.141847	−0.43	0.668	−0.33887	0.217156
	LDACAID	0.276754	0.186177	1.49	0.137	−0.08815	0.641653
	LGNI	−0.12544	0.227078	−0.55	0.581	−0.5705	0.319628
	LPRCIMP	−0.07594	0.088857	−0.85	0.393	−0.2501	0.098212
	LPRCEXP	0.253743	0.133361	1.9	0.057	−0.00764	0.515125
	_cons	0.106933	1.760039	0.06	0.952	−3.34268	3.556547
2003	LUSAAID	−0.01074	0.170045	−0.06	0.95	−0.34402	0.322543
	LDACAID	−0.14033	0.214677	−0.65	0.513	−0.56109	0.28043
	LGNI	−0.57181	0.266659	−2.14	0.032	−1.09445	−0.04917
	LPRCIMP	0.053435	0.103523	0.52	0.606	−0.14947	0.256337
	LPRCEXP	0.082866	0.160102	0.52	0.605	−0.23093	0.39666
	_cons	4.867188	2.061843	2.36	0.018	0.826051	8.908325
2004	LUSAAID	0.080902	0.156054	0.52	0.604	−0.22496	0.386763
	LDACAID	−0.01592	0.199731	−0.08	0.936	−0.40739	0.375542
	LGNI	0.13828	0.254575	0.54	0.587	−0.36068	0.637238
	LPRCIMP	0.009676	0.095477	0.1	0.919	−0.17746	0.196808
	LPRCEXP	−0.10184	0.149775	−0.68	0.497	−0.39539	0.191715
	_cons	0.086257	2.070305	0.04	0.967	−3.97147	4.14398
2005	LUSAAID	0.220188	0.159614	1.38	0.168	−0.09265	0.533026
	LDACAID	0.093614	0.197723	0.47	0.636	−0.29392	0.481144
	LGNI	0.063358	0.260184	0.24	0.808	−0.44659	0.573309
	LPRCIMP	−0.08658	0.101582	−0.85	0.394	−0.28568	0.112514
	LPRCEXP	0.197864	0.177535	1.11	0.265	−0.1501	0.545825
	_cons	−1.11849	2.136403	−0.52	0.601	−5.30576	3.068784

(*Continued*)

Table 7.3 (*Continued*)

Year	Explanatory Variables	Coef.	Std. Err.	z	P > |z|	[95% Conf.	Interval]
2006	LUSAAID	−0.14412	0.171461	−0.84	0.401	−0.48018	0.191938
	LDACAID	0.353683	0.213348	1.66	0.097	−0.06447	0.771838
	LGNI	−0.55493	0.287242	−1.93	0.053	−1.11792	0.008051
	LPRCIMP	0.032275	0.125874	0.26	0.798	−0.21443	0.278983
	LPRCEXP	0.168518	0.17519	0.96	0.336	−0.17485	0.511884
	_cons	3.270442	2.35031	1.39	0.164	−1.33608	7.876966
2007	LUSAAID	0.039969	0.168965	0.24	0.813	−0.2912	0.371135
	LDACAID	0.297859	0.215945	1.38	0.168	−0.12539	0.721104
	LGNI	−0.31431	0.287539	−1.09	0.274	−0.87787	0.24926
	LPRCIMP	0.198656	0.126076	1.58	0.115	−0.04845	0.44576
	LPRCEXP	−0.33187	0.210697	−1.58	0.115	−0.74483	0.081089
	_cons	3.500803	2.435194	1.44	0.151	−1.27209	8.273694
2008	LUSAAID	0.036361	0.121429	0.3	0.765	−0.20163	0.274356
	LDACAID	0.008133	0.186185	0.04	0.965	−0.35678	0.373048
	LGNI	−0.4623	0.234903	−1.97	0.049	−0.9227	−0.0019
	LPRCIMP	0.038896	0.117033	0.33	0.74	−0.19048	0.268276
	LPRCEXP	0.08558	0.167885	0.51	0.61	−0.24347	0.41463
	_cons	3.513962	2.042489	1.72	0.085	−0.48924	7.517166
2009	LUSAAID	0.026735	0.152195	0.18	0.861	−0.27156	0.325032
	LDACAID	0.439448	0.208078	2.11	0.035	0.031624	0.847273
	LGNI	−0.0136	0.276265	−0.05	0.961	−0.55507	0.527873
	LPRCIMP	−0.07572	0.117726	−0.64	0.52	−0.30646	0.155018
	LPRCEXP	0.063262	0.204191	0.31	0.757	−0.33694	0.463468
	_cons	−0.82058	2.450017	−0.33	0.738	−5.62253	3.981363
2010	LUSAAID	0.265578	0.195053	1.36	0.173	−0.11672	0.647874
	LDACAID	0.396387	0.245572	1.61	0.106	−0.08493	0.877701
	LGNI	0.00663	0.304963	0.02	0.983	−0.59109	0.604346
	LPRCIMP	0.049789	0.131376	0.38	0.705	−0.2077	0.30728
	LPRCEXP	−0.20611	0.241318	−0.85	0.393	−0.67908	0.266869
	_cons	−0.51771	2.653312	−0.2	0.845	−5.71811	4.682687
2011	LUSAAID	0.119064	0.153886	0.77	0.439	−0.18255	0.420676
	LDACAID	0.185156	0.224336	0.83	0.409	−0.25453	0.624847
	LGNI	−0.43914	0.272991	−1.61	0.108	−0.97419	0.095915
	LPRCIMP	0.029149	0.117118	0.25	0.803	−0.2004	0.258696
	LPRCEXP	−0.16776	0.20449	−0.82	0.412	−0.56855	0.233031
	_cons	4.393086	2.484313	1.77	0.077	−0.47608	9.26225

(*Continued*)

Table 7.3   (*Continued*)

Year	Explanatory Variables	Coef.	Std. Err.	z	P > |z|	[95% Conf. Interval]	
2012	LUSAAID	0.333822	0.185585	1.8	0.072	−0.02992	0.697562
	LDACAID	0.115759	0.234723	0.49	0.622	−0.34429	0.575808
	LGNI	0.019539	0.301948	0.06	0.948	−0.57227	0.611346
	LPRCIMP	−0.15004	0.12978	−1.16	0.248	−0.4044	0.104326
	LPRCEXP	0.060795	0.231626	0.26	0.793	−0.39318	0.514773
	_cons	0.329205	2.576826	0.13	0.898	−4.72128	5.379692

Source: Estimated by author. L designates natural logs.

Table 7.4   Estimates of PRC Aid Using a Random Effects GLS Estimator

Explanatory Variables	Coef.	Std. Err.	z	P > |z|	[95% Conf. Interval]	
LUSAAID	0.092001	0.042951	2.14	0.032	0.007819	0.176183
LDACAID	0.182025	0.056716	3.21	0.001	0.070863	0.293186
LGNI	−0.18478	0.070714	−2.61	0.009	−0.32337	−0.04618
LPRCIMP	−0.00359	0.029094	−0.12	0.902	−0.06061	0.053433
LPRCEXP	0.045581	0.045978	0.99	0.322	−0.04453	0.135697
_cons	1.198397	0.563021	2.13	0.033	0.094897	2.301897
σ_u	0.109081					
σ_e	2.032612					
ρ	0.002872	(fraction of variance due to u_i)				

Wald chi^2(5) = 95.67   Prob > chi^2 = 0.000
Corr $(u_i, X) = 0$

Source: Estimated by author. L designates natural logs

that significantly explain PRC aid are the competition from US and DAC country aid and the degree of poverty of the recipients. Trade is not as significantly important to the PRC's assistance decision.

Overall, our statistical results point to the competitive importance of assistance from the USA and DAC countries as the primary explanatory variables accounting for PRC assistance. As more data comes available on the buy-back arrangements contained in PRC assistance, these estimates can be updated to determine their overall importance.

Chapter 8

China's Outward Investment Program — A Search for Technology

Maintaining international competitiveness in the current international environment requires rapid scientific and technological innovations. As the flow of foreign direct investment (FDI) and venture capital continues to expand across the world, the pressures to create quicker and more efficient ways to extract the benefits of technological innovation may lead to more innovative methods for its acquisition. This is especially true for countries like the PRC which are rich in foreign reserves but short in the operational research and development (R&D) it needs to alter its external sector from one based on cheap labor to one that is based on innovation and higher value added.

In the 21st century, the primary factor of production is human capital and innovation. Factors such as the productivity of R&D, efficient access to scientific and technical knowledge and establishment of global supply chains are becoming increasingly important to a firm's survival. The past decade has seen a surge in PRC outward investments, as the PRC State-owned enterprises (SOEs) jituan 集团 have seized upon the government's directive to "Going Global."

Despite the fact that the PRC outward FDI (OFDI) is by world standards very small, it has significantly expanded and focused its attention on the acquisition of technology, since it adopted its "going global" program. The PRC's OFDI went from $9.9 billion in 2005 to $77.2 billion in 2012 and, in the first six months of 2013, the PRC's

OFDI was $42.6 billion [MOFCOM, 2013; Heritage Foundation, 2014]. In 2010, the PRC's cumulative FDI abroad (stock) reached $317.21 billion [MOFCOM, 2011].

This impressive growth is a reflection of the PRC's adoption of its National Development and Reform Commission (NDRC) and the Export–Import Bank of China (EIBC) jointly issued directive to encourage overseas investment in specific areas: "(1) resource exploration projects to mitigate the domestic shortage of natural resources; (2) projects that promote the export of domestic technologies, products, equipment and labor; (3) overseas R&D centers to utilize internationally — advanced technologies, managerial skills and professionals and (4) Mergers and acquisitions (M&A) that could enhance the international competitiveness of Chinese enterprises and accelerate their entry into foreign markets [UNCTAD, 2013].

The driver for this OFDI is the State, not the private market. In 2012, official PRC statistics list total PRC OFDI at $87.8 billion, of which the majority originated from centrally-controlled SOEs. While private enterprise's role in OFDI is rising, it is still a minority participant of the total OFDI flows [MOFCOM, 2012].[1] PRC SOE firms operating in the USA and Europe are encouraged to participate in (M&A) or to acquire 100 percent ownership of foreign companies through which they can absorb state-of-the-art technologies and thus "leapfrog" several stages of development and upgrades.[2]

---

[1]The Heritage foundation estimates that over 90 percent of Chinese OFDI by value is SOE investments. According to MOFCOM official statistics, by the end of 2011, SOE's represented 66.2 percent of the country's OFDI stock. In non-financial sectors, OFDI stock from SOEs was $60.17 billion, accounting for 77 percent of the total. Much of the data confusion arises from MOFCOM use of Hong Kong as the final destination of Chinese OFDI. Furthermore, there is confusion about the concept of SOE. MOFCOM attributes the OFDI to 中央企业 (zhongyang qiye), or "central enterprise," which refers specifically to SOEs under the direct control of the central government, as opposed to the more generic 国有企业 (guoyou qiye), which simply means "SOE."

[2]For instance, in 1988, the Shougang (Capital) Iron and Steel Corp. purchased 70 percent of the California-based Mesta Engineering and Design Inc. and thus obtained access to the company's high-tech design capability in steel rolling and casting equipment. See, Chang-hong Pei and Wang Lei, "Chinese

While this could be viewed as intra-firm behavior, it is not. It represents PRC SOE activity and not PRC private TNC M&A activity [Tsang *et al.*, 2008; Tracey, 2007].

Given that the official data presented by the PRC highlights the important role of its SOE in its OFDI activity, we accept their position that the majority of OFDI is done by State actors. A time series of PRC cross-border M&A activity (in millions of US dollars) is presented in Table 8.1. It is noteworthy that by 2012, the value of PRC cross-border M&A was equivalent to 25 percent of total Developed country and 15 percent of total World cross-border M&A investments. The major acquisitions of large state-owned giants are well-detailed, with a focus on central government direction, high-profile deals, and acquisitions of resource-intensive firms [Zhao and Zhang, 2010; Buckley *et al.*, 2008; Shambaugh, 2013].

The PRC's role in OFDI is predominantly in the form of non-financial transnational corporations (TNC) M&As. Table 8.2 presents the top non-financial TNC ranked by foreign assets in 2011. The UNCTAD ranks this data by the Transnationality Index (TNI), which is calculated as the average of the foreign assets to total assets, foreign sales to total sales and foreign employment to total employment. The list of TNCs includes what is often referred to as the "bargain hunters." In many cases, these bargain hunters are in search of "bargains" which represent undervalued or troubled "brands." In acquiring these companies, the PRC does not have to spend decades building up "brand" recognition. For example, Nanjing Automotive acquired British car manufacturer MG Rover's brand in 2005. Geely Automotive, one of the PRC's biggest automotive companies, acquired Ford Motor's Volvo unit in 2010 in

---

Corporate Investment in the United States," *China and World Economy* 5 (May 2001), Chinese Academy of Social Sciences. *http://old.iwep.org.cn/wec/english/ articles/2001_05/5peichanghong.htm*. Another example is Lenovo's purchase of IBM's personal computer division in 2005. With this purchase Lenovo was able to gain managerial and commercial experience in the international PC market, making Lenovo the number 2 global supplier of PC's and other computer equipment.

Table 8.1   Value of Chinese Cross-Border M&As, as Compared to the World and Developed Economies, 1990–2012

Year	China Total (PRC plus Hong Kong) (US$ million)	World (US$ million)	Developed Economies (US$ million)
1990	1,841	98,903	87,188
1991	947	21,094	14,624
1992	2,317	48,106	36,658
1993	1,700	43,623	34,845
1994	2,041	91,769	79,062
1995	1,436	112,527	102,004
1996	1,628	142,557	124,863
1997	5,636	180,751	163,205
1998	6,355	406,427	372,286
1999	7,235	630,807	592,794
2000	37,397	905,214	828,662
2001	1,209	429,374	388,605
2002	18,799	248,446	201,729
2003	1,380	182,874	138,180
2004	2,752	227,221	166,974
2005	11,848	462,253	359,551
2006	20,092	625,320	497,324
2007	−10,262	1,022,725	841,714
2008	36,893	706,543	568,041
2009	28,951	249,732	160,785
2010	44,384	344,029	223,726
2011	49,506	555,173	428,075
2012	45,126	308,055	175,555

Source: UNCTAD, *World Investment Report*, 2013

a $1.8 billion deal.[3] Furthermore, since these TNCs control virtually all intellectual property in the PRC and account for 85 percent of

---

[3] Not all PRC efforts have proven successful. In 2010, Sprint Nextel Corp. excluded Chinese telecommunications-equipment makers Huawei and ZTE from a contract worth billions of dollars largely because of national security concerns about the two companies' ties to the Chinese government and military, and the security implications of integrating their equipment into critical U.S. telecommunications infrastructure. Joann S. Lublin and Shayndi Raice, "Security Fears Kill Chinese Bid in U.S.," *Wall Street Journal*, November 5, 2010. http://online.wsj.com/article/SB10001424052748704353504575596611547810220.html.

Table 8.2 The Top Non-financial TNCs from China, Ranked by Foreign Assets, 2011[a]

Ranking By					Assets		Sales		Employment		
Foreign Assets	TNI[b]	Corporation	Home Economy	Industry[c]	Foreign (US$ m)	Total (US$ m)	Foreign (US$ m)	Total (US$ m)	Foreign[d]	Total	TNI[b] (%)
1	18	Hutchison Whampoa Limited	Hong Kong, China	Diversified	77,291	92,788	23,477	30,023	206,986	250,000	81.4
2	90	CITIC Group	China	Diversified	71,512	514,847	9,923	51,659	30,806	140,028	18.4
5	61	China Ocean Shipping (Group) Company	China	Transport and storage	40,435	52,230	19,454	29,579	7,355	130,000	49.6
10	89	China National Offshore Oil Corp	China	Petroleum expl./ref./distr.	29,802	112,887	19,786	75,518	3,367	98,750	18.7
17	45	Jardine Matheson Holdings Ltd	Hong Kong, China	Diversified	21,486	58,297	28,291	37,967	217,556	330,000	59.1
21	5	Noble Group Ltd	Hong Kong, China	Wholesale trade	17,761	19,943	80,732	80,732	13,477	14,000	95.1
24	100	China National Petroleum Corporation	China	Petroleum expl./ref./distr.	16,954	475,700	8,671	326,790	31,442	1,668,072	2.7
32	60	CLP Holdings Ltd	Hong Kong, China	Utilities (Electricity, gas and water)	14,217	27,595	7,697	11,772	2,057	6,316	49.8

(*Continued*)

Table 8.2 (Continued)

| Ranking By | | Corporation | Home Economy | Industry[c] | Assets | | Sales | | Employment | | TNI[b] (%) |
Foreign Assets	TNI[b]				Foreign (US$ m)	Total (US$ m)	Foreign (US$ m)	Total (US$ m)	Foreign[d]	Total	
34	70	Sinochem Group	China	Petroleum expl./ref./distr.	13,112	40,563	54,861	70,994	7,994	47,022	42.2
36	2	First Pacific Company Ltd	Hong Kong, China	Electrical & electronic equipment	12,500	12,612	5,684	5,684	73,542	73,582	99.7
37	71	New World Development Ltd	Hong Kong, China	Diversified	12,200	29,437	2,273	4,230	14,123	45,000	42.2
40	14	China Resources Enterprises Ltd	Hong Kong, China	Petroleum expl./ref./distr.	11,606	14,635	13,020	14,153	190,000	200,000	88.8
41	93	Sun Hung Kai Properties Ltd	Hong Kong, China	Other services	11,466	53,088	720	8,046	6,242	35,000	16.1
46	11	Li & Fung Ltd	Hong Kong, China	Wholesale trade	10,228	10,920	18,900	20,030	25,106	29,624	90.9
48	8	Shangri-La Asia Ltd	Hong Kong, China	Other consumer services	9,598	9,973	1,647	1,912	27,552	28,900	92.6
51	64	Lenovo Group Ltd	China	Electrical & electronic equipment	9,103	15,861	17,179	29,574	6,238	27,000	46.2

56	34	The Hong Kong and China Gas Co. Ltd	Hong Kong, China	Electricity, gas and water	7,738	10,957	1,606	2,881	1,369	1,938	65.7
58	99	China Mobile (Hong Kong) Limited	China	Tele-communications	7,483	149,653	4,084	81,674		175,336	3.3
60	69	Swire Pacific Ltd	Hong Kong, China	Business services	7,234	37,688	2,633	4,662	37,672	73,867	42.2
66	10	Yue Yuen Industrial Holdings Ltd	Hong Kong, China	Other consumer goods	6,342	6,473	5,529	7,045	451,399	460,000	91.5
73	96	Sinopec — China Petrochemical Corporation	China	Petroleum expl./ref./distr.	5,568	179,813	86,305	387,595	1,000	377,235	8.5
77	83	Power Assets Holdings Ltd	Hong Kong, China	Electricity, gas and water	4,931	12,199		1,311	752	1,861	26.9
79	9	Shenzhen International Holdings Ltd	Hong Kong, China	Construction	4,525	5,138	717	717	4,165	4,729	92.0
80	3	Galaxy Entertainment Group Ltd	Hong Kong, China	Other consumer services	4,519	4,606	5,172	5,291	14,386	15,000	97.3

(*Continued*)

Table 8.2   (*Continued*)

| Ranking By | | Corporation | Home Economy | Industry[c] | Assets | | Sales | | Employment | | TNI[b] (%) |
Foreign Assets	TNI[b]				Foreign (US$ m)	Total (US$ m)	Foreign (US$ m)	Total (US$ m)	Foreign[d]	Total	
81	94	China Minmetals Corp	China	Metal and metal products	4,512	36,227	8,673	54,194	7,990	146,000	11.3
85	6	Guangdong Investment Ltd	Hong Kong, China	Diversified	4,213	4,485	884	920	4,062	4,295	94.9
90	7	Road King Infrastructure Ltd	Hong Kong, China	Transport and storage	3,678	4,086	878	878	1,671	1,832	93.7
91	1	Lee and Man Paper Manufacturing Ltd	Hong Kong, China	Wood and paper products	3,436	3,444	1,892	1,892	7,682	7,700	99.8
92	12	Esprit Holdings Ltd	Hong Kong, China	Other consumer goods	3,381	3,473	4,268	4,344	10,857	14,100	90.9
94	81	ZTE Corp	China	Other consumer goods	3,219	16,934	7,228	13,342	21,069	89,786	32.2

| 98 | 98 | China Railway Construction Corporation Ltd | China | Construction | 3,076 | 66,453 | 2,579 | 68,575 | 23,602 | 241,621 | 6.1 |
| 100 | 41 | TPV Technology Limited | China | Wholesale trade | 2,972 | 5,257 | 7,803 | 11,040 | 17,183 | 29,516 | 61.8 |

Source: UNCTAD. World Investment Report, 2013

[a]All data are based on the companies' annual reports unless otherwise stated; corresponds to the financial year from April 1, 2011 to March 31, 2012.

[b]TNI, the Transnationality Index, is calculated as the average of the following three ratios: foreign assets to total assets, foreign sales to total sales and foreign employment to total employment.

[c]Industry classification for companies follows the United States Standard Industrial Classification as used by the United States Securities and Exchange Commission (SEC).

[d]In a number of cases foreign employment data were calculated by applying the share of foreign employment in total employment of the previous year to total employment of 2011.

[e]In lieu of 2011 figures, 2010 data have been used.

the PRC's technology exports, the PRC's determination to have its overseas firms undertake overseas acquisitions as a route to enhanced R&D would be a rational choice.

According to the OECD [2008a, 2008b], the main economic drivers of economic growth include "the absolute growth of R&D and innovation — related activities." They stress that in the 21st century, one should find great competition in the scientific and technological fields, significant globalization of R&D, more performance of R&D in the services sector and a growing focus on non-technological innovation, widespread policy shifts towards fiscal incentives for R&D and enhanced internationalization and mobility of highly skilled people, including greater participation of women in the HRST (human resources for science and technology) labor force across almost all countries. The leadership of the PRC is aware of this and is therefore on the "fast track" to encourage their overseas firms to acquire more and more foreign firms.

In 2012, PRC M&A deals greater than $1 billion consisted of 20 large SOE transactions which are listed in Table 8.3. The ranking represents a subset of the top 200 M&A deals listed in [UNCTAD, 2013, Appendix Table 17]. The data represents a small subset of the total of 316 M&As completed by the PRC in 2012. The majority of these acquisitions represent far smaller sums of money. The industries represented by China's major acquisitions range from mining industries, oil-extracting industries, telecom companies, environmental sciences and technology companies to banking services and life insurance companies. The acquiring Chinese partners are large SOEs with sufficient capital to complete these transactions. These are not intra-firm transactions as one would expect in a market economy context, but rather acquisitions by China's SOE TNCs.

Receiving far less attention, and for the very reason of their often intentional low profile, has been a string of small-scale acquisitions of developed-country firms by ordinary PRC companies. These acquisitions range from the healthcare, pharmaceutical and computing industries, to manufacturing and agriculture. Analysis of these acquisitions can only be done on a case-by-case basis, as no comprehensive database exists for them. The acquisition of the

Table 8.3   Cross-border M&A Deals Worth Over $1 Billion Completed in 2012 by China

Rank	Value ($ billion)	Acquired Company	Host Economy[a]	Industry of the Acquired Company	Ultimate Acquired Company	Ultimate Host Economy	Industry of the Ultimate Acquired Company	Shares Acquired (Percent)
20	4.8	Petrogal Brasil Ltda	Brazil	Crude petroleum and natural gas	Galp Energia SGPS SA	Portugal	Crude petroleum and natural gas	30
		Acquiring Company	Home Economy[a]	Industry of the Acquiring Company	Ultimate Acquiring Company	Ultimate Home Economy	Industry of the Ultimate Acquiring Company	
		Sinopec International Petroleum Exploration and Production Corp	China	Investors, nec	Sinopec Group	China	Crude petroleum and natural gas	
32	3.5	Acquired Company	Host Economy[a]	Industry of the Acquired Company	Ultimate Acquired Company	Ultimate Host Economy	Industry of the Ultimate Acquired Company	21.35
		Energias de Portugal SA {EDP}	Portugal	Electric services	EDP	Portugal	Electric services	
		Acquiring Company	Home Economy[a]	Industry of the Acquiring Company	Ultimate Acquiring Company	Ultimate Home Economy	Industry of the Ultimate Acquiring Company	
		China Three Gorges International (Europe) SA	Luxembourg	Investors, nec	China Three Gorges Corp	China	Electric services	

(*Continued*)

Table 8.3   (*Continued*)

Rank	Value ($ billion)	Acquired Company / Acquiring Company	Host Economy^a / Home Economy^a	Industry of the Acquired Company / Industry of the Acquiring Company	Ultimate Acquired Company / Ultimate Acquiring Company	Ultimate Host Economy / Ultimate Home Economy	Industry of the Ultimate Acquired Company / Industry of the Ultimate Acquiring Company	Shares Acquired (Percent)
46	3.0	MGN Gas Networks (UK) Ltd	United Kingdom	Natural gas transmission	MGN Gas Networks (UK) Ltd	United Kingdom	Natural gas transmission	100
		Investor Group	Hong Kong, China	Investors, nec	Investor Group	Hong Kong, China	Investors, nec	
55	2.6	AMC Entertainment Holdings Inc	United States	Motion picture theaters, except drive-in	AMC Entertainment Holdings Inc	United States	Motion picture theaters, except drive-in	100
		Dalian Wanda Group Corp Ltd	China	Operators of non-residential buildings	Dalian Wanda Group Corp Ltd	China	Operators of non-residential buildings	

		Acquired Company	Host Economy[a]	Industry of the Acquired Company	Ultimate Acquired Company	Ultimate Host Economy	Industry of the Ultimate Acquired Company	
57	2.5	Devon Energy Corp-Shale Oil & Gas Assets (5)	United States	Crude petroleum and natural gas	Devon Energy Corp	United States	Crude petroleum and natural gas	33.33
		Acquiring Company	Home Economy[a]	Industry of the Acquiring Company	Ultimate Acquiring Company	Ultimate Home Economy	Industry of the Ultimate Acquiring Company	
		Sinopec International Petroleum Exploration & Production Corp	China	Investors, nec	Sinopec Group	China	Crude petroleum and natural gas	
		Acquired Company	Host Economy[a]	Industry of the Acquired Company	Ultimate Acquired Company	Ultimate Host Economy	Industry of the Ultimate Acquired Company	
62	2.3	Swire Properties Ltd	Hong Kong, China	Land subdividers and developers, except cemeteries	John Swire & Sons Ltd	United Kingdom	Deep sea foreign transportation of freight	18
		Acquiring Company	Home Economy[a]	Industry of the Acquiring Company	Ultimate Acquiring Company	Ultimate Home Economy	Industry of the Ultimate Acquiring Company	
		Shareholders	Hong Kong, China	Investors, nec	Shareholders	Hong Kong, China	Investors, nec	

(Continued)

Table 8.3　(*Continued*)

Rank	Value ($ billion)	Acquired Company	Host Economy[a]	Industry of the Acquired Company	Ultimate Acquired Company	Ultimate Host Economy	Industry of the Ultimate Acquired Company	Shares Acquired (Percent)
73	2.2	LME Holdings Ltd	United Kingdom	Security and commodity exchanges	LME Holdings Ltd	United Kingdom	Security and commodity exchanges	100
		Acquiring Company	**Home Economy[a]**	**Industry of the Acquiring Company**	**Ultimate Acquiring Company**	**Ultimate Home Economy**	**Industry of the Ultimate Acquiring Company**	
		HKEx Investment(UK)Ltd	United Kingdom	Investors, nec	HKEX	Hong Kong, China	Security and commodity exchanges	
		Acquired Company	**Host Economy[a]**	**Industry of the Acquired Company**	**Ultimate Acquired Company**	**Ultimate Host Economy**	**Industry of the Ultimate Acquired Company**	
86	2.0	Unicom New Horizon Telecommunications Co Ltd	China	Radiotelephone communications	China United Network	China	Telephone communications, except radiotelephone	100
		Acquiring Company	**Home Economy[a]**	**Industry of the Acquiring Company**	**Ultimate Acquiring Company**	**Ultimate Home Economy**	**Industry of the Ultimate Acquiring Company**	
		China United Network Communications Corp Ltd	China	Telephone communications, except radiotelephone	China Unicom(Hong Kong)Ltd	Hong Kong, China	Telephone communications, except radiotelephone	

87	1.9	Weetabix Ltd	United Kingdom	Cereal breakfast foods	Lion Capital LLP	United Kingdom	Investors, nec	60
		Acquiring Company	Home Economy[a]	Industry of the Acquiring Company	Ultimate Acquiring Company	Ultimate Home Economy	Industry of the Ultimate Acquiring Company	
		Bright Food(Group)Co Ltd	China	Non-commercial research organizations	Bright Food(Group)Co Ltd	China	Non-commercial research organizations	
		Acquired Company	Host Economy[a]	Industry of the Acquired Company	Ultimate Acquired Company	Ultimate Host Economy	Industry of the Ultimate Acquired Company	
103	1.7	ING Management Holdings (Malaysia)Sdn Bhd	Malaysia	Life insurance	ING Groep NV	Netherlands	Life insurance	100
		Acquiring Company	Home Economy[a]	Industry of the Acquiring Company	Ultimate Acquiring Company	Ultimate Home Economy	Industry of the Ultimate Acquiring Company	
		American International Assurance Co Ltd	Hong Kong, China	Life insurance	American Intl Assurance Group	Hong Kong, China	Life insurance	

(Continued)

Table 8.3   (*Continued*)

Rank	Value ($ billion)	Acquired Company	Host Economy[a]	Industry of the Acquired Company	Ultimate Acquired Company	Ultimate Host Economy	Industry of the Ultimate Acquired Company	Shares Acquired (Percent)
113	1.6	Lasalle Investment Management KK-Property Portfolio	Japan	General warehousing and storage	Jones Lang LaSalle Inc	United States	Real estate agents and managers	100
		Acquiring Company	**Home Economy[a]**	**Industry of the Acquiring Company**	**Ultimate Acquiring Company**	**Ultimate Home Economy**	**Industry of the Ultimate Acquiring Company**	
		Investor Group	China	Investors, nec	Investor Group	China	Investors, nec	
118	1.5	Gloucester Coal Ltd	Australia	Bituminous coal and lignite surface mining	Noble Group Ltd	Hong Kong, China	Grain and field beans	100
		Acquiring Company	**Home Economy[a]**	**Industry of the Acquiring Company**	**Ultimate Acquiring Company**	**Ultimate Home Economy**	**Industry of the Ultimate Acquiring Company**	
		Yancoal Australia Pty Ltd	Australia	Bituminous coal and lignite surface mining	Yan Kuang Group Co Ltd	China	Bituminous coal and lignite surface mining	

	122 1.5	130 1.4
Acquiring Company	Talisman Energy(UK)Ltd	China Unicom(Hong Kong)Ltd
Home Economy[a]	United Kingdom	Hong Kong, China
Industry of the Acquiring Company	Crude petroleum and natural gas	Telephone communications, except radiotelephone
Acquired Company	Sinopec International Petroleum Exploration & Production Corp	China United Network Communications Group Co Ltd
Host Economy[a]	China	China
Industry of the Acquired Company	Investors, nec	Telephone communications, except radiotelephone
Ultimate Acquiring Company	Talisman Energy Inc	China Unicom(Hong Kong)Ltd
Ultimate Home Economy	Canada	Hong Kong, China
Industry of the Ultimate Acquiring Company	Crude petroleum and natural gas (49)	Telephone communications, except radiotelephone (4.56)
Ultimate Acquired Company	Sinopec Group	China United Network
Ultimate Host Economy	China	China
Industry of the Ultimate Acquired Company	Crude petroleum and natural gas	Telephone communications, except radiotelephone

(*Continued*)

Table 8.3   (*Continued*)

Rank	Value ($ billion)	Acquired Company	Host Economy[a]	Industry of the Acquired Company	Ultimate Acquired Company	Ultimate Host Economy	Industry of the Ultimate Acquired Company	Shares Acquired (Percent)
136	1.4	Tower Top Development Ltd	China	Operators of non-residential buildings	Yuexiu Property Co Ltd	Hong Kong, China	Land subdividers and developers, except cemeteries	99.99
		Acquiring Company	**Home Economy[a]**	**Industry of the Acquiring Company**	**Ultimate Acquiring Company**	**Ultimate Home Economy**	**Industry of the Ultimate Acquiring Company**	
		Yuexiu REIT 2012 Co Ltd	Hong Kong, China	Real estate investment trusts	Yuexiu Real Estate Investment	Hong Kong, China	Real estate investment trusts	
		Acquired Company	**Host Economy[a]**	**Industry of the Acquired Company**	**Ultimate Acquired Company**	**Ultimate Host Economy**	**Industry of the Ultimate Acquired Company**	
138	1.3	Australia Pacific LNG Pty Ltd	Australia	Crude petroleum and natural gas	ConocoPhillips Co	United States	Crude petroleum and natural gas	10
		Acquiring Company	**Home Economy[a]**	**Industry of the Acquiring Company**	**Ultimate Acquiring Company**	**Ultimate Home Economy**	**Industry of the Ultimate Acquiring Company**	
		China Petrochemical Corp Sinopec Group	China	Crude petroleum and natural gas	Sinopec Group	China	Crude petroleum and natural gas	

147	1.3			100
	Acquiring Company	Anvil Mining NL	Home Economy[a]	Australia	Industry of the Acquiring Company	Copper ores	Ultimate Acquiring Company	Anvil Mining NL	Ultimate Home Economy	Australia	Industry of the Ultimate Acquiring Company	Copper ores

Restructured:

No.	Value	%
147	1.3	100

Acquiring Company	Anvil Mining NL	Home Economy[a] Australia — Industry of the Acquiring Company: Copper ores — Ultimate Acquiring Company: Anvil Mining NL — Ultimate Home Economy: Australia — Industry of the Ultimate Acquiring Company: Copper ores
Acquired Company	MMG Malachite Ltd	Host Economy[a] Hong Kong, China — Industry of the Acquired Company: Non-ferrous die-castings, except aluminum — Ultimate Acquired Company: China Minmetals Corp — Ultimate Host Economy: China — Industry of the Ultimate Acquired Company: Non-durable goods, nec

No.	Value	%
148	1.3	57.26

Acquiring Company	Extract Resources Ltd	Home Economy[a] Australia — Industry of the Acquiring Company: Uranium–radium–vanadium ores — Ultimate Acquiring Company: Extract Resources Ltd — Ultimate Home Economy: Australia — Industry of the Ultimate Acquiring Company: Uranium–radium–vanadium ores
Acquired Company	Taurus Minerals Ltd	Host Economy[a] Hong Kong, China — Industry of the Acquired Company: Investors, nec — Ultimate Acquired Company: Peoples Republic of China — Ultimate Host Economy: China — Industry of the Ultimate Acquired Company: National government

(Continued)

Table 8.3   (*Continued*)

Rank	Value ($ billion)	Acquired Company	Host Economy[a]	Industry of the Acquired Company	Ultimate Acquired Company	Ultimate Host Economy	Industry of the Ultimate Acquired Company	Shares Acquired (Percent)
179	1.1	Kyobo Life Insurance Co Ltd	Korea, Republic of	Life insurance	Kyobo Life Insurance Co Ltd	Korea, Republic of	Life insurance	24
		Acquiring Company	Home Economy[a]	Industry of the Acquiring Company	Ultimate Acquiring Company	Ultimate Home Economy	Industry of the Ultimate Acquiring Company	
		Investor Group	Hong Kong, China	Investors, nec	Investor Group	Hong Kong, China	Investors, nec	
194	1.0	Grande Cache Coal Corp	Canada	Bituminous coal underground mining	Grande Cache Coal Corp	Canada	Bituminous coal underground mining	100
		Acquiring Company	Home Economy[a]	Industry of the Acquiring Company	Ultimate Acquiring Company	Ultimate Home Economy	Industry of the Ultimate Acquiring Company	
		1629835 Alberta Ltd SPV	Canada	Investment offices, nec	Winsway Coking Coal Hldg Ltd	Hong Kong, China	Coal and other minerals and ores	

	195	1.0	100
Acquiring Company	Kalahari Minerals PLC	United Kingdom	Uranium–radium–vanadium ores
Home Economy[a]	China	Uranium–radium–vanadium ores	Kalahari Minerals PLC
Industry of the Acquiring Company	Electric services	Ultimate Acquiring Company	Peoples Republic of China
		United Kingdom	Ultimate Home Economy
	China	Industry of the Ultimate Acquiring Company	Uranium–radium–vanadium ores
China Guangdong Nuclear Power Holding Co Ltd	China	Electric services	Peoples Republic of China	National government

technology and human capital possessed by relatively small-scale research-oriented firms can provide important spillover benefits to PRC companies involved.

The current trend in R&D with the greatest promise of economic growth includes most notably biotechnology and general life sciences, nanotechnology, and environmental sciences and technologies. In terms of expenditure on R&D by biotechnology-active firms, the United States stands far ahead, as its R&D expenditure of just over $14 billion is considerably more than that of all other countries combined. Nanotechnology is a multidisciplinary technology at the atomic or molecular scale encompassing a number of technological fields relating to chemical synthesis, computing and materials and devices at that scale. Internationally comparable data on nanotechnology R&D show that there are no competitive leaders, but inventive output in nanotechnology has grown in recent years.

It should be no surprise that given these R&D activities in the US and Europe, it should be no surprise that this intellectual property is highly demanded by the PRC. According to FBI reports, at least 23 foreign governments actively target the intellectual property of U.S. corporations. Examples of the most targeted regions for information gathering include Silicon Valley, Detroit, North Carolina, Dallas, Boston, Washington, DC and the Pennsylvania-New Jersey area, where many pharmaceutical and biotechnology companies are headquartered. Silicon Valley, according to the FBI, is the most targeted area for economic M&A because of its concentration of electronics, aerospace and biotechnology industries; its national ties to the Far East; and its mobile, multinational workforce.

PRC participation in Greenfield projects in 2012 is at the level of 8 percent of total developed country Greenfield investments and consisting of 438 individual projects, primarily in Africa and Latin America. Most of these projects are equally large scale. A prominent example of these kinds of infrastructure projects includes a $1.5 billion telecom transaction between China's ZTE and Ethiopia. The PRC managed to acquire this infrastructure project in 2006 by offering $1.5 billion in low-interest financing, funded by China's state-owned banks. When faced by a World Bank complaint that Ethiopia granted ZTE monopoly rights, Ethiopia invited ZTE's Chinese rival, Huawei to bid on a subsequent project. Under a 2013 project priced at $1.6 billion, funded by a low-interest loan from China's state-owned banks, Ethiopia accepted Huawei in its telecom sector, thus creating a duopoly controlling this vital sector. Between 1995 and 2012, the Chinese State-Owned Export–Import Bank and the China Development Bank provided approximately $50 billion in low-interest financing for projects in Africa. During the same period, the US state-owned Export–Import Bank has offered approximately $12 billion in low-interest financing for projects in Africa.[4]

If we focus strictly on Chinese state-owned TNC M&A activity, we have a very simple transaction between the state actor and the foreign firm representing the asset that is intended to be acquired. One can begin by introducing the assumption that both parties have asymmetric information on the value of the asset. Part of the asymmetry may arise from the expected positive spillover effect in the local economy after acquisition. In effect, the asset to be acquired has two value components, (1) immediate value, and (2) long-term value arising from the positive spillover. The sequence of this two party transaction can look as follows:

(1) The State, after incurring a search cost of (δ), calculates the value of the spillover effect to be (Ω), which is greater than the expected profitability (π) of the acquired firm; The value of the asset to the State would be:

$$V = (\pi + \Omega) - \delta, \quad \text{where } \Omega > \pi. \tag{8.1}$$

(2) The State offers the target company a purchase package (γ) which is composed of two components, the value of shares $[v(\rho)]$ purchased, where $0 \leq \rho \leq 1$, and a share of the profits of the acquired firm if 100 percent of the shares are not sold $\pi(1 - \rho)$. The latter possibility will include a cost to the targeted company of operating in the PRC. This may be viewed as the

---

[4] *WSJ*. January 6, 2014.

cost associated with a performance clause (ϕ) for a defined period of time or indefinitely equaling $[\beta(\phi)]$. Overall, the offer would be

$$\gamma = [v(\rho)] + [\pi(1 - \rho)] - \beta(\phi). \tag{8.2}$$

(3) The target company observes the purchase package (γ) but not (V).

(4) If the target company rejects the offer, then its payoff is its expected profits (π) from its normal activities, while the State payoff is zero. If the target company accepts the State's offer, its payoff will be $\gamma = [v(\rho)] + [\pi(1 - \rho)] - \beta(\phi)$ and the government gets $V = (\pi + \Omega) - \delta - \gamma$.

Under the scenarios we have outlined above, the PRC TNC in its M&A activity is betting on the fact that not only is $\Omega > \pi$, but also that $(\pi + \Omega) > (\delta + \gamma)$. The empirical literature on the generic issue of "spillover effects" of TNC activity is mixed. We presume that there must be sufficient positive "spillover" effects to justify the large sums of OFDI by PRC state-owned TNCs in their M&A activities. In Section 8.1, we present a brief review of the literature focusing on the spillover effects generated by foreign FDI. The importance of adaptation in the innovation process is the primary byproduct of this literature review. In Section 8.2, we present a reasonable theoretical explanation of PRC OFDI in search for "spillover effects" in a two country model with firms distinguished by their ability to innovate. In Section 8.3, we present a subset of MICRO data on the PRC path to acquire Foreign R&D.

8.1. A Review of FDI and its Spillover Effects

FDI is typically classified into three categories based on the intent of the investment: (i) horizontal, (ii) vertical and (iii) export related. In the first case, traditionally MNCs facing market access difficulties from tariffs, NTBs and or high transaction costs, shift production horizontally to access new markets. In the second case, FDI is motivated by factor cost differentials either upstream or downstream. A simple example would be taking advantage of low labor costs for part of the production process. The third motivation is designed to take advantage of export facilitation to specific markets, like FTA or other regional arrangements where country of origin rules are the deciding factor.

The literature on horizontal FDI is best characterized by the work of Brainard [1993] who explains that foreign affiliates owned by US MNCs primarily serve host markets with a very small share of host country production (13 percent) back to the United States. Likewise, US based affiliates of foreign MNCs export only 2–8 percent of their US production back to their home countries. Markusen [1984] stresses that the size of the local market may be the ultimate driver inducing horizontal FDI. When the potential host country is small, the potential savings in trade costs (with accrue per unit of exports to the country) are insufficient to offset the fixed costs of setting up a production facility there; hence, exports are chosen over FDI as the method for serving the market abroad. However, when a host country is large enough for the fixed costs of the plant to be offset by the trade costs saved, FDI is chosen over exports. Bigger market size of the host country, smaller plant-level fixed costs (smaller plant-level scale economies), and larger trade costs are more conducive to horizontal FDI.

What about the spillover effects? In their recent survey of the empirical literature on spillovers, Görg and Greenaway [2004] conclude that the evidence for generalized spillovers from multinationals located in the same industry might be interpreted at best, as weak. The evidence is stronger when the focus is on more homogeneous groups of firms, when the physical proximity is high and from MNCs located up or down the supply chain.

In contrast to these two productivity spillovers, comparatively little effort has been spent on identifying other indirect benefits from MNCs. Because of substitutability between the presence of MNCs in local market (FDI) and exports, the export decision of domestic firms is influenced by FDI [Aitken *et al.*, 1997; Greenaway *et al.*, 2004].

As [Blyde *et al.*, 2005; Görg and Greenaway, 2004; Kneller and Pisu, 2007] describe, the main difference between "horizontal" and "vertical" spillover is whether each spillover contains general or sector-specific technological knowledge. Horizontal spillovers are likely to involve sector-specific technological knowledge that would benefit competitors. Hence there is greater incentive for the MNCs to prevent this type of spillovers. Possible channels of this spillover are through the acquisition of human capital and imitation of products. Vertical spillovers, by contrast, are more likely to contain general rather than sector specific technological knowledge and would bring benefits to those firms in upstream industries (intermediate goods suppliers) and downstream industries (their buyers) which foreign subsidiaries deal with. These firms represent stakeholders of the subsidiaries of MNCs, not direct competitors, and therefore foreign subsidiaries may have some incentive to share general technological know-how with them, in order to achieve a higher degree of coordination and automation in their production activities.

Another way to classify FDI knowledge spillover is by direction of technology diffusion: technology-exploiting FDI (inward FDI technology transfer) and technology-seeking FDI (outward FDI technology sourcing). Many studies on FDI assume that FDI has knowledge — spillover potential. Firms engage in FDI because they can exploit a technological or other ownership advantage abroad [Kuemmerle, 1999; Le Bas and Sierra, 2002; Keller, 2004; Smeets, 2008]. Most of the traditional literature on FDI refers to this type of investment [Hymer, 1960; Dunning, 1977; Markusen, 2002].

Since the development of subsidiaries or affiliations in another country is often strategic actions of firms, the study of remote knowledge spillovers is not new [Feinberg and Gupta, 2004; Kuemmerle, 1999]. However, scholars have recently pointed out a different type of FDI — technology-seeking FDI — which is motivated by a desire to source or seek external foreign knowledge [Dunning and Narula, 1995; Kuemmerle, 1999; Fosfuri and Motta, 1999; Siotis, 1999; Le Bas and Sierra, 2002]. Firms engaging in technology-seeking FDI try to capture knowledge spillovers from firms in the host countries in which they invest. Knowledge spillovers are expected to flow from local firms to MNCs instead of the other way around.

The comparison of productivity between domestically owned and foreign-owned firms ask whether foreign firms indeed differ from domestic firms. This is because they may operate on different production functions or because they may operate at different points on the same functions. The evidence is almost uniform that there is a higher productivity of foreign-owned plants in both developed and developing countries. Some of that higher productivity, but not all in most comparisons, can be attributed to higher capital intensity or larger scale of production in the foreign owned plants.

Theories of the effect of direct investment on host countries have generally assumed a technological spillover from FDI to the host country economy. Evidence in support of technology transfer is found by [Blomstrom, 1986; Blomstrom and Persson, 1983; Kokko, 1994 for Mexico and by Blomstrom and Sjoholm, 1999 for Indonesia].

Görg and Greenaway [2004] present the details of 40 papers in manufacturing industries in developing, developed, and transition economies. Of those, 22 report unambiguously positive and statistically significant horizontal spillover effects, and 2 show positive and significant effects for only one of several countries analyzed. They point out that all but eight of those reporting unambiguously positive spillovers use cross-sectional data, which may lead to biased results.

Görg and Strobl [2001] argue that panel data analyses are the most appropriate framework for estimating horizontal spillover effects when using firm-level data. First, such framework permits investigation of domestic firms' productivity over a longer time period, rather than at one point in time. Second, panel data allow estimation of spillovers after controlling for other factors. Cross-section data cannot control the time-invariant factor. Hence the differences in productivity aggregated at the sectoral level fail to be controlled even though they might be correlated with foreign presence without being caused by it. This means that coefficients on cross-section estimates are likely to be biased. For example, if productivity is higher in the automobiles sector than in the food sector, multinationals may be attracted to the automobiles sector. Cross-sectional data would show a positive and statistically significant relationship between the level of FDI and productivity consistent with spillovers, even though FDI did not cause high levels of productivity but rather was attracted by them.

Taking this into consideration, one would need to say that the evidence on positive horizontal spillovers seems much weaker. There are only eight studies employing panel framework that find unambiguously positive evidence in the aggregate, and almost all of them are for developed countries.

While many studies of productivity spillovers from FDI assume that they occur mainly in the industry in which the MNC subsidiaries operates, there are other type of effects of FDI outside of the industry in which the subsidiaries are active. Some consider (i) backward linkages, i.e. spillovers to upstream (supply-side) industries and others find (ii) forward linkages, i.e. spillovers to downstream (customer side) industries. Backward linkages may arise from efforts by multinational firms to improve the quality of the intermediate products they buy locally or from the competition among local firms to become the suppliers to the multinationals. MNC subsidiaries have a stronger incentive to provide technological knowledge to their suppliers than to local competitors that produce the same product.[5] Forward linkages, on the other hand, may arise because of the learning of final good producers from foreign owned firms which provide them with superior intermediate inputs. As one of the evidence for this forward linkage, [Larrain et al., 2000] argue that among the most important consequences of the chipmaker Intel's recent FDI into Costa Rica is that (i) intel funded schools that taught local workers certain skills and (ii) intel's FDI served as a signal for other potential foreign investors that it might be time to invest in Costa Rica now.

Rodriguez-Clare [1996] shows how linkages between foreign subsidiaries and indigenous firms may boost the productivity of the latter. Focuses on the intermediate good demand effects of

---

[5]See Kugler [2002] and Blalock and Gertler [2002] for the evidence for such backward linkage.

MNCs, he develops a model with monopolistic competition in the intermediate goods sector. Domestic firms and MNFs use the intermediate goods as inputs in the production of final goods. He assumes that MNFs require more variety of intermediate goods than domestic firms. Hence, the entry of a MNF increases demand for intermediate inputs, which constructs the backward linkage. Because of monopolistic competition in the intermediates sector, the entry of the MNF induces an increase in the variety of available intermediate goods. Final goods producers benefit because of the love of variety for intermediate inputs, which establishes the forward linkage effect.

Markusen and Venables [1999] has a similar setup. However, they explicitly capture the intraindustry competition effect a MNF leads to when it enters the market. Rodriguez-Clare [1996] effectively ignores this effect, considering situations in which MNFs are the only firms producing in one of the two countries. These two studies look only at pecuniary spillovers and competition effects of FDI, not at knowledge spillover effects. Markusen and Venables [1999] argued that contacts between domestic and foreign firms supported by production complementarities and scale economies may enhance the development of domestic sectors with wider consequences for the host region and industry. They also link vertical spillovers to market structure. Backward spillovers may occur if foreign subsidiaries establish a supply arrangement to foster competition in the upstream sector.

Lin and Saggi [2007] explicitly consider vertical technology transfer through backward linkages (from MNFs to their local suppliers). They assume that an MNC can negotiate an exclusivity contract with a number of local suppliers when they decided to enter the market. Only then will the multinational enterprise engage in vertical technology transfer. This model does not consider knowledge spillovers as in the definition of being an externality considered here.

In empirical field, there are a number of empirical studies in this area [Javorcik, 2004; Javorcik and Spatareanu, 2008; Kugler, 2006; Bwalya, 2006; Schoors and van der Tol, 2001]. As Smeets [2008] points out, all of these empirical studies depend on the following simple specification:

$$y_{ijt} = \beta_0 + \beta_1 \text{FDI}_{jt} + \beta_2 \sum_{k \neq j} \left(\alpha_{jkt}^0 \text{FDI}_{kt} \right)$$

$$+ \beta_3 \sum_{k \neq j} \left(\alpha_{jkt}^I \text{FDI}_{kt} \right) + \cdots + \beta_2 X_{it} + B_3 Z_{it} + \varepsilon_{ijt},$$

where α_{jk}^0 is the output share flowing from industry j to industry kj, α_{jk}^i is the share of inputs used by industry j from industry kj, i indexes the firm j, j and k index the industry; t indexes time. y_{ijt} is a measure of productivity of firm i active in sector j at time t, X is a vector of firm-level control variables that are known, to affect productivity (such as own investments in R&D and human capital); Z is a vector of industry-level control variables (for example, market concentration), and ε is an error term. In this model β_1 measures the effect of FDI in firm i's own sector, which can be interpreted as a demonstration effect; β_2 captures the effect of FDI in sector k on the productivity of firm i in sector j, weighted by the share of output flowing from sector j to k (that is, backward linkages); and β_3 captures forward linkages.

The empirical literature attempting to explain PRC state-owned TNC activities is inconclusive and without much theoretical underpinnings [Todo *et al.*, 2011; Chen and Lee, 2012; Li, 2012; Szamosszegi, 2012; Bowman *et al.*, 2013]. We attempt to fill this gap by presenting, in Section 8.2, a reasonable theoretical explanation of PRC OFDI in search for "spillover effects" in a two-country model with firms distinguished by their ability to innovate.

8.2.   Innovation via M&A or Immigration of Skilled S&E Workers?[6]

Consider a world with two countries with two legal enforceable intellectual property (IPR) environments, where an entrepreneur can innovate — with a well-established common law legal structure C^L that enforces IPR rules and that of a transition economy C^T with

---

[6]Pelzman (2015).

a 'work in progress' legal enforcement of IPR. The State actor S^T in the transition economy C^T is attempting to acquire "spillover" effects attached to innovative R&D.[7] The model is divided into two stages: The first stage concerns the problem of inducing "in-country innovation" in the State-dominated economy with questionable IPR enforcement, and the second stage focuses on the economic argument for foreign acquisition of the "spillover effects," either through M&A or by acquiring the skilled labor.

The transition economy is populated by j risk-neutral firms with a strong and powerful State actor that will both create and invest in its enterprises $E_S^{j,T}$ (where S = State and T = transition economy legal structure). The two major distinguishing factors separating transition economy firms and their market counterparts revolve around their ability to acquire an initial wealth, $W^{j,T}$ at capital costs substantially lower than their competition in the market economy, as well as their ability to successfully innovate in the context of a 'work in progress' legal enforcement of IPR.

In order to consider the options available to $E_S^{j,T}$, we begin by focusing on the decision to innovate.

8.2.1. *The Decision to Innovate via Immigration*

There are two firms: One located in C^L and the other in C^T. Assume initially that both firms have constant marginal costs c. In period 1, they can endeavor to initiate an innovation that reduces their marginal costs by x_i, i representing either a firm in L or T environments. For simplicity, assume that research R&D investment has diminishing returns and that the R&D expenditure function is quadratic [Qiu, 1977], such that:

$$V(x_i) = \frac{\sigma x_i^2}{2}, \quad \text{where } \sigma > 0, \tag{8.3}$$

---

[7]The record of PRC acquisitions up to 2012 (presented in Tables 8.1–8.3) supports the idea that S^T is attempting to fill the gap in new innovations created by C^T — the 'work in progress' legal enforcement of IPR.

where the parameter σ measures the efficiency or productivity of the R&D technology.

In order to innovate, each firm has to hire scientists and engineers (S&Es). Once the decision to innovate is made, the next question is the cost of that skilled human capital. In a multi-country context where there is a free flow of skilled labor, one can postulate that C^L and C^T environment firms compete on a regular basis for skilled human capital, and that competition is captured fully in terms of wage competition.[8] One can presume a framework where firm i in C^T offers wages $w_{i,T}^{j,L}(i \neq j)$ for firm j's S&Es and $w_{i,T}^{i,T}$ for their own S&Es. Assuming competitive markets, a scientist or engineer from firm j will switch locations from C^L to C^T if $w_{i,T}^{j,L} > w_{j,L}^{j,L}$, otherwise he or she continues to work for firm j. To attract S&Es from firm j, firm i needs to offer a wage which is higher than $w_{j,L}^{j,L}$ by some τ.

The wage differential τ offered by firm i in C^T must reflect the differential human capital skills and additional expected performance of i. While some of this information is known, the full differential in performance can only be determined with some degree of certainty after the wage contract is offered and the employee comes on board. If an S&E moves to firm i in C^T, this firm obtains an immediate cost reduction equal to x_j accounting for the technical hire, and by the knowledge spillover Ω from knowledge while employed in firm j in C^L. So its marginal production costs will be:

$$c_i^T = c - x_i - \Omega x_j, \qquad (8.4)$$

where the parameter $\Omega \in [0, 1]$ captures the extent of spillovers. The reduction in costs reflected in Equation (8.4) arises because of the assumption that the required human capital to reduce production cost is completely transferable to other firms. Furthermore, we assume that the cost reductions are complementary. Hence, if a firm can motivate an S&E of the competing firms to move, he or she will be able to replicate the original cost reduction in his new firm. For the sake of completeness, one can also assume that knowledge can

---

[8]We assume that the transition economy has reduced or eliminated any restrictions in their policies with respect to foreign skilled labor.

be duplicated within the firm losing its valued scientist or engineer. If firm i in C^T loses an S&E to its local C^T competitors after investing at least the wage differential τ, then we assume that it has already internalized the cost savings so that its costs remain $c - x_i$.

The value to firm i in C^T of attracting foreign skilled workers becomes apparent when we introduce competition between firm i in C^T and firm j in C^L. For simplicity, assume that the two firms produce homogeneous goods. The inverse market-demand schedule of the consuming countries is given by:

$$p = \alpha - \beta(q_i^T + q_j^L); \quad i \neq j; \ \alpha > 0, \tag{8.5}$$

where q_i^T is the quantity of firm i's (in C^T) production. [The homogeneity assumption can be easily transformed by letting $q_j^L = \gamma q_j^L$ where the degree of product differentiation decreases with the parameter γ.]

Let π_i^T represent firm i's profits excluding the cost of innovation. Then given the firm's decisions to undertake R&D,

$$\pi_i^T = p_i^T q_i^T - (c - x_i, -\Omega x_j)q_i^T. \tag{8.6}$$

The two firms choose output to maximize their respective market profits, and the resulting Cournot–Nash equilibrium would be:

$$q_i^* = \frac{1}{4 - \gamma^2}[(\alpha - c)(2 - \gamma) + (2 - \Omega\gamma)x_i + (2\Omega - \gamma)x_j]. \tag{8.7}$$

8.2.2. *The Decision to Acquire R&D*

As an alternative strategy to importing skilled S&E workers, firm i in C^T can begin the process of acquiring via M&A the research firms relevant to its production. Whitney and Gaisford [1999] have suggested that firm i in C^T may be able to acquire the R&D generating firm itself. Incorporating this assumption brings the current discussion closer to the strategic trade policy models of Brander and Spencer [1985], Dixit [1984], Eaton and Grossman [1986], Dixit and Kyle [1985], Branson and Klevorick [1986], Grossman [1986], Gal-Or [1985] and Vives [1984].

As noted above, let Ω denote the "spillover effect" or, in terms of the acquisition, the probability that firm i's agents in C^T successfully penetrate firm j in C^L new technology. The probability that firm i will fail to penetrate firm j is $1 - \Omega$. And the probability where firm i is successful is simply Ω. Given that the marginal cost attainable with previous generation technology is $c - x_i$ and the marginal cost reduction attributable to the new technology post spillover is Ωx_j, firm j would maintain its superior position as long as firm i is prevented from accessing the R&D. Firm j produces more than firm i and earns higher profits because its cost advantages remain intact, when firm i's corporate incursion is unsuccessful. Following Qiu [1977], we assume that $\alpha - (c - x_i) - \Omega x_j$ is strictly positive such that firm i continues to produce even if its attempt to acquire the R&D is unsuccessful. Once firm i manages to succeed in its acquisition of the R&D, the symmetry assumption will guarantee that in both firms, profits, outputs and costs will be identical. All the potential outcomes in this Cournot–Nash Duopoly R&D acquisition model are presented in Table 8.4. A successful bid to penetrate firm j by firm

Table 8.4   Potential Outcomes in a Cournot–Nash Duopoly R&D Acquisition Model

Description	Firm C_i^T Does Not Receive the Cost Saving Technology from Firm C_j^L	Firm C_i^T Does Receive the Cost Saving Technology from Firm C_j^L
Firm C_i^T's MC	$c - x_i$	$c - x_i - \Omega x_j$
Firm C_j^L's MC	$c - x_i - \Omega x_j$	$c - x_i - \Omega x_j$
Firm C_i^T's Output	$\dfrac{(\alpha - x_i - \Omega x_j)}{3\beta}$	$\dfrac{(\alpha - x_i + \Omega x_j)}{3\beta}$
Firm C_j^L's Output	$\dfrac{(\alpha - x_i - 2\Omega x_j)}{3\beta}$	$\dfrac{(\alpha - x_i + \Omega x_j)}{3\beta}$
Firm C_i^T's Profit	$\dfrac{(\alpha - x_i - \Omega x_j)^2}{9\beta}$	$\dfrac{(\alpha - x_i + \Omega x_j)^2}{9\beta}$
Firm C_j^L's Profit	$\dfrac{(\alpha - x_i - 2\Omega x_j)^2}{9\beta}$	$\dfrac{(\alpha - x_i + \Omega x_j)^2}{9\beta}$
Consumer Surplus	$\dfrac{2(\alpha - x_i + 0.5\Omega x_j)^2}{9\beta}$	$\dfrac{2(\alpha - x_i + \Omega x_j)^2}{9\beta}$

i, would increase firm i's Nash equilibrium output by $\frac{2\Omega x_j}{3\beta}$ and its profits by $\frac{4\Omega x_j(\alpha-x_i)}{9\beta}$, reduce firm j's Nash-equilibrium output by $\frac{\Omega x_j}{3\beta}$ and its profits by $\frac{2\Omega x_j(\alpha-x_i+(3/2)x_j)}{9\beta}$ and increase industry output by $\frac{\Omega x_j}{3\beta}$ and consumer surplus by $\frac{2\Omega x_j(\alpha-x_i+(3/4)\Omega x_j)}{9\beta}$.

8.3. Micro Data on the PRC Path to Acquire Foreign R&D

Employment of foreigner experts in China has been on the rise since 2001. While small in numbers relative to the Chinese labor market, its significance is that it is predominantly in economics, technology and management education, science, culture and public health. On the demand side, the definition of "foreign expert" in economy, technology and management experts includes engineers, senior technicians and managerial staff members. In the past 20 years, the number of invited foreign experts has added up to over 2 million, from more than 50 countries and territories. Currently, over 240,000 foreign experts are invited to work in China.[9] There is no data on their distribution by industry and no figure for the ones engaging in S&E activities.

If R&D is an expensive endeavor with enormous risks to investors and, in the case of the PRC, to the State, then there is a strong incentive to acquire proven innovation in the market economies. But the real "bargains" are in R&D operations that have not yet proven their true market value.

The best publicly — available micro data on PRC — outward M&A activity is provided by the Heritage Foundation. In Table 8.5, we present the data for M&A activities by PRC TNCs worth $100 million or more between 2005 and 2013. These deals represent about 25 percent of all the successful M&A deals in 2011. Of equal note are the list of troubled M&A deals presented in Table 8.6. All of these deals are in the technology area. In Table 8.7, we list the smaller PRC transactions as of 2000 in what we call "Heard on the Street." The

---

[9]China's Ministry of Human Resources and Social Security, 2014.

Table 8.5   Cross-Border M&A Deals in Technology Worth More than $100 Million between 2005 and 2013

Year	Investor	Millions	Share Size	Partner/Target	Sector	Subsector	Country
2013	Fosun	$240	96%	Alma Lasers	Technology		Israel
2013	CDH	$110	10%	Mobile World	Technology	Telecom	Vietnam
2013	Mindray Medical	$110	100%	ZONARE Systems	Technology		USA
2013	Shanghai Micro Port Scientific	$290		Wright Medical	Technology		USA
2013	Tencent	$350	6%	Activision	Technology		USA
2013	Huawei	$200			Technology	Telecom	Britain
2012	Huawei	$1,500			Technology	Telecom	Hungary
2012	CIC	$490	7%	Eutelsat	Technology	Telecom	France
2012	Tencent	$330	40%	Epic Games	Technology		USA
2012	Lenovo	$150		Digibras	Technology		Brazil
2012	Huawei	$150			Technology	Telecom	India
2012	Xinwei	$300			Technology	Telecom	Nicaragua
2012	BGI	$120	100%	Complete Genomics	Technology		USA

2011	Lenovo	$180	51%	NEC	Technology		Japan
2011	China Unicom	$500	1%	Telefonica	Technology	Telecom	Spain
2011	Tencent	$400	84%	Riot Games	Technology		USA
2011	ZTE	$200			Technology	Telecom	Brazil
2011	Lenovo	$670	82%	Medion	Technology		Germany
2011	Huawei	$130			Technology	Telecom	Italy
2010	Tencent	$300	10%	Digital Sky Technologies	Technology		Russia
2010	Shanda Games	$100	100%	Eyedentity Games	Technology		S. Korea
2010	Sinochem	$270	50%	DSM	Technology	Medical	Netherlands
2009	Unicom	$1,000	1%	Telefonica	Technology	Telecom	Spain
2009	China Mobile	$500	100%		Technology	Telecom	Pakistan
2008	Wuxi PharmaTech	$160	100%	AppTec Lab Services	Technology		USA
2008	Mindray Medical	$200		Datascope	Technology		USA
2007	China Mobile	$280	89%	Paktel	Technology	Telecom	Pakistan
2007	China Mobile	$180	11%	Paktel	Technology	Telecom	Pakistan
2005	Lenovo	$1,740		IBM	Technology		USA

Source: Heritage Foundation

Table 8.6   Cross-Border Incomplete and Troubled M&A Deals in Technology Worth More than $100 Million between 2005 and 2013

Year	Investor	Millions	Share	Partner	Sector	Subsector	Country
2013	China Mobile	$600	12%	FareasTone	Technology	Telecom	Taiwan
2010	Huawei	$480		2Wire	Technology	Telecom	USA
2010	Huawei	$1,300		Motorola	Technology	Telecom	USA
2010	Huawei and ZTE	$5,000		Sprint	Technology	Telecom	USA
2008	ZTE	$300			Technology	Telecom	Philippines
2008	Huawei	$600	17%	3Com	Technology	Telecom	USA
2008	Great Wall	$300	43%	Iomega	Technology	Telecom	USA
2006	China Mobile	$5,300		Millicom	Technology	Telecom	Luxembourg

Source: Heritage Foundation

Table 8.7 Heard on the Street — PRC TNCs Purchases of Small Foreign Assets

PRC Buyers	Purchase	Equity Stake	Price
Beijing Raisecom Technology Company	Brazil AsGa Acesso S.A	Partial	C$5 per share
Shenzhen Infinova Technology Company	Canada March networks Corporation	100% Value C$90.1 million.	
Futong Group	Futong Group Optical Cable Technology Co., Ltd		$80.36 million
Chaori Solar Energy Technology	Luxembourg Chaori Sky Solar Energy		$6.83 million.
Chengdu Geeya Technology Company	UK Harvard International Company		23 million Pounds
Ningbo Huaxiang Electronics Co	Germany Sellner and IPG		18.7 million euros
Sinochem International	Singapore GMG	51% equity	S$267.98 million
Beijing SL Pharmaceutical Company	Canada Vaccine	85% equity	130 million RMB
Ningbo Lawrence Automotive Interior Company	England Northern Automotive Systems Limited	100% equity	$90 million
Ningbo Huaxiang Electronics Company	Czech Republic WECH Cheb		$70.3 million
Luxshare Precision Industry Company	Taiwan Speed Tech	25% equity	$15 million
Zhejiang Kanglaite Group	Kanglaite, USA		$100 million
Sichuan Ruifeng Investment Management	Canada Windtalkers Energy	90% equity	$383 million
Mmonu (Mengnu) Group	USA Jennifer		$17.37 million
Haichang Group	France Lamont Winery		
Futong Groups	Japan SWCC Showa Holdings	18.58% equity	$64 million
Xinjiang Gold	Germany's Vensys Energy		42.24 million Euros
China Railway Group	Australia Resource house Company		$200 million

(*Continued*)

Table 8.7 (*Continued*)

PRC Buyers	Purchase	Equity Stake	Price
Taiyuan Heavy Machinery Company	Australia Valley		A$130
Guangdong Rising Assets Management Company	Pan-Aust Company	19.9% equity	$140 million
CITIC	Spain Gandara Censa		50 million RMB
Fulida Group	Canada Neucel Specialty Cellulose Ltd.		$250 million
Fushi Copperweld	USA Copperweld		$22.5 million
Beijing E-Town Capital	USA UT Starcom		$25 million
Chongqing Machinery and Electric Company	England Precision Technologies Group		
Shandong Ruyi Technology	Japan Renown Company	41% equity	$56 million
BOE Group	Taiwan JEAN Technology Company		290 million RMB
Zhongrong International Holdings	USA Crimson Oil Exploration Company		$30 million
Shanghai International Port Group	Belgium APM Terminals Company	25% equity	$33.7 million
Shanghai Electric	USA Goss International		$1.5 billion
Shanghai Mechanical and electric	USA Goss International	100% equity	571.06 million RMB
AVIC	Australia FACC	90% equity	100 million Euros
Hisun Group	Germany Grosse Precision Machinery Company		$4.98 million
China Non-ferrous	Germany HP Tec Gmbh	100% equity	

Source: Various newspaper articles

dollar value of these transactions are impossible to confirm. They do suggest that the PRC has been involved in OFDI for a long time.

In order to empirically test the theoretical justifications for PRC TNC overseas activities requires a much richer data set than we can access publicly today. Irrespective of this data constraint, however, the theoretical construct we present here with the available data is a reasonable explanation of the activities by the PRC TNCs in overseas markets.

Bibliography

Aitken, B., Gordon H., and Harrison, A. E. (1997). Spillovers, Foreign Investment, and Export Behavior, *Journal of International Economics*, 43(1–2), pp. 103–132.

Amiti, M. and Freund, C. (2010). The Anatomy of China's Export Growth, in Robert C. Feenstra and Shang-Jin Wei (eds.), *China's Growing Role in World Trade*, Chicago: University of Chicago Press, pp. 35–56.

Amiti, M. and Konings, J. (2007). Trade Liberalization, Intermediate Inputs and Productivity: Evidence from Indonesia, *American Economic Review*, 97(5), pp. 1611–1638.

Antràs, P., Chor, D., Fally, T., and Hillberry, R. (2012). Measuring the Upstreamness of Production and Trade Flows, *American Economic Review*, 102(3), pp. 412–416.

Aristei, D., Castellanu, D., and Franco, C. (2013). Firms' Exporting and Importing Activities: Is There a Two-Way Relationship? *Review of World Economics*, 149, pp. 55–84.

Arkolakis, C., Costinot, A., and Rodriguez-Clare, A. (2012). New Trade Models, Same Old Gains? *American Economic Review*, 102(1), pp. 94–130.

Armington, P. (1969). A Theory of Demand for Products Distinguished by Place of Production, *IMF Staff Papers*, 16, pp. 159–178.

Backer, K. D. and Miroudot, S. (2013). Mapping Global Value Chains, OECD Trade Policy Papers, No. 159, OECD.

Bagwell, K. and Staiger, R. W. (1999). An Economic Theory of GATT, *American Economic Review*, 89(1), pp. 215–248.

Bagwell, K. (2008). Remedies in the World Trade Organization: An Economic Perspective, in Janow, M. E., Donaldson, V.J., and Yanovich, A. (eds.), *The WTO Governance, Dispute Settlement and Developing Countries*. New York: Juris Publishing, Huntington, pp. 733–770.

Bagwell, K. and Staiger, R. W. (2002). *The Economics of the World Trading System*, Cambridge, MA: The MIT Press.

Bagwell, K. and Staiger, R. W. (2003a). Protection and the Business Cycle, *Advances in Economic Analysis and Policy*, 3(1), pp. 1–43.

Bagwell, K. and Staiger, R. W. (2003b). *The Economics of the World Trading System*, Cambridge, MA: The MIT Press.

Bagwell, K. and Staiger, R. W. (2004). Multilateral Trade Negotiations, Bilateral Opportunism and the Rules of the GATT/WTO, *Journal of International Economics*, 63, pp. 1–29.

Bagwell, K. and Staiger, R. W. (2005). Enforcement, Private Political Pressure and the GATT/WTO Escape Clause, *Journal of Legal Studies*, 34(2), pp. 471–513.

Bagwell, K. and Staiger, R. W. (2006). What Do Trade Negotiators Negotiate About? Empirical Evidence From the World Trade Organization, National Bureau of Economic Research (NBER), Working Paper No. 12727, Cambridge, MA.

Balassa, B. (1965). Trade Liberalization and Revealed Comparative Advantage, *The Manchester School of Economic and Social Studies*, 33, pp. 92–123.

Baldwin, R. (2009). The Great Trade Collapse: What Caused it and What Does it Mean? in R. Baldwin (ed.), *The Great Trade Collapse: Causes, Consequences and Prospects*. Available at *www.vox.eu.org*.

Baldwin, R. and Venables, A. (2010). Spiders and Snakes: Offshoring and Agglomeration in the Global Economy, NBER Working Paper Series, No. 16611, Cambridge, M.A.

Baldwin, R. (2011). Trade and Industrialization after Globalization's 2nd Unbundling: How Building and Joining a Supply Chain are Different and Why It Matters, NBER Working Paper Series, No. 17716, Cambridge, M.A.

Bas, M. (2012). Input-Trade Liberalization and Firm Export Decisions: Evidence from Argentina, *Journal of Development Economics*, 97(2), pp. 481–493.

Bas, M. and Strauss-Kahn, V. (2011). Does Importing More Inputs Raise Exports? CEPII Working Paper, No. 2011-15, CEPII, France.

Bayard, T., Orr, J., Pelzman J., and Perez-Lopez J. (1981). MFN Tariff Treatment of Imports from China: Effects on U.S. Employment, *Journal of Policy Modeling*, 3(3), pp. 361–373.

Bayard, T., Orr, J., Pelzman J., and Perez-Lopez J. (1982). U.S.-PRC Trade Normalization: Effects on U.S. and Employment, in Congress of the United States, Joint Economic Committee, *China Under the Four Modernizations, Part Two*, Washington: U.S. GPO, pp. 172–209.

Bernard, A., Eaton, J., Jensen, J. B., and Kortum, S. (2003). Plants and Productivity in International Trade, *American Economic Review*, 93, pp. 1268–1290.

Blalock, G., and Gertler, P. (2002). Technology Diffusion from Foreign Direct Investment through Supply Chains, working paper, Haas School of Business, University of California, Berkeley, June.

Blomstrom, M. (1986). Foreign investment and productive efficiency: The case of Mexico, *Journal of Industrial Economics*, 15, pp. 97–110.

Blomstrom, M., and Persson, H. (1983). Foreign investment and spillover efficiency in an underdeveloped economy: Evidence from the Mexican manufacturing industry, *World Development*, 11, pp. 493–501.

Blyde, J., Kugler, M., and Stein, E. (2005). Exporting vs. Outsourcing by MNC Subsidiaries: Which Determines FDI Spillovers? Paper presented at RES 2005 Conference.

Bowen, H. (1983). On the Theoretical Interpretation of Indices of Trade Intensity and Revealed Comparative Advantage, *Weltwirtschaftliches Archiv*, 119, pp. 464–472.

Bowen, H. and Pelzman, J. (1984). US Export Competitiveness: 1962–1977, *Applied Economics*, 16, pp. 461–473

Bowman, M., Gilligan, G., and Obrien, J. (2013) "China: Investing in the World" *Center for International Finance and Regulation Working Paper*, 2013.

Bown, C. and Crowley, M. A. (2013a). Emerging Economies, Trade Policy, and Macroeconomic Shocks, World Bank Policy Research Working Papers No. 6315, Washington, DC, World Bank.

Bown, C. and Crowley, M. A. (2013b). Import Protection, Business Cycles, and Exchange Rates: Evidence From the Great Recession, *Journal of International Economics*, 90(1), pp. 50–64.

Branstetter, L. and Lardy, N. (2006). China's Embrace of Globalization, NBER Working Paper No. 12373, Cambridge, MA.

Brander, J. A. and Spencer, B. J. (1985). Export Subsidies and International Market Share Rivalry, *Journal of International Economics*, 18(1–2), pp. 83–100

Branson, William H. and Klevorick, Alvin K. (1986). Strategic Behavior and Trade Policy, in Paul Krugman (ed.), *Strategic Trade Policy and the New International Economics*, Cambridge, MA.: MIT Press.

Brainard, S. L. (1993). A simple theory of multinational corporations and trade with a trade-off between proximity and concentration, National Bureau of Economic Research (NBER) Working Paper No. 4269, Cambridge, MA.

Brasili, A., Epifani, P., and Helg, R. (2000). On the Dynamics of Trade Patterns, *De Economist*, 148(2), pp. 233–257.

Buckley, J., Cross, R., Tan, H., Xin, L., and Voss, H. (2008). Historic and Emergent Trends in Chinese Outward Direct Investment, *Management International Review*, 48(6), pp. 715–748.

Brautigam, D. (2010). China, Africa and the International Aid Architecture, Working Papers Series No. 107. Tunis, Tunisia: African Development Bank.

Brautigam, D. (2011). Testimony on China's Growing Role in Africa before the United States Senate Committee on Foreign Relations Subcommittee on African Affairs, November 1, 2011.

Brautigam, D. (2011a). Chinese Development Aid in Africa: What, Where, Why and How Much? in Jane Golley and Ligang Song (eds.), *China Update 2011*, Canberra, Australia: National University.

Bwalya, S. M. (2006). Foreign Direct Investment and Technology Spillovers: Evidence from Panel Data Analysis of Manufacturing Firms in Zambia, *Journal of Development Economics*, 81(2), pp. 514–526.

Cadot, O., Carrere, C., and Strauss-Kahn, V. (2011). Trade Diversification: Drivers and Impacts, in M. Jansen, R. Peters and J.M. Salazar-Xirinachs (eds.), *Trade and Employment: From Myths to Facts*, Geneva: International Labor Office.

Chen, Been-Lon and Shun-Fa Lee. (2012). Intersectoral Spillovers, Relative Prices and Development Traps, *Review of Development Economics*, 16(2), pp. 243–261.

Chinese Ministry of Commerce (MOFCOM). (2010). *Statistical Bulletin of Chinese Outward Foreign Direct Investment.* Beijing, September 2011.

Chinese Ministry of Commerce (MOFCOM). (2012). *Statistical Bulletin of Chinese Outward Foreign Direct Investment.* Beijing, August 2013.

Church, P., Joseph P., Schrader, J., and Schneider, K. (2001). *United States Government Initiatives to Build Trade Related Capacity in Developing and Transition Countries,* prepared for the United States Agency for International Development, October.

Coe, N. M. and Hess, M. (2007). Global Production Networks: Debates and Challenges, paper prepared for the GPERG workshop, University of Manchester, England.

Congressional Research Service (CRS). (2009). *China's Assistance and Government-Sponsored Investment Activities in Africa, Latin America, and Southeast Asia.* Washington DC.

Deardorff, A. (2001a). International Provision of Trade Services, Trade, and Fragmentation, *Review of International Economics*, 9(2), pp. 233–248.

Deardorff, A. (2001b). Fragmentation in Simple Trade Models, *North American Journal of Economics and Finance*, 12, pp. 121–137.

Dedrick, J., Kraemer, K. L., and Linden, G. (2009). Who Profits from Innovation in Global Value Chains?: A Study of the iPod and Notebook OCs, *Industrial and Corporate Change*, 19(1), pp. 81–116.

Deer, L. and Song, L. (2012). China's Approach to Rebalancing: A Conceptual and Policy Framework, *China & World Economy*, 20(1), pp. 1–26.

Dierickx, I. and Cool, K. (1989). Asset Stock Accumulation and Sustainability of Competitive Advantage, *Management Science*, 35(12), pp. 1504–1511.

Dixit, A. (1984). International Trade Policy for Oligopolistic Industries, *Economic Journal*, 94, pp. 1–16.

Dixit, A. K. and Kyle, A. S. (1985). The Use of Protection and Subsidies for Entry Promotion and Deterrence, *American Economics Review*, 75(1), pp. 139–152.

Dunning, J. H. and Narula, R. (1995). The R&D Activities of Foreign Firms in the United States, *International Studies of Management and Organization*, 25(1–2), pp. 39–73.

Dunning, J. (1977). Trade, Location of Economy Activity and MNE: A Search for an Eclectic Approach, in B. Ohlin, P. O. Hesselborn, and P. S. Wijkmaneds (eds.), *The International Allocation of Economic Activity*, London: Macmillan, pp. 395–418.

Eaton, J. and Kortum, S. (2002). Technology, Geography, and Trade, *Econometrica*, 70, pp. 1741–1779.

Eaton, J. and Grossman, G. M. (1986). Optimal Trade and Industrial Policy Under Oligopoly, *Quarterly Journal of Economics*, 101(2), pp. 383–406.

Fair, R. C. and Jaffee, D. M. (1972). Methods of Estimation for Markets in Disequilibrium, *Econometrica*, 40(3), pp. 497–514.

Fally, T. (2012). *Production Staging: Measurement and Facts*. University of Colorado–Boulder.

Feenstra, R. C. and Hiau L. K. (2008.) Export Variety and Country Productivity: Estimating the Monopolistic Competition Model with Endogenous Productivity, *Journal of International Economics*, 74, pp. 500–514.

Feenstra, R. C. (2010). Measuring the Gains from Trade under Monopolistic Competition, *The Canadian Journal of Economics*, 43(1), pp. 1–28.

Feinberg, R. M. (2005). U.S. Antidumping Enforcement and Macroeconomic Indicators Revisited, *Review of World Economics*, 141(4), pp. 612–622.

Feinberg, S. E., and Gupta, A. K. (2004). Knowledge Spillovers and the Assignment of R&D Responsibilities for Foreign Subsidiaries, *Strategic Management Journal*, 25(8–9), pp. 823–845.

Feng, L., Li, Z., and Swenson, D. L. (2012). The Connection between Imported Intermediate Inputs and Exports: Evidence from Chinese Firms, *IAW Discussion Paper*, No. 86.

Ferrarini, B. (2011). Mapping Vertical Trade, Working Paper No. 263, Asian Development Bank.

Finger, J. M. (1996). Legalized Backsliding: Safeguard Provisions in the GATT, in W. Martin and L.A. Winters (eds.), *The Uruguay Round and the Developing Countries*, New York: Cambridge University Press.

Fontagné, L. and Toubal, F. (2010). Trade in intermediate goods and competitiveness Report for the Senate, Paris.

Fosfuri, A., and Massimo, M. (1999). Multinationals without Advantages, *Scandinavian Journal of Economics*, 101(4), pp. 617–30.

Gal-Or, E. (1985). Information Sharing in Oligopoly, *Econometrica*, 53(2), pp. 329–343.

Gereffi, G. (1994). The Organization of Buyer-Driven Global Commodity Chains: How US Retailers Shape Overseas Production Networks, in G. Gereffi and M. Korzeniewicz (eds.), *Commodity Chains and Global Capitalism*, Westport, CT: Praeger, pp. 95–122.

Geweke, John, Robert C. Marshall, and Gary A. Zarkin (1986). Mobility Indices in Continuous Time Markov Chains, *Econometrica*, 54(6), pp. 1407–1423.

Goldberg, P., Khandelwal, A., Pavcnik, N., and Topalova, P. (2009). Imported Intermediate Inputs and Domestic Productivity Growth: Evidence from India, NBER Working Paper No. 14127.

Görg, H., and Strobl, E. (2001). Multinational Companies and Productivity Spillovers: A Meta-Analysis, *Economic Journal*, 111(475), pp. F723–39.

Görg, H. and Greenaway, D. (2004). Much Ado about Nothing? Do Domestic Firms Really Benefit from Foreign Direct Investment? *The World Bank Research Observer*, 19(2), pp. 171–197.

Greenaway, D., Sousa, N., and Wakelin, K. (2004). Do Domestic Firms Learn to Export from Multinationals? *European Journal of Political Economy*, 20(4), pp. 1027–1043.

Grilli, E. (1988). Macro-Economic Determinants of Trade Protection, *World Economy*, 11(3), pp. 313–326.

Grossman, G. and Rossi-Hansberg, E. (2008). Trading Tasks: A Simple Theory of Offshoring, *American Economic Review*, 98(5), pp. 1978–1997.

Grossman, Gene M. (1986). Strategic Export Promotion: A Critique, in Paul Krugman (ed.), *Strategic Trade Policy and the New International Economics*, Cambridge, MA: MIT Press.

Harrigan, J. (2010). Airplanes and Comparative Advantage, *Journal of International Economics*, 82, pp. 181–194.

Harrigan, J. and Venables, A. (2006). Timeliness and Agglomeration, *Journal of Urban Economics*, 59, pp. 300–316.

Hartley, M. J. (1976). The Estimation of Markets in Disequilibrium: The Fixed Supply Case, *International Economic Review*, 17, pp. 687–699.

Heritage Foundation. (2014). *The China Global Investment Tracker.*

Hinloopen, J. and Marrewijk, C. V. (2001). On the Empirical Distribution of the Balassa Index, *Weltwirtschaftliches Archiv*, 137(1), pp. 1–35.

Hsieh, Chang-Tai and Ossa, R. (2011). A Global View of Productivity Growth in China, NBER Working Paper No. 16778 February 2011, Revised July 2015.

Hudson, R. (2004). Conceptualizing Economies and their Geographies: Spaces, Flows and Circuits, *Progress in Human Geography*, 28, pp. 447–471.

Hummels, D. (2007). Transportation Costs and International Trade in the Second Era of Globalization, *Journal of Economic Perspectives*, 21(3), pp. 131–154.

Hummels, D. and Schaur, G. (2012). Time as a Trade Barrier, NBER Working Paper No. 17758, Cambridge, MA.

Hummels, D., Jun, I., and Yi, K.-M. (2001). The Nature and Growth of Vertical Specialization in World Trade, *Journal of International Economics*, 54(1), pp. 75–96.

Hymer, Stephen H. (1960). *The International Operations of National Firms: A Study of Direct Foreign Investment.* Ph.D. diss., M.A. Institute of Technology, Cambridge, MA.

Japan Ministry of Foreign Affairs. (2007). *Japan's Official Development Assistance* White Paper 2007; Japan.

Javorcik, B. S. (2004). Does Foreign Direct Investment Increase the Productivity of Domestic Firms? In Search of Spillovers through Backward Linkages, *American Economic Review*, 94(3), pp. 605–627.

Javorcik, B. S. and Spatareanu, M. (2008). To Share or Not to Share: Does Local Participation Matter for Spillovers from Foreign Direct Investment? *Journal of Development Economics*, 85(1–2), pp. 194–217.

Keesing, Donald B. and Wolf, M. (1980). *Textile Quotas against Developing Countries*, Trade Policy Research Center, London,

Keller, W. (2004). International Technology Diffusion, *Journal of Economic Literature*, 42(3), pp. 752–782.

Kneller, R. and Pisu, M. (2007). Industrial Linkages and Export Spillovers from FDI, *The World Economy*, 30(1), pp. 105–134.

Knetter, M. M. and Prusa, T. J. (2003). Macroeconomic Factors and Antidumping Filings: Evidence from Four Countries, *Journal of International Economics*, 61(1), pp. 1–17.

Koopman, R., Powers, W., Wang, Z., and Wei, S.-J. (2011). Give Credit Where Credit is Due: Tracing Value Added in Global Production Chains, NBER Working Paper Series No. 16426, September 2010, Revised September 2011. Cambridge, MA.

Kokko, A. (1994). Technology, market characteristics, and spillovers, *Journal of Development Economics*, 43, pp. 279–293.

Korkeamäki, T. and Takalo, T. (2010). Valuation of Innovation: The Case of iPhone, MPRA Working Paper, University Library of Munich, Germany.

Krugman, P. (1996). *Pop Internationalism.* Cambridge, MA: MIT Press.

Kuemmerle, W. (1999). The Drivers of Foreign Direct Investment into Research and Development: An Empirical Investigation, *Journal of International Business Studies*, 30, pp. 1–24.

Kuemmerle, Walter. (1999). Foreign Direct Investment in Industrial Research in the Pharmaceutical and Electronics Industries: Results from a Survey of Multinational Firms, *Research Policy* 28(2–3), 179–193.

Kugler, M. (2002). The Diffusion of Externalities from Foreign Direct Investment: Theory ahead of Measurement, working paper, University of Southhampton, Southhampton, United Kingdom.

Kugler, M. (2006). Spillovers from Foreign Direct Investment: Within or between Industries? *Journal of Development Economics*, 80(2), pp. 444–477.

Lancaster, C. (2007). "The Chinese Aid System," Center for Global Development, June 2007 http://www.cgdev.org/sites/default/files/13953_file_ Chinese_aid.pdf

Larrain B. F., Lopez-Calva L. F., and Rodriguez-Clare A. (2000). "Intel: A Case Study of Foreign Direct Investment in Central America", Working Paper No. 58, Center for International Development, Harvard University, December.

Le Bas, C. and Sierra, C. (2002). Location versus Home Country Advantages in R&D Activities: Some Further Results on Multinationals' Location Strategies, *Research Policy*, 31(4), pp. 589–609.

Lederman, D. and Maloney, W. F. (2003). 'Trade Structure and Growth', Policy Research Working Paper No. 3025, World Bank, Washington, DC.

Lemoine, F. and Ünal, D. (2012). The Rebalancing of China's Foreign Trade Paper prepared for the 4th Meeting of the International Policy Advisory Group, 13–14 June, CEPII, Paris.

Li, Tong. Institutional Factors Matter: Perspectives on China's Outward Direct Investment, Milken Institute. December 2012.

Lin, Justin Yifu and Li, Yongjun (2006). *Exports and Economic Growth in China: A Demand Oriented Study.* mimeo.

Lin, P. and Saggi, K. (2007). Multinational Firms, Exclusivity and Backward Linkages, *Journal of International Economics*, 71(1), pp. 206–220.

Linden, G., Kraemer, K. L., and Dedrick, J. (2009). Who Captures Value in a Global Innovation Network? The Case of Apple's iPod, *Communications of the ACM*, 52(3), pp. 140–144.

Ma, A. and Van Assche, A. (2010). The Role of Trade Costs in Global Production Networks — Evidence from China's Processing Trade Regime, Policy Research Working Paper, No. 5490, The World Bank, Washington, DC.

Maddala, G. S. and Nelson, F. (1974). Maximum Likelihood Methods for Models of Market Disequilibrium, *Econometrica*, 42(6), pp. 1013–1030.

Maddala, G. S. (1983a). *Limited-Dependent and Qualitative Variables in Econometrics.* Econometric Society Monographs No. 3, London: Cambridge University Press.

Maddala, G. S. (1983b). Methods of Estimation for Models of Markets with Bounded Price Variation, *International Economic Review*, 24, pp. 361–378.

Markusen, J. (2002). *Multinational Firms and the Theory of International Trade.* Cambridge, MA: MIT Press.

Markusen, J. R. (1984). Multinational, multi-plant economies, and the gains from trade, *Journal of International Economics*, 16(3–4), pp. 205–226.

Markusen, J. and Venables, A. (1999). Foreign Direct Investment as a Catalyst for Industrial Development, *European Economic Review*, 43(2), pp. 335–356.

Melitz, M. J. (2003). The Impact of Trade on Intra-Industry Reallocations and Aggregate Industry Productivity, *Econometrica*, 71, pp. 1695–1725.

Melitz, M. J. and Redding, S. J. (2014). New Trade Models, New Welfare Implications, Working Paper No. 18919, National Bureau of Economic Research.

Miroudot, S., Lanz, R., and Ragoussis, A. (2009). Trade in Intermediate Goods and Services, OECD Trade Policy Papers, No. 93, OECD.

OECD (2005). *OECD Economic Surveys: China*, OECD, Paris.

OECD (2008a). *OECD Reviews of Innovation Policy — China*, OECD, Paris.

OECD (2008b). *OECD Science, Technology and Industry Outlook*, Paris.

OECD (2009). *OECD Reviews of Regulatory Reform — China: Defining the Boundary between the Market and the State*, OECD, Paris.

OECD (2010). *OECD Economic Surveys: China*, OECD Publishing.

OECD (2011a). *Agricultural Policy Monitoring and Evaluation 2011*, OECD, Paris.

OECD (2011b). *Attractiveness for Innovation: Location Factors for International Investment*, OECD Publishing.

OECD (2011c). *OECD Science, Technology and Industry Scoreboard 2011*, OECD Publishing.

OECD (2011d). *Globalisation, Comparative Advantage and the Changing Dynamics of Trade*, OECD Publishing.

Office of the National Counterintelligence Executive (ONCIX) (2009). *Annual Report to Congress on Foreign Economic Collection and Industrial Espionage*. FY 2008, 23 July.

Pelzman, J. and Martin, R. C. (1981). Direct Employment Effects of Increased Imports: A Case Study of the Textile Industry, *Southern Economic Journal*, 48(2), pp. 412–426.

Pelzman, J. (1983). Economic Costs of Tariffs and Quotas on Textile and Apparel Products Imported into the United States: A Survey of the Literature and Implications for Policies, *Weltwirtschafliches Archiv*, 119, pp. 523–542.

Pelzman, J. (1984). The Multifiber Arrangement and Its Effect on the Profit Performance of the U.S. Textile Industry, in Baldwin, R.E. and Anne O. Krueger (eds.), *The Structure and Evolution of Recent U.S. Trade Policy*, The University of Chicago Press. pp. 111–141.

Pelzman, J. (1986a). PRC Textile Trade and Investment: Impact of the U.S. — PRC Bilateral Textile Agreements, in Congress of the United States, Joint Economic Committee, *China's Economy Looks Toward the Year 2000. Volume 2: Economic Openness in Modernizing China*, Washington: U.S. GPO, pp. 384–431.

Pelzman, J. (1986b). Economic Advantages to the PRC from Access to the U.S. Generalized System of Preferences. In Congress of the United States, Joint Economic Committee, *China's Economy Looks Toward the Year 2000. Volume 2: Economic Openness in Modernizing China*, Washington: U.S. GPO, pp. 472–498.

Pelzman, J. (1987a). The Multifiber Arrangement: The Third Reincarnation, in I. William Zartman (ed.), *Positive Sum: Improving North–South Negotiations*, Transaction Books, pp. 149–170.

Pelzman, J. (1987b). The Multifiber Arrangement Round Four: The Refinement Continues, *Law and Policy in International Business*, 19(1), pp. 241–248.

Pelzman, J. (1987c). The MFA: U.S. Refinements or on With the Cartels, Background Paper for the 1987 World Development Report.

Pelzman, J. (1988a). The Multifiber Arrangement: Is There a Future Post Uruguay Round? in Baldwin, R.E. and D. Richardson (eds.), *Issues in the Uruguay Round*, pp. 47–59.

Pelzman, J. (1988b). The Tariff Equivalents of the Existing Quotas under the Multifiber Arrangement, U.S. Department of Labor, Working Paper.

Pelzman, J. (1989). The Textile Industry, in United States International Trade Commission. *The Economic Effects of Significant U.S. Import Restraints, Phase 1*, Pub. No. 2222.

Pelzman, J. (1992). The Redirection of United States Imports, in Kym Anderson, *New Silk Roads: East Asia and World Textile Markets*, New York: Cambridge University Press, pp. 148–166.

Pelzman, J. (1993). "Multinationals And Vietnam's Transition To A Market Economy: Or What Happened To Me On The Way To Rome?," presented at the 2003 *Allied Social Sciences Association Annual Meetings*, Washington DC.

Pelzman, J. and Rees, K. (1998). The Control of Textile and Apparel Trade under the WTO: What is the Track Record? in Gulser Meric and Susan E.W. Nichols (eds.), *The Global Economy at the Turn of the Century*, Vol. III, pp. 811–830.

Pelzman, J. and Rees, K. (1999). The Control of Textile and Apparel Trade under the WTO: Who are the Winners and Losers? in Fatemi, Khosrow and Susan E.W. Nichols (eds.), *Globalization in the 21st Century*, Volume III, pp. 957–972.

Pelzman, J. (2003). *Imported Capital Dependency as an Economic Development Strategy: The Failure of Distortionary Tax Policies In Puerto Rico*, Puerto Rico: Alliance for Tax Equity.

Pelzman, J. and Shoham, A. (2007). WTO Enforcement Issues, *The Global Economy Journal*, 7(1).

Pelzman, J. and Shoham, A. (2009a). Comparison of PRC and Vietnam's Responses to the Elimination of US Textile and Apparel Quotas: Economic and Cultural Perspectives, *International Journal of Business and Emerging Markets*.

Pelzman, J. and Shoham, A. (2009b). WTO DSU — Enforcement Issues, in James Hartigan (ed.), *Frontiers of Economics and Globalization, Trade Disputes and the Dispute Settlement Understanding of the WTO: An Interdisciplinary Assessment*, Volume 6, Chapter 15. London: Emerald Group Publishing Ltd, pp. 369–395.

Pelzman, J. and Shoham, A. (2010). Measuring the Welfare Effects of Country of Origin Rules: A Suggested Methodology, *The Global Economy Journal*, 10(1). Online Aritcle 2.

Pelzman, J. (2015). "PRC Outward Investment in the USA and Europe: A Model of R&D Acquisition, *Review of Development Economics*, 19(1), pp. 1–14.

Proudman, J. and Redding, S. (2000). Evolving Patterns of International Trade, *Review of International Economics*, 8(3), pp. 373–396.

Qiu, Larry D. (1977). On the Dynamic Efficiency of Bertrand and Cournot Equilibria, *Journal of Economic Theory*, 75, pp. 213–229.

Richardson, J. D. (1971a). Constant-Market-Shares Analysis of Export Growth, *Journal of International Economics*, 1, pp. 227–239.

Richardson, J. D. (1971b). Some Sensitivity Tests for a 'Constant-Market-Shares' Analysis of Export Growth, *Review of Economics and Statistics*, 53, pp. 300–304.

Rodriguez-Clare, A. (1996). Multinationals, Linkages and Economic Development, *American Economic Review*, 86(4), pp. 852–873.

Rodrik, D. (2006). What's So Special About China's Exports?, *China & World Economy*, 14(5), pp. 1–19.

Roger, S. (2008). Collecting the Pieces of the FDI Knowledge Spillovers Puzzle, *The World Bank Research Observer*, 23(2), pp. 107–138.

Rose, A. (2012). Protectionism Isn't Countercyclic (Anymore), National Bureau of Economic Research (NBER), Working Paper No. 18062, Cambridge, MA.

Sally, R. (2009). Globalization and the Political Economy of Trade Liberalization in the BRIICS, in Globalization and Emerging Economies: Brazil, Russia, India, Indonesia, China and South Africa, OECD.

Saunders, Phillip C. (2006). China's Global Activism: Strategy, Drivers, and Tools, Institute for National Strategic Studies, National Defense University.

Schoors, K. and van der Tol. B. (2002). Foreign Direct Investment Spillovers within and between Sectors: Evidence from Hungarian Data, Working Paper 157. Department of Economics, Ghent University, Belgium.

Scissor, D. (2011). Chinese State-Owned Enterprises and U.S.-China Economic Relations, Testimony before the U.S.–China Economic and Security Review Commission", March 30.

Schott, P. K. (2008). The Relative Sophistication of Chinese Exports, *Economic Policy*, 53(5), p. 49.

Schwartz, D., Keren, M., and Pelzman, J. (2008). The Ineffectiveness of Location Incentive Programs: Evidence from Puerto Rico and Israel, *Economic Development Quarterly*, 22(2), pp. 167–179.

Shambaugh, D. (2013). *China Goes Global: The Partial Power*. England: Oxford University Press.

Siotis, G. (1999). Foreign Direct Investment Strategies and Firms' Capabilities, *Journal of Economics and Management Strategy*, 8(2), pp. 251–270.

Smeets, R. (2008). Collecting the pieces of the FDI knowledge spillovers puzzle, *The World Bank research observer*, 23(2), pp. 107–138.

Stone, S. F., Cavazos Cepeda, R. H., and Jankowska, A. (2011). Have Changes in Factor Endowments Been Reflected in Trade Patterns? in

Globalization, Comparative Advantage and the Changing Dynamics of Trade, OECD.

Szamosszegi, A. (2012). An Analysis of Chinese Investments in the U.S. Economy, Washington: Capital Trade FDI Study.

Szamosszegi, A. and Kyle, C. (2011). *An Analysis of State-owned Enterprises and State Capitalism in China*, U.S.-China Economic and Security Review Commission, Washington, DC.

Takacs, W. (1981). Pressures for Protectionism: An Empirical Analysis, *Economic Inquiry*, 9(4), pp. 687–693.

The Committee for the Implementation of Textile Agreements (CITA). *Procedures for Considering Requests from the Public for Textile and Apparel Safeguard Actions on Imports from China*, Federal Register, 68(98), pp. 27787–27789.

Todo, Y., Weiying, Z., and Lei-An, Z. (2011). Intra-industry Knowledge Spillovers from Foreign Direct Investment in Research and Development: Evidence from China's 'Silicon Valley', *Review of Development Economics*, 15(3), pp. 569–585.

Tracey, A. J. (2007) The Contract in the Trade Secret Ballroom-A Forgotten Dance Partner? *Texas Intellectual Property Law Journal*, 16(47), pp. 47–89.

Tsang, E. W. K., Yip, P. S. L., and Heng Tob, M. (2008). The Impact of R&D on Value Added for Domestic and Foreign Firms in a Newly Industrialized Economy, *International Business Review*, 17(4), pp. 423–441.

U.N. (2002). *Trade and Development Report*.

UNCTAD (2013). *World Investment Report 2013: Global Value Chains — Investment and Trade for Development*. New York: United Nations Press.

USGAO (1995). *State Trading Enterprises — Compliance with the General Agreement on Tariffs and Trade (GAO-GGD*, Washington, August) paper GAO/GGD-95–208.

United States International Trade Commission (USITC) (1978). *The History and Current Status of the Multifiber Arrangement*. Publication No. 850. Washington, DC.

United States International Trade Commission (USITC) (1999). *Assessment of the Economic Effects of China's Accession to the WTO*. Investigation No. 332-403, Publication 3229. Washington, DC.

U.S. International Trade Commission (USITC) (2004). "Textiles and Apparel: Assessment of the Competitiveness of Certain Foreign Suppliers to the U.S. Market," Investigation No. 332-448, January, Volumes I and II.

Van Assche, A. (2012). Global Value Chains and Canada's Trade Policy: Business as Usual or Paradigm Shift, IRRP Study, No. 32. Available at *www.irp.org*.

Van Assche, A. and Gangnes, B. (2007). Electronics Production Upgrading: Is China Exceptional? CIRANO Scientific Series, 2007s-16.

Vives, Xavier (1984). Duopoly Information Equilibrium, *Journal of Economic Theory*, 34, pp. 71–94.

Whitney, M. E. and Gaisford, J. D. (1999). Why Spy? An Inquiry into the Rationale for Economic Espionage, *International Economic Journal*, 13(2), pp. 103–123.

Winters L. Alan (1984). Separability and the Specification of Foreign Trade Functions, *Journal of International Economics*, 17, pp. 239–263.

Wolf, M., Glismann, H. H., Pelzman, J., and Spinanger, D. (1984). *Costs of Protecting Jobs in Textiles and Clothing*. Thames Essay No. 38, Trade Policy Research Center, London.

World Bank and Development Research Center of the State Council, the People's Republic of China, PRC (2013). *China 2030: Building a Modern, Harmonious, and Creative Society*. Washington.

World Trade Organization (2001), *Accession of the People's Republic of China*, WT/L/432, 23, WTO, Geneva.

Zhao, Zhongxiu and Kevin Honglin Zhang (2010). FDI and Industrial Productivity in China: Evidence from Panel Data in 2001–06, *Review of Development Economics*, 14(3), pp. 656–665.

Index

A

a threat thereof, 194
Accession Agreement, 195
ACT, 194, 196
actual threat of serious damage, 193
actual threat thereof, 185, 188
ad hoc, 276
affirmative determination, 262
Africa, 1–2, 15, 275, 277, 286, 316–317
agreed limits, 182
Agreement on Textiles and Clothing, 183
Agreement on the Interpretation and Application of Articles VI, XVI and XXIII of the GATT (Subsidies Code), 265
agriculture, 100, 102, 105, 107, 110
Aid Data, 277
Aitken, 319
Amiti and Freund, 17, 92
Amiti and Konings, 92
animal or vegetable fats, 130
Anti-Monopoly Law, 243
antidumping (AD), 243–245, 250–251, 254–255, 257, 262–266, 273
Antràs, 96–97
Argentina, 245
Aristei, 72
Arkolakis, 6

Armington, 201–202, 208
Arms and Ammunition, 156
Arrangement Regarding International Trade in Textiles, 180
Article XXIII of the GATT, 187, 189
Articles of Iron or Steel, 150
"Articles" of Lead, Zinc Tin and other Base metals, 150
Articles of leather, 134
Articles of stones, 147
ASEAN, 106, 241
Asia, 15
Asia-Pacific Trade Agreement, 241
Asian, 10, 13
assistance, 283
ATC, 183–187, 194
Australia, 52, 72, 241
autos, 2

B

Backer and Miroudot, 96–97
backward, 100
backward linkages, 322
Bagwell and Staiger, 244
Balassa, 115–116
Baldwin, 19–20, 113
Baldwin and Venables, 19
Bangladesh, 241
bargain hunters, 297

bargains, 297
barriers to trade, 20
Bas, 72
Bas and Strauss-Kahn, 72
base metals and articles, 254–255
basic metals, 28, 150
basic metals and fabricated metal
    products, 52, 95, 108, 110
Bayard, 5
bedding, 156
Bernard, 6
bilateral imbalances, 6
bilateral investment agreements
    (BIT), 20
Blalock, 322
Blomstrom, 321
Blyde, 319
Boston, 316
Bowen, 115
Bowen and Pelzman, 116–117
Bowman, 324
Bown and Crowley, 244
Brainard, 319
Brander, 327
brands, 297
Branson, 327
Branstetter and Lardy, 92
Brasili, 122
Brautigam, 281–282
Brazil, 52, 72, 190, 245
        Brazilian, 282
bright line standard, 185
bright-line, 188
Brunei, 241
Buckley, 297
budget line, 276
business services, 108
business to business services, 91
buyer-driven, 94
Bwalya, 323

C

calls, 185–186, 188
Cambodia, 31
Canada, 72, 194

capital intensity of the industry, 257
carbon steel wire rods, 265
Carded Cotton Yarn, 218
Caribbean, 15, 194
Category 351/651, 189
Category 352/652 (Cotton and
    Man-made Fiber Underwear), 188
Category 434, 190
Category 435, 191
caused, or threatens to cause, 262
ceiling and oscillating fans, 266
CES, 6
CES price indexes, 7
chain, 21
Chang-hong Pei, 296
chemical and allied industries, 254
chemical products, 254
chemicals, 28, 31, 164
chemicals and metals sectors, 257
chemicals and minerals, 28
chemicals and non-metallic mineral,
    31
chemicals and non-metallic
    mineral products, 102, 105,
    107–108, 110
chemicals and non-metallic mineral
    products sector, 31, 52
chemicals and other mineral
    products, 95
Chen, 324
Chile, 241
China, 5, 10, 13, 91
China Development Bank, 317
China National Textiles Import and
    Export Company, 232
China's export competitiveness, 17
China's footprint, 19
China's RCA, 17, 120
China's Textile and Apparel industry,
    17
China's total exports, 13, 15
China–Asia integration, 10
Chinatex, 232
Chinese SOEs, 31
Chinese SSC, 243

Chinese State-Owned Export–Import
    Bank, 317
Chinese Taipei, 110
Chinese value-added network, 10
Church, 240
clocks and watches, 156
clothing, 164
codification of transactions, 29
Coe and Hess, 19
Columbia, 241
Committee for the Implementation of
    Textile Agreements (CITA), 185,
    188–192
commodity and country
    diversification, 119
commodity composition, 116
commodity composition effect, 117
comparable stage of economic
    development, 263
comparative advantage, 115–116
competitive advantage, 257
competitive residual (CR), 117–118
competitiveness, 19, 113, 116,
    165–166
competitiveness effect, 158, 164, 166
competitiveness of Chinese firms, 15
computers, 2
computing machinery, 28
COMTRADE, 120, 123
concentration of products, 16
Constant Market Share (CMS), 3,
    116–119, 158, 166
constrained, 197
constructed value, 262
construction, 2, 97
contingency measures, 250–251, 257
contingent protection, 243–245,
    250–251
cost-benefit analysis, 4
Costa Rica, 188–190, 241
costs associated with non-tariff
    measures, 20
Cotton and Man-made Fiber
    Pajamas and other Nightwear, 189
cotton dresses, 218

cotton sweaters, 218
counter-trade, 134
countervailing, 3
countervailing duties (CVD), 3, 245,
    250, 257, 264–266, 273
country specific heterogeneous
    technology, 6
country under the Agreement, 265
Court of Appeals for the Federal
    Circuit, 266
Court of International Trade (CIT),
    196
cross-category mobility, 122
crowding-out theory, 170
CRS, 277
customer services, 96
customs area agreements, 241

D

Dallas, 316
Deardorff, 72
decomposition, 3
Dedrick, 20
Deer and Song, 6
deferential and more favorable, 186
Department of Aid to Foreign
    Countries, 283
Department of Commerce (DOC),
    262, 264–266
design, 91
designated consultation levels, 182
Detroit, 316
developing world, 2
Development Assistance Committee
    (DAC), 2, 277, 282–283, 291, 294
Dierickx and Cool, 20
digital entertainment, 2
direct value-added coefficients, 24
direct value-added share, 22
dispute resolution, 241
Dispute Settlement Body (DSB), 187,
    192, 193
Dispute Settlement Understanding
    (DSU), 187, 189
distance, 29

distance to final demand, 99
diversification, 16
diversification issue, 16
Dixit, 327
domestic and foreign content of
    exports, 23
domestic content in a country's gross
    exports, 26
domestic content of exports, 23
domestic education, 19
domestic value (DV) added, 24, 26
Dominican Republic, 188
downstream activities, 31
downstream processed products, 1
dumping, 3, 262
dumping margin, 262
Dunning, 320
Dutch Disease, 119
dynamic comparative advantage, 1
dynamic demand, 165

E

Eaton, 327
Eaton and Kortum, 6
economies of scale, 255
El Salvador, 189, 190
Electric Golf Cars from Poland, 263
electrical and optical equipment, 31,
    93, 95, 97, 100–102, 104, 107–111,
    122
electrical equipment industry, 28
electrical machinery, 28
electricity, gas and water supply, 100
embodied technology, 91
Ethiopia, 282, 317
EU, 17, 102, 243
EU28, 13
EU15, 102
EU27, 102
European Community (EC), 181
exceptional circumstances, 180
exploration, 31
explosives, 134
export competitiveness, 123
export diversification, 119

export driver, 10
export related, 318
Export–Import Bank, 317
Export–Import Bank of China
    (EIBC), 296
exports of goods and services, 10
exposure to trade, 257

F

Fabrics of Yarns of Different Colors,
    218
factors of production, 263
Fair and Jaffee, 204
fair market value, 262–263
Fally, 96–97
Feenstra, 119
Feenstra and Kee, 119
Feinberg, 244, 320
Feng *et al.*, 72
Ferrarini, 100
financial intermediation, 100
Finger, 262
fixed I–O technical coefficients, 29
flexibility, 181
flexibility provisions, 181
Fontagné and Toubal, 92
food products and beverages, 100
footprint, 10, 13
footwear, 147
Ford Motor's Volvo, 297
foreign aid, 2, 283
foreign assistance, 276
foreign content, 28
foreign direct investment (FDI), 1,
    20, 31, 277, 282, 295, 318, 320
foreign expert, 329
foreign value (FV) added, 24, 26, 29
forward, 94–95, 100
forward linkages, 322
Fosfuri, 320
fragmentation, 28, 97
free and fair trading environment, 245
Free Trade Agreements (FTAs), 241
freight and insurance costs, 20
Furskins, 134

G

1947 GATT agreement, 244
Görg, 319, 321
Gaisford, 327
Gal-Or, 327
GATT, 181, 184
GATT Article VI (5), 245
GATT/WTO, 114
GDP, 10
Geely Automotive, 297
generalized least squares estimator (GLS), 291
generalized linear model (GLM), 291
geographic concentration, 123
Gereffi, 93
Germany, 52, 72, 91
Gertler, 322
Geweke, 122
Ghosh inverse, 97
global, 15, 20
global competition, 114
global economy, 19
global factory, 29
global footprint, 3
global network, 19
global producers and suppliers, 20
"global" quotas, 181
global value-added, 31
global value-added chains, 1, 29, 91, 170
global value-added network, 20
global-buying syndicates, 96
global-production network, 96
global-production value chain, 96
global-supply production networks, 96
globalization, 19, 29
going global, 4, 295
Goldberg, 92
Greenaway, 319, 321
Greenfield, 316
Grilli, 244
gross exports, 24
gross trade creation, 200
Grossman, 327
Grossman and Rossi-Hansberg, 20, 92

growing footprint, 8
Gulf Cooperative Council, 241
Gupta, 320

H

Harrigan, 31
Harrigan and Venables, 31
Hartley, 203
Heard on the Street, 329
Heckscher–Ohlin, 119
Herfindahl, 154, 156, 158, 164
Herfindahl indexes, 119, 123, 126, 134, 139, 147, 150
Heritage Foundation, 296, 329
high technology intensive, 28
high value-added industries, 2
higher value-added products, 6
Hinloopen and Van Marrewijk, 122
Honduran, 190
Honduras, 188–191
Hong Kong, 107, 179, 181–182, 192, 194, 241
horizontal, 318–319
horizontal spillovers, 320
hotels and restaurants, 97
HRST (human resources for science and technology), 304
HS 50 — Silk, 167
HS 53 — Vegetable Fibers, 167
HS 54 — Man-made Fibers, 167
HS 55 — Man-made Staple Fibers, 167
HS 58 — Special Woven Fabric, 167
HS 59 — Coated Fabric, 167
HS 61, 62 and 63 — Apparel, 167
HS2, 126
Hsieh and Ossa, 6, 8–9
HS — VI and VII, 257
Huawei, 282, 298, 317
Hudson, 19
human capital, 19
Hummels, 31, 93
Hummels and Schaur, 31
Hymer, 320

I

IBM, 297
iceberg trade cost, 7
Iceland, 241
ICIO, 96
ICT,
ideological affinity, 285
imported inputs, 16
India, 2, 5, 10, 13, 170, 176, 190–193,
    196, 200, 205–206, 208, 218, 230,
    241, 243, 245
Indian, 170, 176, 192–193, 196, 200,
    206
indirect value-added exports, 26
Indonesia, 72, 92
industrial component parts, 257
information and communications
    technology (ICT), 19–20, 113–114,
    170
information management software,
    20
infrastructure-development, 2
initial product specialization effect,
    165
inorganic chemical compounds, 134
Input–Output (I–O), 21
inter-Asian connection, 10
inter-country I–O tables, 21
intermediate goods, 19
intermediate inputs, 10
intermediate products, 2, 52
intermediates, 72
international fragmentation of
    production, 19
international production networks,
    19
International Trade Commission
    (ITC), 263, 265
intra-firm trade, 31
intra-industry, 52
iPad, 20
iPhone, 20, 23
Iron and Steel, 150
iron and steel mill products (ISM),
    273

J

Jamaica, 189–190
Japan, 10, 13, 29, 31, 52, 108, 156,
    179, 237, 241
Japan Ministry of Foreign Affairs, 277
Javorcik, 323
jointly-agreed reasonable departures,
    181
just-in-time, 31
jute, 182

K

Keesing and Wolf, 181
Keller, 91, 320
Klevorick, 327
Kneller, 319
Knetter and Prusa, 244
knowledge spillovers, 320
Kokko, 321
Koopman, 21–26, 93
Korea, 10, 13, 29, 109–110, 156, 179,
    181, 194, 241
    Korean, 110
Korkeamaki and Takalo, 20
Krugman, 116
Kuemmerle, 320
Kugler, 322–323
Kyle, 240, 327

L

Lancaster, 276
large country effect, 10, 13
Larrain, 322
Latin America, 1–2, 15, 275, 277, 282,
    286, 316
Le Bas, 320
leather or furskin goods, 134
Lederman and Maloney, 119
Lee, 324
legalized backsliding, 262
Lemoine and Ünal, 6
Lenovo, 297
Leontief inverse, 93, 96
Leontief inverse matrix, 22

less developed country (LDC), 197, 284
less than the fair market value (LTFMV), 262
Li, 324
LIBOR, 281
Lin, 323
Lin and Li, 10
Linden, 20
linear-production function, 6
linen, 182
live animals, 126
Long-Term Arrangement Regarding International Trade in Cotton Textiles (LTA), 179
low technology segments, 72
lowering trade barriers through negotiations, 240
Lublin, 298

M

Ma and Van Assche, 29
Macau, 241
machinery and electrical appliances, 254
machinery and equipment, nec, 52, 97, 100
Machinery and Mechanical Appliances, 154
machinery, and basic metals industries, 28
Maddala, 199, 203–204
Maddala and Nelson, 203
made in the world, 96
Malaysia, 2, 10, 13, 31
Maldives, 241
manufactures of straw, 134
manufacturing, 150
manufacturing and recycling, 122
manufacturing nec, 100
mark-ups by importers and wholesalers, 20
market distribution, 116
market distribution effect, 117
marketing, 31, 96

Markusen, 319–320, 323
material injury, 245, 262–263
medium-to-low technology, 52
medium-high technology sector, 31
Melitz, 6, 119
Melitz and Redding, 6
Memorandum of Understanding (MOU), 195
Memorandum of Understanding between the Governments of The United States of America and the People's Republic Of China concerning Trade in Textile and Apparel Products, 195
Men and Boys' Cotton Trousers and Shorts, 209
Men and Boys' non-knit MMF Shirts, 209
Men's and Boy's Wool Coats Other Than Suit Type, 190
Men's Coats, 190
merger and acquisition (M&A), 2, 304, 316
metals and metal products, 254
Mexican, 195
Mexico, 2, 194, 245
MFA II, 181
MFA III, 181
MFA IV, 182
MG Rover's, 297
military equipment, 2
Mineral products, 134
Minerals, 160
minimum consultation levels, 182
mining, 28
Mining and quarrying, 100
Ministry of Commerce, 283
Miroudot, 91
Miscellaneous Manufactured Articles, 156
miscellaneous manufactured products (MSC), 273
MMF Nightwear and Pajamas, 209
MMF Skirts, 218, 230
MMF Underwear, 209

modality, 29
modules, 29
modulization, 29
MOFCOM, 296
Most Favored Nation (MFN), 1, 5,
    233, 240
motor vehicle, 28
Motta, 320
Multi Fiber Arrangement (MFA), 17
    122, 134, 147, 166–167, 170,
    179–184, 194–196, 199, 201,
    203–206, 218, 230
multilateral and bilateral investment
    agreements, 20

N

Nanjing Automotive, 297
Narula, 320
National Development and Reform
    Commission (NDRC), 296
National treatment, 240
Natural or Cultured Pearls, 147
natural resource, 1
networks, 20
New Zealand, 241
non-convertible, 166
non-electrical equipment, 164
non-market economy (NME), 3, 240,
    244, 263–266
non-MFA fibers, 182
non-OECD, 119
non-performing asset, 116
North Carolina, 316
Norway, 241
notification, 185

O

ODA-like, 282
OECD Inter-Country Input–Output,
    96
OECD–WTO, 120
OECD–WTO Trade, 20
OECD–WTO-TiVA, 21–26
Official Development Assistance
    (ODA), 276–277, 282

offshore processing, 5
Omnibus Trade and Competitiveness
    Act of 1988 (OTCA), 264
OOF, 281–282
OOF-like, 281–282
operations, 96
Optical, Photographic and
    Cinematographic, 156
ordinary least squares (OLS), 197
Organisation for Economic
    Co-operation and Development
    (OECD), 2, 20, 31, 102–103, 107,
    119, 122–123, 196, 231, 233, 241,
    243, 276, 283, 304
Original brand name manufacturing
    (OBM), 236
original equipment manufacturing
    (OEM), 236
other products and castings (ISO),
    273
other services, 100
output inverse, 97
outward FDI (OFDI), 295–297, 318

P

Pakistan, 2, 241
parents, 19
Pelzman, 5, 100, 179–180, 183, 264
Pelzman and Martin, 233
Pelzman and Rees, 183
Pelzman and Reese, 5
Pelzman and Shoham, 5, 19, 147,
    243
Pennsylvania-New Jersey, 316
People's Republic of China (PRC), 1,
    5, 10, 12–13, 72, 196, 205–206,
    208–209, 230, 232–233, 237, 263
Persson, 321
Peru, 241
Philippines, 2, 170
pipe products (ISP), 273
Pisu, 319
Plastic and Rubber Articles, 134
plastic and rubber products, 254
Playsuits and Sunsuits, 209, 218

polarization, 123
post, 207
PRC M&A, 304
PRC OFDI, 318
PRC SOE, 297
PRC TNC, 318
PRC's footprint in exports, 15
PRC-LDC, 283
prepared foodstuffs, 130
prepared foodstuffs of meat and fish, 130
prepared foodstuffs of vegetable fruit nuts, 130
price competitiveness, 13
price to market, 166
process technology, 91
procurement, 96
producer-driven value chains, 93
product diversification, 17
production networks, 20
production standardization, 28
productive technology, 91
Products of the Chemicals or Allied Industries, 134
Proudman and Redding, 122
provisional Cotton Textile Committee, 179
Pulp of Wood or Fibrous Cellulosic Material, 139

Q

Qiu, 325, 328

R

Raice, 298
rail, 154
ramie, 182
Raw Hides and Skins, 134
raw materials, 2
RCA indexes, 120, 123
reasonable departures, 181
"real" spillover effects, 9
recovery, 31
recycling, 100
refining, 31

Regional Comprehensive Economic Partnership, (RCEP), 241
Reliance on tariffs to protect sensitive sectors, 241
remote, 126
Report of the Working Party on the Accession of China to the World Trade Organization, 195
research, 91
research and development (R&D), 20, 91, 96, 295, 304, 316, 318
residual competitiveness, 117
restraint limits, 182
retail, 31
revealed comparative advantage (RCA), 3, 17, 112, 114–116, 118–120, 123, 126, 134, 139, 147, 150, 154, 156, 158
Ricardian, 119
Richardson, 117
Rodriguez-Clare, 322–323
Rodrik, 10
roll-backs, 182
Rose, 244
rubber and plastics, 28
Russia, 52, 72, 91, 240
R&D technology, 326

S

§204 of the Agricultural Act, 178
safeguard, 244–245, 250, 257
safeguard actions, 257
Saggi, 323
Sally, 240
Saudi Arabia, 52, 72
Schoors, 323
Schwartz, 100
Scissor, 240
sector level gross exports, 24
sector level value-added exports, 24
self-sufficient, 10
sensitive, 181
separability of the production function, 29
series damage, 188

serious damage, 185, 188–194
services, 2, 19
Shambaugh, 297
ships, 154
Short-Term Arrangement (STA)
   Regarding International Trade in
   Cotton Textiles, 178–179
Sierra, 320
Silicon Valley, 316
silk, 182
silk and non-cotton vegetable fibers,
   182
similarly situated third country, 263
Singapore, 241
Siotis, 320
six digit HS classification, 160
Sjoholm, 321
skilled labor, 2
skills, 96
Smeets, 320, 323
Socialism with Chinese
   characteristics, 239
sophistication, 16
sophistication issue, 17
source country, 31
source industry, 31
South Africa, 245
South Korea, 182, 241
Southeast Asia, 275, 277, 286
Soviet type, 5
Soviet Union, 275, 283
Spatareanu, 323
special consideration, 186
specific business functions, 96
specific limits, 182
Spencer, 327
spillover, 1–2, 318–319, 325
spillover effects, 6, 8, 10, 31, 275, 318,
   324–325
Sprint Nextel Corp, 298
Sri Lanka, 241
standard methodology, 262
start-up, 3
State Supervised Capitalism (SSC),
   239–240, 243, 276

state-owned enterprises (SOEs), 15,
   232–233, 240, 295, 297
Statement of Serious Damage, 185
Strobl, 321
Supply and Marketing Cooperatives
   (SMCs), 231–232
supply chains, 19–20
surges, 182
surrogate country, 263
Switzerland, 241
Szamosszegi, 240, 324

T

Taiwan, 29, 179, 181–182, 194
Takacs, 244
Tariff Act of 1930, 265
tariffs, 20
technical textiles, 232
technological spillovers, 19
technologically advanced inputs, 92
technology, 6
technology-exploiting FDI (inward
   FDI technology transfer), 320
technology-seeking FDI (outward FDI
   technology sourcing), 320
telecommunications, 20
television and communication
   equipment, 28
temporary, 180
"temporary" relief, 178
Tenth Five-Year Plan, 234
textile and apparel, 3, 5, 93–94, 134,
   166
textile and apparel industry, 94
textile and apparel trade, 5
Textile and Textile Articles, 139, 254
textiles, 164
Textiles Monitoring Body (TMB),
   183, 187–190, 192–194
textiles, leather and footwear, 97,
   100
textiles, textile products, leather and
   footwear, 102, 105, 109
Thailand, 2, 10, 13, 31, 111, 188
threat of serious damage, 189, 192

threat of such damage, 190
threatened injuries, 263
tied aid, 3, 275
TNC M&A, 297
TNCs, 297–298, 318
Tobit, 203
Tobit analysis, 200
Tobit method, 199
Todo, 324
total trade expansion, 200
Toys, 156
Trade Act of 1974, 263
Trade Agreements Act of 1979,
    264–265
trade competitiveness, 119
trade contingency measures, 250
trade creation, 199–200
trade diversification, 119
trade diversion, 199–200
transaction costs, 20
transitional product-specific
    safeguard, 244
transitional safeguards, 185–186
transnational networks, 114
Transnationality Index (TNI), 297
transparency, 240
transport, 31
transport and port costs, 20
transport and storage, post and
    telecommunication, 108
transport equipment, 97, 100, 164
transportation costs, 29
transportation equipment, 93
transportation equipment sector, 72
transportation hubs, 29
trilateral FTA, 241
Turkey, 188, 245

U

U.S. Peace Corps, 277
unconstrained, 197
UNCTAD, 296–297, 304
underwear, 188
United States, 2, 5, 13, 243
upstream activities, 31

upstream business services, 31
upstream linkages or looking
    backward, 26
upstream value-added, 31
upstreamness, 97
US, 2, 17, 31, 91, 102, 294
US Antidumping Act of 1921, 263
US Court of International Trade
    (USCIT), 265–266, 273
US Trade Act of 1974, 263
US Treasury Department, 263
USITC, 273
USITC [1978], 179
USITC [2004], 234–235
utility function (U), 286

V

$VAS\_\hat{E}$, 23
Vague (OF), 282
value-added, 19, 21, 120
value-added exports, 23
value-added exports to the world, 26
value-added production chains, 170
value-added shares (VAS), 22–23, 25
Value-added trade, 23
value-added trade matrix, 24
Van Assche, 29, 31
Van Assche and Gangnes, 29
van der Tol, 323
vehicles, aircraft and vessels, 154
Venables, 323
vertical, 318–319
vertical and horizontal value-added
    linkages, 91
vertical foreign direct-investment, 31
vertical spillovers, 320
Vietnam, 2, 31, 147, 170, 176, 196,
    200, 205–206, 208–209, 218
    Vietnamese, 170, 196
Vives, 327

W

W/G Cotton trousers/slacks/shorts,
    230
Walrasian, 204

Wang Lei, 296
"water" in their bilateral quota
    agreements, 183
Washington, DC, 316
weight-to-value, 31
Western Europe, 2
what you do, 19
what you sell, 19
Whitney, 327
wholesale and retail trade, hotels and
    restaurants, 95, 101–102, 104,
    107–111
Winters, 202, 208
Women and Girl MMF Coats, 209
Women and Girl MMF Slacks,
    Breeches and Shorts, 209
Women and Girls' not-knit MMF
    Shirts and Blouses, 209
Women's and Girls' Wool Coats, 191,
    192
Women's Coats, 191
Wood and Articles of Wood, 134
wood, paper, paper products, 100

Works of Art, 156
world trade, 116
World Trade Organization
    (WTO), 19, 183–184, 187, 194–195,
    232, 239–241, 243–245, 254, 263,
    266
world-trading network, 10
Woven Blouses, 192–193
Woven Wool Shirts and Blouses,
    192
WTO DSU, 189

X
Xinjiang, 232

Y
youth volunteers, 277

Z
Zhang, 297
Zhao, 297
ZTE, 282, 298, 316–317

Printed in the United States
By Bookmasters